THREEFOLD GOLD

PURE. REFINED.

COMPILED BY RAY COMFORT

BRIDGE LOGOS FOUNDATION

Alachua, Florida 32615

Bridge-Logos
Alachua, FL 32615 USA

Threefold Gold
by Ray Comfort

Printed in the United States of America.

Library of Congress Catalog Card Number: 2011934114
International Standard Book Number: 978-088270-803-4

Table of Contents

Dedications

Jonathan Edwards

Dedicated to
Ken and Win Hibbert (my in-laws)
for their example of godliness,
and for allowing me to marry
their beautiful daughter, Sue.

Dwight Lyman Moody

My sincere thanks to
Trisha Ramos
for her editorial research.

Charles H. Spurgeon

Dedicated to
Ken and Win Hibbert (my in-laws)
for their example of godliness,
and for allowing me to marry
their beautiful daughter, Sue.

EDWARDS GOLD

Compiled by Ray Comfort

Introduction to Sinners in the Hands of an Angry God

by Ray Comfort

Edwards Gold would not be "gold" unless we included his most famous sermon: *Sinners in the Hands of an Angry God*. Although it is a famous sermon, many have not taken the time to sit and read it. Edwards believed that in order to have the most effective evangelism one must awaken the unconverted sinner with what the Scriptures teach about hell. In one sermon on Hebrews 9:12, he wrote, "The consideration of hell commonly is the first thing that rouses sleeping sinners. By this means their sins are set in order before them and their conscience stares them in the face." [Edwards' manuscript sermon on Hebrews 9:12; Jesus Christ is both the only priest and sacrifice by which eternal redemption is obtained for believers, nd, p.15.]

Many pastors today believe most of the members to be genuinely saved, but Jonathan Edwards was convinced that many in his congregation were not saved. He begins "Sinners in the Hands of an Angry God" with this short sentence that proves he was concerned about the individuals sitting under his teachings week after week, "This awful subject may be of awakening to unconverted persons in *this congregation*" (italics mine). Edwards uses other striking words towards his hearers, "How terrifying should it be to you . . . How frightful should it be to you . . . How awful may the thought well be to you . . . How awful and doleful may it be to you . . . How frightful may it be to you every night . . . How can you live in such circumstances without living in continual terror." *[The Works of Jonathan Edwards, Occasional Sermons,* p. 826] In Edwards' mind, preaching on hell and the judgment of God was essential to saving the lost.

Jonathan Edwards first preached *Sinners in the Hands of an Angry God,* in his own congregation in June of 1741 and then one month later taught it in another church in Enfield, Connecticut. When Edwards delivered his sermon, *Sinners in the Hands of an Angry God,* the response was overwhelming. The congregation shrieked, some moaned, and others lifted their voices and cried out to God for mercy on their depraved souls.

Stephen Williams gives a detailed account in his diary about the remarkable effect of terror that Jonathan's preaching had on the Enfield congregation the day that he preached *Sinners in the Hands of an Angry God:*

> We went over to Enfl-- where we met dear Mr E-- of N--H-- who preached a most awakening sermon from these words—Duet 32:35 and before the sermon was done—there was a great moaning & crying out through the whole House—What shall I do to be Saved—oh I am going to hell—Oh what shall I do for Christ &c. &c. So yt ye minister was obliged to desist—ye shrieks & crys were piercing & Amazing—after Some time of waiting the Congregation were Still so yt a prayer was made by Mr W. 7 after that we descend from the pulpit and discoursd with the people—Some in one place and Some in another—

> and *Amazing and Astonishing ye power God was seen*— & Several Souls were hopefully wrought of their countenances yt receivd comfort—oh yt God wd strengthen and confirm—we sung an hymn & prayd & dismissed ye Assembly. *[A Sketch of the Strict Congregational Church of Enfield,* Connecticut, (Hartford: Oliver Means, 1899). *P. 19.* Taken from *Jonathan Edwards 1703-1758, A Biography* by Ola Elizabeth Winslow, (New York: Farrar, Sterns, & Giroux, 1973).]

Edwards was not manipulative or fiery in his preaching style. He was calm and collected and each sermon was jam-packed with truth from God's Word. John MacArthur has this to say about his demeanor in the pulpit:

> He read his message in a carefully controlled tone just so that his primary appeal would be to his hearers' minds, not their emotions. The force of his delivery lay not in his voice or gestures but in his lucid, powerful reasoning and intense conviction. Many consider him the greatest philosopher-theologian to have graced the American scene. [Quote taken from the foreward to *Sinners in the Hands of an Angry God–Made Easier to Read* by John Jeffery Fanella.]

Even though Edwards was one of the greatest theologians and philosophers that quite possibly America has ever seen, his sermons were extremely understandable to the average hearer. J.I. Packer comments on Edwards' style of delivery, "[He] studied plainness of style, concealing his learning beneath a deliberately bald clarity of statement." (J.I. Packer, *A Quest for Godliness: The Puritan Vision of the Christian Life* [Wheaton, Ill, Crossway Books, 1190], 313).

Sinners in the Hands of an Angry God[1]

Jonathan Edwards (1703-1758)

Enfield, Connecticut, July 8, 1741

Deuteronomy 32:35

Their foot shall slide in due time.

In this verse is threatened the vengeance of God on the wicked unbelieving Israelites, who were God's visible people, and who lived under the means of grace; but who, notwithstanding all God's wonderful works towards them, remained (as in verse 28) void of counsel, having no understanding in them. Under all the cultivations of heaven, they brought forth bitter and poisonous fruit; as in the two verses next preceding the text. The expression I have chosen for my text, their foot shall slide in due time, seems to imply the following things, relating to the punishment and destruction to which these wicked Israelites were exposed.

1 There is a sure way to make a joke fall flat. It's to say, "This is the funniest joke you've ever heard!" It sets the bar too high. The first time I read this sermon, I was underwhelmed. The sermon's reputation had set the bar very high. I was expecting to find myself flat on the floor, weeping, groaning, and filled with the fear of God. It just didn't happen, and it confirmed the fact that God doesn't need eloquence to speak to the lost. He can take our words and, at any time He pleases, put the full force of a lightning bolt behind them. That's what He did with this famous sermon the day that it was first preached.

1. That they were always exposed to destruction; as one that stands or walks in slippery places is always exposed to fall. This is implied in the manner of their destruction coming upon them, being represented by their foot sliding. The same is expressed, Psalm 73:18, "Surely thou didst set them in slippery places; thou castedst them down into destruction."

2. It implies that they were always exposed to sudden unexpected destruction. As he that walks in slippery places is every moment liable to fall, he cannot foresee one moment whether he shall stand or fall the next; and when he does fall, he falls at once without warning: Which is also expressed in Psalm 73:18-19, "Surely thou didst set them in slippery places; thou castedst them down into destruction: How are they brought into desolation as in a moment!"

3. Another thing implied is, that they are liable to fall of themselves, without being thrown down by the hand of another; as he that stands or walks on slippery ground needs nothing but his own weight to throw him down.

4. That the reason why they are not fallen already and do not fall now is only that God's appointed time is not come. For it is said, that when that due time, or appointed time comes, their foot shall slide. Then they shall be left to fall, as they are inclined by their own weight. God will not hold them up in these slippery places any longer, but will let them go; and then, at that very instant, they shall fall into destruction; as he that stands on such slippery declining ground, on the edge of a pit, he cannot stand alone, when he is let go he immediately falls and is lost.[2]

2 Sinners are often shocked when death comes close to them. It's as though they had never taken the time to face reality. One of the first signs of an awakening soul is that they face their own mortality—that life itself is a slippery place.

The observation from the words that I would now insist upon is this: "There is nothing that keeps wicked men at any one moment out of hell, but the mere pleasure of God." By the mere pleasure of God, I mean His sovereign pleasure, His arbitrary will, restrained by no obligation, hindered by no manner of difficulty, any more than if nothing else but God's mere will had in the least degree, or in any respect whatsoever, any hand in the preservation of wicked men one moment. The truth of this observation may appear by the following considerations.

1. There is no want [lack] of power in God to cast wicked men into hell at any moment. Men's hands cannot be strong when God rises up. The strongest have no power to resist him, nor can any deliver out of his hands. He is not only able to cast wicked men into hell, but He can most easily do it. Sometimes an earthly prince meets with a great deal of difficulty to subdue a rebel, who has found means to fortify himself, and has made himself strong by the numbers of his followers. But it is not so with God. There is no fortress that is any defense from the power of God. Though hand join in hand, and vast multitudes of God's enemies combine and associate themselves, they are easily broken in pieces. They are as great heaps of light chaff before the whirlwind; or large quantities of dry stubble before devouring flames. We find it easy to tread on and crush a worm that we see crawling on the earth; so it is easy for us to cut or singe a slender thread that any thing hangs by: thus easy is it for God, when He pleases, to cast His enemies down to hell. What are we that we should think to stand before Him, at whose rebuke the earth trembles, and before whom the rocks are thrown down?

2. They deserve to be cast into hell; so that divine justice never stands in the way, it makes no objection against

God's using His power at any moment to destroy them. Yea, on the contrary, justice calls aloud for an infinite punishment of their sins. Divine justice says of the tree that brings forth such grapes of Sodom, "Cut it down, why cumbereth[3] it the ground?" Luke 13:7. The sword of divine justice is every moment brandished over their heads, and it is nothing but the hand of arbitrary mercy, and God's mere will, that holds it back.

3. They are already under a sentence of condemnation to hell. They do not only justly deserve to be cast down thither, but the sentence of the law of God, that eternal and immutable rule of righteousness that God has fixed between Him and mankind, is gone out against them, and stands against them; so that they are bound over already to hell. John 3:18, "He that believeth not is condemned already." So that every unconverted man properly belongs to hell; that is his place; from thence he is, John 8:23, "Ye are from beneath." And thither he is bound; it is the place that justice, and God's word, and the sentence of His unchangeable law assign to him.[4]

4. They are now the objects of that very same anger and wrath of God[5] that is expressed in the torments of hell. And the reason why they do not go down to hell at each moment, is not because God, in whose power they are, is not then very angry with them; as He is with many miserable creatures now tormented in hell, who there feel and bear the fierceness of His

---

3 Not only doing no good, but wasting ground.

4 This is why it's essential to use the Law of God to bring the knowledge of sin—taking sinners through the Ten Commandments to show the righteousness of God. As long as a sinner remains in ignorance as to the holiness of God, he will not see hell as being just. See Mark 10:17 and Romans 3:21-24, Romans 3:19, 20; Romans 7:7, 13.

5 The Law shows the sinner that God is a Judge. He is not a divine butler or his friend. The sinner is an enemy of God in his mind, a child of wrath, who by his daily sins stores up God's just wrath that will be revealed on the Day of Judgment.

wrath. Yea, God is a great deal more angry with great numbers that are now on earth: yea, doubtless, with many that are now in this congregation, who it may be are at ease, than He is with many of those who are now in the flames of hell.

So that it is not because God is unmindful of their wickedness, and does not resent it, that He does not let loose His hand and cut them off. God is not altogether such an one as themselves, though they may imagine Him to be so. The wrath of God burns against them, their damnation does not slumber; the pit is prepared, the fire is made ready, the furnace is now hot, ready to receive them; the flames do now rage and glow. The glittering sword is whet [sharpened], and held over them, and the pit hath opened its mouth under them.

5. The devil stands ready to fall upon them, and seize them as his own, at what moment God shall permit him. They belong to him; he has their souls in his possession, and under his dominion. The Scripture represents them as his goods, Luke 11:21. The devils watch them; they are ever by them at their right hand; they stand waiting for them, like greedy hungry lions that see their prey, and expect to have it, but are for the present kept back. If God should withdraw his hand, by which they are restrained, they would in one moment fly upon their poor souls. The old serpent is gaping for them; hell opens its mouth wide to receive them; and if God should permit it, they would be hastily swallowed up and lost.[6]

6. There are in the souls of wicked men those hellish principles reigning, that would presently kindle and flame out into hell fire, if it were not for God's

6 The sinner mistakenly thinks that God's silence is evidence of the condoning of his sin. It is rather evidence of His patience with him.

restraints. There is laid in the very nature of carnal men, a foundation for the torments of hell. There are those corrupt principles, in reigning power in them, and in full possession of them, that are seeds of hell fire. These principles are active and powerful, exceedingly violent in their nature, and if it were not for the restraining hand of God upon them, they would soon break out, they would flame out after the same manner as the same corruptions, the same enmity does in the hearts of damned souls, and would beget the same torments as they do in them. The souls of the wicked are in Scripture compared to the troubled sea, Isaiah 57:20. For the present, God restrains their wickedness by His mighty power, as He does the raging waves of the troubled sea, saying, "Hitherto shalt thou come, but no further" (Job 38:11); but if God should withdraw that restraining power, it would soon carry all before it. Sin is the ruin and misery of the soul; it is destructive in its nature; and if God should leave it without restraint, there would need nothing else to make the soul perfectly miserable. The corruption of the heart of man is immoderate and boundless in its fury; and while wicked men live here, it is like fire pent up by God's restraints, whereas if it were let loose, it would set on fire the course of nature; and as the heart is now a sink of sin, so if sin was not restrained, it would immediately turn the soul into a fiery oven, or a furnace of fire and brimstone.[7]

7. It is no security to wicked men for one moment, that there are no visible means of death at hand. It is no security to a natural man, that he is now in health, and that he does not see which way he should now

---

7 If Jonathan Edwards preached this sermon in most of today's churches, he would be silenced within minutes and condemned as being a hatemonger. Yet every word of this sermon is soaked in biblical truth.

immediately go out of the world by any accident, and that there is no visible danger in any respect in his circumstances. The manifold and continual experience of the world in all ages, shows this is no evidence, that a man is not on the very brink of eternity, and that the next step will not be into another world. The unseen, unthought-of ways and means of persons going suddenly out of the world are innumerable and inconceivable. Unconverted men walk over the pit of hell on a rotten covering, and there are innumerable places in this covering so weak that they will not bear their weight, and these places are not seen. The arrows of death fly unseen at noon-day; the sharpest sight cannot discern them. God has so many different unsearchable ways of taking wicked men out of the world and sending them to hell, that there is nothing to make it appear, that God had need to be at the expense of a miracle, or go out of the ordinary course of His providence, to destroy any wicked man, at any moment. All the means that there are of sinners going out of the world, are so in God's hands, and so universally and absolutely subject to His power and determination, that it does not depend at all the less on the mere will of God, whether sinners shall at any moment go to hell, than if means were never made use of, or at all concerned in the case.

8. Natural men's prudence and care to preserve their own lives, or the care of others to preserve them, do not secure them a moment. To this, divine providence and universal experience do also bear testimony. There is this clear evidence that men's own wisdom is no security to them from death; that if it were otherwise we should see some difference between the wise and politic men of the world, and others, with regard to their liableness to early and unexpected death: but

how is it in fact? Ecclesiastes. 2:16, "How dieth the wise man? as the fool."

9. All wicked men's pains and contrivance that they use to escape hell, while they continue to reject Christ, and so remain wicked men, do not secure them from hell one moment. Almost every natural man that hears of hell, flatters himself that he shall escape it; he depends upon himself for his own security; he flatters himself in what he has done, in what he is now doing, or what he intends to do. Every one lays out matters in his own mind how he shall avoid damnation, and flatters himself that he contrives well for himself, and that his schemes will not fail. They hear indeed that there are but few saved, and that the greater part of men that have died heretofore are gone to hell; but each one imagines that he lays out matters better for his own escape than others have done. He does not intend to come to that place of torment; he says within himself, that he intends to take effectual care, and to order matters so for himself as not to fail.

   But the foolish children of men miserably delude themselves in their own schemes, and in confidence in their own strength and wisdom; they trust to nothing but a shadow.[8] The greater part of those who heretofore have lived under the same means of grace, and are now dead, are undoubtedly gone to hell; and it was not because they were not as wise as those who are now alive: it was not because they did not lay out matters as well for themselves to secure their own escape. If we could speak with them, and inquire of them, one by one, whether they expected, when alive, and when they used to hear about hell, ever to

8 Most of the time, the trust that sinners have is in themselves. Ask any unsaved person if he thinks that he is morally good, and he will be quick to answer that he is (see Proverbs 20:6). Rarely will one say that they have a wicked heart. This is because they are ignorant of the spiritual nature of the moral Law.

be the subjects of misery: we doubtless, should hear one and another reply, "No, I never intended to come here: I had laid out matters otherwise in my mind; I thought I should contrive well for myself—I thought my scheme good. I intended to take effectual care; but it came upon me unexpected; I did not look for it at that time, and in that manner; it came as a thief—Death outwitted me: God's wrath was too quick for me. Oh, my cursed foolishness! I was flattering myself, and pleasing myself with vain dreams of what I would do hereafter; and when I was saying, Peace and safety, then sudden destruction came upon me."[9]

10. God has laid himself under no obligation, by any promise to keep any natural man out of hell one moment. God certainly has made no promises either of eternal life, or of any deliverance or preservation from eternal death, but what are contained in the covenant of grace, the promises that are given in Christ, in whom all the promises are yea and Amen.[10] But surely they have no interest in the promises of the covenant of grace who are not the children of the covenant, who do not believe in any of the promises, and have no interest in the Mediator of the covenant.

So that, whatever some have imagined and pretended about promises made to natural men's earnest seeking and knocking, it is plain and manifest, that whatever pains a natural man takes in religion, whatever prayers he makes, till he believes in Christ, God is under no manner of obligation to keep him a moment from eternal destruction.

So that, thus it is that natural men are held in the hand of God, over the pit of hell; they have deserved the fiery pit, and are

9 1 Thessalonians 5:3
10 2 Corinthians 1:20

already sentenced to it; and God is dreadfully provoked, His anger is as great towards them as to those that are actually suffering the executions of the fierceness of His wrath in hell, and they have done nothing in the least to appease or abate that anger, neither is God in the least bound by any promise to hold them up one moment; the devil is waiting for them, hell is gaping for them, the flames gather and flash about them, and would fain lay hold on them, and swallow them up; the fire pent up in their own hearts is struggling to break out: and they have no interest in any Mediator, there are no means within reach that can be any security to them. In short, they have no refuge, nothing to take hold of; all that preserves them every moment is the mere arbitrary will, and uncovenanted, unobliged, forbearance of an incensed God.[11]

Application

The use of this awful subject may be for awakening unconverted persons in this congregation.[12] This that you have heard is the case of every one of you that are out of Christ. That world of misery, that take of burning brimstone, is extended abroad under you. There is the dreadful pit of the glowing flames of the wrath of God; there is hell's wide gaping mouth open; and you have nothing to stand upon, nor any thing to take hold of; there is nothing between you and hell but the air; it is only the power and mere pleasure of God that holds you up.

---

11 The root cause of almost all sin is idolatry. Those who are of the world have their own concept of what they believe God is like. The very hint of God being "incensed" is offensive to them.

12 The subject of God's wrath and the reality of hell *is* an "awful" subject. "Awful" can mean "extremely bad" or "unpleasant" or it can mean "inspiring fear" or "dreadful." As Christians we can want to avoid the subject of hell because it isn't pleasant. At the same time, the justice of God should inspire a healthy fear—to know that ultimate justice will ultimately be done. Every mass murderer who has gotten away with his terrible crimes will be brought to justice, and will finally receive that which he deserves.

You probably are not sensible of this; you find you are kept out of hell, but do not see the hand of God in it; but look at other things, as the good state of your bodily constitution, your care of your own life, and the means you use for your own preservation. But indeed these things are nothing; if God should withdraw His hand, they would avail no more to keep you from falling, than the thin air to hold up a person that is suspended in it.

Your wickedness makes you as it were heavy as lead, and to tend downwards with great weight and pressure towards hell; and if God should let you go, you would immediately sink and swiftly descend and plunge into the bottomless gulf, and your healthy constitution, and your own care and prudence, and best contrivance, and all your righteousness, would have no more influence to uphold you and keep you out of hell, than a spider's web would have to stop a falling rock. Were it not for the sovereign pleasure of God, the earth would not bear you one moment; for you are a burden to it; the creation groans with you; the creature is made subject to the bondage of your corruption, not willingly; the sun does not willingly shine upon you to give you light to serve sin and Satan; the earth does not willingly yield her increase to satisfy your lusts; nor is it willingly a stage for your wickedness to be acted upon; the air does not willingly serve you for breath to maintain the flame of life in your vitals, while you spend your life in the service of God's enemies. God's creatures are good, and were made for men to serve God with, and do not willingly subserve [be helpful or useful] to any other purpose, and groan when they are abused to purposes so directly contrary to their nature and end. And the world would spew you out, were it not for the sovereign hand of Him who hath subjected it in hope. There are the black clouds of God's wrath now hanging directly over your heads, full of the dreadful storm, and big with thunder; and were it not for the restraining hand of God, it would immediately burst forth upon you.[13] The sovereign pleasure of God, for the present, stays His rough wind; otherwise it would come with fury, and your destruction would come like a whirlwind, and you would be like the chaff on the summer threshing floor.

The wrath of God is like great waters that are dammed for the present; they increase more and more, and rise higher and higher, till an outlet is given; and the longer the stream is stopped, the more rapid and mighty is its course, when once it is let loose. It is true, that judgment against your evil works has not been executed hitherto; the floods of God's vengeance have been withheld; but your guilt in the meantime is constantly increasing, and you are every day treasuring up more wrath; the waters are constantly rising, and waxing more and more mighty; and there is nothing but the mere pleasure of God, that holds the waters back, that are unwilling to be stopped, and press hard to go forward. If God should only withdraw His hand from the floodgate, it would immediately fly open, and the fiery floods of the fierceness and wrath of God, would rush forth with inconceivable fury, and would come upon you with omnipotent power; and if your strength were ten thousand times greater than it is, yea, ten thousand times greater than the strength of the stoutest, sturdiest devil in hell, it would be nothing to withstand or endure it.

The bow of God's wrath is bent, and the arrow made ready on the string, and justice bends the arrow at your heart, and strains the bow, and it is nothing but the mere pleasure of God, and that of an angry God, without any promise or obligation at all, that keeps the arrow one moment from being made drunk with your blood.[14] Thus all you that never

---

13 The wrath of God *abides* on the sinner. See John 3:36.

14 It is the Law of God that is the enemy of the sinner. This is a good judge who has just seen evidence of the life of a young girl that has been cruelly snuffed out by the unrepentant rapist that stands before him. If the judge is truly good, he will be incensed with anger towards such a heinous criminal.

passed under a great change of heart, by the mighty power of the Spirit of God upon your souls; all you that were never born again, and made new creatures, and raised from being dead in sin, to a state of new, and before altogether never experienced light and life, are in the hands of an angry God. However you may have reformed your life in many things, and may have had religious affections, and may keep up a form of religion in your families and closets, and in the house of God, it is nothing but His mere pleasure that keeps you from being this moment swallowed up in everlasting destruction. However unconvinced you may now be of the truth of what you hear, by and by you will be fully convinced of it. Those that are gone from being in the like circumstances with you, see that it was so with them; for destruction came suddenly upon most of them; when they expected nothing of it, and while they were saying, "Peace and safety," now they see that those things on which they depended for peace and safety, were nothing but thin air and empty shadows.

The God that holds you over the pit of hell, much as one holds a spider, or some loathsome insect over the fire, abhors you,[15] and is dreadfully provoked: His wrath towards you burns like fire; He looks upon you as worthy of nothing else, but to be cast into the fire; He is of purer eyes than to bear to have you in His sight; you are ten thousand times more abominable in His eyes, than the most hateful venomous serpent is in ours. You have offended Him infinitely more than ever a stubborn rebel did his prince; and yet it is nothing but His hand that holds you from falling into the fire every moment. It is to be ascribed to nothing else that you did not go to hell the last night; that you were suffered to awake again in this world, after you closed your eyes to sleep. And there is no other

15 God's abhorrence of the wicked is difficult to reconcile with John 3:16 (and other passages) because we separate "hatred" from the judicial righteousness of God: "The Lord tries the righteous: but the wicked and him that loves violence his soul hates" (Psalm 11:5, AKV). "The foolish shall not stand in your sight: you hate all workers of iniquity" (Psalm 5:5, AKV). God's hatred is without sin.

reason to be given, why you have not dropped into hell since you arose in the morning, but that God's hand has held you up. There is no other reason to be given why you have not gone to hell, since you have sat here in the house of God, provoking His pure eyes by your sinful wicked manner of attending His solemn worship. Yea, there is nothing else that is to be given as a reason why you do not this very moment drop down into hell.

O sinner! Consider the fearful danger you are in:[16] it is a great furnace of wrath, a wide and bottomless pit, full of the fire of wrath, that you are held over in the hand of that God, whose wrath is provoked and incensed as much against you, as against many of the damned in hell. You hang by a slender thread, with the flames of divine wrath flashing about it, and ready every moment to singe it, and burn it asunder; and you have no interest in any Mediator, and nothing to lay hold of to save yourself, nothing to keep off the flames of wrath, nothing of your own, nothing that you ever have done, nothing that you can do, to induce God to spare you one moment. And consider here more particularly:

1. Whose wrath it is: it is the wrath of the infinite God. If it were only the wrath of man, though it were of the most potent prince, it would be comparatively little to be regarded. The wrath of kings is very much dreaded, especially of absolute monarchs, who have the possessions and lives of their subjects wholly in their power, to be disposed of at their mere will. Proverbs. 20:2, "The fear of a king is as the roaring of a lion: Whoso provoketh him to anger, sinneth against his own soul." The subject that very much enrages an arbitrary prince, is liable to suffer the most extreme torments that human art can invent, or human power

16 Our agenda isn't to convince the careless world to "believe" in God. Every sane person already believes in His existence (see Romans 1:20). It is to show them that they are in great danger and that they need a Savior.

can inflict. But the greatest earthly potentates in their greatest majesty and strength, and when clothed in their greatest terrors, are but feeble, despicable worms of the dust, in comparison of the great and almighty Creator and King of heaven and earth. It is but little that they can do, when most enraged, and when they have exerted the utmost of their fury. All the kings of the earth, before God, are as grasshoppers; they are nothing, and less than nothing: both their love and their hatred is to be despised. The wrath of the great King of kings, is as much more terrible than theirs, as His majesty is greater. Luke 12:4-5, "And I say unto you, my friends, Be not afraid of them that kill the body, and after that, have no more that they can do. But I will forewarn you whom you shall fear: Fear him, which after he hath killed, hath power to cast into hell: yea, I say unto you, Fear him."

2. It is the fierceness of His wrath that you are exposed to. We often read of the fury of God; as in Isaiah. 59:18, "According to their deeds, accordingly he will repay fury to his adversaries." So Isaiah 66:15, "For behold, the LORD will come with fire, and with his chariots like a whirlwind, to render his anger with fury, and his rebuke with flames of fire." And in many other places. So, in Revelation 19:15 we read of "the wine press of the fierceness and wrath of Almighty God." The words are exceeding terrible. If it had only been said, "the wrath of God," the words would have implied that which is infinitely dreadful: but it is "the fierceness and wrath of God." The fury of God! The fierceness of Jehovah! Oh, how dreadful that must be! Who can utter or conceive what such expressions carry in them! But it is also "the fierceness and wrath of almighty God." As though there would be a very great manifestation of His almighty power

in what the fierceness of His wrath should inflict, as though omnipotence should be as it were enraged, and exerted, as men are wont to exert their strength in the fierceness of their wrath. Oh! then, what will be the consequence! What will become of the poor worms that shall suffer it! Whose hands can be strong? And whose heart can endure? To what a dreadful, inexpressible, inconceivable depth of misery must the poor creature be sunk who shall be the subject of this!

Consider this, you that are here present, that yet remain in an unregenerate state. That God will execute the fierceness of His anger, implies, that He will inflict wrath without any pity. When God beholds the ineffable extremity of your case, and sees your torment to be so vastly disproportioned to your strength, and sees how your poor soul is crushed, and sinks down, as it were, into an infinite gloom; He will have no compassion upon you, He will not forbear the executions of His wrath, or in the least lighten His hand; there shall be no moderation or mercy, nor will God then at all stay His rough wind; He will have no regard to your welfare, nor be at all careful lest you should suffer too much in any other sense, than only that you shall not suffer beyond what strict justice requires. Nothing shall be withheld, because it is so hard for you to bear. Ezekiel 8:18, "Therefore will I also deal in fury: mine eye shall not spare, neither will I have pity; and though they cry in mine ears with a loud voice, yet I will not hear them." Now God stands ready to pity you; this is a day of mercy; you may cry now with some encouragement of obtaining mercy.[17] But when once the day of mercy

17 How tragic that so many who profess to be Christians are not running the streets pleading with the lost to take advantage of the day of mercy. The time will come and the sun of God's patience will set upon this world, and the lost will find themselves in the dark and terrible wrath of Almighty God, with no means of escape.

is past, your most lamentable and dolorous cries and shrieks will be in vain; you will be wholly lost and thrown away of God, as to any regard to your welfare. God will have no other use to put you to, but to suffer misery; you shall be continued in being to no other end; for you will be a vessel of wrath fitted to destruction; and there will be no other use of this vessel, but to be filled full of wrath. God will be so far from pitying you when you cry to him, that it is said he will only "laugh and mock," Proverbs 1:25-26, &c.

How awful are those words, Isaiah 63:3, which are the words of the great God. "I will tread them in mine anger, and will trample them in my fury, and their blood shall be sprinkled upon my garments, and I will stain all my raiment." It is perhaps impossible to conceive of words that carry in them greater manifestations of these three things, viz. contempt, and hatred, and fierceness of indignation. If you cry to God to pity you, He will be so far from pitying you in your doleful case, or showing you the least regard or favor, that instead of that, He will only tread you under foot. And though he will know that you cannot bear the weight of omnipotence treading upon you, yet He will not regard that, but He will crush you under His feet without mercy; He will crush out your blood, and make it fly, and it shall be sprinkled on His garments, so as to stain all His raiment. He will not only hate you, but He will have you in the utmost contempt: no place shall be thought fit for you, but under His feet to be trodden down as the mire of the streets.

3. The misery you are exposed to is that which God will inflict to that end, that He might show what that wrath of Jehovah is. God hath had it on His heart to show to angels and men, both how excellent His love is, and also how terrible His wrath is. Sometimes earthly

kings have a mind to show how terrible their wrath is, by the extreme punishments they would execute on those that would provoke them. Nebuchadnezzar, that mighty and haughty monarch of the Chaldean empire, was willing to show his wrath when enraged with Shadrach, Meshach, and Abednego; and accordingly gave orders that the burning fiery furnace should be heated seven times hotter than it was before; doubtless, it was raised to the utmost degree of fierceness that human art could raise it. But the great God is also willing to show his wrath, and magnify his awful majesty and mighty power in the extreme sufferings of his enemies. Romans 9:22, "*What if God, willing to shew his wrath, and to make his power known, endured with much long-suffering the vessels of wrath fitted to destruction?*" And seeing this is His design, and what He has determined, even to show how terrible the unrestrained wrath, the fury and fierceness of Jehovah is, He will do it to effect. There will be something accomplished and brought to pass that will be dreadful with a witness. When the great and angry God hath risen up and executed His awful vengeance on the poor sinner, and the wretch is actually suffering the infinite weight and power of His indignation, then will God call upon the whole universe to behold that awful majesty and mighty power that is to be seen in it. Isaiah 33:12-14, "*And the people shall be as the burnings of lime, as thorns cut up shall they be burned in the fire. Hear ye that are far off, what I have done; and ye that are near, acknowledge my might. The sinners in Zion are afraid; fearfulness hath surprised the hypocrites,*" &c.

Thus it will be with you that are in an unconverted state, if you continue in it; the infinite might, and majesty, and terribleness of the omnipotent God shall be magnified upon you, in the ineffable strength of your torments. You shall be tormented in the presence of the holy angels, and in the presence of the Lamb; and when you shall be in this state of suffering, the glorious inhabitants of heaven shall go forth and look on the awful spectacle, that they may see what the wrath and fierceness of the Almighty is; and when they have seen it, they will fall down and adore that great power and majesty. Isaiah 66:23-24, "And it shall come to pass, that from one new moon to another, and from one Sabbath to another, shall all flesh come to worship before me, saith the Lord. And they shall go forth and look upon the carcasses of the men that have transgressed against me; for their worm shall not die, neither shall their fire be quenched, and they shall be an abhorring unto all flesh."

4. It is everlasting wrath.[18] It would be dreadful to suffer this fierceness and wrath of Almighty God one moment; but you must suffer it to all eternity. There will be no end to this exquisite horrible misery. When you look forward, you shall see a long forever, a boundless duration before you, which will swallow up your thoughts, and amaze your soul; and you will absolutely despair of ever having any deliverance, any end, any mitigation, any rest at all. You will know certainly that you must wear out long ages, millions of millions of ages, in wrestling and conflicting with this almighty merciless vengeance; and then when you have so done, when so many ages have actually been spent by you in this manner, you will know that all is

18 There are some who dismiss the *everlasting* nature of God's justice as being totally out of proportion to their sins. They believe that sinners are threatened with an infinite punishment for finite crimes, and that is unjust. However, what they are not taking into account is that God will withdraw the dimension of time. Those who die in their sins will be treated with perfect equity and find themselves in the dimension of eternity, with no recourse, damned from all that is good and pleasurable.

> but a point to what remains. So that your punishment will indeed be infinite. Oh, who can express what the state of a soul in such circumstances is! All that we can possibly say about it, gives but a very feeble, faint representation of it; it is inexpressible and inconceivable: For "who knows the power of God's anger?"

How dreadful is the state of those that are daily and hourly in the danger of this great wrath and infinite misery! But this is the dismal case of every soul in this congregation that has not been born again, however moral and strict, sober and religious, they may otherwise be. Oh that you would consider it, whether you be young or old! There is reason to think, that there are many in this congregation now hearing this discourse that will actually be the subjects of this very misery to all eternity. We know not who they are, or in what seats they sit, or what thoughts they now have. It may be they are now at ease, and hear all these things without much disturbance, and are now flattering themselves that they are not the persons, promising themselves that they shall escape. If we knew that there was one person, and but one, in the whole congregation, that was to be the subject of this misery, what an awful thing would it be to think of! If we knew who it was, what an awful sight would it be to see such a person! How might all the rest of the congregation lift up a lamentable and bitter cry over him! But, alas! instead of one, how many is it likely will remember this discourse in hell? And it would be a wonder, if some that are now present should not be in hell in a very short time, even before this year is out. And it would be no wonder if some persons, that now sit here, in some seats of this meeting-house, in health, quiet and secure, should be there before tomorrow morning. Those of you that finally continue in a natural condition that shall keep out of hell longest will be there in a little time! Your damnation does not slumber; it will come swiftly, and, in all probability, very suddenly upon many of you. You have reason to wonder that you are not already in hell. It is doubtless the case of some whom you have seen and known, that never deserved hell more than you, and that heretofore appeared as likely to have been now alive as you. Their case is past all hope; they are crying in extreme misery and perfect despair; but here you are in the land of the living and in the house of God, and have an opportunity to obtain salvation. What would not those poor damned hopeless souls give for one day's opportunity such as you now enjoy!

And now you have an extraordinary opportunity, a day wherein Christ has thrown the door of mercy wide open, and stands in calling and crying with a loud voice to poor sinners; a day wherein many are flocking to Him, and pressing into the kingdom of God.[19] Many are daily coming from the east, west, north and south; many that were very lately in the same miserable condition that you are in, are now in a happy state, with their hearts filled with love to Him who has loved them, and washed them from their sins in His own blood, and rejoicing in hope of the glory of God. How awful is it to be left behind at such a day! To see so many others feasting, while you are pining and perishing! To see so many rejoicing and singing for joy of heart, while you have cause to mourn for sorrow of heart, and howl for vexation of spirit! How can you rest one moment in such a condition? Are not your souls as precious as the souls of the people at Suffield, where they are flocking from day to day to Christ?

Are there not many here who have lived long in the world, and are not to this day born again? And so are aliens from the commonwealth of Israel, and have done nothing ever since they have lived, but treasure up wrath against the day

19 The preaching of the Law of God and its ensuing justice makes a sinner thirst for righteousness. He who finds himself crawling in the desert of sin, under the burning heat of the Law of a holy God, is the one who most appreciates the cool and thirst-quenching waters of the gospel.

of wrath? Oh, sirs, your cases, in an especial manner, are extremely dangerous. Your guilt and hardness of heart is extremely great. Do you not see how generally persons of your years are passed over and left, in the present remarkable and wonderful dispensation of God's mercy? You had need to consider yourselves, and awake thoroughly out of sleep. You cannot bear the fierceness and wrath of the infinite God. And you, young men, and young women, will you neglect this precious season which you now enjoy, when so many others of your age are renouncing all youthful vanities, and flocking to Christ? You especially have now an extraordinary opportunity; but if you neglect it, it will soon be with you as with those persons who spent all the precious days of youth in sin, and are now come to such a dreadful pass in blindness and hardness. And you, children, who are unconverted, do not you know that you are going down to hell, to bear the dreadful wrath of that God, who is now angry with you every day and every night? Will you be content to be the children of the devil, when so many other children in the land are converted, and are become the holy and happy children of the King of kings?

And let every one that is yet out of Christ, and hanging over the pit of hell, whether they be old men and women, or middle aged, or young people, or little children, now hearken to the loud calls of God's word and providence. This acceptable year of the Lord, a day of such great favor to some, will doubtless be a day of as remarkable vengeance to others. Men's hearts harden, and their guilt increases apace at such a day as this, if they neglect their souls; and never was there so great danger of such persons being given up to hardness of heart and blindness of mind. God seems now to be hastily gathering in his elect in all parts of the land; and probably the greater part of adult persons that ever shall be saved, will be brought in now in a little time, and that it will be as it was on the great out-pouring of the Spirit upon the Jews in the apostles' days; the election will obtain, and the rest will be blinded. If this should be the case with you, you will eternally curse this day, and will curse the day that ever you were born, to see such a season of the pouring out of God's Spirit, and will wish that you had died and gone to hell before you had seen it. Now undoubtedly it is, as it was in the days of John the Baptist, the axe is in an extraordinary manner laid at the root of the trees, that every tree which brings not forth good fruit, may be hewn down and cast into the fire.[20] Therefore, let every one that is out of Christ, now awake and fly from the wrath to come. The wrath of Almighty God is now undoubtedly hanging over a great part of this congregation.

Let every one fly out of Sodom: " Escape for thy life; look not behind thee, neither stay thou in all the plain; escape to the mountain, lest thou be consumed."[21]

20 Matthew 3:10

21 Genesis 19:17

Introduction to the Resolutions of Jonathan Edwards

by
Ray Comfort

Jonathan Edwards wrote his resolutions before he became the great theologian that we know him as today. Many of his resolutions were written before the age of 19 and during a short period of just under eight months, from December 18, 1722 to August 17, 1723.

It has been said that he conscientiously practiced the resolutions for the rest of his days. This is what makes Edwards so infectious. His entire life was dominated by a blistering zeal to live a holy life for the glory of God. Edwards wrote seventy resolutions of things that he was resolved to do in his daily life.

If George Whitefield was the "lightning rod" of the Great Awakening, then Jonathan Edwards was the "conductor." He was the brains behind the Great Awakening. He provided theological substance and depth to the revivals. He read all seventy of his resolutions once a week as part of his spiritual discipline.

The Resolutions of Jonathan Edwards (1722-1723)

Resolutions 1 through 21 were written by Edwards in one sitting in New Haven in 1722.

Being sensible that I am unable to do anything without God's help, I do humbly entreat Him by his grace to enable me to keep these Resolutions, so far as they are agreeable to His will, for Christ's sake.

Remember to read over these Resolutions once a week.

1. Resolved, that I will do whatsoever I think to be most to God's glory, and my own good, profit and pleasure, in the whole of my duration, without any consideration of the time, whether now, or never so many myriad's of ages hence. Resolved to do whatever I think to be my duty and most for the good and advantage of mankind in general. Resolved to do this, whatever difficulties I meet with, how many and how great soever.[22]

2. Resolved, to be continually endeavoring to find out some new invention and contrivance to promote the aforementioned things.

22 There is a fine dividing line between these sorts of resolutions and legalism. The difference is seen in our motives, which are governed by our understanding of both Law and grace. The Law leaves us helpless, clinging for life itself by grace alone. Nothing we can offer God in the area of self-improvement can in itself please Him. Sanctification for the Christian has nothing to do with justification. It springs solely from the fuel of gratitude for His amazing grace.

3. Resolved, if ever I shall fall and grow dull, so as to neglect to keep any part of these Resolutions, to repent of all I can remember, when I come to myself again.[23]

4. Resolved, never to do any manner of thing, whether in soul or body, less or more, but what tends to the glory of God; nor be, nor suffer it, if I can avoid it.

5. Resolved, never to lose one moment of time; but improve it the most profitable way I possibly can.

6. Resolved, to live with all my might, while I do live.[24]

7. Resolved, never to do anything, which I should be afraid to do, if it were the last hour of my life.[25]

8. Resolved, to act, in all respects, both speaking and doing, as if nobody had been so vile as I, and as if I had committed the same sins, or had the same infirmities or failings as others; and that I will let the knowledge of their failings promote nothing but shame in myself, and prove only an occasion of my confessing my own sins and misery to God.[26]

9. Resolved, to think much on all occasions of my own dying, and of the common circumstances which attend death.[27]

---

23 Our relationship, as the bride of Christ, is likened to marriage. If my marriage becomes dull and lifeless, it is an insult to my spouse. God has proved His love for us through the Cross (see Romans 5:8). Dullness is an insult to the Spirit of grace.

24 This is something we must resolve to do, especially in the area of evangelism. May God give us energy to reach out to the lost.

25 This is a wonderful attitude in which we should live. It is to walk in a healthy sobriety and fear of God.

26 Always keep a short account with God. Never let unconfessed sin sit as stagnant water in your soul. Talk often with God about those sins that "so easily beset"—wandering eyes, secret envy, hidden conceit, unbridled appetite, etc. The more you keep them in the light, the easier they are to confess to God. Never forget that cleansing is a mere confession away. You don't need a priest for this, if you have a Savior. His blood is sufficient. See 1 John 1:9.

27 It is wise for the Christian to keep in mind the most important moment of his life—his death. It keeps us close to the Savior.

10. Resolved, when I feel pain, to think of the pains of martyrdom, and of hell.[28]

11. Resolved, when I think of any theorem in divinity to be solved, immediately to do what I can towards solving it, if circumstances don't hinder.

12. Resolved, if I take delight in it as a gratification of pride, or vanity, or on any such account, immediately to throw it by.[29]

13. Resolved, to be endeavoring to find out fit objects of charity and liberality.

14. Resolved, never to do anything out of revenge.[30]

15. Resolved, never to suffer the least motions of anger to irrational beings.

16. Resolved, never to speak evil of anyone, so that it shall tend to his dishonor, more or less, upon no account except for some real good.[31]

17. Resolved, that I will live so as I shall wish I had done when I come to die.

18. Resolved, to live so at all times, as I think is best in my devout frames, and when I have clearest notions of things of the gospel, and another world.

19. Resolved, never to do anything, which I should be afraid to do, if I expected it would not be above an hour, before I should hear the last trump.

---

28 Thinking of the suffering of the lost or of the martyrs brings our suffering into perspective.

29 It is a testimony to our wickedness that we can still, in the light of the Cross, have delight in any sin.

30 If you want a test of your godliness, look objectively at your attitude when you are wronged by someone.

31 Our flesh gravitates to gossip like steel to a magnet. We are naturally attracted to it. We must turn the magnet around so that we are repulsed by the slightest gossip.

20. Resolved, to maintain the strictest temperance in eating and drinking.[32]

21. Resolved, never to do anything, which if I should see in another, I should count a just occasion to despise him for, or to think any way the more meanly of him.

22. Resolved, to endeavor to obtain for myself as much happiness, in the other world, as I possibly can, with all the power; might, vigor, and vehemence, yea violence, I

---

32 I once saw an attractive woman on a panel, with a number of very large ladies. She said that she was once extremely overweight, but that she realized what the problem was when she thought about the liberation of the Jews from Nazi concentration camps. She said that none of those who came out of the death camps were overweight. Not one. No one had a genetic disposition towards obesity, or "large" bones, or had inherited an overweight body from a parent and stayed overweight in the camp, or who had some sort of "obesity syndrome." They were all skin and bone, because they were deprived of food. She said her problem was simply a lack of self-control. She ate too much. The women on the panel almost ate her alive. If I can't see my feet, I need to quickly deal with my run-away mouth. Either I'm eating too much or I'm eating the wrong sort of food. My overweight problem is not a good witness to a critical world. We are called to be blameless. Obesity reveals a lack of self-control on my part, and self-control is a fruit of the Spirit (see Gal. 5:23). But the issue is more than to do with my Christian testimony. Obesity will eventually cause me great suffering. If I overload my truck, it's just a matter of time until the tires blow. In time I will bring upon myself terrible diseases, and a horrible death. If I give myself to my appetite, I may as well be cutting my own throat.

Ten Practical Ways to Fight the Appetite:

1. Say "No" to the convenience (and pleasure) of fast food.
2. Serve food on a smaller plate, and it will look like more.
3. Leave a potato or something on your plate, and put it in the refrigerator for later when you feel hungry.
4. Get a bike and make yourself ride it regularly.
5. Keep your mind busy. We tend to eat when we are bored.
6. When hunger comes, have a large hot drink. Then have another until it curbs your appetite.
7. Don't stuff yourself to the full. Every time you do, you will stretch your stomach just a little more.
8. Fast one or two meals each week. This will help to teach you self-control. You can do this—memorize and quote out loud, "I can do all things through Christ who strengthens me" (Philippians 4:13).
9. Buy (and eat) plenty of fresh vegetables—and don't shop when you are hungry. You will be tempted to buy what appeals to your eyes.
10. Pray that God gives you a very tender conscience, so that you will know when you are sinning in regard to food. Then take it a day at a time.

am capable of, or can bring myself to exert, in any way that can be thought of.[33]

23. Resolved, frequently to take some deliberate action, which seems most unlikely to be done, for the glory of God, and trace it back to the original intention, designs and ends of it; and if I find it not to be for God's glory, to repute it as a breach of the 4th Resolution.

24. Resolved, whenever I do any conspicuously evil action, to trace it back, till I come to the original cause; and then both carefully endeavor to do so no more, and to fight and pray with all my might against the original cause of it.[34]

25. Resolved, to examine carefully, and constantly, what that one thing in me is, which causes me in the least to doubt of the love of God; and to direct all my forces against it.[35]

26. Resolved, to cast away such things, as I find do abate my assurance.[36]

27. Resolved, never willfully to omit anything, except the omission be for the glory of God; and frequently to examine my omissions.

28. Resolved, to study the Scriptures so steadily, constantly and frequently, as that I may find, and plainly perceive myself to grow in the knowledge of the same.[37]

29. Resolved, never to count that a prayer, nor to let that pass as a prayer, nor that as a petition of a prayer, which is so

---

33 Some people are so earthly-minded, they are no heavenly use.

34 God is not aware of confessed sin. It is because of this truth, that we can gratefully remember what we have been forgiven.

35 There is no more effective way to doubt the love of God, than to forget the horror of the Cross.

36 Unbelief is a subtle sin. It is to doubt the very character of God. It is to call him a liar (see 1 John 5:10). We are so wicked, we tend to believe the lies of the devil, rather than to believe the truths of God's Word.

37 Resolve to read the Bible daily, and let its holy light expose any hidden darkness.

made, that I cannot hope that God will answer it; nor that as a confession, which I cannot hope God will accept.

30. Resolved, to strive to my utmost every week to be brought higher in religion, and to a higher exercise of grace, than I was the week before.

31. Resolved, never to say anything at all against anybody, but when it is perfectly agreeable to the highest degree of Christian honor, and of love to mankind, agreeable to the lowest humility, and sense of my own faults and failings, and agreeable to the golden rule; often, when I have said anything against anyone, to bring it to, and try it strictly by the test of this Resolution.

32. Resolved, to be strictly and firmly faithful to my trust, that that in Proverbs 20:6, "A faithful man who can find?" may not be partly fulfilled in me.

33. Resolved, always to do what I can towards making, maintaining, establishing and preserving peace, when it can be without over-balancing detriment in other respects.[38] (December 26, 1722.)

34. Resolved, in narrations never to speak anything but the pure and simple verity.

35. Resolved, whenever I so much question whether I have done my duty, as that my quiet and calm is thereby disturbed, to set it down, and also how the question was resolved.[39] (December 18, 1722.)

36. Resolved, never to speak evil of any, except I have some particular good call for it. (December 19, 1722.)

37. Resolved, to inquire every night, as I am going to bed, wherein I have been negligent, what sin I have

---

38 This is the character of a true peacemaker—a child of God. See Matthew 5:9.

39 The Christian life begins and ends with discipline.

committed, and wherein I have denied myself: also at the end of every week, month, and year.[40] (December 22 and 26, 1722.)

38. Resolved, never to speak anything that is ridiculous, sportive, or matter of laughter on the Lord's day.[41] (Sabbath evening, December 23, 1722.)

39. Resolved, never to do anything that I so much question the lawfulness of, as that I intend, at the same time, to consider and examine afterwards, whether it be lawful or no; except I as much question the lawfulness of the omission.[42]

40. Resolved, to inquire every night, before I go to bed, whether I have acted in the best way I possibly could, with respect to eating and drinking. (January 7, 1723.)

41. Resolved, to ask myself at the end of every day, week, month, and year, wherein I could possibly in any respect have done better. (January 11, 1723.)

42. Resolved, frequently to renew the dedication of myself to God, which was made at my baptism; which I solemnly renewed, when I was received into the communion of the church; and which I have solemnly remade this twelfth day of January, 1723.

43. Resolved, never henceforward, till I die, to act as if I were

---

40 God bless Jonathan Edwards for his honesty of heart. Those who maintain the doctrine of sinless perfection may have forgotten that we commit sin by failing to love our neighbor as much as we love ourselves. It is a serious violation of the moral Law to walk by a sinner and fail to have deep concern for his salvation. Who of us outside of Christ could live up to such a Law?

41 While we have liberty of conscience regarding how we spend the Sabbath, we should esteem it a special day of the week.

42 This is the proper use of the moral Law. It is a light that helps us to know what is pleasing to God. The Christian isn't a "worker of lawlessness," as is the false convert (see Matthew 7:21-23).

any way my own, but entirely and altogether God's, agreeable to what is to be found in Saturday, January 12 (1723).

44. Resolved, that no other end but religion, shall have any influence at all on any of my actions; and that no action shall be, in the least circumstance, any otherwise than the religious end will carry it. (January12, 1723.)

45. Resolved, never to allow any pleasure or grief, joy or sorrow, nor any affection at all, nor any degree of affection, nor any circumstance relating to it, but what helps religion. (January 12 and 13, 1723.)

46. Resolved, never to allow the least measure of any fretting uneasiness at my father or mother. Resolved to suffer no effects of it, so much as in the least alteration of speech, or motion of my eye; and to be especially careful of it, with respect to any of our family.

47. Resolved, to endeavor to my utmost to deny whatever is not most agreeable to a good, and universally sweet and benevolent, quiet, peaceable, contented, easy, compassionate, generous, humble, meek, modest, submissive, obliging, diligent and industrious, charitable, even, patient, moderate, forgiving, sincere temper; and to do at all times what such a temper would lead me to. Examine strictly every week, whether I have done so. (Sabbath morning, May 5, 1723.)

48. Resolved, constantly, with the utmost niceness and diligence, and the strictest scrutiny, to be looking into the state of my soul, that I may know whether I have truly an interest in Christ or no; that when I come to die, I may not have any negligence respecting this to repent of. (May 26, 1723.)

49. Resolved, that this never shall be, if I can help it.

50. Resolved, I will act so as I think I shall judge would have been best, and most prudent, when I come into the future world. (July 5, 1723.)

51. Resolved, that I will act so, in every respect, as I think I shall wish I had done, if I should at last be damned. (July 8, 1723.)

52. I frequently hear persons in old age say how they would live, if they were to live their lives over again. Resolved, that I will live just so as I can think I shall wish I had done, supposing I live to old age.[43] (July 8, 1723.)

53. Resolved, to improve every opportunity, when I am in the best and happiest frame of mind, to cast and venture my soul on the Lord Jesus Christ, to trust and confide in Him, and consecrate myself wholly to Him; that from this I may have assurance of my safety, knowing that I confide in my Redeemer.[44] (July 8, 1723.)

54. Whenever I hear anything spoken in conversation of any person, if I think it would be praiseworthy in me, resolved to endeavor to imitate it. (July 8, 1723.)

55. Resolved, to endeavor to my utmost to act as I can think I should do, if I had already seen the happiness of heaven, and hell torments. (July 8, 1723.)

56. Resolved, never to give over, nor in the least to slacken my fight with my corruptions, however unsuccessful I may be.[45]

---

43 Teach me to number my days that I might apply my heart to wisdom (See Psalm 90:12.). Don't chase anything of this world. It is chasing the wind. Apply all your energies to eternity.

44 Can you say "I love Jesus"? This is the beginning and end of Christianity. See 1 Corinthians 16:22.

45 Don't give up the fight against your greatest enemy—the flesh. If you win "the battle of the flesh," you win the war. The world will have no attraction to you, and the devil will have no foothold on you. Fight it daily. It wants to take the helm, and it will steer you to hell.

57. Resolved, when I fear misfortunes and adversities, to examine whether I have done my duty, and resolve to do it; and let it be just as providence orders it, I will as far as I can, be concerned about nothing but my duty and my sin. (June 9, and July 13 1723.)

58. Resolved, not only to refrain from an air of dislike, fretfulness, and anger in conversation, but to exhibit an air of love, cheerfulness and benignity. (May 27, and July 13, 1723.)

59. Resolved, when I am most conscious of provocations to ill nature and anger, that I will strive most to feel and act good-naturedly; yea, at such times, to manifest good nature, though I think that in other respects it would be disadvantageous, and so as would be imprudent at other times.[46] (May 12, July 2, and July 13.)

60. Resolved, whenever my feelings begin to appear in the least out of order, when I am conscious of the least uneasiness within, or the least irregularity without, I will then subject myself to the strictest examination.[47] (July 4 and 13, 1723.)

61. Resolved, that I will not give way to that listlessness which I find unbends and relaxes my mind from being fully and fixedly set on religion, whatever excuse I may have for it—that what my listlessness inclines me to do, is best to be done, etc. (May 21, and July 13, 1723.)

62. Resolved, never to do anything but duty; and then according to Ephesians 6:6-8, do it willingly and cheerfully as unto the Lord, and not to man; "knowing that whatever good thing any man doth, the same shall he receive of the Lord." (June 25 and July 13, 1723.)

---

46 Life's daily trials are the litmus test of godly character.

47 We should search our souls with the eye of a surgeon, with scalpel in hand.

63. On the supposition, that there never was to be but one individual in the world, at any one time, who was properly a complete Christian, in all respects of a right stamp, having Christianity always shining in its true luster, and appearing excellent and lovely, from whatever part and under whatever character viewed: Resolved, to act just as I would do, if I strove with all my might to be that one, who should live in my time.[48] (January 14 and July 3, 1723.)

64. Resolved, when I find those "groanings which cannot be uttered" (Romans 8:26), of which the Apostle Paul speaks, and those "breakings of soul for the longing it hath," of which the Psalmist speaks (Psalm 119:20), that I will promote them to the utmost of my power, and that I will not be weary of earnestly endeavoring to vent my desires, nor of the repetitions of such earnestness.[49] (July 23 and August 10, 1723.)

65. Resolved, very much to exercise myself in this all my life long, viz. with the greatest openness I am capable of, to declare my ways to God, and lay open my soul to him: all my sins, temptations, difficulties, sorrows, fears, hopes, desires, and every thing, and every circumstance; according to Dr. Manton's 27th Sermon on Psalm 119.[50] (July 26, and August 10 1723.)

66. Resolved, that I will endeavor always to keep a benign aspect, and air of acting and speaking in all places, and in all companies, except it should so happen that duty requires otherwise.

67. Resolved, after afflictions, to inquire, what I am the better for them, what good I have got by them, and what I might have got by them.

---

48 Jesus is our model of imitation.

49 Nothing fuels "groanings" in prayer like meditation of the fate of the lost.

50 Too many think nothing of an hour of workout at the gym, and begrudge an hour of godly exercise in the prayer closet. Muscle degenerates in time. Godliness has eternal permanency.

68. Resolved, to confess frankly to myself all that which I find in myself, either infirmity or sin; and, if it be what concerns religion, also to confess the whole case to God, and implore needed help.[51] (July 23 and August 10, 1723.)

69. Resolved, always to do that, which I shall wish I had done when I see others do it. (August 11, 1723.)

70. Let there be something of benevolence, in all that I speak.[52] (August 17, 1723.)

51 This is honesty in relationship. No marriage is healthy where secrets are kept from a spouse.

52 It should be evident to all, that love is the fountain from which we drink.

EDWARDS GOLD

R.C. Sproul, in his Foreword to *Altogether Lovely* a work by Jonathan Edwards on the glory and excellency of Christ, has this to say about Edwards' incredible life:

> Augustine has been esteemed as the greatest thinker of the first millennium of Christian history. Those who followed him had the advantage of standing on his shoulders. In my judgment, however, the two most prodigious thinking of all time are Aquinas and Edwards. Aquinas was more prolific in his literary productions than Edwards, but, in terms of intellectual brilliance, Edwards was at least his peer, if not his superior. He was to theology what Newton and Einstein were to physics. The value of Edwards' work is not found merely in his lucid and penetrating mind. What is most singular is his combination of rational analysis with spiritual ardor. He was a man whose heart was aflame with love[53] and devotion for the sweetness and excellence of Christ. His work exudes authentic religious

53 The world twists the motives of Christians, who love enough to warn of hell. Such talk is deemed to be hate speech, and yet it is a sign of true concern and compassion. It is those who call themselves Christians who don't warn the world of the reality of hell, that are the ones to whom the world should direct its disdain. Disdain is what they will have for them on the Day of Judgment. Jesus rebuked the hypocritical Pharisees because He cared for them. Had He not, He would have remained silent. Who knows how many of His hypocritical hearers turned from their sin at His rebuke and were there with the 3,000 on the day of Pentecost.

affection. He was, above all things, a lover of God who made the seeking of His Kingdom the chief business of his life.

Safety in Christ

There is in Christ Jesus an abundant foundation of peace and safety for those who are in fear and danger. The fears and dangers to which men are subject are of two kinds: temporal and eternal. Men are frequently in distress from fear of temporal evils. We live in an evil world, where we are liable to an abundance of sorrows and calamities. A great part of our lives is spent in sorrowing for present or past evils, and in fearing those which are future. What poor, distressed creatures are we when God is pleased to send His judgments among us! If He visits a place with mortal and prevailing sickness, what terror seizes our hearts! If any person is taken sick and trembles for his life, or if our near friends are at the point of death, or in many other dangers how fearful is our condition! Now there is sufficient foundation for peace and safety to those exercised with such fears and brought into such dangers. But Christ is a refuge in all trouble; there is a foundation for rational support and peace in Him, whatever threatens us. He whose heart is fixed, trusting in Christ, need not be afraid of any evil tidings. As the mountains are round about Jerusalem, so Christ is round about them that fear Him.

(Jonathan Edwards, *Altogether Lovely*, pp 81-82)

Justice and the Law

If we are in Christ Jesus, justice and the law have its course with respect to our sins without our hurt. The foundation of the sinner's fear and distress is the justice and the law of God, they are against him and they are unalterable, they must have their course. Every jot and tittle of the law must be fulfilled, heaven and earth shall be destroyed rather than justice should not take place; there is no possibility of sin's escaping justice.[54] But, yet, if the distressed, trembling soul who is afraid of justice would fly to Christ, He would be a safe hiding place. Justice and the threatening of the law will take their course as fully while he is safe and untouched, as if he were to be eternally destroyed. Christ bears the stroke of justice and the curse of the law falls fully upon Him.

(Jonathan Edwards, *Altogether Lovely,* p 85)

Christ, Our Burden Bearer

Those who are in trouble and distressing fear, if they come to Jesus Christ, have this to ease them of their fears: that Christ has promised them that He will protect them; that they come upon His invitation; that Christ has pledged His faith for their security if they will close with Him; and that He is engaged by covenant to God the Father that He will save those afflicted and distressed souls that come to Him.

(Jonathan Edwards, *Altogether Lovely,* p 83)

54 It is probably divine design that the Law of God is preceded in Psalms by talk of the majesty of God's sun. Nothing is hid from the heat thereof. Such is the penetrating ray of eternal justice. It will search out and burn up every shadow of sin.

Christ by His own free act, has made Himself the surety of such. He has voluntarily put Himself in their stead; and, if justice has anything against them, He has undertaken to answer for them.[55] By His own act He has engaged to be responsible for them, so that if they have exposed themselves to God's wrath, and to the stroke of justice, it is not their concern, but His, how to answer or satisfy for what they have done. Let there be never so much wrath they have deserved, they are as safe as if they never deserved any, because He has undertaken to stand for them, let it be more or less. If they are in Christ Jesus, the storm does of course light on Him, and not on them; as when we are under a good shelter, the storm that otherwise come upon our heads lights upon the shelter.
(Jonathan Edwards, *Altogether Lovely,* p 84)

Christ bears all that vengeance that belongs to the sin that has been committed by him [the sinner], and there is no need of its being borne twice over. His temporal sufferings, by reason of the infinite dignity of His person, are fully equivalent to the eternal sufferings of a mere creature. And then His sufferings answer for him who flees to Him as well as if they were his own, for indeed they are his own by virtue of the union between Christ and him. Christ has made Himself one with them. He is the head, and they are the members.[56] Therefore, if Christ suffers for the believer, there is no need of his suffering; and what needs he to be afraid? . . . The threatening "thou shall surely die"[57] is properly fulfilled in the death of Christ. . . . Therefore if those who are afraid will go to Jesus Christ, they need to fear nothing from the threatening of the law. The threatening of the law

---

55 Our perspective of the gospel changes completely when we understand the position of the Law of God. God and justice cannot be separated. It was the Law that demanded a sacrifice. It was the Law that put Jesus on the Cross. It is the Law that sinners must face on the day of wrath. He is the Savior from the Law, for all who repent and trust in Him alone.

56 It is for this reason that we should feel the divine heartbeat of God. The living Body of Christ on this earth must have the same passion as the Savior had when He walked this earth. He is the head, we are the members, and we must therefore seek and save that which is lost.

57 Ezekiel 3:18, 33:8, 14

has nothing to do with them.[58]
(Jonathan Edwards, *Altogether Lovely,* pp 85-86)

The wounded soul is sensible that he has affronted the majesty of God, and looks upon God as a vindicator of his honor, as a jealous God that will not be mocked, an infinitely great God that will not bear to be affronted, who will not suffer His authority and majesty to be trampled on, that will not bear that His kindness should be abused. A view of God in this light terrifies awakened souls. They think how exceedingly they have sinned, how they have sinned against light, against frequent and long-continued calls and warnings; and how they have slighted mercy, and been guilty of turning the grace of God into lasciviousness, taking encouragement from God's mercy to go on in sin against Him. They fear that God is so affronted at the contempt and slight which they have cast upon Him that He, being careful of His honor will never forgive them, but will punish them. But if they go to Christ, the honor of God's majesty and authority will not be in the least hurt by their being freed and made happy. For what Christ has done has repaired God's honor to the full.
(Jonathan Edwards, *Altogether Lovely,* p 86)

God hates our sins,[59] but not more than He delights in Christ's obedience which He performed on account. This is a sweet savor to Him, a savor of rest. God is abundantly compensated, and desires no more. Christ's righteousness is of infinite worthiness and merit.
(Jonathan Edwards, *Altogether Lovely,* p 87)

58 How wonderful that God has made provision for sinners who are so easily beset by sin. We have instant cleansing through the blood of Jesus Christ (see 1 John 1:9), and therefore can have boldness on the "day of wrath."

59 A testimony to our depravity is seen in how often we open the door to sin, and invite it in as a guest. How many of us can say that we truly hate sin? Rather, we love it, and if it wasn't for the redeeming work of the Holy Spirit, we would gladly allow it to take permanent residence in our sinful hearts. Such revelations keep us on our knees at the foot of the bloodied Cross.

Peace With Christ

A terrified conscience, therefore, may have rest here, and abundant satisfaction that he [the sinner] is safe in Christ, and that there is not the least danger but that he shall be accepted, and that God will be at peace with Him in Christ.
(Jonathan Edwards, *Altogether Lovely* p 87)

There is free admittance for all sinners into God's favor through this risen Savior. There is enough done, and God is satisfied. He has declared and sealed it by the resurrection of Christ, who is alive and lives for evermore, and is making intercession for poor, distressed souls that come unto him.[60]
(Jonathan Edwards, *Altogether Lovely* p 88)

Christ has the dispensation of safety and in His own hands, so that we need not fear but that, if are united to Him, we may be safe. God has given all power in heaven and in earth to give eternal life to whomsoever comes to Him.
(Jonathan Edwards, *Altogether Lovely* p 88)

Christ Has Pity on Sinners Who Come to Him

Christ's love, and compassion, and gracious disposition are such that we may be sure He is inclined to receive all who come to Him. If He should not do it, He would fail of

60 Never console a distressed sinner, if he becomes alarmed at your words of warning. Sinners should be distressed, as should any criminal who has seriously transgressed civil law. It is rather a good sign to see concern that the Judge is deeply offended by sin.

His own undertaking, and also of His promise to the Father, and to us; and His wisdom and faithfulness will not allow of that. But He is so full of love and kindness that He is disposed to nothing but to receive and defend us if we come to Him. Christ is exceedingly ready to pity us. His arms are open to receive us.[61] He delights to receive distressed souls that come to Him and to protect them. He would gather them as a hen gathereth her chickens under her wings, it is a work that He exceedingly rejoices in because He delights in acts of love, and pity, and mercy.
(Jonathan Edwards, *Altogether Lovely,* pp 88-89)

You will certainly be accepted of the Father if your soul lays hold of Jesus Christ. Christ is chosen and anointed of the Father, and sent forth for this very end: to save those that are in danger and fear. He is greatly beloved of God, even infinitely, and He will accept those that are in Him. Justice and the law will not be against you, if you are in Christ. That threatening, "in the day that thou eatest thereof thou shalt surely die,"[62] in the proper sense of it, will not touch you. The majesty and honor of God are not against you. You need not be afraid, but that you shall be justified, if you come to Him; there is an act of justification already past and declared for all who come to Christ by the resurrection of Christ. And as soon as ever you come you are by that declared free.
(Jonathan Edwards, *Altogether Lovely,* p 90)

If you come to Christ, it will be a sure sign that Christ loved you from all eternity, and that He died for you; and you may be sure that, if He died for you, He will not lose the end of His death, for the dispensation of life is committed unto Him.
(Jonathan Edwards, *Altogether Lovely,* p 90)

---

61 The clearest proof of the arms of the Savior being open to us is seen at the Cross. The nails were only temporary but most necessary restraints, until such a time as He would gather His own.
62 Genesis 2:17

There is none like Christ, "the God of Jeshurun, who rideth upon the heaven in thy help, and in his excellency on the sky; the eternal God is thy refuge, and underneath are everlasting arms."[63] He in whom you trust is a buckler to all that trust in Him. O, prize that Savior who keeps your soul in safety, while thousands of others are carried away by the fury of God's anger, and are tossed with raging and burning tempests into hell! O, how much better is your case than theirs! And to whom is it owing but to the Lord Jesus Christ? Remember what was once your case, and what it is now, and prize Jesus Christ.[64]

(Jonathan Edwards, *Altogether Lovely,* pp 90-91)

A Word for Those Who Are Lacking Assurance

And let those Christians who are in doubts and fears concerning their condition renewedly fly to Jesus Christ, who is a hiding place from the wind and a covert from the tempest. Most Christians are at times afraid whether they shall not miscarry at last. Such doubtings are always through some want of the exercise of faith, and the best remedy for them is a renewed resort of the soul to this hiding place; the same act which at first gave comfort and peace, will give peace again. They that clearly see the sufficiency of Christ, and the safety of committing themselves to him to save them from what they fear, will rest in it that Christ, will defend them. Be directed therefore at such times to do as the psalmist. "In God I will praise His word, in God I have put my trust. I will not fear what flesh can do unto me."[65]

(Jonathan Edwards, *Altogether Lovely,* pp 90-91)

63 Deuteronomy 33:26-27a

64 Think often of the reality of hell. Such sobering thoughts of our redemption produce the explosive fuel of gratitude, and motivate us to reach out to the lost.

65 Psalm 56:4

Finding Contentment and Satisfaction in God Alone

There is provision in Christ for the satisfaction and full contentment of the needy and thirsty soul.
(Jonathan Edwards, *Altogether Lovely,* p 91)

Sinners who are thoroughly awakened are sensible of their great want. Multitudes of men are not sensible of their miserable needy condition. There are many who are thus poor, and think themselves rich and increased in goods. Indeed, there are no natural men that have true contentment; they are all restless and crying, "Who will show us any good?" but multitudes are not sensible how exceedingly necessitous is their condition. But the thoroughly awakened soul sees that he is very far from true happiness, that those things which he possesses will never make him happy; that for all his outward possessions he is wretched and miserable and poor and blind and naked. He becomes sensible of the short continuance and uncertainty of those things, and their insufficiency to satisfy a troubled conscience. He wants something else to give him peace and ease. If you would tell him that he might have a kingdom, it would not quiet him; he desires to have his sins pardoned, and to be at peace with his Judge. He is poor, and he becomes as a beggar; he comes and cries for help. (See Jeremiah 12:1)
(Jonathan Edwards, *Altogether Lovely,* pp 95-96)

The carnal soul imagines that earthly things are excellent; one thinks riches most excellent, another has the highest esteem of honor, and to another carnal pleasure appears the most excellent; but the soul cannot find contentment in any of these things, because it soon finds an end to their excellency. Worldly men imagine that there is true excellency and true happiness in those things which they are pursuing. They think that if they could but obtain them they should be happy and when they obtain them and cannot find happiness they look for happiness in something else and are still upon the pursuit.[66]

(Jonathan Edwards, *Altogether Lovely*, p 96)

Feast on God

"Persons need not, and ought not, to set any bounds to their spiritual and gracious appetites...and with respect to those [spiritual] appetites, self-denial has nothing to do; but here they may give themselves an unbounded liberty . . . There is no such thing as inordinateness in holy affections; there is no such thing as excess in longings after the discoveries of the beauty of Christ Jesus, greater degrees of holiness, or the enjoyment of communion with God. Men may be as covetous as they please after spiritual riches, as eager as they please to heap up treasure in heaven, as ambitious as they please of spiritual and eternal honor and glory, and as voluptuous as they please with respect to spiritual pleasure. Persons neither need nor ought to keep those inclinations and desires from increasing to any degree whatsoever, and there cannot be a too frequent or too powerful exercise of them. . . . Persons may indulge them as much as they please; they may give themselves their full swing . . . by all means, endeavor to raise and to obtain satisfaction for holy inclinations; delight yourselves in the Lord. . . . One would think you should not need urging to indulge your appetites and to enjoy your pleasures. Carnal men, by all

---

66 While it may be true that some don't find happiness in the pleasures of sin, Scripture does ask the question, "Why are they all so happy that deal treacherously?" (See Jeremiah 12:1) Sinners can find happiness without Jesus. However, they cannot find righteousness without Him, and righteousness is what they will need on the Day of Judgment. See Proverbs 10:2, 11:4.

the arguments that can be used, can scarcely be restrained from indulging their carnal appetites. 'Tis a shame that the saints should need a great many arguments to move them to promote their spiritual appetites."[67]

(An excerpt from a *Sermon Spiritual Appetites Need No Bounds* by Jonathan Edwards.)

True Repentance

Holy practice is the most decisive evidence of the reality of our repentance. When the Jews professed repentance, confessing their sins to John while he was preaching the baptism of repentance for the remission of sins, he directed them to the best way of obtaining and exhibiting proper evidence of the truth of their repentance, when he said to them "Bring forth fruits meet for repentance."[68] Agreeable to this was the practice of the Apostle Paul.[69] Pardon and mercy are often promised to him who, as an evidence of true repentance, forsakes his sins, Proverbs 28:13. Isaiah 56:7, and many other places.[70]

(Jonathan Edwards, *A Treatise Concerning Religious Affections*, p 288)

Christ promises us eternal life, on condition of our coming to Him; but he requires such a coming as that to which He

---

67 When it comes to the things of this world, we must be careful to keep the foot close to the brake. We must be temperate and moderate in our appetites and pursuits, but not in the Kingdom of God. We are free to accelerate to the full. We cannot love God, pray, witness, or believe too much. It is a good thing for the soul to "delight itself in fatness" (Isaiah 55:2a).

68 Matthew 3:8

69 See Acts 26:20

70 It is frustrating to meet so many who profess faith in Jesus because they have "asked Him into their heart," and yet there is no fruit. These people often blaspheme while they talk to you. One evident barometer of spirituality is to ask if he is reading the Bible every day. You will usually find that he isn't. Then ask if he thinks that he is a good person. Usually he will, and that reveals that he has never seen his sins in their true light. He needs the Law to awaken him.

directed the young man, who came to inquire what he should do that he might have eternal life: Christ bid him "go and sell that thou hast . . . and come and follow me."[71] Had he really consented, the proper evidences of his having done so would have been his actually doing as he was commanded.

(Jonathan Edwards, *A Treatise Concerning Religious Affections,* p 289)

He who, on the credit of what he hears of a future world, forsakes all at least so far as there is occasion, making every thing subservient to his everlasting interest, is the only person who can with propriety be said to venture on the report of the gospel; and this is the proper evidence of a real trust in Christ for salvation.

(Jonathan Edwards, *A Treatise Concerning Religious Affections,* p 289)

Real saints, or those persons who are sanctified by the Spirit of God, are in the New Testament called spiritual persons; and their being spiritual is spoken of as their peculiar character, and that wherein they are distinguished from those who are not sanctified. Those who are spiritual are set in opposition to those who are carnal, or natural, that is, in a state of nature. "The natural man receiveth not the things of the Spirit of God, for they are foolishness unto him; neither can he know them, because they are spiritually discerned. But he that is spiritual, judges all things."[72]

(Jonathan Edwards, *A Treatise Concerning Religious Affections,* p 108)

---

71 Matthew 19:21

72 1 Corinthians 2:14-15a. Edwards uses the term "real saints" to differentiate from the oxymoron of false saints. Paul spoke of "false brethren," and the Bible teaches the reality of true and false conversion. For an understanding of this truth, freely listen to "True and False Conversion" on www.livingwaters.com.

True Christian Compassion

Some persons evidence great love to men, as it respects their temporal welfare, but appear to have no concern for their spiritual and everlasting happiness. Others, on the contrary, pretend to have great love for the souls of men, while they have no concern for their temporal comfort. The appearance of great concern for the souls of men costs nothing; but in order to promote their temporal ease and comfort, it is necessary to part with money. But true Christian love to the brethren extends both to their spiritual and temporal interests; and in this it resembles the love and compassion of Jesus Christ. He showed mercy to the souls of men by preaching the gospel to them, and to their bodies by going about doing good, healing all manner of sickness and disease among the people. We have a remarkable instance of His compassion to the souls, and the bodies of men, shown to the same individuals: "And Jesus, when he came out, saw much people, and was moved with compassion toward them, because they were as sheep not having a shepherd; and he began to teach them many things."[73] In the sequel, we have an account of His compassion to their bodies. They had been a long time without food, and He fed five thousand of them with five loaves and two fishes. Now if the compassion of professing Christians does not operate in the same ways, it is evidently not true Christian compassion.[74]

(Jonathan Edwards, *A Treatise Concerning Religious Affections*, p 243)

73 Mark 6:34

74 A good way to let your light shine before men, both in the temporal and the eternal, is to offer to buy a hamburger for the person to whom you are witnessing. This not only shows your love for him, but it stops his mouth while you talk to him.

Safety, Fullness, and Sweet Refreshment in Christ

The mind never has any satiety, but Christ's excellency is always fresh and new, and tends as much to delight after it has been seen a thousand or ten thousand years as when it was seen the first moment.

(Jonathan Edwards,*A Treatise Concerning Religious Affections,* p 97)

The way to keep our first love is to never forget the Cross, and the way to never forget the Cross is to remember how much we have been forgiven. A revelation of our sinful state before God will produce a perpetual and overwhelming gratitude for the mercy of God in Christ. – Ray Comfort

The excellency of Jesus Christ is the suitable food for the rational soul. The soul that comes to Christ feeds upon this, and lives upon it. It is that bread, which down from heaven, of which he that eats shall not die; it is angels' food, it is that wine and milk that is given without money and without price. This is that fatness with which the believing soul delights itself. Here the soul may be satisfied and the hungry soul may be filled with goodness. The delight and contentment that is found here passes understanding and is full of unspeakable glory. It is impossible for those who have tasted of this fountain and know the sweetness of it, ever to forsake it. The soul has found the river of the water of life, it desires no other drink. It has found the tree of life and it desires no other fruit.

(Jonathan Edwards,*A Treatise Concerning Religious Affections*, pp 97-98)

The key to being satisfied in Christ is to "keep your heart with all diligence, for out of it spring the issues of life" (Proverbs 4:22-24). We live in an age that bombards the eyes with the promise of lust-filled pleasure; so guard your heart from the poison of demonic seduction. If the enemy has your eyes, he has your heart. Instead, be often on your knees, soak in the Word, and walk in the fear of God. Be eternity-minded. We cannot be friends of the world and friends of God. We cannot drink fresh water and bitter. – Ray Comfort

Christ, by being thus the way to the Father, is the way to true happiness and contentment. John 10:9: "I am the door: by me if any man enter in, he shall be saved, and shall go in and out, and find pasture." Hence I would take occasion to invite needy, thirsty souls to come to Jesus. "In the last day, that great day of the feast, Jesus stood and cried, saying, 'If any man thirst, let him come unto me and drink.'"[75] You that have not yet come to Christ are in a poor necessitous condition; you are in a parched wilderness, in a dry and thirsty land. And if you are thoroughly awakened, you are sensible that you are in distress and ready to faint for want of something to satisfy your souls. Come to Him who is "as rivers of water in a dry place." There are plenty and fullness in Him. He is like a river that is always flowing; you may live by it forever and never be in want. Come to Him who has such excellency as is sufficient to give full contentment to your soul, who is a person of transcendent glory and ineffable beauty, where you may entertain the view of your soul forever without weariness, and without being cloyed. Accept of the offered love of Him who is the only begotten Son of God, and His elect, in whom His soul delighteth. Through Christ, come to God the Father, from whom you have departed by sin. He is the way, the truth, and the life. He is the door, by which if any man enters he shall be saved.

(Jonathan Edwards, *A Treatise Concerning Religious Affections,* pp 99-100)

75 John 7:37

The Effects of Sin

Sin is the most evil and odious thing, as well as the most mischievous and fatal. It is the most mortal poison; it above all things hazards life and endangers the soul, exposes it to the loss of all happiness, and to the suffering of all misery, and brings the wrath of God.

(Jonathan Edwards, *A Treatise Concerning Religious Affections*, p 101)

The Comparison of the Believer and Unbeliever

Sinners are not wearied with sin from any dislike to it or dislike of it. There is no sinner that is burdened with sin in the sense in which a godly man carries his indwelling sin as his daily and greatest burden, because he loathes it and longs to get rid of it. He would fain be at a great distance from it, and have nothing more to do with it. He is ready to cry out as Paul did, "Oh, wretched man that I am! Who shall deliver me from the body of this death?"[76] The unregenerate man has nothing of this nature, for sin is yet his delight. He dearly loves it. If he be under convictions, his love to sin in general is not mortified. He loves it as well as ever; he hides it still as a sweet morsel under his tongue.

(Jonathan Edwards, *A Treatise Concerning Religious Affections*, p 102)

76 Romans 7:24

It is against nature for any unregenerate man or woman to hate sin. It is his life's breath. He is a thoughtless moth to the flame of sin. He cannot and will not depart from his darling sins without the help of God. It is God who "grants" us repentance to the acknowledging of the truth. – Ray Comfort

Christ: The Only Remedy

There is no remedy but in Jesus Christ; there is nothing else will give you true quietness. If you could fly into heaven, you would not find it there; if you should take the wings of the morning, and dwell in the uttermost parts of the earth, in some solitary place in the wilderness, you could not fly from your burden. So that if you do not come to Christ, you must either continue still weary and burdened, or, which is worse, you must return to your old dead sleep, to a state of stupidity; and not only so, but you must be everlastingly wearied with God's wrath.God.

(Jonathan Edwards, *A Treatise Concerning Religious Affections*, p 106)

To serve sin is to serve stupidity. To run at hell as though it was Heaven and reject Heaven as though it was hell itself is insanity. It's only when we come to Christ that we receive "a sound mind" (2 Timothy 1:7). – Ray Comfort

Rest and Feasting for the Weary Soul

They who come to Christ do not come to a resting place after they have been wandering in a wilderness, but they come to a banqueting house where they may rest, and where they may feast. They cease from their former troubles and toils, and they enter upon a course of delights and spiritual joys.

(Jonathan Edwards, *Altogether Lovely*, p 107)

Christ not only delivers from fears of hell and of wrath, but He gives hopes of heaven and the enjoyment of God's love. He delivers from inward tumults and inward pain, from that guilt of conscience, which is as a worm gnawing within, and He gives delight and inward glory. He brings us out of a wilderness of pits and drought and flying spirits. He brings us into a pleasant land, a flowing with milk and honey. He delivers us out of prison and lifts us off from the dunghill and He sets us among princes and causes us to inherit the throne of glory.[77]

(Jonathan Edwards, *Altogether Lovely*, p 107)

77 One of the great errors of the modern evangelicalism is the neglect of God's Law to bring to knowledge of sin. Instead, evangelists and preachers have used the benefits of Christianity to supposedly lure sinners to the Savior. We do have "delight and inward glory," but these wonderful benefits come to us *because* we trust in God. Even though we are not yet in the promised land of Heaven, we have "joy and peace in believing" (Romans 15:13). We have joy unspeakable because we believe the exceeding great and precious promises of God. But to use these benefits as bait when we fish for men is to pervert the motive for which one should come to Christ. We come to Him as guilty criminals, pleading for mercy because we have sinned against God by violating His Law. Any other motive can result in the tragedy of a false conversion.

Come to Christ Anew

There are quiet rest and sweet refreshment in Christ for God's people that are weary. The saints themselves, while they remain in this imperfect state and have so much remains of sin in their hearts, are liable still to many troubles and sorrows, and much weariness and have often need to resort anew unto Christ for rest. . . . There is rest and sweet refreshment in Christ for those that are wearied with persecutions. [78] It has been the lot of God's Church in this world for the most part to be persecuted. It has had now and then some lucid of peace and outward prosperity, but generally it has otherwise. This has accorded with the first prophecy concerning Christ: "I will put enmity between thee and the woman and between thy seed and her seed."[79] Those two seeds have been at enmity ever since the time of Abel. Satan has borne great malice against the Church of God, as so have those that are his seed. Oftentimes God's people have been persecuted to an extreme degree, have been put to the most exquisite torments that wit art could devise, and thousands of them have been tormented to death. But even in such a case there are rest and refreshment to be found in Christ Jesus.

(Jonathan Edwards, *Altogether Lovely,* pp 107-108)

There is in Christ rest for God's people when exercised with afflictions. If a person labors under great bodily weakness, or under some disease that causes frequent and strong pains, such things will tire out so feeble a creature as man. It may, to such an one, be a comfort and an effectual support to think that he

78 Those who call themselves by the name of "Christian," and yet fail to live godly in Christ, won't have persecution. They are friends of the world and the world loves its own. The Scriptures say, "Let everyone who names the name of Christ depart from iniquity" (2 Timothy 2:19, NKJV). We cannot serve God and the devil. Those who believe they can will find to the contrary, when they stand before God on Judgment Day and hear, "I never knew you; depart from Me, you who practice lawlessness!'" (Matthew 7:23, NKJV).

79 Genesis 3:15

has a Mediator who knows by experience what pain is; who by His pain has purchased eternal ease and pleasure for him, and who will make his brief sufferings to work out a far more exceeding delight, to be bestowed when he shall rest from his labors and sorrows.
(Jonathan Edwards, *Altogether Lovely*, p 108)

Christ is the joy of the soul, and if the soul be but rejoiced and filled with divine light, such joy no man can take away; whatever outward misery there be the spirit will sustain it.[80]
(Jonathan Edwards, *Altogether Lovely*, p 108)

Jonathan Edwards and Apologetics for the Law in Evangelism

(Excerpted from "A Treatise Concerning Religious Affections" by Jonathan Edwards.)

Many persons seem to be prejudiced against affections and experiences that come in such a method, as has been much insisted on by many divines; first, such awakenings, fears, and awful apprehensions, followed with such legal humbling, in a sense of total sinfulness and helplessness, and then, such and such light and comfort. They look upon all such schemes, laying

80 Those who see the wickedness of their own sinful heart, catch a glimpse of God's mercy and love expressed in the Cross, and therefore have a feast of joy at such unmerited love. Those who have a shallow understanding of their sin, will have a shallow understanding of God's love, and not swim in the depth of the joy of sins forgiven.

down such methods and steps, to be of men's devising; and particularly if high affections of joy follow great distress and terror, it is made by many an argument against those affections. But such prejudices and objections are without reason or Scripture. Surely it cannot be unreasonable to suppose that, before God delivers persons from a state of sin and exposedness to eternal destruction, He should give them some considerable sense of the evil He delivers them from; that they may be delivered sensibly, and understand their own salvation, and know something of what God does for them.[81] As men that are saved are in two exceeding different states, first a state of condemnation, and then a state of justification and blessedness: and as God, in the work of the salvation of mankind, deals with them suitably to their intelligent rational nature, so it seems reasonable, and agreeable to God's wisdom that men who are saved should be in these two states sensibly; first, that they should, sensibly to themselves, be in a state of condemnation, and so in a state of woeful calamity and dreadful misery, and so afterwards sensibly in a state of deliverance and happiness; and that they should be first sensible of their absolute extreme necessity, and afterwards of Christ's sufficiency and God's mercy through Him.[82]

And that it is God's manner of dealing with men, to lead them into a wilderness, before he speaks comfortably to them, and so to order it that they shall be brought into distress, and made to see their own helplessness and absolute dependence on His power and grace, before He appears to work any great deliverance for them, is abundantly manifest by the Scripture. Then is God wont to "repent himself for his servants, when he

---

81 Without an understanding of the purpose of the moral Law, the entire gospel presentation crumbles and becomes meaningless to the lost. It remains "foolishness" to them. Without the Law they don't flee to the Cross, and God becomes nothing more than a divine butler, and the sinner, his master. Removal of the Law from the nature of God leaves nothing but a dumb idol with no moral dictate, and any talk of God being angry at sin is deemed to be unloving.

82 If there is no wrath of the Law then there is no need for the mercy of Calvary. How can any sinner understand the mercy of God if he doesn't understand the condemnation of the Law?

seeth that their power is gone, and there is none shut up, or left," and when they are brought to see that their false gods cannot help them, and that "their rock in whom they trusted" is vain.[83] Before God delivered the children of Israel out of Egypt, they were prepared for it, by being made to "see that they were in an evil case,"[84] and made to cry "unto God by reason of their bondage."[85] And before God wrought that great deliverance for them at the Red Sea, they were brought into great distress, the wilderness had shut them in, they could not turn to the right hand nor the left; the Red Sea was before them, and the great Egyptian host behind, and they were brought to see that they could do nothing to help themselves, and that if God did not help them, they would be immediately swallowed up; and then God appeared, and turned their cries into songs.[86] So, before they were brought to their rest, and to enjoy the milk and honey of Canaan, God led them through a great and terrible wilderness, that he might humble them and teach them what was in their heart, and so do them good in their latter end.[87] The woman that had the issue of blood twelve years was not delivered until she had first "spent all her living upon physicians, neither could be healed of any," and so was left helpless, having no more money to spend; and then she came to the Great Physician, without any money or price, and was healed by Him.[88] Before Christ would answer the request of the woman of Canaan, He first seemed utterly to deny her, and humbled her, and brought her to own herself worthy to be called a dog; and then He showed her mercy, and received her as a dear child.[89] The Apostle Paul, after a remarkable deliverance, wrote, "We were pressed out of measure, above strength, insomuch that we despaired even of life: But we had the sentence of death in ourselves, that we

83 Deuteronomy 32:36-37

84 See Exodus 5:19

85 See Exodus 2:23

86 Those who are forgiven much, love much. Individuals who find themselves shut up by the Law, with no means of escape, can fully appreciate the deliverance of the gospel.

87 See Deuteronomy 2:2, 16

88 Luke 8:43-44

89 Matthew 15:22-28

should not trust in ourselves, but in God which raiseth the dead."[90] There was first a great tempest; the ship was covered with the waves, and just ready to sink, and the disciples were brought to cry to Jesus, "Lord save us, we perish;" and then the winds and seas were rebuked, and there was a great calm.[91] The leper, before he is cleansed, must have his mouth stopped by a covering on his upper lip, and was to acknowledge his great misery and utter uncleanness by rending his clothes and crying, "Unclean, unclean."[92] And backsliding Israel, before God heals them, are brought to acknowledge that they have sinned, and have not obeyed the voice of the Lord, and to see that they lie down in their shame, and that confusion covers them, and that "in vain is salvation hoped for from the hills, and from the multitude of mountains," and that God only can save them.[93] Joseph, who was sold by his brethren, and therein was a type of Christ, brings his brethren into great perplexity and distress, and brings them to reflect on their sin, and to say, "We are verily guilty;"[94] and at last to resign up themselves entirely into his hands for bondmen; and then reveals himself to them, as their brother and their savior.

And if we consider those extraordinary manifestations which God made of himself to saints of old, we shall find that He commonly first manifested himself in a way which was terrible, and then by those things that were comfortable. So it was with Abraham; first, a horror of great darkness fell upon him, and then God revealed Himself to him in sweet promises.[95] So it was

90 2 Corinthians 1:8-9

91 See Matthew 8:24-26

92 Leviticus 13:45. The Law shows us that sin is exceedingly sinful, that we are all as an unclean thing and that our righteous deeds are as filthy rags in His sight. It stops our mouth and leaves the whole world guilty before God (see Romans 3:20). It is when we see the holiness of God that we (like Job) lay our hand upon our mouth and say. "I have heard of You by the hearing of the ear, but now my eye sees You. Therefore I abhor myself, and repent in dust and ashes" (Job 42:5-4, NKJV.)

93 See Jeremiah 3:23-25

94 Genesis 42:21

95 See Genesis 15:12-16

with Moses at Mount Sinai; first, God appeared to him in all the terrors of His dreadful majesty, so that Moses said, "I exceedingly fear and quake,"[96] and then He made all His goodness to pass before him, and proclaimed His name, "The LORD God, merciful and gracious."[97] So it was with Elijah; first there is a stormy wind and earthquake and devouring fire, and then a still, small voice.[98] So it was with Daniel; he first saw Christ's countenance as lightning, that terrified him, and caused him to faint away; and then he is strengthened and refreshed with such comfortable words as these, "O Daniel, a man greatly beloved."[99] So it was with the Apostle John.[100] And there is an analogy observable in God's dispensations and deliverances which He works for His people, and the manifestations which He makes of himself to them, both ordinary and extraordinary.

(End of excerpts from A *Treatise Concerning Religious Affections* by Jonathan Edwards.)

Many Things in Scripture Show God's Ordinary Way of Working Salvation

But there are many things in Scripture, which do more directly show that this is God's ordinary manner in working salvation for the souls of men, and in the manifestations God makes of himself and of His mercy in Christ, in the ordinary works of His grace on the hearts of sinners. The servant that owed his prince ten thousand talents is first held to his debt,

96 Hebrews 12:21
97 Exodus 34:6
98 1 Kings 19:11-12
99 Daniel, Chapter 10
100 Revelation, Chapter 1

and the king pronounces sentence of condemnation upon him, and commands him to be sold, and his wife and children, and payment to be made; and thus he humbles him, and brings him to own the whole of the debt to be just, and then forgives him all. The prodigal son spends all he has, and is brought to see himself in extreme circumstances, and to humble himself, and own his unworthiness, before he is relieved and feasted by his father.[101] Old deep-rooted wounds must be searched to the bottom, in order to heal: and the Scripture compares sin, the wound of the soul, to this, and speaks of healing this wound without thus searching of it as vain and deceitful.[102] Christ, in the work of His grace on the hearts of men, is compared to rain on the new mown grass, grass that is cut down with a scythe,[103] representing His refreshing, comforting, influences on the wounded spirit. Our first parents, after they had sinned, were first terrified with God's majesty and justice, and had their sin with its aggravations set before them by their Judge, before they were relieved by the promise of the Seed of the woman. Christians are spoken of as those "who have fled for refuge to lay hold upon the hope set before us,"[104] which representation implies great fear and sense of danger preceding. To the like purpose, Christ is called "an hiding place from the wind, and a covert from the tempest; as rivers of water in a dry place, as the shadow of a great rock in a weary land."[105] And it seems to be the natural import of the word gospel, glad tidings, that it is news of deliverance and salvation, after great fear and distress. There is also reason to suppose that God deals with particular believers as He dealt with His church, which He first made to hear His voice in the law, with terrible thunders and lightnings, and kept under that schoolmaster to prepare her for Christ; and then comforted her with joyful sound of the gospel from Mount Zion. So likewise, John the Baptist

---

101 Luke, Chapter 15. It is the Law that shows the sinner that his desires are for that which is unclean, and causes him come to his senses, and to seek the Father.
102 See Jeremiah 8:11-12
103 See Psalm 72:6
104 Hebrews 6:18
105 Isaiah 32:2

came to prepare the way for Christ, and prepare men's hearts for His reception, by showing them their sins, and by bringing the self-righteous Jews off from their own righteousness, telling them that they were "a generation of vipers," and showing them their danger of "the wrath to come," telling them that "the axe is laid unto the root of the trees."[106]

(*The Works of Jonathan Edwards*, edited by Edward Hickman, 1839.)

And if it be indeed God's manner (as I think the foregoing considerations show that it undoubtedly is), before He gives men the comfort of a deliverance from their sin and misery, to give them a considerable sense of the greatness and dreadfulness of those evils, and their extreme wretchedness by reason of them; surely it is not unreasonable to suppose that persons, at least oftentimes, while under these views, should have great distresses and terrible apprehensions of mind; especially if it be considered what these evils are that they have a view of, which are no other than great and manifold sins against the infinite majesty of the great Jehovah, and the suffering of the fierceness of His wrath to all eternity. And the more so still, when we have many plain instances in Scripture of persons that have actually been brought into great distress by such convictions before they have received saving consolations: as the multitude at Jerusalem, who were "pricked in their heart, and said unto Peter and the rest of the apostles, Men and brethren, what shall we do?";[107] and the Apostle Paul, who trembled and was astonished before he was comforted; and the jailer, when "he called for a light, and sprang in, and came trembling, and fell down before Paul and Silas, and brought them out, and said, Sirs, what must I do to be saved?"[108]

(*The Works of Jonathan Edwards*, edited by Edward Hickman, 1839.)

106 Luke 3:7-9. May God raise up more preachers, who like John, are not afraid to reprove even kings for their transgression of the moral Law.

107 Acts 2:37

108 Acts 16:29-30. See www.FreeWonderfulBook.com for further understanding of these principles.

It is of God that Christ becomes ours, that we are brought to Him, and are united to Him. It is of God that we receive faith to close with Him, that we may have an interest in Him. "For by grace ye are saved, through faith; and that not of yourselves, it is the gift of God."[109] It is of God that we actually receive all the benefits that Christ has purchased. It is God that pardons and justifies, and delivers from going down to hell; and into his favor the redeemed are received, when they are justified. So it is God that delivers from the dominion of sin, cleanses us from our filthiness, and changes us from our deformity. It is of God that the redeemed receive all their true excellency, wisdom, and holiness; and that two ways, as the Holy Ghost by whom these things are immediately wrought is from God, proceeds from Him, and is sent by Him; and also as the Holy Ghost himself is God, by whose operation and indwelling the knowledge of God and divine things, a holy disposition and all grace, are conferred and upheld. And though means are made use of in conferring grace on men's souls, yet it is of God that we have these means of grace, and it is He that makes them effectual. It is of God that we have the Holy Scriptures; they are His word. It is of God that we have ordinances, and their efficacy depends on the immediate influence of His Spirit. The ministers of the gospel are sent of God, and all their sufficiency is of Him. "We have this treasure in earthen vessels, that the excellency of the power may be of God, and not of us."[110] Their success depends entirely and absolutely on the immediate blessing and influence of God.[111]

(Jonathan Edwards, *God Glorified in Man's Dependence,* Sermon 1)

There was scarcely a single person in the town, old or young, left unconcerned about the great things of the eternal world.

109 Ephesians 2:8

110 2 Corinthians 4:7

111 For of Him and through Him and to Him are all things. Without Him, we can know nothing, do nothing, and we are nothing. This should give us great confidence when it comes to reaching the lost. God provides the seed; He provides the sower, the growth, and those who reap. All He desires from us is a willingness to do His will.

Those who were wont to be the vainest and loosest, and those who had been most disposed to think and speak slightly of vital and experimental religion, were now generally subject to great awakenings. And the work of conversion was carried on in a most astonishing manner, and increased more and more; souls did as it were come by flocks to Jesus Christ. From day to day, for many months together, might be seen evident instances of sinners brought "out of darkness into his marvellous light,"[112] and delivered out of an horrible pit, and from the miry clay, and set their feet upon a rock, with a new song of praise to God in their mouths.[113] This work of God, as it was carried on, and the number of true saints multiplied, soon made a glorious alteration in the town: so that in the spring and summer following 1735, the town seemed to be full of the presence of God: it never was so full of love, nor of joy, and yet so full of distress, as it was then. There were remarkable tokens of God's presence in almost every house. It was a time of joy in families on account of salvation being brought unto them; parents rejoicing over their children as new born, and husbands over their wives, and wives over their husbands. The goings of God were then seen in His sanctuary. God's day was a delight, and His tabernacles were amiable. Our public assemblies were then beautiful: the congregation was alive in God's service, every one earnestly intent on the public worship, every hearer eager to drink in the words of the minister as they came from his mouth; the assembly in general were, from time to time, in tears while the word was preached; some weeping with sorrow and distress, others with joy and love, others with pity and concern for the souls of their neighbors. [114]
(Jonathan Edwards, *Narrative of Surprising Conversions*, p 348)

When this work first appeared, and was so extraordinarily carried on amongst us in the winter, others round about us

112 1 Peter 2:9

113 See Psalm 40:2-3

114 May God grant us genuine revival, in this day and age, when Christianity to many is either a mockery or their faith in Christ is nothing more than a "form of godliness." Work towards revival, believe God for it, and always keep in mind that with Him, nothing shall be impossible.

seemed not to know what to make of it. Many scoffed at and ridiculed it; and some compared what we called conversion, to certain distempers. But it was very observable of many, who occasionally came amongst us from abroad with disregardful hearts, that what they saw here cured them of such a temper of mind. Strangers were generally surprised to find things so much beyond what they had heard, and were wont to tell others that the state of the town could not be conceived of by those who had not seen it. The notice that was taken of it by the people who came to town on occasion of the court that sat here in the beginning of March, was very observable. And those who came from the neighborhood to our public lectures, were for the most part remarkably affected. Many who came to town, on one occasion or other, had their consciences smitten, and awakened; and went home with wounded hearts, and with those impressions that never wore off till they had hopefully a saving issue; and those who before had serious thoughts, had their awakenings and convictions greatly increased. There were many instances of persons who came from abroad on visits, or on business, who had not been long here before, to all appearance, they were savingly wrought upon; and partook of that shower of divine blessing which God rained down here, and went home rejoicing; till at length the same work began evidently to appear and prevail in several other towns in the county.

(Jonathan Edwards, *Narrative of Surprising Conversions,* p 348-349)

In the month of March, the people in South-Hadley began to be seized with deep concern about the things of religion; which very soon became universal. The work of God has been very wonderful there; not much, if any thing, short of what it has been here, in proportion to the size of the place. About the same time, it began to break forth in the west part of Suffield, (where it also has been very great,) and it soon spread into all parts of the town. It next appeared at Sunderland, and soon overspread the town: and I believe was, for a season, not less remarkable than it was here. About the same time it began to appear in a part of

Deerfield, called Green River, and afterwards filled the town, and there has been a glorious work there. It began also to be manifest in the south part of Hatfield, in a place called the Hill, and the whole town, in the second week in April, seemed to be seized, as it were at once, with concern about the things of religion; and the work of God has been great there. There has been also a very general awakening at West-Springfield, and Long Meadow; and in Enfield there was for a time a pretty general concern amongst some who before had been very loose persons. About the same time that this appeared at Enfield, the Rev. Mr. Bull, of Westfield, informed me, that there had been a great alteration there, and that more had been done in one week, than in seven years before. Something of this work likewise appeared in the first precinct in Springfield, principally in the north and south extremes of the parish. And in Hadley old town, there gradually appeared so much of a work of God on souls, as at another time would have been thought worthy of much notice. For a short time there was also a very great and general concern, of the like nature, at Northfield. And wherever this concern appeared, it seemed not to be in vain: but in every place God brought saving blessings with Him, and His word attended with His Spirit (as we have all reason to think) returned not void. It might well be said at that time, in all parts of the county, who are these that fly as a cloud, and as doves to their windows?

As what other towns heard of and found in this, was a great means of awakening them; so our hearing of such a swift and extraordinary propagation, and extent of this work, did doubtless for a time serve to uphold the work amongst us. The continual news kept alive the talk of religion, and did greatly quicken and rejoice the hearts of God's people, and much awakened those who looked on themselves as still left behind, and made them the more earnest that they also might share in the great blessings that others had obtained.

(Jonathan Edwards, *Narrative of Surprising Conversions*, p 349)

I am very sensible, how apt many would be, if they should see the account I have here given, presently to think with themselves that I am very fond of making a great many converts, and of magnifying the matter; and to think that, for want of judgment, I take every religious pang, and enthusiastic conceit, for saving conversion. I do not much wonder if they should be apt to think so; and, for this reason, I have forborne to publish an account of this great work of God, though I have often been solicited. But having now a special call to give an account of it, upon mature consideration I thought it might not be beside my duty to declare this amazing work, as it appeared to me to be indeed divine, and to conceal no part of the glory of it; leaving it with God to take care of the credit of His own work, and running the venture of any censorious thoughts, which might be entertained of me to my disadvantage. That distant persons may be under as great advantage as may be to judge for themselves of this matter, I would be a little more large and particular.

(Jonathan Edwards, *Narrative of Surprising Conversions*, p 350)

The drift of the Spirit of God in His legal strivings with persons, have seemed most evidently to be, to bring to a conviction of their absolute dependence on His sovereign power and grace, and an universal necessity of a mediator. This has been effected by leading them more and more to a sense of their exceeding wickedness and guiltiness in His sight; their pollution, and the insufficiency of their own righteousness; that they can in no wise help themselves, and that God would be wholly just and righteous in rejecting them and all that they do, and in casting them off forever. There is however, a vast variety, as to the manner and distinctness of such convictions. As they are gradually more and more convinced of the corruption and wickedness of their hearts: they seem to themselves to grow worse and worse, harder and blinder, and more desperately wicked, instead of growing better. They are ready to be discouraged by it, and oftentimes never think themselves so far off from good, as when they are nearest. Under the sense that the Spirit of God gives them of their sinfulness, they often think that they differ from all others;

their hearts are ready to sink with the thought, that they are the worst of all, and that none ever obtained mercy who were so wicked as they.

(Jonathan Edwards, *Narrative of Surprising Conversions*, p 351)

The way that grace seems sometimes first to appear, after legal humiliation, is in earnest longings of soul after God and Christ: to know God, to love Him, to be humble before Him, to have communion with Christ in His benefits; which longings, as they express them, seem evidently to be of such a nature as can arise from nothing but a sense of the superlative excellency of divine things, with a spiritual taste and relish of them, and an esteem of them as their highest happiness and best portion. Such longings as I speak of, are commonly attended with firm resolutions to pursue this good forever, together with a hoping, waiting disposition. When persons have begun in such frames, commonly other experiences and discoveries have soon followed, which have yet more clearly manifested a change of heart. [115]

(Jonathan Edwards, *Narrative of Surprising Conversions*, p 354)

Sometimes disconsolate souls have been revived, and brought to rest in God, by a sweet sense of His grace and faithfulness, in some special invitation or promise; in which nevertheless there is no particular mention of Christ, nor is it accompanied with any distinct thought of Him in their minds: but yet, it is not received as out of Christ, but as one of the invitations or promises made of God to poor sinners through his Son Jesus. And such persons afterwards have had clear and distinct discoveries of Christ, accompanied with lively and special actings of faith and love towards Him.

---

115 The beginnings of the way of salvation for any sinner, is the realization that he is helpless to save himself. Until that happens, a wise preacher will hold back on the good news of the gospel. There must be a thirst for the quenching of water to be appreciated. Mercy is only for those who know that they are condemned. This is clearly the principle and purpose behind Edward's most famous sermon, *Sinners in the Hands of an Angry God.*

Frequently, when persons have first had the gospel-ground of relief discovered to them, and have been entertaining their minds with the sweet prospect, they have thought nothing at that time of their being converted. To see, that there is an all-sufficiency in God, and such plentiful provision made in Christ, after they have been borne down, and sunk with a sense of their guilt and fears of wrath, exceedingly refreshes them. The view is joyful to them; as it is in its own nature glorious, gives them quite new and delightful ideas of God and Christ, greatly encourages them to seek conversion. This begets in them a strong resolution to devote themselves and their whole lives to God and His Son, and patiently to wait till God shall see fit to make all effectual; and very often entertain a strong persuasion, that He will in His own time do it for them.

(Jonathan Edwards, *Narrative of Surprising Conversions,* p 354)

I therefore proceed to give an account of the manner of persons being wrought upon; and here there is a vast variety, perhaps as manifold as the subjects of the operation; but yet in many things there is a great analogy in all. Persons are first awakened with a sense of their miserable condition by nature, the danger they are in of perishing eternally, and that it is of great importance to them that they speedily escape and get into a better state. Those who before were secure and senseless, are made sensible how much they were in the way to ruin, in their former courses. Some are more suddenly seized with convictions—it may be, by the news of others' conversion, or something they hear in public, or in private conference—their consciences are smitten, as if their hearts were pierced through with a dart. Others are awakened more gradually; they begin at first to be something more thoughtful and considerate, so as to come to a conclusion in their minds, that it is their best and wisest way to delay no longer, but to improve the present opportunity. They have accordingly set themselves seriously to meditate on those things that have the most awakening tendency, on purpose to obtain convictions; and so their awakenings have increased, till a sense of their misery, by God's Holy Spirit setting in therewith, has had fast hold of them. Others who before had been somewhat religious, and concerned for their salvation, have been awakened in a new manner; and made sensible that their slack and dull way of seeking, was never likely to attain that purpose.

(Jonathan Edwards, *Narrative of Surprising Conversions*, p 350)

Whatever minister has a like occasion to deal with souls, in a flock under such circumstances, as this was in the last year, I cannot but think he will soon find himself under a necessity, greatly to insist upon it with them, that God is under no manner of obligation to show mercy to any natural man, whose heart is not turned to God: and that a man can challenge nothing either in absolute justice or by free promise, from any thing he does before he has believed on Jesus Christ, or has true repentance begun in him.[116] It appears to me, that if I had taught those who came to me under trouble, any other doctrine, I should have taken a most direct course utterly to undo them. I should have directly crossed what was plainly the drift of the Spirit of God in His influences upon them; for if they had believed what I said, it would either have promoted self-flattery and carelessness, and so put an end to their awakenings; or cherished and established their contention and strife with God, concerning His dealings with them and others, and blocked up their way to that humiliation before the Sovereign Disposer of life and death, whereby God is wont to prepare them for His consolations. And yet those who have been under awakenings have oftentimes plainly stood in need of being encouraged, by being told of the infinite and all-sufficient mercy of God in Christ and that it is God's manner to succeed diligence, and to bless His own means, that so awakenings and encouragements, fear and hope, may be duly mixed, and proportioned to preserve their minds in a just medium between the two extremes of self-flattery and despondence, both which tend to slackness and negligence, and in the end to security. I think I have found that no discourses have been more remarkably blessed, than those in

116 The only obligation God has towards humanity is to see that justice is done. He is not obligated in the slightest to show us mercy; otherwise it would not be mercy.

which the doctrine of God's absolute sovereignty, with regard to the salvation of sinners, and His just liberty, with regard to answering the prayers, or succeeding the pains, of natural men, continuing such, have been insisted on. I never found so much immediate saving fruit, in any measure, of any discourses I have offered to my congregation, as some from these words, "that every mouth may be stopped";[117] endeavoring to show from thence, that it would be just with God for ever to reject and cast off mere natural men.

(Jonathan Edwards, *Narrative of Surprising Conversions*, p 353-354)

There is a vast difference, as observed, in the degree, and also in the particular manner, of persons' experiences, both at and after conversion; some have grace working more sensibly in one way, others in another. Some speak more fully of a conviction of the justice of God in their condemnation; others, more of their consenting to the way of salvation by Christ; and some, more of the actings of love to God and Christ. Some more of acts of affiance, in a sweet and assured conviction of the truth and faithfulness of God in His promises; others, more of their choosing and resting in God, as their whole and everlasting portion; and of their ardent and longing desire after God, to have communion with Him; and others, more of their abhorrence to themselves for their past sins, and earnest longings to live to God's glory for the time to come. But it seems evidently to be the same work, the same habitual change wrought in the heart, it all tends the same way, and to the same end; and it is plainly the same Spirit that breathes and acts in various persons. There is an endless variety in the particular manner and circumstances in which persons are wrought on; and an opportunity of seeing so much will show that God is further from confining himself to a particular method in His work on souls, than some imagine. I believe it has occasioned some good people amongst us, who were before too ready to make their own experience a rule to others, to be less censorious and more extended in their charity;

117 Romans 3:19

and this is an excellent advantage indeed. The work of God has been glorious in its variety; it has the more displayed the manifold and unsearchable wisdom of God, and wrought more charity among His people.

(Jonathan Edwards, *Narrative of Surprising Conversions*, p 357)

God Glorified in Man's Dependence

(Sermon by Jonathan Edwards)

Compiled from http://www.apuritansmind.com jonathanedwards/ JonathanEdwards-Sermons GodGlorifiedMansDependence.htm.

All the good of the fallen and redeemed creature is concerned in these four things [wisdom, righteousness, sanctification, and redemption], and cannot be better distributed than into them; but Christ is each of them to us, and we have none of them any otherwise than in him. He is made of God unto us wisdom: in Him are all the proper good and true excellency of the understanding.

Wisdom was a thing that the Greeks admired; but Christ is the true light of the world; it is through Him alone that true wisdom is imparted to the mind. It is in and by Christ that we have righteousness: it is by being in Him that we are justified, have our sins pardoned, and are received as righteous into God's favor. It is by Christ that we have sanctification: we have in Him true excellency of heart as well as of understanding; and He is made unto us inherent as well as imputed righteousness. It is by Christ that we have redemption or the actual deliverance from all misery, and the bestowment of all happiness and glory. Thus we have all our good by Christ, who is God.[118]

Another instance wherein our dependence on God for all our good appears, is this, that it is God that has given us Christ, that we might have these benefits through Him; He of God is made unto us wisdom, righteousness, etc.[119]

So that in this verse is shown our dependence on each person in the Trinity for all our good. We are dependent on Christ the Son of God, as He is our wisdom, righteousness, sanctification, and redemption.[120] We are dependent on the Father, who has given us Christ, and made Him to be these things to us. We are dependent on the Holy Ghost, for it is of Him that we are in Christ Jesus; it is the Spirit of God that gives faith in Him, whereby we receive Him, and close with Him.

There is an absolute and universal dependence of the redeemed on God. The nature and contrivance of our redemption is such, that the redeemed are in every thing directly, immediately, and entirely dependent on God: they are dependent on Him for all, and are dependent on Him every way.[121]

The redeemed have all their good of God. God is the great author of it. He is the first cause of it; and not only so, but He is the only proper cause. It is of God that we have our Redeemer. It is God that has provided a Savior for us. Jesus Christ is not only of God in His person, as He is the only begotten Son of God, but He is from God, as we are concerned in Him, and in His office

---

118 One of the enemy's greatest strategies is to blind the world's eyes as to the identity of Jesus of Nazareth. The many verses that tell us God was manifest in the flesh, and that all things were made by Jesus of Nazareth have to be read again and again, so that we understand the great truth that He was God in human form. See Colossians 1:15-20.

119 1 Corinthians 1:29-30

120 ibid

121 This dependency is the strongest of consolations, because the One on whom we are dependent is dependable.

of Mediator. He is the gift of God to us: God chose and anointed Him, appointed Him His work, and sent Him into the world. And as it is God that gives, so it is God that accepts the Savior. He gives the purchaser, and He affords the thing purchased.

It is of God that we actually receive all the benefits that Christ has purchased. It is God that pardons and justifies, and delivers from going down to hell; and into His favor the redeemed are received, when they are justified. So it is God that delivers from the dominion of sin, cleanses us from our filthiness, and changes us from our deformity. It is of God that the redeemed receive all their true excellency, wisdom, and holiness.

It is of God that we have the Holy Scriptures; they are His word. It is of God that we have ordinances, and their efficacy depends on the immediate influence of His Spirit. The ministers of the gospel are sent of God, and all their sufficiency is of Him. "We have this treasure in earthen vessels, that the excellency of the power may be of God, and not of us."[122] Their success depends entirely and absolutely on the immediate blessing and influence of God.

It was of mere grace that God gave us His only begotten Son. The grace is great in proportion to the excellency of what is given. The gift was infinitely precious, because it was of a person infinitely worthy, a person of infinite glory; and also because it was of a person infinitely near and dear to God.

The grace in bestowing this gift is great in proportion to our unworthiness to whom it is given; instead of deserving such a gift, we merited infinitely ill of God's hands. He gave Him to dwell amongst us; He gave Him to us incarnate, or in our nature; and in the like though sinless infirmities. He gave Him to us in a low and afflicted state; and not only so, but as slain, that He might be a feast for our souls.

122 2 Corinthians 4:7

The grace of God in bestowing this gift is most free. It was what God was under no obligation to bestow. He might have rejected fallen man, as He did the fallen angels. It was what we never did anything to merit; it was given while we were yet enemies, and before we had so much as repented. It was from the love of God who saw no excellency in us to attract it; and it was without expectation of ever being requited for it. And it is from mere grace that the benefits of Christ are applied to such and such particular persons. Those that are called and sanctified are to attribute it alone to the good pleasure of God's goodness, by which they are distinguished. He is sovereign, and hath mercy on whom He will have mercy.
We stand in need of grace, not only to bestow glory upon us, but to deliver us from hell and eternal wrath. Under the first covenant we depended on God's goodness to give us the reward of righteousness; and so we do now; but we stand in need of God's free and sovereign grace to give us that righteousness; to pardon our sin, and release us from the guilt and infinite demerit of it.

Man was created holy, for it became God to create holy all His reasonable creatures. It would have been a disparagement to the holiness of God's nature if He had made an intelligent creature unholy. But now when fallen man is made holy, it is from mere and arbitrary grace.

We are not only indeed more dependent on the grace of God, but our dependence is much more conspicuous, because our own insufficiency and helplessness in ourselves is much more apparent in our fallen and undone state, than it was before we were either sinful or miserable. We are more apparently dependent on God for holiness, because we are first sinful, and utterly polluted, and afterward holy.[123]

---

123 Too many who profess the new birth, are strangers to holiness. They couldn't define the word if their life depended on it; which it does: "Follow peace with all men, and holiness, without which no man shall see the Lord" (Hebrews 12:14).

And we are not only without any true excellency, but are full of, and wholly defiled with, that which is infinitely odious. All our good is more apparently from God, because we are first naked and wholly without any good, and afterwards enriched with all good.

All we have, wisdom, the pardon of sin, deliverance from hell, acceptance into God's favor, grace, and holiness, true comfort and happiness, eternal life and glory, is from God by a Mediator; and this Mediator is God; which Mediator we have an absolute dependence upon, as He through whom we receive all. . . . God not only gives us the Mediator, and accepts His mediation, and of His power and grace bestows the things purchased by the Mediator; but He the Mediator is God.

Our blessings are what we have by purchase; and the purchase is made of God, the blessings are purchased of Him, and God gives the purchaser; and not only so, but God is the purchaser. Yea, God is both the purchaser and the price; for Christ, who is God, purchased these blessings for us, by offering up himself as the price of our salvation. He purchased eternal life by the sacrifice of himself.

We have the greater occasion to take notice of God's all-sufficiency, when all our sufficiency is thus every way of Him. We have the more occasions to contemplate Him as an infinite good, and as the fountain of all good. Such a dependence on God demonstrates His all-sufficiency. So much as the dependence of the creature is on God, so much the greater does the creature's emptiness in himself appear; and so much the greater the creature's emptiness, so much the greater must the fullness of the being be who supplies him. Our having all of God, shows the fullness of His power and grace; our having all through Him, shows the fullness of His merit and worthiness; and our having all in Him, demonstrates His fullness of beauty, love, and happiness.

And the redeemed, by reason of the greatness of their dependence on God, have not only so much the greater occasion, but also obligation to contemplate and acknowledge the glory and fullness of God. How unreasonable and ungrateful should we be if we did not acknowledge that sufficiency and glory which we absolutely, immediately, and universally depend upon!

So much the more men exalt themselves, so much the less will they surely be disposed to exalt God.

Though God be pleased to lift man out of that dismal abyss of sin and woe into which he was fallen, and exceedingly to exalt him in excellency and honor, and to a high pitch of glory and blessedness, yet the creature hath nothing in any respect to glory of; all the glory evidently belongs to God, all is in a mere, and most absolute, and divine dependence on the Father, Son, and Holy Ghost.

Hence those doctrines and schemes of divinity that are in any respect opposite to such an absolute and universal dependence on God, derogate from His glory, and thwart the design of our redemption. And such are those schemes that put the creature in God's stead, in any of the mentioned respects that exalt man into the place of Father, Son, or Holy Ghost, in any thing pertaining to our redemption. However they may allow of a dependence of the redeemed on God, yet they deny a dependence that is so absolute and universal. They own an entire dependence of God for some things, but not for others; they own that we depend on God for the gift and acceptance of a Redeemer, but deny so absolute a dependence on Him for the obtaining of an interest in the Redeemer. They own an absolute dependence on the Father for giving His Son, and on the Son for working out redemption, but not so entire a dependence on the Holy Ghost for conversion, and a being in Christ, and so coming to a title to His benefits. They own a dependence on God for means of grace, but not absolutely for the benefit and success of those means; a partial dependence on the power of God, for obtaining and exercising holiness, but not a mere dependence on the arbitrary and sovereign grace of God. They own a dependence on the free grace of God for a reception into his favor, so far that it is without any proper merit, but not as it is without being attracted, or moved with any excellency. They own a partial dependence on Christ, as He through whom we have life, as having purchased new terms of life, but still hold that the righteousness through which we have life is inherent in ourselves, as it was under the first covenant. Now whatever scheme is inconsistent with our entire dependence on God for all, and of having all of Him, through Him, and in Him, it is repugnant to the design and tenor of the gospel, and robs it of that which God accounts its luster and glory.

Faith is a sensibleness of what is real in the work of redemption; and the soul that believes doth entirely depend on God for all salvation, in its own sense and act. Faith abases men, and exalts God; it gives all the glory of redemption to Him alone. It is necessary in order to saving faith, that man should be emptied of himself, be sensible that he is "wretched, and miserable, and poor, and blind, and naked." Humility is a great ingredient of true faith: he that truly receives redemption, receives it as a little child: "Whosoever shall not receive the kingdom of heaven as a little child, he shall not enter therein."[124] It is the delight of a believing soul to abase itself and exalt God alone: that is the language of it. "Not unto us, O LORD, not unto us, but unto thy name give glory."[125]

Let us be exhorted to exalt God alone, and ascribe to Him all

124 Mark 10:15

125 Psalm 115:1a. Saving faith is a hidden mystery to the unsaved. They assume that when we speak of "faith in God" that it is a mere belief in His existence. But when the Bible speaks of a faith that saves, it is a *trust* in God for our eternal salvation. However, it is a faith that *begins* with an intellectual acknowledgment of our need for His mercy. If a person trusts a parachute, the very fact that he put it on is, in itself, an intellectual acknowledgment of his need of it. He is "emptied of himself." In other words he has given up trying to save himself, and instead entirely trusts in the parachute. The trust that saves us *begins* with the belief that we are wretched and under His wrath.

the glory of redemption. Let us endeavor to obtain, and increase in, a sensibleness of our great dependence on God, to have our eye to Him alone, to mortify a self-dependent and self-righteous disposition. Man is naturally exceeding prone to exalt himself, and depend on his own power or goodness; as though from himself he must expect happiness. He is prone to have respect to enjoyments alien from God and His Spirit, as those in which happiness is to be found. But this doctrine should teach us to exalt God alone; as by trust and reliance, so by praise. "But he that glorieth, let him glory in the Lord."[126] Hath any man hope that he is converted, and sanctified, and that his mind is endowed with true excellency and spiritual beauty? That his sins are forgiven, and he [is] received into God's favor, and exalted to the honor and blessedness of being His child, and an heir of eternal life? Let him give God all the glory, who alone makes him to differ from the worst of men in this world, or the most miserable of the damned in hell. Hath any man much comfort and strong hope of eternal life, let not his hope lift him up, but dispose him the more to abase himself, to reflect on his own exceeding unworthiness of such a favor, and to exalt God alone.[127] Is any man eminent in holiness, and abundant in good works, let him take nothing of the glory of it to himself, but ascribe it to Him, "For we are his workmanship, created in Christ Jesus unto good works."[128]

126 2 Corinthians 2:17

127 Praise comes easy to those who have seen the Cross.

128 Ephesians 2:10

The Vain Self-Flatteries of the Sinner

(Sermon by Jonathan Edwards)

Compiled from http://www.apuritansmind.com/jonathan edwards/JonathanEdwards-Sermons-VainSelfFlattery.htm.

"For he flattereth himself in his own eyes, until his iniquity be found to be hateful."[129]

In the previous verse, David says, "The transgression of the wicked saith within my heart, that there is no fear of God before his eyes."[130] That is, when he saw that the wicked went on in sin, in an allowed way of wickedness, it convinced him, that he was not afraid of those terrible judgments, and of that wrath with which God hath threatened sinners. If the sinner were afraid of these, he could never go on so securely in sin, as he doth.

It was a strange thing that men, who enjoyed such light as they did in the land of Israel, who read and heard those many awful threatenings which were written in the book of the law, should not be afraid to go on in sin. But saith the Psalmist, "They flatter themselves in their own eyes: they have something or other which they make a foundation of encouragement, whereby they persuade themselves that they shall escape those judgments, and that makes them put far away the evil day."[131]

In this manner he proceeds, until his iniquity be found to be hateful; that is, until he finds by experience that it is a more dreadful thing to sin against God, and break His holy commands, than he imagined. He thinks sin to be sweet, and hides it as a

129 Psalm 36:2
130 Psalm 36:1
131 See Psalm 36:2.

sweet morsel under his tongue. He loves it and flatters himself in it, till at length he finds, by experience, that it is bitter as gall and wormwood. Though he thinks the commission of sin to be lovely, yet he will find the fruit of it to be hateful, and what he cannot endure. "At the last it biteth like a serpent, and stingeth like an adder."[132]

Here observe, the subject spoken of is the wicked man, of whom the Psalmist had been speaking in the foregoing verse.[133] His action in flattering himself in his own eyes; i.e., he makes himself and his case to appear to himself, or in his own eyes, better than it is.

Wicked men generally flatter themselves with hopes of escaping punishment, till it actually comes upon them.[134] There are but few sinners who despair, who give up the cause and conclude with themselves, that they shall go to hell. Yet there are but few who do not go to hell. It is to be feared that many go to hell every day out of this country. Yet very few of them suffer themselves to believe that they are in any great danger of that punishment.

They go on sinning and traveling in the direct road to the pit; yet by one they persuade themselves that they shall never fall into it.

---

132 Proverbs 23:32

133 Psalm 36:1

134 We all tend to flatter ourselves in some way. Many a person, who thought he had a good singing voice, has been brought back to reality after hearing a recording of himself singing. We also tend to think that we look better than we do. The unflattering objectivity of a mirror brings us back to reality. God gave humanity a faithful mirror for the unsaved to see reality:

"For if anyone is a hearer of the word and not a doer, he is like a man observing his natural face in a mirror; for he observes himself, goes away, and immediately forgets what kind of man he was. But he who looks into the perfect law of liberty and continues *in it*, and is not a forgetful hearer but a doer of the work, this one will be blessed in what he does" (James 1:23-25, NKJV).

The Law shows a sinner himself as he is in the sight of God. Without it, he flatters and puffs himself up in his own conceit. Self-righteousness is nothing but self-flattery, caused by an overdose of self-deceit.

It is very evident that sinners flatter themselves that they shall escape punishment, otherwise they would be in dreadful and continual distress. They could never live and go about so cheerfully as they now do. Their lives would be filled with sorrow and mourning, and they would be in continual uneasiness and distress, as much as those that are exercised with some violent pain of body. But it is apparent that men are careless and secure, that they are not much concerned about future punishment, and that they cheerfully pursue their business and recreations. Therefore they undoubtedly flatter themselves, that they shall not be eternally miserable in hell, as they are threatened in the Word of God.

It is evident that [sinners] flatter themselves with hopes that they shall escape punishment. Otherwise they would certainly be restrained, at least from many of those sins in which they now live. They would not proceed in willful courses of sin. The transgression of the wicked convinced the Psalmist, and is enough to convince everyone, that there is no fear of God before his eyes, and that he flatters himself in his own eyes. It would be impossible for men allowably from day to day to do those very things which they know are threatened with everlasting destruction, if they did not some way encourage themselves [that] they should nevertheless escape that destruction.

Some [sinners] flatter themselves with a secret hope that there is no such thing as another world. They hear a great deal of preaching, and a great deal of talk about hell, and the eternal judgment. But those things do not seem to them to be real. They never saw hell, nor the devils and damned spirits. And therefore are ready to say to themselves, "How do I know that there is any such thing as another world?" When the beasts die, there is an end of them, and how do I know but that it will be so with me? Perhaps all these things are nothing but the inventions of men, nothing but cunningly devised fables. Some flatter themselves that death is a great way off, and that they shall hereafter have much opportunity to seek salvation. And they think if they earnestly seek it, though it be a great while hence, they shall obtain [it]. Although they see no reason to conclude that they shall live long, and perhaps they do not positively conclude that they shall, yet it doth not come into their minds that their lives are really uncertain, and that it is doubtful whether they will live another year. Such a thought as this doth not take any hold of them. And although they do not absolutely determine that they shall live to old age or to middle age, yet they secretly flatter themselves with such an imagination. They are disposed to believe so. They act upon it and run the venture of it.

Some flatter themselves that they lead moral and orderly lives, and therefore think that they shall not be damned. They think with themselves that they live not in any vice, that they take care to wrong no man, are just and honest dealers, that they are not addicted to hard drinking, or to uncleanness, or to bad language; that they keep the Sabbath strictly, are constant attendants on the public worship, and maintain the worship of God in their families. Therefore they hope that God will not cast them into hell. They see not why God should be so angry with them as that would imply, seeing they are so orderly and regular in their walk! They see not that they have done enough to anger Him to that degree. And if they have angered Him, they imagine they have also done a great deal to pacify Him.

If they be not as yet converted, and it be necessary that they should experience any other conversion in order to their salvation, they hope that their orderly and strict lives will move God to give them converting grace. They hope that surely God will not see those that live as they do, go to hell. Thus they flatter themselves, as those "which trusted in themselves that they were righteous."[135]

---

135 Luke 18:19

Hell is full of good intenders who never proved to be true performers: "Go thy way for this time; when I have a convenient season, I will call for thee."[136]

Men often have a dependence on their own righteousness, and as long as they live are never brought off from it. Multitudes uphold themselves with their own intentions till all their prospects are dashed in pieces by death. They put off the work that they have to do till such a time. And when that comes, they put it off to another time; until death, which cannot be put off, overtakes them.

All men know that they must die, and all that sit under the light of the gospel have been told many a time, that after this there is an other world, that there are but two states in that other world—a state of eternal happiness, and a state of eternal misery—that there is but one way of escaping the misery and obtaining the blessedness of eternity, which is by obtaining an interest in Christ, through faith in Him, and that this life is the only opportunity of obtaining an interest in Christ. Yet men are so much given to flatter themselves in those ways which we have mentioned, that there are but few that seasonably take care of their salvation. Indeed they cannot but be in some measure concerned about their souls. Yet they flatter themselves with one thing or other, so that they are kept steadily and uninterruptedly going on in the broad way to destruction.

Is it because you are outwardly of an orderly life and conversation, that you think you shall be saved? How unreasonable is it to suppose that God should be so obliged by those actions, which he knows are not done from the least respect or regard to Him, but wholly with a private view! Is it because you are under great advantages that you are not much afraid but that you shall some

136 Acts 24:25

time or other be converted, and therefore neglect yourselves and your spiritual interests? And were not the people of Bethsaida, Chorazin and Capernaum, under as great advantages as you, when Christ himself preached the gospel to them, almost continually, and wrought such a multitude of miracles among them? Yet He says, that it shall be more tolerable in the Day of Judgment for Sodom and Gomorrah, than for those cities.[137]

Do you expect you shall be saved, however you neglect yourselves, because you were born of godly parents? Hear what Christ saith, "Think not to say within yourselves, we have Abraham to our father."[138]

If you think yourselves already converted, and that encourages you to give yourselves the greater liberty in sinning, this is a certain sign that you are not converted.

Wherefore abandon all these ways of flattering yourselves. No longer follow the devil's bait and let nothing encourage you to go on in sin; but immediately and henceforth seek God with all your heart, and soul, and strength.

137 Matthew 10:15
138 Matthew 3:9

The Excellency of Christ

(Sermon by Jonathan Edwards)

Compiled from: http://www.apuritansmind.com

There do meet in Jesus Christ infinite highness and infinite condescension. Christ, as He is God, is infinitely great and high above all. He is higher than the kings of the earth, for He is King of kings, and Lord of lords.[139] He is higher than the heavens, and higher than the highest angels of heaven. So great is He, that all men, all kings and princes, are as worms of the dust before Him. All nations are as the drop of the bucket, and the light dust of the balance, yea, and angels themselves are as nothing before Him. He is so high, that He is infinitely above any need of us, above our reach that we cannot be profitable to Him, and above our conceptions that we cannot comprehend Him. "What is his name, and what is his Son's name, if thou canst tell?"[140] Our understandings, if we stretch them never so far, cannot reach up to His divine glory. "It is high as heaven; what canst thou do?"[141] Christ is the Creator and great Possessor of heaven and earth. He is sovereign Lord of all. He rules over the whole universe, and does whatsoever pleaseth Him. His knowledge is without bound. His wisdom is perfect, and what none can circumvent. His power is infinite, and none can resist Him. His riches are immense and inexhaustible. His majesty is infinitely awful.[142]

---

139 Titus 6:15

140 Proverbs 30:4

141 Job 11:8

142 Never before have we been able to probe the universe and search out creation to see its magnificence. Therefore, of all generations we should be the ones filled with awe in worship at the feet of Jesus Christ, who created all these things. Yet the opposite is true. We are part of the most sinful, God-defying, blasphemous generation that ever lived. This may be because of the sexual revolution of the 1960s, coupled with the unbridled access to sin that modern technology and the Internet have made available, and the more this world loves the darkness, the

And yet He is one of infinite condescension. None are so low or inferior, but Christ's condescension is sufficient to take a gracious notice of them. He condescends not only to the angels, humbling himself to behold the things that are done in heaven, but He also condescends to such poor creatures as men, and that not only so as to take notice of princes and great men, but of those that are of meanest rank and degree, "the poor of this world,"[143] Such as are commonly despised by their fellow creatures, Christ does not despise: "Base things of the world, and things that are despised, hath God chosen."[144] Christ condescends to take notice of beggars[145] and people of the most despised nations. In Christ Jesus is neither "Barbarian, Scythian, bond nor free"[146] He that is thus high condescends to take a gracious notice of little children: "Suffer little children . . . to come unto me."[147] Yea, which is more, His condescension is sufficient to take a gracious notice of the most unworthy, sinful creatures, those that have no good deservings, and those that have infinite ill-deservings.[148]

Yea, so great is His condescension, that it is not only sufficient to take some gracious notice of such as these, but sufficient for everything that is an act of condescension. His condescension is great enough to become their friend, to become their companion, to unite their souls to Him in spiritual marriage. It is enough to take their nature upon Him, to become one of them, that He may be one with them. Yea, it is great enough to abase himself yet lower for them, even to expose himself to shame and spitting; yea, to yield up himself to an ignominious death for them. And what act of condescension can be conceived of greater? Yet such an act as this, has His condescension yielded to, for those that

---

more they will hate the light.

143 James 2:5

144 I Corinthians 1:28

145 Luke 16:22

146 Colossians 3:12

147 Matthew 19:14

148 The Incarnation was the opposite of everything for which this sinful world stands. God became a humble person—born in a cowshed, gravitating to the lowly and poor, riding on a donkey, dying on a cross, and confounding this proud world by granting everlasting life through the despised doorway of humility of heart.

are so low and mean, despicable and unworthy!

Such a conjunction of infinite highness and low condescension, in the same person, is admirable. We see, by manifold instances, what a tendency a high station has in men, to make them to be of a quite contrary disposition. If one worm be a little exalted above another, by having more dust, or a bigger dunghill, how much does he make of himself! What a distance does he keep from those that are below him! And a little condescension is what he expects should be made much of, and greatly acknowledged. Christ condescends to wash our feet, but how would great men (or rather the bigger worms), account themselves debased by acts of far less condescension!

There meet in Jesus Christ, infinite justice and infinite grace. As Christ is a divine person, He is infinitely holy and just, hating sin, and disposed to execute condign punishment for sin. He is the Judge of the world, and the infinitely just judge of it, and will not at all acquit the wicked, or by any means clear the guilty.[149]

And yet He is infinitely gracious and merciful. Though His justice be so strict with respect to all sin, and every breach of the law, yet He has grace sufficient for every sinner, and even the chief of sinners.[150] And it is not only sufficient for the most unworthy to show them mercy, and bestow some good upon them, but to bestow the greatest good. Yea, it is sufficient to bestow all good upon them, and to do all things for them. There is no benefit or blessing that they can receive, so great but the grace of Christ is sufficient to bestow it on the greatest sinner that ever lived; and

---

149 Nahum 1:3, Exodus 34:7. In the first decade of the 21st century, Mexican drug lords murdered thousands of innocent people and reigned by terror. In September of 2010, they killed their fifth mayor of a city, by tying his hands and slashing his face with a machete. It is a mystery how anyone can believe in the existence of God and yet not believe in the retribution of hell for those who do such things to their fellow man. Throughout the world, horrors take place every day in every corner, but the strong consolation for those who believe God's Word is that there will be a day of ultimate justice. May God hasten that day.

150 Titus 1:15

not only so, but so great is His grace, that nothing is too much as the means of this good. It is sufficient not only to do great things, but also to suffer in order to do it, and not only to suffer, but to suffer most extremely even unto death, the most terrible of natural evils, and not only death, but the most ignominious and tormenting, and every way the most terrible that men could inflict; yea, and greater sufferings than men could inflict, who could only torment the body. He had sufferings in His soul, which were the more immediate fruits of the wrath of God against the sins of those He undertakes for.

In the person of Christ do meet together infinite glory and lowest humility. Infinite glory and the virtue of humility, meet in no other person but Christ. They meet in no created person, for no created person has infinite glory, and they meet in no other divine person but Christ.

But however He is thus above all, yet He is lowest of all in humility. There never was so great an instance of this virtue among either men or angels, as [was] Jesus. None ever was so sensible of the distance between God and Him, or had a heart so lowly before God, as the man Christ Jesus.[151]

And yet He was the most marvelous instance of meekness, and humble quietness of spirit, that ever was, agreeable to the prophecies of Him: "All this was done, that it might be fulfilled which was spoken by the prophet, saying, Tell ye the daughter of Sion, Behold, thy King cometh unto thee, meek, and sitting upon an ass, and a colt the foal of an ass."[152] And agreeable to what Christ declares of himself: "I am meek and lowly in heart."[153] And agreeable to what was manifest in His behavior, for there never was such an instance seen

---

151 See Matthew 11:29. Jesus of Nazareth was "only begotten." There was never a man like this man. He *always* did those things that pleased the Father. No other human being can rightly claim moral perfection in thought, word, and in deed.

152 Matthew 21:4-5

153 Matthew 11:29

on earth of a meek behavior, under injuries and reproaches, and towards enemies, who when he was reviled, reviled not again. He had a wonderful spirit of forgiveness, was ready to forgive His worst enemies, and prayed for them with fervent and effectual prayers. With what meekness did He appear in the ring of soldiers that were contemning and mocking Him. He was silent, and opened not His mouth, but went as a lamb to the slaughter. Thus is Christ a lion in majesty and a lamb in meekness.

There are conjoined in the person of Christ infinite worthiness of good, and the greatest patience under sufferings of evil. He was perfectly innocent, and deserved no suffering. He deserved nothing from God by any guilt of His own, and He deserved no ill from men. Yea, He was not only harmless and undeserving of suffering, but He was infinitely worthy — worthy of the infinite love of the Father, worthy of infinite and eternal happiness, and infinitely worthy of all possible esteem, love, and service from all men. And yet He was perfectly patient under the greatest sufferings that ever were endured in this world. "(He) endured the cross, despising the shame."[154] He suffered not from His Father for His faults, but ours. He suffered from men not for His faults, but for those things on account of which He was infinitely worthy of their love and honor, which made His patience the more wonderful and the more glorious.[155]

There is no such conjunction of innocence, worthiness, and patience under sufferings, as in the person of Christ.

Christ is the Lord of all things in two respects: He is so as God-man and mediator, and thus His dominion is appointed, and given Him of the Father. Having it by delegation from God, He is

154 Hebrews 12:2

155 Our songs, our praises, our preaching, and even our deepest thoughts about God fall infinitely short of expressing who and what He is. Only occasionally do we get a fleeting glimpse of His breathtaking magnificence. Such realms of the Spirit leave us with our mouth shut, and head bowed in a holy worship.

as it were the Father's vicegerent. But He is Lord of all things in another respect, viz. as He is [by His original nature] God. So He is by natural right the Lord of all, and supreme over all as much as the Father. Thus, He has dominion over the world, not by delegation, but in His own right. He is not an under God, as the Arians suppose,[156] but to all intents and purposes, supreme God. And yet in the same person is found the greatest spirit of obedience to the commands and laws of God that ever was in the universe, which was manifest in His obedience here in this world. . . . Never anyone received commands from God of such difficulty, and that were so great a trial of obedience, as Jesus Christ. One of God's commands to Him was, that He should yield himself to those dreadful sufferings that He underwent. . . . Never was there such an instance of obedience in man or angel as this, though He was at the same time supreme Lord of both angels and men.

In the person of Christ are conjoined absolute sovereignty and perfect resignation. This is another unparalleled conjunction. Christ, as He is God, is the absolute sovereign of the world, the sovereign disposer of all events . . . But yet Christ was the most wonderful instance of resignation that ever appeared in the world. He was absolutely and perfectly resigned when He had a near and immediate prospect of His terrible sufferings, and the dreadful cup that He was to drink. The idea and expectation of this made His soul exceeding sorrowful, even unto death, and put Him into such an agony that His sweat was as it were great drops or clots of blood, falling down to the ground. But in such circumstances He was wholly resigned to the will of God.[157]
In Christ do meet together self-sufficiency and an entire trust and reliance on God, which is another conjunction

156 "Arianism" is also often used to refer to the theological belief, which began in the 4th century, that regarded Jesus as a created being.
157 Our resignation should be to reach this world with the gospel. May God help us to have our own Gethsemane experience—where we may sweat drops of blood at the thought of evangelism, but overcome our fears with "nevertheless, not My will, but Yours be done" (Luke 22:42, NKJV).

peculiar to the person of Christ. As He is a divine person, He is self-sufficient, standing in need of nothing. All creatures are dependent on Him, but He is dependent on none, but is absolutely independent.

The strict justice of God, and even His revenging justice, and that against the sins of men, never was so gloriously manifested as in Christ. He manifested an infinite regard to the attribute of God's justice, in that when He had a mind to save sinners, He was willing to undergo such extreme sufferings, rather than that their salvation should be to the injury of the honor of that attribute. And as He is the Judge of the world, He does himself exercise strict justice; He will not clear the guilty, nor at all acquit the wicked in judgment. Yet how wonderfully is infinite mercy towards sinners displayed in Him! And what glorious and ineffable grace and love have been and are exercised by Him, towards sinful men! Though He be the just Judge of a sinful world, yet He is also the Savior of the world. Though He be a consuming fire to sin,[158] yet He is the light and life of sinners.

So the immutable truth of God, in the threatenings of His law against the sins of men, was never so manifested as it is in Jesus Christ; for there never was any other so great a trial of the unalterableness of the truth of God in those threatenings, as when sin came to be imputed to His own Son. And then in Christ has been seen already an actual complete accomplishment of those threatenings, which never has been nor will be seen in any other instance, because the eternity that will be taken up in fulfilling those threatenings on others, never will be finished. Christ manifested an infinite regard to this truth of God in His sufferings.

Christ's humiliation was great, in being born in such a low condition, of a poor virgin, and in a stable. His humiliation was

---

158 Hebrews 12:29

great, in being subject to Joseph the carpenter, and [to] Mary His mother, and afterwards living in poverty, so as not to have where to lay His head, and in suffering such manifold and bitter reproaches as He suffered, while He went about preaching and working miracles. But His humiliation was never so great as it was, in His last sufferings, beginning with His agony in the garden, till He expired on the Cross. Never was He subject to such ignominy as then, never did He suffer so much pain in His body, or so much sorrow in His soul. Never was He in so great an exercise of His condescension, humility, meekness, and patience, as He was in these last sufferings. Never was His divine glory and majesty covered with so thick and dark a veil. Never did He so empty himself and make himself of no reputation, as at this time. And yet, never was His divine glory so manifested, by any act of His, as in yielding himself up to these sufferings. When the fruit of it came to appear, and the mystery and ends of it to be unfolded in its issue, then did the glory of it appear, [and] then did it appear as the most glorious act of Christ that ever He exercised towards the creature.[159]

He never in any act gave so great a manifestation of love to God, and yet never so manifested His love to those that were enemies to God, as in that act. Christ never did anything whereby His love to the Father was so eminently manifested, as in His laying down His life, under such inexpressible sufferings, in obedience to His command, and for the vindication of the honor of His authority and majesty; nor did ever any mere creature give such a testimony of love to God as that was. And yet this was the greatest expression of His love to sinful men who were enemies to God: "When we were enemies, we were reconciled to God by the death of his Son."[160] The greatness of Christ's

159 It is a wonderful paradox that in the darkness of suffering such light should shine. It is there that we see the brilliance of God's holy character; how far we fall short of this. When trials come to us, we tend to yield up hidden sin. The heat of tribulation manifests dross rather than gold, and makes us infinitely thankful for mercy.

160 Romans 5:10

love to such, appears in nothing so much as in its being dying love. That blood of Christ that fell in great drops to the ground, in His agony, was shed from love to God's enemies, and His own. That shame and spitting, that torment of body, and that exceeding sorrow, even unto death, which He endured in His soul, was what He underwent from love to rebels against God to save them from hell, and to purchase for them eternal glory. Never did Christ so eminently show His regard to God's honor, as in offering up himself a victim to justice. And yet in this above all, He manifested His love to them who dishonored God, so as to bring such guilt on themselves, that nothing less than His blood could atone for it.[161]

Christ never so eminently appeared for divine justice, and yet never suffered so much from divine justice, as when He offered up himself a sacrifice for our sins. In Christ's great sufferings, did His infinite regard to the honor of God's justice distinguishingly appear, for it was from regard to that, that He thus humbled himself. And yet in these sufferings, Christ was the mark of the vindictive expressions of that very justice of God. Revenging justice then spent all its force upon Him, on account of our guilt, which made Him sweat blood, and cry out upon the Cross, and probably rent his vitals—broke His heart, the fountain of blood, or some other blood vessels—and by the violent fermentation turned His blood to water. For the blood and water that issued out of His side, when pierced by the spear, seems to have been extravasated blood, and so there might be a kind of literal fulfillment of Psalm 22:14, "I am poured out like water, and all my bones are out of joint: my heart is like wax, it is melted in the midst of my bowels." And this was the way and means by which Christ stood up for the honor of God's justice, namely, by thus suffering its terrible executions. For when He had undertaken for sinners, and had substituted himself in their stead, divine justice could have its due honor no other way than by His suffering its

161 We must preach the blood of the Cross, despite it being held in contempt by this wicked world. It is the center point of the gospel.

revenges. In this the diverse excellencies that met in the person of Christ appeared, viz. His infinite regard to God's justice, and such love to those that have exposed themselves to it, as induced Him thus to yield himself a sacrifice to it.

Christ's holiness never so illustriously shone forth as it did in His last sufferings, and yet He never was to such a degree treated as guilty. Christ's holiness never had such a trial as it had then, and therefore never had so great a manifestation. When it was tried in this furnace, it came forth as gold, or as silver purified seven times.[162] His holiness then above all appeared in His steadfast pursuit of the honor of God, and in His obedience to Him. For His yielding himself unto death was transcendently the greatest act of obedience that ever was paid to God by anyone since the foundation of the world.

Christ never so greatly manifested His hatred of sin, as against God, as in His dying to take away the dishonor that sin had done to God.[163] Yet never was He to such a degree subject to the terrible effects of God's hatred of sin, and wrath against it, as He was then. In this appears those diverse excellencies meeting in Christ, viz. love to God, and grace to sinners.

Christ never was so dealt with, as unworthy, as in His last sufferings, and yet it is chiefly on account of them that He is accounted worthy. He was therein dealt with as if He had not been worthy to live: they cry out, "Away with him, away with him, crucify him."[164] And they prefer Barabbas before Him. And He suffered from the Father, as one whose demerits were infinite, by reason of our demerits that were laid upon Him. And yet it was especially by that act of His subjecting himself to those sufferings, that He merited, and on the account of which chiefly He was accounted worthy of the glory of His exaltation. "He

---

162 The fiery trials revealed no dross from the Son of God. His character was pure gold.

163 Nothing keeps us at the foot of the Cross more than our love of sin.

164 John 19:15

humbled himself, and became obedient unto death, . . . wherefore God also hath highly exalted him."[165] And we see that it is on this account chiefly, that He is extolled as worthy by saints and angels in the context: "Worthy," say they, "is the Lamb that was slain."[166] This shows an admirable conjunction in Him of infinite dignity, and infinite condescension and love to the infinitely unworthy.

Christ in His last sufferings suffered most extremely from those towards whom He was then manifesting His greatest act of love.[167] He never suffered so much from His Father (though not from any hatred to Him, but from hatred to our sins), for He then forsook Him, or took away the comforts of His presence. Then "it pleased the LORD to bruise him; he hath put him to grief."[168] And yet He never gave so great a manifestation of love to God as then, as has been already observed. So Christ never suffered so much from the hands of men as He did then, and yet never was in so high an exercise of love to men. He never was so ill-treated by His disciples, who were so unconcerned about His sufferings that they would not watch with Him one hour in His agony. And when He was apprehended, all forsook Him and fled, except Peter, who denied Him with oaths and curses.[169] And yet then He was suffering, shedding His blood, and pouring out His soul unto death for them. Yea, He probably was then shedding His blood for some of them that shed His blood, for whom He prayed while they were crucifying Him; and who were probably afterwards brought home to Christ by Peter's preaching.[170] This shows an admirable meeting of justice and grace in the redemption of Christ.

In His last sufferings, Christ sapped the very foundations of Satan's kingdom. He conquered His enemies in their own

165 Philippians 2:8-9a

166 Revelation 5:12

167 We have no idea how many who cried out "Crucify Him!" were part of the three thousand that were saved at Pentecost. In an instant, the mercy of God can take a bloodthirsty Saul of Tarsus and make him an apostle of love.

168 Isaiah 53:10

169 Matthew 26:74-75

170 See Luke 23:34; Acts 2:23, 36-37, 41; 3:17; 4:4.

territories, and beat them with their own weapons; as David cut off Goliath's head with his own sword.

Thus Christ appeared at the same time, and in the same act, as both a lion and a lamb. He appeared as a lamb in the hands of His cruel enemies, as a lamb in the paws and between the devouring jaws of a roaring lion. Yea, He was a lamb actually slain by this lion: and yet at the same time, as the Lion of the tribe of Judah, He conquers and triumphs over Satan, destroying His own devourer, as Samson did the lion that roared upon Him, when He rent him as He would a kid. And in nothing has Christ appeared so much as a lion, in glorious strength destroying His enemies, as when He was brought as a lamb to the slaughter. In His greatest weakness He was most strong; and when He suffered most from His enemies, He brought the greatest confusion on His enemies. Thus this admirable conjunction of diverse excellencies was manifest in Christ, in His offering up himself to God in His last sufferings.

Fallen man is in a state of exceeding great misery, and is helpless in it. He is a poor weak creature, like an infant cast out in its blood in the day that it is born. But Christ is the Lion of the tribe of Judah: He is strong, though we are weak; He has prevailed to do that for us which no creature else could do. Fallen man is a mean despicable creature, a contemptible worm, but Christ, who has undertaken for us, is infinitely honorable and worthy. Fallen man is polluted, but Christ is infinitely holy; fallen man is hateful, but Christ is infinitely lovely. Fallen man is the object of God's indignation, but Christ is infinitely dear to Him. We have dreadfully provoked God, but Christ has performed that righteousness which is infinitely precious in God's eyes.[171]

---

171 The difference between the sinfulness of man and God is seen in the moral Law. It is a two-edged sword that divides the sinfulness of man from the holiness of God.

And here is not only infinite strength and infinite worthiness, but infinite condescension, and love and mercy, as great as power and dignity. If you are a poor, distressed sinner, whose heart is ready to sink for fear that God never will have mercy on you, you need not be afraid to go to Christ, for fear that He is either unable or unwilling to help you. Here is a strong foundation, and an inexhaustible treasure, to answer the necessities of your poor soul. Here is infinite grace and gentleness to invite and embolden a poor, unworthy, fearful soul to come to it. If Christ accepts of you, you need not fear but that you will be safe, for He is a strong Lion for your defense. And if you come, you need not fear but that you shall be accepted, for He is like a Lamb to all that come to Him, and receives then with infinite grace and tenderness. It is true He has awful majesty, He is the great God, and infinitely high above you. But there is this to encourage and embolden the poor sinner, that Christ is man as well as God. He is a creature, as well as the Creator, and He is the most humble and lowly in heart of any creature in heaven or earth. This may well make the poor unworthy creature bold in coming to Him. You need not hesitate one moment; but may run to Him, and cast yourself upon Him. You will certainly be graciously and meekly received by Him.[172]

Though He is a lion, He will only be a lion to your enemies, but He will be a lamb to you.[173] It could not have been conceived, had it not been so in the person of Christ, that there could have been so much in any Savior that is inviting and tending to encourage sinners to trust in Him. Whatever your circumstances are, you need not be afraid to come to such a Savior as this. Be you never so wicked a creature, here is worthiness enough; be you never so poor, and mean, and ignorant a creature, there is no danger of being despised, for though He be so much greater than you, He is also immensely more humble than you. Any one of you that

---

172 How can anyone read the gospels and not fall in love with the Savior? He is a lighthouse in the dark and terrifying storms of life.

173 The essence of the gospel is to kiss the Son, least He become angry and you perish when His wrath is kindled but a little. (See Psalm 2:12.)

is a father or mother, will not despise one of your own children that comes to you in distress: much less danger is there of Christ despising you, if you in your heart come to Him.

What are you afraid of, that you dare not venture your soul upon Christ? Are you afraid that He cannot save you: that He is not strong enough to conquer the enemies of your soul? But how can you desire one stronger than the "mighty God," as Christ is called?[174] Is there need of greater than infinite strength? Are you afraid that He will not be willing to stoop so low as to take any gracious notice of you? But then, look on Him, as He stood in the ring of soldiers, exposing His blessed face to be buffeted and spit upon by them. Behold Him bound with His back uncovered to those that smote Him. And behold Him hanging on the Cross! Do you think that He that had condescension enough to stoop to these things, and that for His crucifiers, will be unwilling to accept of you if you come to Him? Or, are you afraid that if He does accept you, that God the Father will not accept of Him for you?

But consider, will God reject His own Son, in whom His infinite delight is, and has been, from all eternity, and who is so united to Him, that if He should reject Him He would reject himself?

And is not Christ a person honorable enough to be worthy that you should be dependent on Him? Is He not a person high enough to be appointed to so honorable a work as your salvation?

Was it not a great thing for Him, who was God, to take upon Him human nature: to be not only God, but man thenceforward to all eternity? But would you look upon suffering for sinners to be a yet greater testimony of love to sinners, than merely doing, though it be ever so extraordinary a thing that He has done? And would you desire that a Savior should suffer more than Christ has suffered for sinners? What is there wanting, or what would you add if you could, to make Him more fit to be your Savior?

174 Isaiah 9:6

O thou poor distressed soul! whoever thou art, consider that Christ mentions thy very case, when He calls to them who labor and are heavy laden! How he repeatedly promises you rest if you come to Him! In the 28th verse [of the 11th chapter of Matthew] He says, "I will give you rest." And in the 29th verse, "Ye shall find rest unto your souls." This is what you want. This is the thing you have been so long in vain seeking after. O how sweet would rest be to you, if you could but obtain it! Come to Christ, and you shall obtain it. And hear how Christ, to encourage you, represents himself as a lamb! He tells you, that He is meek and lowly in heart, and are you afraid to come to such a one![175]

Whatsoever there is or can be desirable in a friend, is in Christ, and that to the highest degree that can be desired.

Would you choose for a friend a person of great dignity? It is a thing taking with men to have those for their friends who are much above them, because they look upon themselves honored by the friendship of such. Thus, how taking would it be with an inferior maid to be the object of the dear love of some great and excellent prince. But Christ is infinitely above you, and above all the princes of the earth, for He is the King of kings. So honorable a person as this offers himself to you, in the nearest and dearest friendship.[176]

And would you choose to have a friend not only great but good? In Christ infinite greatness and infinite goodness meet together, and receive luster and glory one from another. His greatness is rendered lovely by His goodness. The greater anyone is without goodness, so much the greater evil. But when infinite goodness is joined with greatness, it renders it a glorious and adorable

175 It is important that the sinner comes to the savior heavy laden with the guilt of sin, and not with the weight and burden of problems.

176 Until we find peace through the Cross, we are enemies of God in our minds through wicked works. The Psalmist cried, "Your enemies take *your name* in vain." (Psalm 139:20, NKJV). It is good to explain to sinners who say that they believe in God, that if they have taken His name in vain, they are making themselves His enemy.

greatness. So, on the other hand, His infinite goodness receives luster from his greatness.

And how glorious is the sight, to see him who is the great Creator and supreme Lord of heaven and earth, full of condescension, tender pity and mercy, towards the mean and unworthy! His almighty power, and infinite majesty and self-sufficiency, render His exceeding love and grace the more surprising.

Though it be taking with men to have a near and dear friend of superior dignity, yet there is also an inclination in them to have their friend a sharer with them in circumstances. Thus is Christ.

Though He be the mighty God, yet He has, as it were, brought himself down to be upon a level with you, so as to become man as you are, that He might not only be your Lord, but your brother, and that He might be the more fit to be a companion for such a worm of the dust.

One design of God in the gospel is to bring us to make God the object of our undivided respect, that He may engross our regard every way, that whatever natural inclination there is in our souls, He may be the center of it: that God may be all in all. But there is an inclination in the creature, not only to the adoration of a Lord and Sovereign, but to complacence in some one as a friend, to love and delight in some one that may be conversed with as a companion. And virtue and holiness do not destroy or weaken this inclination of our nature. But so has God contrived in the affair of our redemption, that a divine person may be the object even of this inclination of our nature. And in order hereto, such a one is come down to us, and has taken our nature, and is become one of us, and calls himself our friend, brother, and companion. "For my brethren and companions' sakes, will I now say, Peace be within thee."[177]

---

177 Psalm 122:8

But is it not enough in order to invite and encourage you to free access to a friend so great and high, that He is one of infinite condescending grace, and also has taken your own nature, and is become man? But would you, further to embolden and win you, have Him a man of wonderful meekness and humility? Why, such a one is Christ! He is not only become man for you, but far the meekest and most humble of all men, the greatest instance of these sweet virtues that ever was, or will be. And besides these, He has all other human excellencies in the highest perfection.

By your choosing Christ for your friend and portion, you will obtain these two infinite benefits:

1. Christ will give Himself to you, with all those various excellencies that meet in Him, to your full and everlasting enjoyment. He will ever after treat you as His dear friend, and you shall ere long be where He is, and shall behold His glory, and dwell with Him, in most free and intimate communion and enjoyment.
2. By your being united to Christ, you will have a more glorious union with and enjoyment of God the Father, than otherwise could be. For hereby the saints' relation to God becomes much nearer: they are the children of God in a higher manner than otherwise could be.

When believers get to heaven, Christ will conform them to himself, as He is set down in His Father's throne, so they shall sit down with Him on His throne, and shall in their measure be made like Him.

When the saints shall see Christ's glory and exaltation in heaven, it will indeed possess their hearts with the greater admiration and adoring respect, but it will not awe them into any separation, but will serve only to heighten their surprise and joy, when they find Christ condescending to admit them to such intimate access, and so freely and fully communicating himself to them. So that if we choose Christ for our friend and portion, we shall hereafter be so received to Him, that there shall be nothing to hinder the fullest enjoyment of Him, to the satisfying the utmost cravings of our souls. We may take our full swing at gratifying our spiritual appetite after these holy pleasures.

Christ, who is a divine person, by taking on Him our nature, descends from the infinite distance and height above us, and is brought nigh to us, whereby we have advantage for the full enjoyment of Him. And, on the other hand, we, by being in Christ, a divine person, do as it were ascend up to God, through the infinite distance, and have hereby advantage for the full enjoyment of Him also.

This was the design of Christ, that He and His Father, and His people, might all be united in one: "That they all may be one; as thou, Father, *art* in me, and I in thee, that they also may be one in us: that the world may believe that thou hast sent me. And the glory which thou gavest me, I have given them, that they may be one, even as we are one: I in them, and thou in me, that they may be made perfect in one."[178] Christ has brought it to pass, that those whom the Father has given Him should be brought into the household of God, that He, His Father, and His people should be as one society, one family, [and] that the church should be as it were admitted into the society of the blessed Trinity.[179]

178 John 17:21-23

179 The Church is a chaste virgin, espoused in a glorious love relationship to the Savior that will find consummation at His return.

The End of the Wicked Contemplated by the Righteous

(Sermon by Jonathan Edwards)

Compiled from http://www.apuritansmind.com/jonathanedwards/JonathanEdwards-Sermons-EndOfTheWicked.htm

When the saints in glory shall see the wrath of God executed on ungodly men, it will be no occasion of grief to them, but of rejoicing.[180]

It is not only the sight of God's wrath executed on those wicked men who are of the antichristian church, which will be occasion of rejoicing to the saints in glory; but also the sight of the destruction of all God's enemies: whether they have been the followers of antichrist or not, that alters not the case, if they have been the enemies of God, and of Jesus Christ. All wicked men will at last be destroyed together, as being united in the same cause and interest, as being all of Satan's army. They will all stand together at the Day of Judgment, as being all of the same company.

God glorifies himself in the eternal damnation of the ungodly men. God glorifies himself in all that He doth; but He glorifies himself principally in His eternal disposal of His intelligent creatures, some are appointed to everlasting life, and others left to everlasting death.[181]

There are many now in the world who proudly lift up themselves

180 While something in us grieves that any sinner would end up in hell, we can't help but rejoice at the thought that Hitler and other evil men will receive ultimate justice for their unspeakable wickedness.

181 Some may cringe at the thought that God would be glorified "in the eternal damnation of the ungodly men." However, justice served by a judge upon a wicked and unrepentant criminal reflects the judge's good character. On the Day of Judgment perfect righteousness will be exalted and God will be glorified, because all humanity will see that justice is served.

against God. There are many open opposers of the cause and interest of Christ. "They set their mouth against the heavens, and their tongue walketh through the earth" (See Psalm 73:9). (See Psalm 73:9.) Then God will show his glorious power in destroying these enemies.

We ought now to seek and be concerned for the salvation of wicked men, because now they are capable subjects of it. Wicked men, though they may be very wicked, yet are capable subjects of mercy. It is yet a day of grace with them, and they have the offers of salvation. Christ is as yet seeking their salvation; He is calling upon them, inviting and wooing them, He stands at the door and knocks. He is using many means with them, is calling them, saying, "Turn ye, turn ye, why will ye die?" The day of His patience is yet continued to them; and if Christ is seeking their salvation, surely we ought to seek it.

God is wont now to make men the means of one another's salvation; yea, it is His ordinary way so to do. He makes the concern and endeavors of His people the means of bringing home many to Christ. Therefore they ought to be concerned for and endeavor it. But it will not be so in another world; there wicked men will be no longer capable subjects of mercy. The saints will know that it is the will of God [that] the wicked should be miserable to all eternity. It will therefore cease to be their duty any more to seek their salvation, or to be concerned about their misery.

The vengeance inflicted on many of the wicked will be a manifestation of God's love to the saints. One way whereby God shows His love to the saints is by destroying their enemies. God hath said, "He that toucheth you, toucheth the apple of mine eye."[182] And it is often mentioned in Scripture, as instance of the great love of God to His people, that His wrath is so awakened, when they are wronged and injured. Thus Christ hath promised that God will avenge His own elect,[183] and hath said, "Whoso

182 See Zechariah 2:8.

183 Luke 18:7

shall offend one of these little ones which believe in me, it were better for him that a millstone were hanged about his neck, and *that* he were drowned in the depth of the sea."[184]

So the saints in glory will see the great love of God to them, in the dreadful vengeance which He shall inflict on those who have injured and persecuted them; and the view of this love of God to them will be just cause of their rejoicing.[185] Thus, in the text, heaven and the holy apostles and prophets are called to rejoice over their enemies, because God hath avenged them of them.

[Sinner], how destitute of any comforting consideration your condition will be, if you perish at last. You will have none to pity you. Look which way you will, before or behind, on the right hand or left, look up to heaven, or look about you in hell, and you will see none to condole your case, or to exercise any pity towards you, in your dreadful condition. You must bear these flames, you must bear that torment and amazement, day and night, forever, and never have the comfort of considering that there is so much as one that pities your case; there never will one tear be dropped for you.[186]

Jesus Christ, the Redeemer, will have no pity on you [after this life]. Though He had so much love to sinners, as to be willing to lay down His life for them, and offers you the benefits of His blood, while you are in this world, and often calls upon you to accept them; yet then He will have no pity upon you. You never will hear any more instructions from Him; He will utterly refuse to be your instructor: on the contrary, He will be your judge, to pronounce sentence against you.

---

184 Matthew 18:6

185 How fearful shall this day be for those, who, in the name of God, set afire the flames that burned the martyrs, and tortured those who stood for the name of Jesus Christ.

186 Meditate often on the terrors of everlasting damnation. Such thoughts will not only fuel the flame of gratitude for mercy, but they will drive you to overcome your fears and reach out to a world bound for hell.

You will find none that will pity you in hell. The devils will not pity you, but will be your tormentors, as roaring lions or hellhounds to tear you in pieces continually. And other wicked men who shall be there will be like devils; they will have no pity on you, but will hate, and curse, and torment you. And you yourselves will be like devils; you will be like devils to yourselves, and will be your own tormentors.

Perhaps there are now some godly people, to whom you are near and dear, who are tenderly concerned for you, are ready to pity you under all calamities, and willing to help you; and particularly are tenderly concerned for your poor soul, and have put up many fervent prayers for you. How will you bear to hear these singing for joy of heart, while you are crying for sorrow of heart and howling for vexation of spirit, and even singing the more joyful for the glorious justice of God which they behold in your eternal condemnation![187]

You that have godly parents, who in this world have tenderly loved you, who were wont to look upon your welfare as their own, and were wont to be grieved for you when any thing calamitous befell you in this world, and especially were greatly concerned for the good of your souls, industriously sought, and earnestly prayed for your salvation; how will you bear to see them in the kingdom of God, crowned with glory? Or how will you bear to see them receiving the blessed sentence, and going up with shouts and songs, to enter with Christ into the kingdom prepared for them from the foundation of the world, while you are amongst a company of devils, and are turned away with the most bitter cries, to enter into everlasting burnings, prepared for the devil and his angels?

You that have godly husbands, or wives, or brethren, or sisters, with whom you have been wont to dwell under the same roof,

187 The fate of the ungodly is twofold. It is not only to inherit the endurance of hell, but it is to miss the eternal pleasures of Heaven.

and to eat at the same table, consider how it will be with you, when you shall come to part with them, when they shall be taken and you left: "I tell you, in that night, there shall be two men in one bed; the one shall be taken, and the other left. Two women shall be grinding together; the one shall be taken, and the other left. Two men shall be in the field; the one shall be taken and the other left."[188] However you may wail and lament, when you see them parted from you, they being taken and you left, you will see in them no signs of sorrow, that you are not taken with them; that you ascend not with them to meet the Lord in the air, but are left below to be consumed with the world, which is reserved unto fire, against the day of the perdition of ungodly men.

God makes it the duty of all the godly now to be concerned for your salvation.[189]

But now God makes it the duty of all the godly, to love you with a sincere good-will and earnest affection. God doth not excuse men from loving you, nor your ill qualities: though you are wicked and undeserving, yet God makes it the duty of all sincerely to wish well to you; and it is a heinous sin in the sight of God for any to hate you. He requires all to be concerned for your salvation, and by all means to seek it. It is their duty now to lament your danger, and to pray for mercy to you, that you may be converted and brought home to Christ.[190]

---

188 Luke 17:34-36

189 There is no place for complacency within the heart of any person who has truly been saved. The salvation of the lost was the priority of the Church of the Book of Acts, and should be the number one priority of the Church at the end of the age.

190 We are to pray *for* and preach *to* the ungodly. The word "preach" comes from the Greek word *keruss*—"to herald (as a public crier)"[1] and is used 61 times in Scripture. According to Rick Renner in his book *Sparkling Gems from the Greek*: "[The keruss] was the message proclaimed by the *kerux*, who was *the official spokesman or herald of a king*. Because the *kerux* was *the appointed official representative of the king or government*, his specific job was to announce with a clear and unquestionable voice the desires, dictates, orders, recent events, news, policy changes, or message that the king or government wished to express to the people. The position of this *kerux* . . . was viewed to be the highest, most noble, privileged position in the kingdom."

And there is not only the command of God, God hath not only made it the duty of others to seek your salvation, but hath given encouragement to others to seek it. He gives encouragement that they may obtain help for you by their prayers, and that they may be instrumental of your spiritual good. God reveals it to be His manner, to make our sincere endeavors a means of each other's good. How different is the case with you from what it is with those that are already damned! And how happy an opportunity have you in your hands, if you would but improve it!

Now you live where there is a certain order of men appointed to make it the business of their lives to seek your salvation. Now you have ministers, not to rise up in judgment against you; but in Christ's stead, to beseech you to be reconciled to God.[191] God hath not only made it the duty of all to wish well to your souls, and occasionally to endeavor to promote your spiritual interests, but He hath set apart certain persons, to make it their whole work, in which they should spend their days and their strength.

Christ himself is now seeking your salvation. He seeks it by the aforementioned means, by appointing men to make it their business to seek it; He seeks it by them; they are His instruments, and they beseech you in Christ's stead, to be reconciled to God. He seeks it in commanding our neighbors to seek it. Christ is represented in Scripture, as wooing the souls of sinner's. He uses means to persuade them to choose and accept of their own salvation. He often invites them to come to Him that they may have life, that they may find rest to their souls; to come and take of the water of life freely. He stands at the door and knocks; and ceases not, although sinners for a long time refuse him. He bears repeated repulses from them, and yet mercifully continues knocking, saying, "Open to me, that I may come in and sup with you, and you with me."[192] At the doors of many sinners He stands thus knocking for many years together. Christ

191 2 Corinthians 5:20
192 See Revelation 3:20

is become a most importunate suitor to sinners, that He may become their sovereign. He is often setting before them the need they have of Him, the miserable condition in which they are, and the great provision that is made for the good of their souls and He invites them to accept of this provision, and promises it shall be theirs upon their mere acceptance.

You have Christ's internal calls and knockings. All the persons of the Trinity are now seeking your salvation. God the Father hath sent His Son, who hath made way for your salvation, and removed all difficulties, except those that are within your own heart. And He is waiting to be gracious to you; the door of His mercy stands open to you; He hath set a fountain open for you to wash in from sin and uncleanness. Christ is calling, inviting, and wooing you; and the Holy Ghost is striving with you by His internal motions and influences.

If you now repent, before it be too late, the saints and angels in glory will rejoice at your repentance. If you repent not till it is too late, they will, as you have heard, rejoice in seeing justice executed upon you. But if you now repent, they will rejoice at your welfare, that you who were lost, are found; that you who were dead, are alive again.[193] They will rejoice that you are come to so happy a state already, and that you are in due time to inherit eternal happiness.[194] So that if now you will improve your opportunity, there will be a very different occasion of joy in heaven concerning you, than that of which the doctrine speaks; not a rejoicing on occasion of your misery, but on occasion of your unspeakable blessedness.

193 There are those who erroneously say that repentance is a work, and is therefore not to be preached to the ungodly. Repentance is God-given (see 2 Timothy 2:25), and it *must* be preached to the unsaved, as Paul said of his own proclamation: "Testifying both to the Jews, and also to the Greeks, repentance toward God, and faith toward our Lord Jesus Christ" (Acts 20:21).
194 See Luke 15:10.

The Warnings of Scripture Are in the Best Manner Adapted to the Awakening and Conversion of Sinners

(Sermon by Jonathan Edwards)

Compiled from http://www.apuritansmind.com/jonathan edwards/JonathanEdwards-Sermons-TheWarningsOf Scriptures.htm

"And he said unto him, If they hear not Moses and the prophets, neither will they be persuaded, though one rose from the dead" (Luke 16:32).

Sinners are apt to find fault with the means of grace which they enjoy, and to say with themselves, "If I had ever seen hell, or had ever heard the cries of the damned, or had ever seen a person who had felt hell-torments, or had seen them at a distance, that would awaken me; then I would forsake all my sins, and would do whatever I could to escape hell. But now I am only told of hell in the Bible and by ministers; and there never was any in this world that saw or felt it: so that I am ready to think it is mere delusion and fancy.[195] How do I know that there is any hell?" How do I know but that when I die there will be an end of me?"[196]

---

195 The knowledge of how sinners respond shows that Edwards practiced what he preached, in that he was involved in personal witnessing.

196 The existence of hell is unreasonable until the Law does its wonderful work and shows sin to be exceedingly sinful. Once sin is seen for the evil that it is, it leaves the sinner thinking that if God is good, how can there *not* be a hell?

He knows far better what the eternity of these torments is than any of them, He can better tell us how awful a thing eternity is. He knows better what the future judgment of sinners will be, when the Lord Jesus shall come in flaming fire to take vengeance on them that know not God, and obey not the gospel.[197] He knows far better than they how much the torment of the wicked will then be increased.

We have the truth upon surer grounds from God's testimony than we could have it from the testimony of one rising from the dead. Suppose one should rise from the dead, and tell us of the dreadfulness of hell-torments. How precarious a foundation would that be to build upon, in a matter of such importance, unless we consider it as confirmed by divine testimony. We should be uncertain whether there were not some delusion in the case. We know that it is impossible for God to lie.[198] And we may know that the matter is just as He declares it to us. But if one should come from the dead, we could not be so sure that we were no way imposed upon. We could not be so sure that he who testified was not himself subject to some delusion. We could not be sure that the matter was not strained too high, and represented greater than it really is.

The warnings of God's Word have greatly the advantage, by reason of the greatness and majesty of Him who speaks. The speeches and declarations of those who are great, excellent, and honorable, have a greater tendency to move the affections, than the declarations of others who are less excellent. Things spoken by a king affect more than the same things spoken by a mean man.

---

197 The fruit of salvation is an obedient heart: "Though he were a Son, yet learned he obedience by the things which he suffered; and being made perfect, he became the author of eternal salvation unto *all them that obey him* . . . " (Hebrews 5:8-9, italics added).

198 See Hebrews 6:18. He who has the word of a king, has a sure word. We have the highest authority on earth telling us of the reality of hell—the Word of God.

But God is infinitely greater than kings; He is universal king of heaven and earth, the absolute sovereign of all things. Now, what can have a greater tendency to strike the mind and move the heart, than to be warned by this great and glorious being? Shall we be unmoved when He speaks who made heaven and earth by the word of His power? If His immediate speeches, declarations, and warning, will not influence us, what will? "Hear, O heavens, and give ear, O earth, for the LORD hath spoken."[199] That is to the present purpose which we have in Matthew 21:37, "But last of all he sent unto them his son, saying, They will reverence my son." He sent His servants before, but they did not regard them. He therefore sent His son, who was a much greater and more honorable messenger, and said, "Surely they will regard Him."

What if God should send messengers from the dead to warn us, even many in succession, and men should reject them. We should justly argue, that it would have a much greater tendency to make men regard and obey the counsel, if He would send His Son, or come himself. But God has sent His Son, and therein He hath come himself. He came down from heaven, and took upon Him our nature, and dwelt among us, teaching and warning us concerning hell and damnation.

Now, which has the greatest tendency to influence men, to have one of the departed spirits sent back into its body to warn them, or to have God himself assume a body and warn them?

Men are apt to think, that if they had lived in Christ's time, and had seen and heard Him, and had seen His miracles, that they would have effectually convinced and turned them from sin. But how was it in fact? How few were there brought to repentance by all His discourses and miracles. How hard-hearted were they! Some were very much affected for a little

---

199 Isaiah 1:2

while; but how few constant steady followers had He. He was, notwithstanding His miracles, rejected, despised, and even murdered by the people among whom He dwelt. And they were men of the same natures as sinners in these days.[200]

The Scripture is full of instances, sufficient to convince us, that if the Word of God will not awaken and convert sinners, nothing will.

The warnings of the Word of God are, as you have heard, better and more powerful means than if one should rise from the dead to warn us, and tell us our danger, and the dreadfulness of the wrath of God. You have also heard, that if these means will not answer the end of awakening and leading sinners to repentance, no other will; neither the working of miracles, nor the hearing of God speak with an audible voice from heaven, nor anything else.[201]

Let all make use of the means which God hath instituted. They are the best and only means by which we may expect to obtain salvation. We shall be most inexcusable therefore if we neglect them. Let us attend to the Word of God, read and hear it carefully, consider it thoroughly, and daily walk by it. Let us be diligent in this work. The Word of God is a great price put into our hands to get wisdom and eternal salvation.[202] Let us therefore improve it while we have it, as we know not how soon we may be deprived of

---

200 It is the gospel arrow that is thrust by the bow of the moral Law by the hand of the Spirit of God that convinces men of their sin. Paul said, "For I am not ashamed of the gospel of Christ: for it is the power of God unto salvation to every one that believeth; to the Jew first, and also to the Greek" (Romans 1:16).

201 Even when Lazarus was raised from the dead, some didn't believe on Him: "Then many of the Jews who had come to Mary, and had seen the things Jesus did, believed in Him. But some of them went away to the Pharisees and told them the things Jesus did" (John 11:45-46, NKJV).

202 Make sure you read your Bible every day. Man doesn't live by bread alone, but by every word of God. (See Luke 4:4.) You have the Word of God, so soak your soul in it, daily.

it; lest Christ say to us, "If thou hadst known, even thou, at least in this thy day, the things which belong unto thy peace! but now they are hid from thine eyes."[203]

God Makes Men Sensible of Their Misery Before He Reveals His Mercy and Love

(Sermon by Jonathan Edwards)

Compiled from http://www.apuritansmind.com/jonathanedwards/JonathanEdwards-Sermons-GodMakesMenSensibleMisery.htm

"I will go and return to my place, till they acknowledge their offence, and seek my face: in their affliction they will seek me early" (Hosea 5:15).

It is God's manner to make men sensible of their misery and unworthiness, before He appears in His mercy and love to them.[204]

So before God brought the children of Israel into Canaan, He led them about in a great and terrible wilderness through a train

203 Luke 19:42

204 This was the standard doctrine of the great men of God who reached out to the lost. No one wants to be "found" if they don't know they're "lost." No one appreciates a cure if they don't understand that they have a disease, and no one wants the mercy of God if they don't understand that they have violated the Law of God.

of difficulties and temptations for forty years, that He might teach them their dependence on Him, and the sinfulness of their own hearts. "He found him in a desert land, and in the waste howling wilderness; he led him about, he instructed him, he kept him as the apple of his eye."[205] God brought them into those trials and difficulties in the wilderness to humble them, and let them see what was in their hearts, that they might be convinced of their own perverseness by the many discoveries of it under those temptations, and so that they might be sensible that it was not for their righteousness that God made them His people, and gave them Canaan, seeing it was so evident that they were a stiff-necked people.[206] "And thou shalt remember all the way which the LORD thy God led thee these forty years in the wilderness, to humble thee, *and* to prove thee, to know what *was* in thine heart, whether thou wouldest keep his commandments, or no. And he humbled thee, and suffered thee to hunger, and fed thee with manna, which thou knewest not, neither did thy fathers know; that he might make thee know that man doth not live by bread only, but by every word that proceedeth out of the mouth of the LORD doth man live."[207]

It is God's manner, when He will bestow signal blessings in answer to prayer, to make men seek them and pray for them with a sense of sin and misery.

It is God's usual method before remarkable discoveries of His mercy and love to them, especially by spiritual mercies, in a special manner to humble them, and make them sensible of their misery and helplessness in themselves, and of their vileness and unworthiness, either by some remarkably humbling dispensation of His providence or influence of His Spirit.[208]

---

205 Deuteronomy 32:10

206 "You brought us into the net; you laid affliction on our backs. You have caused men to ride over our heads; we went through fire and through water; but You brought us out to rich *fulfillment*" (Psalm 66:11-13, NKJV). God doesn't take us through fire to burn us, but to purify us. He doesn't takes us through water to drown us, but to wash us.

207 Deuteronomy 8:2-3

208 One sign of an awakening sinner is an appreciation for his or her helplessness in the face of death. There are few atheists in a 7.5 plus earthquake, or in severe turbulence.

To show particularly that it is God's manner to make men sensible of their misery and unworthiness before He reveals His saving love and mercy to their souls. The mercy of God, which He shows to a sinner when He brings Him home to the Lord Jesus Christ, is the greatest and most wonderful exhibition of mercy and love, of which men are ever the subjects. He first brings them to reflect upon themselves, and consider and be sensible what they are, and what condition they are in. What has already been said proves this. There is a harmony between God's dispensations. And as we see that this is God's manner of dealing with men when He gives them other great and remarkable mercies and manifestations of His favor, it is a confirmation that it is His method of proceeding with the souls of men, when about to reveal His mercy and love to them in Jesus Christ.

First, God makes men consider and be sensible of what sin they are guilty. Before, it may be, they were very regardless of this. They went on sinning, and never reflected upon what they did. [They] never considered or regarded what or how many sins they committed. They saw no cause why they should trouble their minds about it. But when God convinces them, He brings them to reflect upon themselves. He sets their sins in order before their eyes. He brings their old sins to their minds, so that they are fresh in their memory—things which they had almost forgotten.[209] And many things, which they used to regard as light offenses, which were not wont to be a burden to their consciences, nor to appear worthy to be taken notice of, they are now made to reflect upon. Thus they discover of what a multitude of transgressions they have been guilty, which they have heaped up till they are grown up to Heaven. There are some sins especially, of which they have been guilty, which are ever before them, so that they cannot get them out of their minds. Sometimes when

209 Never underestimate the power of a stirred conscience. The Law, in the hand of the Spirit of God, says to the deadened conscience "Come forth!" And that which has been seared suddenly comes to life and does its duty. (See Romans 2:15.)

men are under conviction, their sins follow them, and haunt them like a specter.

God makes them sensible of the sin of their hearts, how corrupt and depraved their hearts are. And there are two ways in which He does this. One is by setting before them the sins of their lives. They are so set in order before them, they appear so many and so aggravated, that they are convinced what a fountain of corruption there is in their hearts. Their sinful natures appear by their sinful lives. There is sin enough, which every man has committed, to convince him, that he is sold under sin, that his heart is full of nothing but corruption, if God by His Spirit leads him rightly to consider it.

Another way which God sometimes makes use of, is to leave men to such internal workings of corruption under the temptations which they have in their terrors and fears of hell, as shows them what a corrupt and wicked heart they have. God sometimes brings this good out of this evil, to make men see the corruption of their nature by the workings of it under temptations, which they have in their terrors about damnation. God leads them through the wilderness to prove them, and let them know what is in their hearts, as He did the children of Israel, as we have already observed.

We must not go and be wicked on purpose that we may get good by it. It will be very absurd, as well as horridly presumptuous, for us so to do. Though God sometimes in His sovereign mercy makes those workings of corruption, and a spirit of opposition and enmity against God, a means of showing them the vileness of their own hearts, and so to turn to their good. But it is God's manner to show men the plague of their own hearts by some means or other, before He reveals His redeeming love to their souls. While sinners are unconvinced, sin lies hid. They take no notice of it. But God makes the law effectual to bring men's own sins of heart and life to be reflected on, and observed. "I was alive without the law once: but when the commandment came, sin revived."[210] Then sin appeared and came to light, which was not before observed.

God convinces sinners of the dreadful danger they are in by reason of their sin. Having their sins set before them, God makes them sensible of the relation which their sin has to misery.

God makes them sensible that His displeasure is very dreadful. Before they heard often about the anger of God, and the fierceness of His wrath, but they were not moved by it. But now they are made sensible that "it is a fearful thing to fall into the hands of the living God."[211] They are made in some measure sensible of the dreadfulness of hell.[212] They are led with fixedness of impression to think what a dismal thing it will be to have God an enraged enemy, setting to work the misery of a soul, and how dismal it will be to dwell in such torment forever without hope. "The sinners in Zion are afraid; fearfulness hath surprised the hypocrites. Who among us shall dwell with the devouring fire? who among us shall dwell with everlasting burnings?"[213]

Other sinners are told of hell, but convinced sinners often have hell, as it were, in their view. Their being impressed with a sense of the dreadfulness of its misery, is the cause why it works upon their imagination oftentimes, and it will seem as though they saw the dismal flames of hell; as though they saw God in implacable wrath exerting His fury upon them; as though they heard the cries and shrieks of the damned.

---

210 Romans 7:9. The word "commandment" is a direct reference to the moral Law—the Ten Commandments. Its function is to show us our sinful hearts in the light of God's holiness.

211 Hebrews 10:31

212 It is a good thing when the guilty criminal suddenly has a fear of the judge, and the power he holds in his hand. "And I say unto you my friends, Be not afraid of them that kill the body, and after that have no more that they can do. But I will forewarn you whom ye shall fear: Fear him, which after he hath killed hath power to cast into hell; yea, I say unto you, Fear him" (Luke 12:4-5).

213 Isaiah 33:14

They are made in some measure sensible of the connection there is between their sins and that wrath, or how their sin and guilt exposes them to that wrath, of the dreadfulness of which they have such lively apprehensions, and so fear takes hold of them. They are afraid that will be their portion. And they are sensible that they are in a miserable and doleful condition by reason of sin. Many things in the Scriptures make it evident that this is God's method. The account we have of our first parents confirms it. They had a sense of guilt and danger, before Christ was revealed to them. They were guilty, and were afraid of God's wrath, and ran and hid themselves. They were terribly afraid when they heard God coming. And doubtless their sense of their guilt and fear, when they were brought before God, and were called to an account, and God asked them what they had done, and whether they had eaten of that tree, whereof He commanded them that they should not eat, prepared them for a discovery of mercy. God made them sensible of their guilt and danger before He revealed to them the covenant of grace.

The expression of flying for refuge, by which coming to Christ is signified, implies that before they come, they are in fear of some evil.[214] They apprehend themselves in danger, and this fear gives wings to their feet. "The name of the LORD is a strong tower."[215]

They are made sensible of the desert of their sin: that their sin deserves that wrath of God to which it exposes them. They are not only sensible of the dreadfulness of God's wrath, how fearful a thing it would be to fall into the hands of the living God, and to sustain the eternal expressions of His fierce anger, as well as of the connection between their sins and this wrath, and how their sins expose them to it, but God is also wont, before He comforts them, to show them that their sins deserve this wrath. By a clear discovery of the connection between their sin and God's wrath,

214 This is what is so often missing in today's "converts." They are not fleeing from wrath to come because they haven't been warned that there is wrath to come.
215 Proverbs 18:10

they are sensible of their danger of hell, of which many are in a measure sensible, who are wholly insensible of their desert of hell. The threatenings of the law make them afraid indeed, that God will punish sins. Yet they have no thorough apprehension of their desert of the punishment threatened, and therefore many, who are afraid, murmur against God. They charge Him foolishly with being hard and cruel. But it is God's manner before He speaks peace to them, and reveals His redeeming love and mercy in Jesus Christ, to make them sensible that they also deserve it.

Very commonly when men are first made sensible of their danger, their mouths are open against God and His dealings, that is, their hearts are full of murmurings. But it is God's manner before He comforts and reveals His mercy and love to them, to stop their mouths, and make them acknowledge their guilt, or their desert of the threatened punishment. Rom. 3:19, 20, "Now we know that what things soever the law saith, it saith to them who are under the law: that every mouth may be stopped, and all the world may become guilty before God. Therefore by the deeds of the law there shall no flesh be justified in his sight: for by the law *is* the knowledge of sin."[216]

God would convince men of their guilt before He reveals a pardon to them. Now a man cannot be said to be thoroughly sensible of his guilt, till he is sensible that he deserves hell. A man must be sensible that he is guilty of death, or guilty of damnation, to use the scriptural mode of expression, before God will reveal to him his freedom from damnation. A sense of guilt consists in two things: in a sense of sin, and in a sense of the relation which sin has to punishment. Now the relation which sin has to punishment is also twofold. First, the connection that it has with punishment, by which it exposes to it, and brings it. Second, its desert of punishment. When a man is truly convinced of his desert of the punishment to which his sin exposes him, then he may be said to be thoroughly sensible of his guilt. Then he

216 Romans 3:19-20

is become guilty, in the sense of our text, and in the sense of Romans 3:20.

How is it that a sinner is made sensible of his desert of God's wrath? A natural man may have a sense of this, though not the same sense which a person may have after conversion, because a natural man cannot have a true sight of sin, and of the evil of it. A man cannot truly know the evil of sin against God, except it be by a discovery of His glory and excellence.[217] Then he will be sensible how great an evil it is to sin against Him.

What principle in man is assisted in convincing him of his desert of eternal punishment? No new principle is infused. Natural men have only natural principles, and therefore all that is done by the Spirit of God before regeneration is by assisting natural principles. . . . That the principle, which is assisted in making natural men sensible of their desert of wrath, is natural conscience; though man has lost a principle of love to God, and all spiritual principles, by the fall, yet natural conscience remains.

Now there are two things, which are the proper work of natural conscience. One is to give man a sense of right and wrong. A natural man has no sense of the beauty and amiability of virtue, or of the turpitude and odiousness of vice. But yet every man has that naturally within, which testifies to him that some things are right, and others wrong. Thus if a man steals, or commits murder, there is something within, which tells him that he has done wrong. He knows that he has not done right. Rom. 2:14, 15, "For when the Gentiles, which have not the law, do by nature the things contained in the law, these, having not the law, are a law unto themselves: which shew the work of the law written in their hearts, their conscience also bearing witness,

217 "Indeed you are called a Jew, and rest on the law, and make your boast in God, and know His will, *and approve the things that are excellent, being instructed out of the law*." (Romans 2:17-18, NKJV, italics added).

and their thoughts the mean while accusing, or else excusing, one another."[218]

And the other work of natural conscience is to suggest the relation there is between right and wrong, and a retribution. Man has that in him, which suggests to him, when he has done ill, a relation between that ill and punishment. If a man has done that which his conscience tells him is wrong, is unjust, his conscience tells him that he deserves to be punished for it.

Thus natural conscience has a twofold power; a teaching or accusing, and a condemning power. The Spirit of God, therefore, assists natural conscience the more thoroughly to do this, its work, and so convinces a man of sin. Conscience naturally suggests, when he has done a known evil, that he deserves punishment, and being assisted to its work thoroughly, a man is convinced that he deserves eternal punishment. Though natural conscience does remain in the man since the fall, yet it greatly needs assistance in order to [do] its work. It is greatly hindered in doing its work by sin. Everything in man, which is part of his perfection, is hindered and impaired by sin. A faculty of reason remains since the fall, but it is greatly impaired and blinded. So natural conscience remains, but sin, in a great degree, stupefies it, and hinders it in its work. Now when God convinces a sinner, He assists his conscience against the stupefaction of sin, and helps it to do its work more freely and fully. The Spirit of God works immediately upon men's consciences. In conviction their consciences are awakened. They are convinced in their consciences. Their consciences smite them and condemn them.[219]

---

218 Romans 2:14-15. Then watch Paul use the Law further on in Romans 2: "You, therefore, who teach another, do you not teach yourself? You who preach that a man should not steal, do you steal? You who say, 'Do not commit adultery,' do you commit adultery? You who abhor idols, do you rob temples? You who make your boast in the law, do you dishonor God through breaking the law? For '*the name of God is blasphemed among the Gentiles because of you*,' as it is written" (Romans 2:21-24).

219 See Romans 2:14-15.

It may be inquired how God assists natural conscience so as to convince the sinner of his desert of hell? I answer, in general, it is by light. The whole work of God is carried on in the heart of man from his first convictions to his conversion by light. It is by discoveries that are made to his soul. But by what light is it, that a sinner is made sensible that he deserves God's wrath? It is some discovery that he has, which makes him sensible of the heinousness of disobeying and casting contempt upon God. The light which gives evangelical humiliation, and which makes man sensible of the hateful and odious nature of sin, is a discovery of God's glory and excellence and grace.

But what is it that a natural man sees of God, which makes him sensible that sin against God deserves His wrath. For He sees nothing of the excellence and loveliness of God's glory and grace? I answer, particularly it seems to be a discovery of God's awful and terrible greatness. Natural men cannot see anything of God's loveliness, His amiable and glorious grace, or anything which should attract their love, but they may see His terrible greatness to excite their terror.

The principal outward means, which the Spirit of God makes use of in this work of convincing men of their desert of hell… is the law. The Spirit of God in all His work upon the souls of men, works by His word. And in this whole work of conviction of sin, that part of the word is principally made use of; viz. the Law. It is the Law that makes men sensible of their sin; and it is the Law, attended with its awful threatenings and curses, which gives a sense of the awful greatness, the authority, the power, the jealousy of God. Wicked men are made sensible of the tremendous greatness of God, as it were, in the same manner in which the children of Israel were, viz. by the thunders, and earthquake, and devouring fire, and sound of the trumpet, and terrible voice at Mount Sinai. All the people who were in the camp trembled, and they said, "Let not God speak with us, lest we die."[220] So that it is the law, which God makes use of in assisting the natural conscience to do its work. "Wherefore the law was our schoolmaster to bring us unto Christ."[221] It is the law which God makes use of, to make men sensible of their guilt, and to stop their mouths. "Now we know that whatsoever things the law saith, it saith to them that are under the law, that every mouth may be stopped, and all the world may become guilty before God."[222] It is the law, which kills men as to trusting in their own righteousness. "For I was alive without the law once: but when the commandment came, sin revived, and I died."[223] "For I through the law am dead to the law."[224] Conviction, which precedes conversion, is of sin and misery. But men are not thoroughly sensible of their sin or guilt, till they are sensible they deserve hell; nor thoroughly sensible of their misery, till they are sensible they are helpless.

It is God's manner to make men sensible of their helplessness in their own strength. It is usual with sinners, when they are first made sensible of their danger of hell, to attempt by their own strength to save themselves. They in some measure see their danger, and endeavor to work out their own deliverance. They are striving to make themselves better. They strive to convert themselves, to work their hearts into a believing frame, and to exercise a saving trust in Christ. Having heard that if ever they believe, they must put their trust in Christ, and in Him alone, for salvation, they think they will trust in Christ and cast their souls upon Him. And this they endeavor to do in their own strength. This is very common with persons upon a sick bed, when they are afraid that they shall die and go to hell, and are told that they must put their trust in Christ alone for salvation. They attempt to do it in their own strength. So sinners will be striving without

220 Exodus 20:19
221 Galatians 3:24
222 Romans 3:19
223 Romans 7:9
224 Galatians 2:19

a sense of their insufficiency in themselves to bring their own hearts to love God, and to choose Him for their portion, and to repent of their sins. Or they strive to make themselves better so that God may be more willing to convert them and give them His grace, and enable them to believe in Christ, and love God, and repent of their sins. But before God appears to them as their help and deliverance, it is His manner to make them sensible that they are utterly helpless in themselves. They are brought to despair of help from themselves. There is a death to all their hopes from themselves.

Before God opens the prison doors, He makes them see that they are shut up, that they are close prisoners, and that there is no way in which they can escape. Christ tells us in Isaiah 61:1 that He was sent to bind up the broken-hearted, and to proclaim liberty to captives, and the opening of the prison to them that are bound. Christ was sent to open the prison to them that are not only really, but sensibly, bound. "But before faith came, we were kept under the law, shut up unto the faith, that should afterwards be revealed."[225] God makes men sensible that they are in a forlorn condition, that they are wretched, and miserable, and blind, and naked, before He comforts them. Christ tells us in John 9:39, "For judgment I am come into this world, that they which see not might see; and that they which see might be made blind"; meaning, partly at least, by those that see, those who think they see: having respect to the Pharisees, who were proud of their knowledge, and by the blind, those who are sensibly blind.

God oftentimes makes use of men's own experience to convince them that they are helpless in themselves. When they first set out in seeking salvation, it may be they thought it an easy thing to be converted. They thought they should presently bring themselves to repent of their sins, and believe in Christ, and accordingly they strove in their own strength with hopes of success. But they

225 Galatians 3:23

were disappointed. And so God suffers them to go on striving to open their own eyes, and mend their own hearts. But they find no success. They have been striving to see for a long time, yet they are as blind as ever; and can see nothing. It is all Egyptian darkness. They have been striving to make themselves better; but they are bad as ever. They have often striven to do something that is good, to be in the exercise of good affections, which should be acceptable to God, but they have no success. And it seems to them, that instead of growing better, they grow worse and worse. Their hearts are fuller of wicked thoughts than they were at first. They see no more likelihood of their conversion than there was at first. So God suffers them to strive in their own strength, till they are discouraged, and despair of helping themselves. The prodigal son first strove to fill his belly with the husks that the swine did eat. But when he despaired of being helped in that way, then he came to himself, and entertained thoughts of returning to his father's house.

God sometimes, by a particular assistance of the understanding, enables men to see so much of their own hearts, as at once causes them to despair of helping themselves. He sometimes convinces them by their own trials, suffering them to try a long time to effect their own salvation, until they are discouraged. By revealing to them their own hearts, He sometimes enables them to perceive that they are so remote from the exercise of love to God, of faith, and of every other Christian grace, as well as from the possession of the least degree of spiritual light that they despair of ever bringing themselves to it. It is God's ordinary manner, before He reveals His redeeming mercy to the souls of men, to make them sensible of their sinfulness and danger, of their desert of the divine wrath, and of their utter helplessness in themselves. It is God's manner to convince men of sin, before He convinces them of righteousness.[226]

226 While God has chosen the foolishness of preaching (Law and grace) to save those who believe, the salvation of every sinner is *His* work, from the providence of the seed to the maturity of the harvest. We simply have the honor of putting the God-made seed in the Spirit-prepared soil of the hearts of men, and reaping

The very nature and design of the gospel show that this is the will of God, that those who have the discoveries of His love, should also have the discoveries of those other attributes. For this was the very end of Christ's laying down His life, and coming into the world, to render the glory of God's authority, holiness, and justice, consistent with His grace in pardoning and justifying sinners, that while God thus manifested His mercy, we might not conceive any unworthy thoughts of Him with respect to those other attributes. Seeing, therefore, that this is the very end of Christ's coming into the world, we may conclude that those who are actually redeemed by Christ, and have a true discovery of Christ made to their souls, have a discovery of God's terribleness and justice to prepare them for the discovery of His love and mercy.

Even the man Christ Jesus was first made sensible of the wrath of God, before His exaltation to that transcendent height of enjoyment of the Father's love. And this is one reason that God gives sinners a sense of His wrath against their sins, and of His justice, before He gives them the discoveries of His redeeming love.

Unless a man be thus convinced of his sin and misery before God makes him sensible of His redeeming love and mercy, he cannot be sensible of that love and mercy as it is, viz. that it is free and sovereign. When God reveals His redeeming grace to men, and makes them truly sensible of it, He would make them sensible of it as it is.

God's grace and love towards sinners is in itself very wonderful, as it redeems from dreadful wrath. But men cannot be sensible of this until they perceive in some adequate degree how dreadful the wrath of God is.

God's redeeming grace and love in Christ is free and sovereign, as it is altogether without any worthiness in those who are the objects of it. But men cannot be sensible of this, until they are sensible of their own unworthiness.

---

the results of the work of God.

The grace of God in Christ is wonderful, as it saves and redeems from so many and so great sins, and from the punishment they have deserved. But sinners cannot be sensible of this till they are in some measure sensible of their sinfulness, and brought to reflect upon the sins of their lives, and to see the wickedness of their hearts.

The heart of man is not prepared to receive the mercy of God in Christ, as free and unmerited, till he is sensible of his own demerit. Indeed the soul is not capable of receiving a revelation or discovery of the redeeming grace of God in Christ, as redeeming grace, without being convinced of sin and misery. He must see his sin and misery before he can see the grace of God in redeeming him from that sin and misery.

Until the sinner is convinced of his sin and misery, he is not prepared to receive the redeeming mercy and grace of God, as through a mediator, because he does not see his need of a mediator till he sees his sin and misery.

The redeeming mercy and grace of God is mercy and grace in Christ.

It is the will of God, that as all the spiritual comforts which His people receive are in and through Christ, so they should be sensible that they receive them through Christ, and that they can receive them in no other way. It is the will of God that His people should have their eyes directed to Christ, and should depend upon Him for mercy and favor, [so] that whenever they receive comforts through His purchase, they should receive them as from Him. And that because God would glorify His Son as mediator, as the glory of man's salvation belongs to Christ, so it is the will of God that all the people of Christ, all who are saved by Him, should receive their salvation as of Him, and should attribute the glory of it to Him. None who will not give the glory of salvation to Christ, should have the benefit of it. Upon this

account God insists upon it, and it is absolutely necessary, that a sinner's conviction of his sin, and misery, and helplessness in himself, should precede or accompany the revelation of the redeeming love and grace of God.
When the soul stands trembling at the brink of the pit, and despairs of any help from itself, it is prepared joyfully to receive tidings of deliverance.

The gospel then, if it be heard spiritually, will be glad tidings indeed, the most joyful which the sinner ever heard. The love of God and of Christ to the world, and to him in particular, will be admired, and Christ will be most precious. To remember what danger he was in, what seas surrounded him, and then to reflect how safe he now is in Christ, and how sufficient Christ is to defend him and to answer all his wants, will cause the greater exultation of soul.

As they are hereby made sensible how free and sovereign the mercy of God is towards them and how great His grace in saving them, and as they more highly prize the mercy and love of God made known to them, all will dispose them to magnify the name of God, to exalt the love of God the Father in giving His Son to them, and to exalt Jesus Christ by their praise, who laid down His life for them to redeem them from all iniquity. They are ready to say, "How miserable should I have been, had not God had pity upon me, and provided me a Savior! In what a miserable condition should I have been, had not Christ loved me, and given himself for me! I must have endured that dreadful wrath of God; I must have suffered the punishment which I had deserved by all that great sin and wickedness of which I have been guilty."

God's Sovereignty in the Salvation of Men

(Sermon by Jonathan Edwards)

Compiled from http://www.apuritansmind.com/jonathanedwards/JonathanEdwards-Sermons-GodsSoveriegntySalvationMen.htm

The absolute, universal, and unlimited sovereignty of God requires, that we should adore Him with all possible humility and reverence. It is impossible that we should go to excess in lowliness and reverence of that being, who may dispose of us to all eternity, as He pleases.[227]

Those who are in a state of salvation are to attribute it to sovereign grace alone, and to give all the praise to Him, who maketh them to differ from others. Godliness is no cause for glorying, except it be in God. "That no flesh should glory in his presence. But of him are ye in Christ Jesus, who of God is made unto us wisdom, and righteousness, and sanctification, and redemption: that, according as it is written, He that glorieth, let him glory in the Lord."[228]

They should exalt God the Holy Ghost, who of sovereign grace has called them out of darkness into marvelous light; who has by His own immediate and free operation, led them into an understanding of the evil and danger of sin, and brought them off from their

227 Our hearts are so hardened by sin, it takes the grace of God to open our eyes to see the genius of His creative hand, and further grace to open our eyes to the love expressed in the Cross. Each of us knows intuitively that God made this world, but it is only when He opens the eyes of our understanding that we begin to fully appreciate His mighty power.

228 1 Corinthians 1:29-31. Anyone who believes Scripture cannot argue about being saved by grace: "and that *not of yourselves*: it is the gift of God. (See Ephesians 2:8-9, italics added.)

own righteousness, and opened their eyes to discover the glory of God, and the wonderful riches of God in Jesus Christ, and has sanctified them, and made them new creatures. When they hear of the wickedness of others, or look upon vicious persons, they should think how wicked they once were, and how much they provoked God, and how they deserved for ever to be left by Him to perish in sin, and that it is only sovereign grace which has made the difference. Many sorts of sinners are there enumerated; fornicators, idolaters, adulterers, effeminate, abusers of themselves with mankind.[229] And then in the eleventh verse, the apostle tells them, "Such were some of you; but ye are washed, but ye are sanctified, but ye are justified, in the name of the Lord Jesus, and by the Spirit of our God."[230]

The people of God have the greater cause of thankfulness, more reason to love God, who hath bestowed such great and unspeakable mercy upon them of His mere sovereign pleasure.

Let us, therefore, labor to submit to the sovereignty of God. God insists, that His sovereignty be acknowledged by us, and that even in this great matter, a matter which so nearly and infinitely concerns us, as our own eternal salvation. This is the stumbling-block on which thousands fall and perish; and if we go on contending with God about His sovereignty, it will be our eternal ruin. It is absolutely necessary that we should submit

229 See 1 Corinthians 6:9-10

230 1 Corinthians 6:11. As Christians, we are told to be loving and kind to everyone, because we understand that there but for the mercy of God, go I, so we are "to speak evil of no one, to be peaceable, gentle, showing all humility to all men. For we ourselves were also once foolish, disobedient, deceived, serving various lusts and pleasures, living in malice and envy, hateful and hating one another. But when the kindness and the love of God our Savior toward man appeared, not by works of righteousness which we have done, but according to His mercy He saved us" (Titus 3:2-5, NKJV). Who of us isn't on the list of "wicked" people given in 1 Corinthians 6:10? Maybe we weren't homosexuals or were guilty of extortion, or perhaps we didn't go to drunken parties or have sex out of marriage. But more than likely every one of us have lusted after someone, and are therefore guilty of adultery in God's eyes (see Matthew 5:27-28), or taken something that belonged to someone else, and are therefore a thief in His eyes. More than likely each of us are guilty of idolatry and covetousness, so we can't point a holier-than-thou finger at another soul, because we are guilty ourselves.

to God, as our absolute sovereign, and the sovereign over our souls; as one who may have mercy on whom He will have mercy, and harden whom He will.[231]

Do not presume upon the mercy of God, and so encourage yourself in sin. Many hear that God's mercy is infinite, and therefore think, that if they delay seeking salvation for the present, and seek it hereafter, that God will bestow His grace upon them. . . . If you put off salvation till hereafter, salvation will not be in your power. . . . Seeing, therefore, that in this affair you are so absolutely dependent on God, it is best to follow His direction in seeking it, which is to hear his voice today: "To day if ye will hear his voice, harden not your hearts."[232]

Beware also of discouragement. Take heed of despairing thoughts, because you are a great sinner, because you have persevered so long in sin, have backslidden, and resisted the Holy Ghost.[233] Remember that, let your case be what it may, and you ever so great a sinner, if you have not committed the sin against the Holy Ghost, God can bestow mercy upon you without the least prejudice to the honor of His holiness, which you have offended, or to the honor of His majesty, which you have insulted, or of His justice, which you have made your enemy, or of His truth, or of any of His attributes. Let you be what sinner you may, God can, if He pleases, greatly glorify himself in your salvation.

231 See Romans 9: 18. This isn't an issue of Calvinism or Arminianism. It is an issue of salvation by works or by grace.

232 Hebrews 3:15

233 We must never even *think* of backsliding. God forbid that any of us could consider trampling the blood of Jesus Christ underfoot. Whoever puts his hand to the plow *and even looks back* isn't fit for the Kingdom (see Luke 9:62). Cultivate the fear of God and look straight ahead. Keep your eyes on the Cross and on the Day of Judgment.

Pardon for the Greatest Sinners

(Sermon by Jonathan Edwards)

Compiled from http://www.apuritansmind.com/jonathanedwards/JonathanEdwards-Sermons-PardonSinners.htm

"For thy name's sake, O LORD, pardon my iniquity; for it is great" (Psalm 25:11).

He pleads for pardon for God's name's sake. He has no expectation of pardon for the sake of any righteousness or worthiness of his for any good deeds he had done, or any compensation he had made for his sins; though if man's righteousness could be a just plea, David would have had as much to plead as most.

But he begs that God would do it for His own name's sake,[234] for His own glory, for the glory of His own free grace, and for the honor of His own covenant-faithfulness.

The psalmist pleads the greatness of his sins as an argument for mercy. He not only doth not plead his own righteousness, or the smallness of his sins; he not only doth not say, Pardon mine iniquity, for I have done much good to counterbalance it; or, Pardon mine iniquity, for it is small, and thou hast no great reason to be angry with me; mine iniquity is not so great, that thou hast any just cause to remember it against me; mine offence is not such but that thou mayest well enough overlook it: but on the contrary he says, Pardon mine iniquity, for it is great; he pleads the greatness of his sin, and not the smallness of it; he enforces his prayer with this consideration, that his sins are very heinous.[235]

---

234 The Scriptures many times use the phrase "My name's sake." It doesn't simply mean that God is protecting His name from being marred. Rather, it is because of His Name that He does certain things—He holds back His wrath, pardons, etc. The phrase is indicative of His holy character. "For my name's sake" is an indication of who God is, and because of who He is, we can be assured that He will always keep His promises.

235 No sin is small in God's eyes, such is the greatness of His holiness. We would

But how could he make this a plea for pardon? I answer, because the greater his iniquity was, the more need he had of pardon. It is as much as if he had said, "Pardon mine iniquity, for it is so great that I cannot bear the punishment; my sin is so great that I am in necessity of pardon; my case will be exceedingly miserable, unless thou be pleased to pardon me." He makes use of the greatness of his sin, to enforce his plea for pardon, as a man would make use of the greatness of calamity in begging for relief. When a beggar begs for bread, he will plead the greatness of his poverty and necessity. When a man in distress cries for pity, what more suitable plea can be urged than the extremity of his case? And God allows such a plea as this: for He is moved to mercy towards us by nothing in us but the miserableness of our case. He doth not pity sinners because they are worthy, but because they need His pity.[236]

To suppose mercy without supposing misery, or pity without calamity, is a contradiction: therefore men cannot look upon themselves as proper objects of mercy, unless they first know themselves to be miserable;[237] and so, unless this be the case, it is impossible that they should come to God for mercy. They must be sensible that they are the children of wrath; that the law is against them,[238] and that they are exposed to the curse of it: that the wrath of God abideth on them; and that He is angry with them every day while they are under the guilt of sin.

They must be sensible that it is a very dreadful thing to be the object of the wrath of God; that it is a very awful thing to have Him for their enemy; and that they cannot bear His wrath. They must be sensible that the guilt of sin makes them miserable

---

have dismissed Adam's transgression as a misdemeanor, but in God's eyes it was worthy of capital punishment. How fearful it is to fall into the hands of the living God, and how consoling it is to be sheltered from wrath in Jesus Christ.

236 God's love for us isn't drawn out by something in us, but something in God.

237 "Miserable" in this context, doesn't mean "unhappy," but "wretched."

238 Sinners are ignorant today that "the Law is against them." They somehow see the Law as being *for* them—merely a standard by which God gave them to live.

creatures, whatever temporal enjoyments they have; that they can be no other than miserable, undone creatures, so long as God is angry with them; that they are without strength, and must perish, and that eternally, unless God help them. They must see that their case is utterly desperate, for any thing that any one else can do for them; that they hang over the pit of eternal misery; and that they must necessarily drop into it, if God have not mercy on them.[239]

They must be sensible that they are not worthy that God should have mercy on them. They who truly come to God for mercy, come as beggars, and not as creditors: they come for mere mercy. for sovereign grace, and not for any thing that is due.

Therefore, they must see that the misery under which they lie is justly brought upon them, and that the wrath to which they are exposed is justly threatened against them; and that they have deserved that God should be their enemy, and should continue to be their enemy. They must be sensible that it would be just with God to do as He hath threatened in His holy law[240], viz. make them the objects of His wrath and curse in hell to all eternity. They who come to God for mercy in a right manner are not disposed to find fault with His severity; but they come in a sense of their own utter unworthiness, as with ropes about their necks, and lying in the dust at the foot of mercy.

They must come to God for mercy in and through Jesus Christ alone. All their hope of mercy must be from the consideration of what He is, what He hath done, and what He hath suffered; and that there is no other name given under heaven, among men, whereby we can be saved, but that of Christ; that He is the Son of God, and the Savior of the world; that His blood cleanses from

239 How differently we would approach the lost if we *really* believed this. Shame on us for having hard and apathetic hearts when it comes to the unsaved.

240 The Law works wrath. It thunders its precepts and flashes with holy indignation. Its purpose if to terrify sinners and put the fear of God in them, as it did with Israel on the day God gave it to His people.

all sin,[241] and that He is so worthy, that all sinners who are in Him may well be pardoned and accepted. It is impossible that any should come to God for mercy, and at the same time have no hope of mercy.[242]

"By him all that believe are justified from all things, from which ye could not be justified by the law of Moses."[243] All the sins of those who truly come to God for mercy, let them be what they will, are satisfied for, if God be true who tells us so; and if they be satisfied for, surely it is not incredible, that God should be ready to pardon them. So that Christ having fully satisfied for all sin, or having wrought out a satisfaction that is sufficient for all, it is now no way inconsistent with the glory of the divine attributes to pardon the greatest sins of those who in a right manner come unto Him for it. God may now pardon the greatest sinners without any prejudice to the honor of His holiness.

The holiness of God will not suffer Him to give the least countenance to sin, but inclines Him to give proper testimonies of His hatred of it. But Christ having satisfied for sin, God can now love the sinner, and give no countenance at all to sin, however great a sinner He may have been. It was a sufficient testimony of God's abhorrence of sin that He poured out His wrath on His own dear Son, when He took the guilt of it upon himself. Nothing can more show God's abhorrence of sin than this. If all mankind had been eternally damned, it would not have been so great a testimony of it.

The sufferings of Christ fully satisfy justice. The justice of God, as the supreme governor and Judge of the world, requires the punishment of sin. The supreme Judge must judge the world

241 See 1 John 1:7.

242 No one should be assured of their own salvation if they do not believe in the exclusivity of Jesus Christ. To say that a man or woman can be saved outside of the mercy of God in Christ is to call God a liar, and corrupt the message of the gospel.

243 Acts 13:39. The Law could not save because that's not its purpose. A mirror cannot cleanse. It simply sends us to the water.

according to a rule of justice. God doth not show mercy as a judge, but as a sovereign; therefore His exercise of mercy as a sovereign, and His justice as a judge, must be made consistent one with another; and this is done by the sufferings of Christ, in which sin is punished fully, and justice answered.[244]

Christ will not refuse to save the greatest sinners, who in a right manner come to God for mercy[245]; for this is His work. It is His business to be a Savior of sinners; it is the work upon which He came into the world; and therefore He will not object to it. He did not come to call the righteous, but sinners to repentance.[246]

The whole contrivance of the way of salvation is for this end, to glorify the free grace of God. God had it on His heart from all eternity to glorify this attribute; and therefore it is, that the device of saving sinners by Christ was conceived. The greatness of divine grace appears very much in this, that God by Christ saves the greatest offenders. The greater the guilt of any sinner is, the more glorious and wonderful is the grace manifested in His pardon: "Where sin abounded, grace did much more abound."[247]

The Redeemer is glorified, in that He proves sufficient to redeem those who are exceeding sinful, in that His blood proves sufficient to wash away the greatest guilt, in that He is able to save men to the uttermost, and in that He redeems even from the greatest misery. It is the honor of Christ to save the greatest sinners, when they come to Him, as it is the honor of a physician that he cures the most desperate diseases or wounds. Therefore, no doubt, Christ will be willing to save the greatest sinners, if they come to Him; for He will not be backward to glorify himself,

244 It is beneficial to use legal terms when explaining the gospel to the unsaved—that God is indeed a judge; that we are criminals that have violated God's Law; that Christ paid our fine so that our case could be dismissed, etc.

245 The "right manner," is with a humble heart. Humility doesn't justify itself in the face of guilt. It hangs its head low in shame, and pleads for mercy.

246 See Matthew 9:13.

247 Romans 5:20. This is why sin must be made to abound, using God's Law. It *magnifies* His grace.

and to commend the value and virtue of His own blood. Seeing He hath so laid out himself to redeem sinners, He will not be unwilling to show, that He is able to redeem to the uttermost.[248]

The proper use of this subject is, to encourage sinners whose consciences are burdened with a sense of guilt, immediately to go to God through Christ for mercy. If you go in the manner we have described, the arms of mercy are open to embrace you.

You need not be at all the more fearful of coming because of your sins, let them be ever so black. If you had as much guilt lying on each of your souls as all the wicked men in the world, and all the damned souls in hell; yet if you come to God for mercy, sensible of your own vileness, and seeking pardon only through the free mercy of God in Christ, you would not need to be afraid; the greatness of your sins would be no impediment to your pardon. Therefore, if your souls be burdened, and you are distressed for fear of hell, you need not bear that burden and distress any longer.[249] If you are but willing, you may freely come and unload yourselves, and cast all your burdens on Christ, and rest in Him.

But, says one, I fear I have committed sins that are peculiar to reprobates. I have sinned against light, and strong convictions of conscience; I have sinned presumptuously; and have so resisted the strivings of the Spirit of God, that I am afraid I have committed such sins as none of God's elect ever commit. I cannot think that God will ever leave one whom He intends to save, to go on and commit sins against so much light and conviction, and with such horrid presumption. Others may say, I have had risings of heart against God; blasphemous thoughts, a spiteful and malicious spirit; and have abused mercy and the strivings

248 The truth that God saves us to the "uttermost" has been the deathbed comfort of every saint who has been ushered into eternity.

249 Don't let the world tell you not to preach on the subject of hell. On the Day of Judgment they will realize that they should have utterly encouraged us to shout its warning from the house tops.

of the Spirit, trampled upon the Savior, and my sins are such as are peculiar to those who are reprobated to eternal damnation. To all this I would answer, There is no sin peculiar to reprobates but the sin against the Holy Ghost. Do you read of any other in the Word of God? And if you do not read of any there, what grounds have you to think any such thing? What other rule have we, by which to judge of such matters, but the divine word? If we venture to go beyond that, we shall be miserably in the dark. When we pretend to go further in our determinations than the Word of God, Satan takes us up, and leads us. It seems to you that such sins are peculiar to the reprobate, and such as God never forgives. But what reason can you give for it, if you have no word of God to reveal it? Is it because you cannot see how the mercy of God is sufficient to pardon, or the blood of Christ to cleanse from such presumptuous sins? If so, it is because you never yet saw how great the mercy of God is; you never saw the sufficiency of the blood of Christ, and you know not how far the virtue of it extends. Some elect persons have been guilty of all manner of sins, except the sin against the Holy Ghost; and unless you have been guilty of this, you have not been guilty of any that are peculiar to reprobates.

But when once any sinner is willing to come to Christ, mercy is as ready for him as for any.[250] There is no consideration at all had of his sins; let him have been ever so sinful, his sins are not remembered; God doth not upbraid him with them.

But had I not better stay till I shall have made myself better, before I presume to come to Christ. I have been, and see myself to be very wicked now; but am in hopes of mending myself, and rendering myself at least not so wicked: then I shall have more courage to come to God for mercy. In answer to this, consider how unreasonably you act. You are striving to set up yourselves for your own saviors; you are striving to get something of your own, on the account of which you may the more readily be accepted. So that by this it appears that you do not seek to be

250 The prodigal son's father ran to greet his wayward son.

accepted only on Christ's account. And is not this to rob Christ of the glory of being your only Savior? Yet this is the way in which you are hoping to make Christ willing to save you.

You can never come to Christ at all, unless you first see that He will not accept of you the more readily for any thing that you can do. You must first see, that it is utterly in vain for you to try to make yourselves better on any such account.[251] You must see that you can never make yourselves any more worthy, or less unworthy, by any thing which you can perform.

If ever you truly come to Christ, you must see that there is enough in Him for your pardon, though you be no better than you are. If you see not the sufficiency of Christ to pardon you, without any righteousness of your own to recommend you, you never will come so as to be accepted of Him. The way to be accepted is to come, not on any such encouragement, that now you have made yourselves better, and more worthy, or not so unworthy, but on the mere encouragement of Christ's worthiness, and God's mercy.

If ever you truly come to Christ, you must come to Him to make you better. You must come as a patient comes to his physician, with his diseases or wounds to be cured. Spread all your wickedness before Him, and do not plead your goodness; but plead your badness, and your necessity on that account: and say, as the psalmist in the text, not "Pardon mine iniquity for it is not so great as it was," but, "Pardon mine iniquity, for it is great."

251 This is the tragic deception of believing that religious works commend us to God. Such a belief blinds the minds of millions who think that they are going to merit eternal life.

Christians: A Chosen Generation, A Royal Priesthood, A Holy Nation, A Peculiar People

(Sermon by Jonathan Edwards)

Compiled from http://www.apuritansmind.com/jonathanedwards/JonathanEdwards-Sermons-ChristiansChosenGeneration.htm

The truly godly are very different in their disposition from others. They hate those things that the rest of the world love, and love those things for which the rest of the world have no relish, insomuch that others are ready to wonder that they should place any happiness in a strict observance of the self-denying duties of religion. They wonder what delight they can take in spending so much time in meditation and prayer, and that they do not place happiness in those things which themselves do: "Wherein they think it strange that ye run not with them to the same excess of riot; speaking evil of you."[252] But the reason is, they are of a different race, and so derive different dispositions.[253]

It is ordinary to see those who are of different families, of a different temper. The natural temper of parents is commonly

252 1 Peter 4:4

253 Never be discouraged when the world hates you or separates you from its company because you belong to Jesus Christ. It is an honor to be counted as one of His, and any persecution is merely confirmation of the many warnings in Scripture that this world loves the darkness and hates the light.

in some degree transmitted to their posterity. Indeed, all agree in many things, for all are of the same blood originally. All are descended from the same Adam, and the same Noah. But Christians are born again of another stock, different from all the rest of the world.[254]

The precious treasures of kings are not to be compared to those precious things which Christ will give His saints in another world: the gold tried in the fire that Christ has purchased with His own blood, those precious jewels, those graces and joys of His Spirit, and that beauty of mind with which He will endow them. Kings' possessions are very extensive, especially were they thus when kings were generally absolute, and their whole dominions, their subjects and their fortunes, were looked upon as their possessions. But these fall short of the extensive possessions of the saints, who possess all things. They are the heirs of God, and all that is God's is theirs so far as it can contribute to their happiness. "He that overcometh shall inherit all things; and I will be his God, and he shall be my son."[255] "Therefore let no man glory in men, for all things are yours; whether Paul, or Apollos, or Cephas, or the world, or life, or death, or things present, or things to come; all are yours."[256]

In seeking conversion, you seek a kingdom. You who are poor, you who are children, have opportunity to obtain a kingdom,

---

254 It is because we are not of this world that we should truly be alien to it—to its fleeting fashions and lustful passions. Those who have passed from death to life hold the world in contempt, because it is fueled by lust, greed, pride and selfish ambition. These things are offensive to the Christian because they are offensive to the Spirit of which he is born. He is truly a fish out of water when it comes to this sinful world. It has no life for him.

255 Revelation 21:7

256 1 Corinthians 3:-21-22. Nothing in this life can begin to be compared to the treasure that we have in Jesus Christ. He is the source of life itself, and He dwells in those who have repented and trusted alone in His mercy. How guilty sinners will cry out in anguish when they realize that that they rejected everlasting life, and rather chose to enjoy the passing pleasures of sin. They rejected the everlasting joy of Heaven and unwillingly embrace the terrors of hell. There is no anecdotal comparison to express such foolishness.

to advance yourselves to higher dignity, to more substantial honors, to greater possessions, to more precious treasures, to be clothed in robes of richer splendor, and to fill a loftier throne, than those enjoyed by the greatest earthly monarchs. It is a crown that you are to run for, an incorruptible crown, to be given you by the great King of Heaven, and to be worn by you as long as His throne shall endure. What encouragement is here afforded to the saints under afflictions and reproaches. What are they, to the worth and honor of a heavenly kingdom? When you shall have a crown of glory placed on your head, and be seated on Christ's throne, and shine forth as the light, and are seated at His royal banquet, then you will suffer no more forever. All trouble, all reproach, shall be driven away; you will be too high to be reached by the malice of men and devils, and shall soon forget all your sorrows.[257]

The Christian gives himself to God freely as of mere choice. He does it heartily; he desires to be God's, and to belong to no other. He gives all the faculties of his soul to God. He gives God his heart, and it is offered to God as a sacrifice in two ways.

Of these, the first is when the heart is broken for sin. A sacrifice, before it can be offered, must be wounded and slain. The heart of a true Christian is first wounded by a sense of sin, of the great evil and danger of it, and is slain with godly sorrow and true repentance. When the heart truly repents, it dies unto sin. Repentance is compared unto a death in the Word of God. "Knowing this, that our old man is crucified with *him*, that the body of sin might be destroyed, that henceforth we should not serve sin. For he that is dead is freed from sin. For in that he died, he died unto sin once: but in that he liveth, he liveth unto

257 Our joy comes from faith in the promises of a faithful Creator. These awaiting pleasures are both sure and steadfast, because it is impossible for God to lie. Do you believe that? If you don't, then you have no basis to call yourself a Christian, because you insult the character of God with your unbelief. Without faith it is impossible to please Him (Hebrews 11:6). Jesus commanded "Have faith in God" (Mark 11:22), and if you do trust Him—if you do believe that God is faithful—you should have joy unspeakable right now as evidence of that faith, and the joy of the Lord will be your strength (Nehemiah 8:10).

God. Now if we be dead with Christ, we believe that we shall also live with him. Likewise reckon ye also yourselves to be dead indeed unto sin, but alive unto God through Jesus Christ our Lord."[258] "I am crucified with Christ: nevertheless I live; yet not I, but Christ liveth in me: and the life which I now live in the flesh I live by the faith of the Son of God, who loved me, and gave himself for me."[259] As Christ, when He was offered was offered broken upon the Cross, so there is some likeness to this when a soul is converted, the heart is offered to God slain and broken: "The sacrifices of God are a broken spirit: a broken and a contrite heart, O God, thou wilt not despise."[260]

The second way is when a Christian offers his heart to God, flaming with love. The sacrifice of old was not only to be slain, but to be burnt upon the altar. It was to ascend in flame and smoke, and so to be a sweet savor to God.[261]

"I will praise the name of God with a song, and will magnify him with thanksgiving. This also shall please the Lord better than an ox or bullock that hath horns and hoofs."[262] Praises are therefore in Hosea called calves of our lips, because they are like calves offered in sacrifice: "Take with you words, and turn to the LORD: say unto him, Take away all iniquity, and receive *us* graciously: so will we render the calves of our lips."[263] Only true Christians offer those sacrifices. However, hypocrites pretend to praise God, and to offer thanksgiving to Him. Yet they, being insincere, offer not sacrifices with which God is well pleased. They offer not spiritual sacrifices, and therefore they are not of the spiritual priesthood. In Heaven especially are the saints a

---

258 Romans 6:6-11

259 Galatians 2:20

260 Psalm 51:17

261 This love for God is not passive. Rather, it *runs* to do His will. It delights to please Him, and nothing pleases God like one sinner who comes to repentance. That brings joy to Heaven. So follow in the steps of the one you say that you love, by obeying His command to preach the gospel to every creature. Obedience is evidence of love.

262 Psalm 69:30-31

263 Hosea 14:2

holy priesthood upon this account, whose work it is forever to offer these sacrifices to God, who cease not day nor night to praise God and sing forth their ardent joyful hallelujahs. They sing a new song, a song that never will end, and never will grow old.[264]

Though the obedience of saints has no merit, yet it is pleasing and acceptable to God. It is as a sweet-smelling savor, and is compared to sacrifices, and preferred before them: "And Samuel said, Hath the LORD as *great* delight in burnt-offerings and sacrifices, as in obeying the voice of the LORD? Behold, to obey *is* better than sacrifice, *and* to hearken than the fat of rams."[265] Christians, by offering obedience to God in their lives and conversation, do what the apostle calls offering their bodies to be a living sacrifice, holy and acceptable to God, as their reasonable service.[266] They offer their bodies, that is they dedicate their bodies to holy uses and purposes. They yield their members as instruments of righteousness unto holiness. The soul, while here, acts externally by the body. And in this Christians serve God. They yield their eyes, their ears, their tongues, their hands, and feet, as servants to God, to be obedient to the dictates of His Word, and of His Holy Spirit in the soul.[267]

Let all who profess themselves Christians take heed that they do not defile themselves and profane their sacred character. There was great strictness required of old of the priests, lest they should defile themselves and profane their office, and it was regarded as a dreadful thing to profane it. So holy a God hath threatened in

---

264 We will have eternity to sing God's praises, but we have such a short time to preach His gospel.

265 I Samuel 15:22

266 See Romans 12:1

267 The last member of our body that wants to yield to God is the tongue. It is a world of iniquity, a flame, set on fire by hell. That is, if it's not yielded to God. But those that are Christ's have presented themselves as a living sacrifice, and a different fire is upon their tongue—it has been taken from the very altar of God and it burns with a passion for the lost. It preaches in season and out of season. Those who have life among those who are dead in sin, cannot but speak that which they have seen and heard.

the New Testament: "If any man defile the temple of God, him shall God destroy."[268] As Christians are here called the temple of God, so it is said in 1 Peter 2:5 that you are "a spiritual house, an holy priesthood." Avoid the commission of all immoralities, or things that have a horrid filthiness in them, things that will dreadfully profane the sacred name by which you are called, and the sacred station wherein you are set.[269]

Take heed of every sin: and allowing any sin whatever is a dreadful presumption of your holy character.

See that you well execute your office. Offer up your heart in sacrifice. Get and keep a near access to God. Come with boldness.[270] Offer up a heart broken for sin; offer it up flaming with love to God; offer praise to God. Praise God for his glorious excellency, and for His love and mercy. Consider what great things you have to praise God for: the redemption of Jesus Christ, His sufferings, His obedience, and the gift of that holiness, which makes you like unto God.

Be much in offering up your prayers to God, and see that all your offerings are offered upon the right altar, otherwise they will be abominable to God. Offer your hearts to God through Jesus Christ. In His name present the sacrifice of praise, obedience, charity, and of prayer on the golden altar perfumed with the incense of Christ's merits. Your reward will be to have this honor in heaven, to be exalted to that glorious priesthood, to be made a priest unto God forever and ever.

268 1 Corinthians 3:17

269 Be careful to maintain a godly character. Stay away from gossip, unclean talk, inordinate affection, and any "jesting" (see Ephesians 5:4). You battle a very real enemy who wants to destroy your testimony, through compromise with sin.

270 Nothing takes away boldness in prayer like unconfessed sin. Guilt cringes. If you fall in some way, be quick to get onto your knees and pour your heart out to God. Keep your conscience tender, stay in the Word of God, and be very afraid of any subtle hypocrisy.

God's Sovereignty in the Salvation of Men

(Sermon by Jonathan Edwards)

Compiled from http://www.apuritansmind.com/jonathanedwards/JonathanEdwards-Sermons-GodsSoveriegntySalvationMen.htm

But otherwise there is no sinner, let him be ever so great, but God can save him without prejudice to any attribute; if he has been a murderer, adulterer, or perjurer, or idolater, or blasphemer, God may save him if He pleases, and in no respect injure His glory. Though persons have sinned long, have been obstinate, have committed heinous sins a thousand times, even till they have grown old in sin, and have sinned under great aggravations: let the aggravations be what they may; if they have sinned under ever so great light; if they have been backsliders, and have sinned against ever so numerous and solemn warnings and strivings of the Spirit, and mercies of His common providence: though the danger of such is much greater than of other sinners, yet God can save them if He pleases, for the sake of Christ, without any prejudice to any of His attributes.[271] He may have mercy on whom He will have mercy. He may have mercy on the greatest of sinners, if He pleases, and the glory of none of His attributes will be in the least sullied. Such is the sufficiency of the satisfaction and righteousness of Christ, that none of the divine attributes stand in the way of the salvation of

---

271 Thank God for the incredible testimony of God's grace in the life of Saul of Tarsus. This murderous fanatic, who tortured and even killed Christians thinking that he was doing God a service, was stopped in his tracks and saved by the grace of God. His mercy is far greater than any of us can comprehend. Had we been there when Saul's merciless hand gave consent to kill Christians, perhaps we would have said, "No Lord, not him." But God is "rich" in mercy to poor poor sinners bound for hell, of which we were a part.

any of them. Thus the glory of any attribute did not at all suffer by Christ's saving some of His crucifiers.

God may save any of them without prejudice to the honor of His holiness. God is an infinitely holy being. The heavens are not pure in His sight. He is of purer eyes than to behold evil, and cannot look on iniquity. And if God should in any way countenance sin, and should not give proper testimonies of His hatred of it, and displeasure at it, it would be a prejudice to the honor of His holiness.[272] But God can save the greatest sinner without giving the least countenance to sin. If He saves one, who for a long time has stood out under the calls of the gospel, and has sinned under dreadful aggravations; if He saves one who, against light, has been a pirate or blasphemer, He may do it without giving any countenance to their wickedness; because His abhorrence of it and displeasure against it have been already sufficiently manifested in the sufferings of Christ. It was a sufficient testimony of God's abhorrence against even the greatest wickedness that Christ, the eternal Son of God died for it. Nothing can show God's infinite abhorrence of any wickedness more than this. If the wicked man himself should be thrust into hell, and should endure the most extreme torments which are ever suffered there, it would not be a greater manifestation of God's abhorrence of it, than the sufferings of the Son of God for it.

God may save any of the children of men without prejudice to the honor of His majesty. If men have affronted God, and that ever so much, if they have cast ever so much contempt on

---

272 Sin draws wrath like fiery lightning from the heavens. Holy wrath thunders with indignation, and the storm of God's fury against all unrighteousness will one day be released upon guilty sinners. What a fearful thing will be to fall into the hands of the living God! And if His love dwells within us, we will with a sense of urgency warn sinners that they may shelter in the safety of the Savior. Are you doing that? Are you warning this world? Have you overcome your natural fears with the supernatural love of God? Don't wait. Just do it. Pray as you go, and God will speak through you. He will take your jawbone and use it to slay a thousand. Compromise with sin or any irrational fear, and you will not only lose your strength, but you will end up blind to the state of the lost, and with your hands bound by your adversary.

His authority; yet God can save them, if He pleases, and the honor of His majesty not suffer in the least. If God should save those who have affronted Him, without satisfaction, the honor of His majesty would suffer. For when contempt is cast upon infinite majesty, its honor suffers, and the contempt leaves an obscurity upon the honor of the divine majesty, if the injury is not repaired. But the sufferings of Christ do fully repair the injury. Let the contempt be ever so great, yet if so honorable a person as Christ undertakes to be a mediator for the offender, and in the mediation suffer in his stead, it fully repairs the injury done to the majesty of heaven by the greatest sinner.

God may save any sinner whatsoever consistently with His justice. The justice of God requires the punishment of sin. God is the supreme Judge of the world, and He is to judge the world according to the rules of justice. It is not the part of a judge to show favor to the person judged; but he is to determine according to a rule of justice without departing to the right hand or left. God does not show mercy as a judge, but as a sovereign. And therefore when mercy sought the salvation of sinners, the inquiry was how to make the exercise of the mercy of God as a sovereign, and of His strict justice as a judge, agree together. And this is done by the sufferings of Christ, in which sin is punished fully, and justice answered. Christ suffered enough for the punishment of the sins of the greatest sinner that ever lived. So that God, when He judges, may act according to a rule of strict justice, and yet acquit the sinner, if he be in Christ. Justice cannot require any more for any man's sins, than those sufferings of one of the persons in the Trinity, which Christ suffered. "Whom God hath set forth to be a propitiation through faith in his blood, to declare his righteousness . . . that he might be just, and the justifier of him which believeth in Christ."[273]

---

273 Romans 3:25-26. Turn a deaf ear to the accuser of the brethren. If you are in Christ, God knows nothing of your sins. He has blotted them out, cast them into the sea of His forgetfulness, and removed them as far as the east is from the west. There is no condemnation to those who are in Christ Jesus. Not one jot or tittle of the Law can point the smallest of its fingers at any Christian.

God can save any sinner whatsoever, without any prejudice to the honor of His truth. God passed His word, that sin should be punished with death, which is to be understood not only of the first, but of the second death. God can save the greatest sinner consistently with His truth in this threatening; for sin is punished in the sufferings of Christ, inasmuch as He is our surety, and so is legally the same person, and sustained our guilt, and in His sufferings bore our punishment.[274]

274 It is good to explain the gospel to sinners with reference to human law. God is a judge. We are guilty criminals, condemned by the Law to God's prison, without parole. But Jesus paid our fine in full. That means that God can legally dismiss our case. He can commute our death sentence and allow us to live, because another paid our fine.

~Biography of~

Jonathan Edwards: A Puritan Paradox

1703–1758

Puritan Pastor and missionary to the Indians, Jonathan Edwards was a multifaceted man. A dozen authors could sit down now and each write an essay on Edwards, yet the reader would think he were reading about a dozen different—and equally interesting—men.

Who was this austere man, this reticent Puritan whose preaching was a moving force behind the emotionally charged Great Awakening; the man whose brilliance and impact on American history and modern Western thought is praised by both religious and secular scholars; the man whose voluminous writings on philosophy, psychology, and science, as well as theology, are to this day being studied, contemplated, and expounded upon; the man referred to both as "the last Puritan" and the "theologian of the heart"? Who was this paradox of a man, Jonathan Edwards?

As we read Edwards's works and works on Edwards, we are struck by how extraordinary a man he was. Just when we think we have him pegged as a rational, bookish intellectual, we read his fiery words in support of the emotionally charged Colonial revivals and are forced to reassess our views—to try to harmonize a dichotomy.

As we reflect on the legacy Edwards left to Christendom and to the Western world, we grow curious. "What made Edwards tick?" is a simple enough question, but the answer is complex. To gain an understanding of Jonathan Edwards before we read his words, we will eclipse our look at him to two prominent facets: his uncanny melding of rational dissection and spiritual fervor, and his faith in Christ.

To even begin to understand Jonathan Edwards, we must start by turning back time, beyond the wilds of his colonial New England, to the grimy streets of 17th Century London, and examine his heritage.

An Edwards Family History

London in 1625 was battling a scourge called "the plague." The plague had been a part of life in London for decades when it hit especially hard in 1625. In that year alone, it claimed the lives of about 35,000 Londoners, among them the Reverend Richard Edwards, great-great grandfather of Jonathan Edwards.

Reverend Edwards's widow, Anne, married James Cole, a cooper (barrel maker) and religious dissenter—a Puritan. In 1635 Anne, Mr. Cole, Anne's son William Edwards, and the cooper's daughter Abigail, set sail for the New World—a far better adventure than meeting their fate in an English debtors' prison. They arrived in Massachusetts but joined a party bound for the settlement in Connecticut. There young William learned his stepfather's trade, built the family business, and later passed it on to his son, Richard Edwards. It is in Richard Edwards, the son and grandson of Puritan coopers, that history records the first real glimmerings of the Edwards intellect and faith lived out.

Richard Edwards, Jonathan's grandfather, was born in Hartford, Connecticut, in 1647. Apparently not content to make barrels for a living, Richard established himself as a successful merchant and was appointed as the Queen's attorney. At around 20 years of age, he married Elizabeth Tuthill, who three months later confessed to him that she was pregnant by another man. In the midst of this scandalous situation, Richard Edwards followed his Christian faith and, in obedience to the Bible, he did the honorable thing; rather than divorce Elizabeth on the spot, he paid the customary fornication fine for a child conceived out of wedlock, essentially admitting he was guilty of a crime he did not commit. Richard Edwards took the blows of a tarnished reputation, both to obey the Lord and to hinder a worse outcome from being heaped upon his new wife.

After Elizabeth's illegitimate child was born and placed with its maternal grandparents, the conflicts in the Edwards's home continued. Family tradition holds that Elizabeth was insane. True or not, Elizabeth doubtless carried the baggage of her upbringing into her marriage—and that upbringing included shocking violence. Her brother killed one of their sisters with an axe and another sister committed infanticide. Something was terribly wrong in the Tuthill home. Whatever that "something" was, it undoubtedly had a strong influence on the character and behavior of Elizabeth Tuthill Edwards.

We will never know for certain whether Richard contributed to the couple's troubles, since the same family tradition that claims Elizabeth was insane holds Richard up as a man of great Christian virtue, including an unusual fortitude during times of domestic turbulence. We can, however, be certain that Elizabeth ignited more fires of contention than would a woman solidly rooted in reality—and in God's Word. Elizabeth's bouts of depression would not have started a rumor about her sanity, though her abandonment of her husband and their seven children for several years, her terrible temper, her threats to murder Richard, and her wicked tongue certainly would have.

Richard's long-suffering finally wore thin. In 1691, Richard Edwards, grandfather of Jonathan Edwards, faced another scandal and divorced Elizabeth, making theirs one of the earliest divorces in Colonial America. The following year he married Mary Talcott and together they added four surviving children to Richard's seven.

The first of Richard Edwards's eleven children was Timothy, born to Elizabeth in 1669. In Timothy we see even more clearly the brilliant intellect that bore such fruit in Jonathan Edwards. For one year, Timothy attended Harvard College. In his second year, he was barred from the college, likely due to the scandal of his parents' impending divorce, for which he was called to testify against his mother. A Reverend Pelatiah Glover took over as Timothy's tutor and, in 1691, the young man traveled to Cambridge to take his exams. In one day, Timothy took and passed the exams for both the bachelor's and the master's degrees.

Timothy Edwards married Esther Stoddard, daughter of the Reverend Solomon Stoddard, powerful pastor of the largest church in Massachusetts outside Boston, the Congregational Church in Northampton. Known for his fire and brimstone preaching, he was also the most notable revival preacher in the area.

Timothy and Esther moved to East Windsor (now South Windsor), Connecticut, where Timothy aided in assembling a new church. And so began Timothy Edwards's notoriously rocky sixty-three years as Puritan evangelical pastor of the Congregational Church—and as a revival preacher second only to his father-in-law, Solomon Stoddard.

Timothy Edwards, Jonathan's father, was obsessive and controlling. Although understandable considering his chaotic upbringing, these traits were a source of great tension between him and his congregation, yet in them we spy the spring from which poured forth his son's steadfastness and self-discipline.

The Birth of the Last Puritan

Jonathan Edwards was born in East Windsor, Connecticut, on October 5, 1703, the fifth of eleven children born to Timothy and Esther, and the only boy. Along with his ten sisters, Jonathan received his early education at home. Like their brother, the Edwards girls were highly intelligent, quick witted, and opinionated. Two of the girls died young. Another, Mary, cared first for her grandparents and then for her parents, never marrying. The other six girls married pastors and other men of good position—quite a step up socially from the Puritan cooper who assembled his family and fled across the Atlantic to avoid debtors' prison in England.

Jonathan's home schooling included the classics, the Bible, Christian theology, and ancient languages. Little did Edwards know it when he began his Latin studies at the age of seven, but that same year a baby girl named Sarah Pierpont was born, and seventeen years later they would wed.

Growing up as the son and grandson of renowned revival preachers, it is no wonder that Edwards describes a boyhood of great spiritual interest. As a lad of about nine, he witnessed a time of spiritual awakening sweep through his father's congregation. Likely prompted by this, little Jonathan built a prayer booth in the swamp. He recounts how he would meet with other boys to talk about religious things and to pray and admits his affinity for things religious. This period of youthful piety was not to last, however, and Edwards later wrote what should be an admonition to all:

> My affections seemed to be lively and easily moved, and I seemed to be in my element, when engaged in religious duties. And I am ready to think, many are deceived with such affections, and such a kind of delight, as I then had in religion, and mistake it for grace. But in process of time, my convictions and affections wore off; and I entirely lost all those affections and delights, and left off secret prayer, at least as to any constant performance of it; and returned like a dog to his vomit, and went on in ways of sin.

Edwards spent his undergraduate (1716-1720) and graduate years (1720-1722) at Yale College. Exceptionally intelligent, he engrossed himself in current issues in theology and philosophy, well on his way to one day being known as America's greatest philosopher. He wrote mainly on natural philosophy and metaphysics, while studying debates between the Calvinism of his faith and those movements that opposed it: Arianism, Arminianism, Deism, and Socinianism among them.

Edwards's academic career is a study in determined brilliance. He graduated first in his class and delivered the Valedictory Oration, yet he was the poorer in spirit, admitting great spiritual struggles during this time. He was a gifted seventeen-year-old—the son and grandson of Puritan preachers well known for the revivals that broke out under their preaching—and yet he did not possess saving faith in Christ.

It was in 1719, when he was only sixteen, that he wrote *Of Insects,* but it was two years later, in 1721, that we see an indication of the prolific writer Edwards would become when he wrote *Of the Rainbow* and *Of Light Rays*, and began several other works. Edwards was now eighteen, possessed of a razor-sharp rationality and soaring intellect. It was during his eighteenth year that he experienced a spiritual awakening, two years before he completed his *Resolutions*.

A Puritan's Resolve

In the eighteenth century, it was common practice for educated people to write a list of resolutions that were usually aimed at improving character and godliness, with the intention of following them as guidelines for a lifetime.

As a comparison, a contemporary of Jonathan Edwards, Benjamin Franklin—the embodiment of the Age of Reason—had a list of thirteen resolutions, which he described as a list of virtues, each followed by a precept. Written in his late twenties, Franklin's resolutions were compact and epigrammatic in style and focused on self-improvement and becoming a better citizen:

1. Temperance: Eat not to dullness; drink not to elevation.
5. Frugality: Make no expense but to do good to others or yourself; i.e., waste nothing.
13. Humility: Imitate Jesus and Socrates.

Franklin's intention was to master one virtue before going on to the next. Relying on his will, he had trouble keeping his short list of resolutions.

The aim of a Puritan's resolutions, however, had mainly to do with sanctification: growing in holiness. Jonathan Edwards composed seventy resolutions to this end and he followed them the rest of his life. The date of the first of Edwards's resolutions is unknown, but the last of them, number seventy, was composed on August 17, 1723—about a month before he received his master's degree at the age of nineteen.

Edwards began his *Resolutions* with these words:

> Being sensible that I am unable to do anything without God's help, I do humbly entreat Him by His grace to enable me to keep these *Resolutions*, so far as they are agreeable to His will, for Christ's sake.
>
> Remember to read over these *Resolutions* once a week.
>
> 1. Resolved, that I will do whatsoever I think to be most to God's glory, and my own good, profit and pleasure, in the whole of my duration, without any consideration of the time, whether now, or never so many myriads of ages hence. Resolved to do whatever I think to be my duty, and most for the good and advantage of mankind in general. Resolved to do this, whatever difficulties I meet with, how many and how great soever.
>
> 24. Resolved, whenever I do any conspicuously evil action, to trace it back, till I come to the original cause; and then both carefully endeavor to do so no more, and to fight and pray with all my might against the original of it.
>
> 28. Resolved, to study the Scriptures so steadily, constantly, and frequently, as that I may find, and plainly perceive myself to grow in the knowledge of the same.
>
> 70. Let there be something of benevolence in all that I speak.

The ransacking of the soul, the digging up and exposing of sin in his life, and the firm resolve to eradicate it that permeated Edwards's *Resolutions,* were common practices among the Puritans, who were committed to following the biblical commands to submit themselves to God and to carefully and honestly scrutinize their own hearts. Until his death, Edwards the Puritan reviewed, evaluated, and abided by his seventy resolutions. To this end he was aided not only by his extraordinary self-discipline, but by remaining dependent upon Christ.

The Conversion of a Puritan

About his time at college, Jonathan Edwards noted that he endured tremendous struggles with temptations to sin. He repeated his resolutions, put his overt sin behind him, and turned to his religion, though he describes a lifeless practice of it, devoid of any sweetness or emotion that he had earlier experienced. Although Edwards questions whether he had saving faith at this time, he does point out that he was driven to find it: "I made seeking my salvation the main business of my life"; Jonathan Edwards, staunch Calvinist, doubted God's sovereignty in salvation.

Edwards finally did come to grips with the sovereignty of God, abandoning his objections to it and instead finding what he called "a delightful conviction" and accepting it as "an exceeding pleasant, bright, and sweet doctrine." Though he remembered being convicted of this, he admitted he was not sure how this turn of mind came about.

It was probably the spring or summer of 1721 that Jonathan Edwards had a strong conversion experience. It came while reading 1 Timothy 1:17, "Now unto the King eternal, immortal, invisible, the only wise God, be honor and glory forever and ever, Amen." Edwards wrote,

> As I read the words, there came into my soul, and was as it were diffused through it, a sense of the glory of the Divine Being; a new sense, quite different from anything I ever experienced before.

He describes a growing awareness of the beauty of God:

> . . . my sense of divine things gradually increased, and became more and more lively, and had more of that inward sweetness. The appearance of everything was altered: there seemed to be, as it were, a calm, sweet cast, or appearance of divine glory, in almost everything. . . . God's excellency, His wisdom, His purity and love, seemed to appear in everything; in the sun, moon and stars; in the clouds, and blue sky; in the grass, flowers, trees; in the water, and all nature. . . .

Where most men would have been content to remain in such a state, Edwards was not.

> I felt then a great satisfaction as to my good estate. But that did not content me. I had vehement longings of soul after God and Christ, and after more holiness; wherewith my heart seemed to be full, and ready to break: which often brought to my mind, the words of the Psalmist, Psalm 119:20, "My soul breaketh for the longing it hath. . . ." Spent most of my time in thinking of divine things, year after year. And used to spend abundance of my time in walking alone in the woods, and solitary places, for meditation, soliloquy, and prayer, and converse with God. And it was always my manner, at such times, to sing forth my contemplations.

This man, who spent much of his time in contemplating spiritual things, conversing with God, and in singing songs of praise to Him, bore a striking spiritual resemblance to the young girl Sarah Pierpont.

Sarah Pierpont Edwards: A Transcendence of Spirit—A Sweetness of Communion with God

In 1723, when he was nearing twenty years old, Jonathan Edwards wrote an apostrophe for the thirteen-year-old girl whose faith in and relationship with God he so admired. He inscribed "On Sarah Pierpont" on the flyleaf of a book, which he gave to her.

> They say there is a young lady in [New Haven] who is beloved of that almighty Being, who made and rules the world, and that there are certain seasons in which this great Being, in some way or other invisible, comes to her and fills her mind with exceeding sweet delight, and that she hardly cares for anything, except to meditate on Him—that she expects after a while to be received up where He is, to be raised out of the world and caught up into Heaven; being assured that He loves her too well to let her remain at a distance from Him always. There she is to dwell with Him, and to be ravished with His love, favor and delight, forever. Therefore, if you present all the world before her, with the richest of its treasures, she disregards it and cares not for it, and is unmindful of any pain or affliction. She has a strange sweetness in her mind, and sweetness of temper, uncommon purity in her affections; is most just and praiseworthy in all her actions; and you could not persuade her to do anything thought wrong or sinful, if you would give her all the world, lest she should offend this great Being. She is of a wonderful sweetness, calmness, and universal benevolence of mind; especially after those times in which this great God has manifested himself to her mind. She will sometimes go about, singing sweetly, from place to [place], and seems to be always full of joy and pleasure, and no one knows for what. She

> loves to be alone, and to wander in the fields and on the mountains, and seems to have someone invisible always conversing with her.

This short dedication contains a breath of Edwards's own longing to immerse himself in the Lord, to know Him and fill his mind and heart with Him. Sarah, both as a young girl and later as Mrs. Jonathan Edwards, had a powerful spiritual impact on him. He, in turn, succeeded in winning Sarah's heart and four years after penning his prose poem, they were wed in New Haven, Connecticut, on July 28, 1727.

In 1726, Jonathan Edwards headed to Northampton to become assistant pastor under his grandfather, Solomon Stoddard, the great revival preacher. When Stoddard died in 1729, Edwards took over the Congregational Church of Northampton as sole pastor and Sarah Edwards became a full-fledged pastor's wife.

In Sarah Pierpont Edwards, we see a living example of the meshing of contrary forces so striking in the life of Jonathan Edwards. Sarah Edwards was his spiritual equal—and the standard toward which he reached—while his opposite in personality.

Born January 9, 1710, Sarah Pierpont was the daughter of the Reverend James Pierpont of New Haven—a founder of what was later named Yale University. As a girl, Sarah enjoyed wandering the fields and mountains, seemingly with an unseen companion, sweetly singing and communing with God. She is said to have conversed more with God than with any of His creatures and was known for her remarkable joy, which baffled others, but Edwards, having tasted the sweetness of such communion himself, understood it well.

Both Jonathan and Sarah were deeply committed to Christ; in fact, it was Sarah's devotion to the Lord that drew Jonathan to her, yet they were as different in personality as they were similar in convictions. Sarah Edwards, the epitome of the Christian wife that other renowned men of God sought after and prayed for, was not only a model of Christian virtue and devotion to both God and her husband, she was no wallflower. Intelligent and beautiful, Sarah Edwards was as sociable as Jonathan was reserved. Jonathan, the introverted scholar, was not terribly adept socially and he was content to spend many hours daily in his study. Sarah thoroughly enjoyed conversation with others and entertaining her husband's many guests. Described as a woman of uncommon beauty, Sarah was known for her gentle spirit, kindness, and deep devotion to God and to her husband. Sarah Edwards was stylish and cultured. Not only did she wear rouge and chintz dresses (boldly patterned and fashionable in Europe at the time), she presumably adorned herself with the beauty marks she kept in an engraved silver box. Jonathan, himself a man of genteel tastes, wore spectacles, a calamanco vest made of Flanders wool woven with satin twill, and a beaver hat. Add to that, silver buckles at his knees and a cane in his hand and we see how our theologian must have cut a dashing figure.

The Edwards family table was set with damask tablecloths and napkins and china plates and cups, and their walls were ornamented with mirrors and small pictures. Despite such luxuries, most items in their home were functional. Though their inclinations were refined, the Edwardses were not flamboyant, nor were they spendthrifts.

Jonathan and Sarah raised their eight daughters and three sons to be well-educated, sophisticated intellectuals. The family maintained the biblical view of marriage: The woman was the weaker vessel while at the same time men and women were equal, though with different roles, and marriage for the Edwardses was a partnership. This equality may have been biblical, but it was unusual for the time—so much so that it tends to be misunderstood and misrepresented by secular scholars today, who like to see it as a sign that the Edwardses were "less Christian," demonstrating through their marriage more of a secular breakthrough in gender issues. The Edwardses would have been affronted by this misinterpretation of biblical gender roles.

Jonathan Edwards—among many others—portrays Sarah as a paragon of godliness. Through his eyes we see her as the height of virtue, purity, piety, and sweetness and might think he was at least partially blind with love, but others who met Sarah all gave similar reports. George Whitefield prayed for a wife like Sarah Edwards and said he could not recall a "sweeter couple" than Jonathan and Sarah Edwards. "I think I love Mr. Edwards & his Wife because I see so much of [the] Image of God in them," wrote John Walley. Joseph Emerson depicted the Edwards family as "the most agreeable Family I was ever acquainted with. Much of the Presence of God there."

A good deal has been written about Sarah Edwards, and much of it utterly fantastic, with little basis in reality. When we read Sarah's own words, however, we see she was a normal woman whose only unusual experiences had to do with her periods of special communion with God—a communion that arose from her solid faith in God and in her active striving to obey Him and to know Him. Sarah Edwards, the woman who profoundly affected Jonathan Edwards, was a woman of unusual faith in and dependence upon Christ and who spent much time in meditating upon His beauties.

Toward the end of 1738, and twice again in 1740, Sarah Edwards experienced periods of rapturous transcendence. Resting in God and finding great joy in Him, she dedicated herself to God's service and His glory, renouncing the world and surrendering all to Him. Afterwards, Sarah would find herself—sometimes for hours on end—swept up in thoughts of God's love, joy, and light, all the while going about her daily tasks as mistress of a large household.

Although Sarah Edwards had a deep and uncommon communion

with God, she also possessed the usual foibles of the flesh. On January 24, 1742, the day before Jonathan left for a two-week preaching tour to Leicester, he reprimanded Sarah for her inconsiderate words to another pastor. The following day he set out, yet Sarah still carried the guilt of her transgression and the sting of her husband's rebuke.

Other ministers came to Northampton to preach during Edwards's absence, among them Samuel Buell, whose preaching was outstanding. This caused Sarah—loyal wife of the regular pastor—great jealousy. Turning this over to God, she was filled with peace. Her sense of God's greatness and excellence grew and her inner peace turned to ineffable joy. She continued on in a state of ecstasy over God's glory in excess of a week, at times being physically overwhelmed by it, yet carrying out her usual duties in taking care of her home and family. She once declared, "Oh how good is it to work for God in the daytime, and at night to lie down under His smiles!"

Upon the return of her husband, Sarah reported her experiences to him. Edwards was deeply stirred by hearing her news and found these periods of her transcendence so strikingly different from her normal experiences that he asked his wife to detail them in writing. Later that year, he added her account to his work, *Some Thoughts Concerning the Present Revival of Religion in New England* (1743), a book he wrote in response to the attacks on the revivals and revival supporters.

Sarah recounts how she was chastised by her husband for her imprudent words to Mr. Williams of Hadley, and describes how she turned to God for help:

> On Tuesday night, Jan. 19, 1742, I felt very uneasy and unhappy, at my being so low in grace. I thought I very much needed help from God, and found a spirit of earnestness to seek help of Him, that I might have more

> holiness. When I had for a time been earnestly wrestling with God for it, I felt within myself great quietness of spirit, unusual submission to God, and willingness to wait upon Him, with respect to the time and manner in which He should help me, and wished that He should take His own time, and His own way, to do it.

She goes on to describe how she viewed her imprudence as stemming from a lack of trusting in God. Words from Romans 8:34-35 came to her mind, "Who is He that condemneth? It is Christ that died, yea rather, that is risen again, who is even at the right hand of God, who also maketh intercession for us. Who shall separate us from the love of Christ? Shall tribulation, or distress, or persecution, or famine, or nakedness, or peril, or sword?" She then says it "occasioned great sweetness and delight in my soul" and excused herself so that she might be alone with God. She read the rest of Romans 8 and explains her experience:

> Melted and overcome by the sweetness of this assurance, I fell into a great flow of tears, and could not forbear weeping aloud. It appeared certain to me that God was my Father, and Christ my Lord and Savior, that He was mine and I His.

This period of sweetness continued for several days. Whereas most today would see this as a sign of God's blessing and one's own special holiness, Sarah Edwards, so much like her husband, recognized that her heart was filled with sin, not the grace of God. And so Sarah strove to eradicate sin from her heart.

At one point, while a number of people interested in spiritual things were in her home and Sarah was going about her household duties, she happened to enter a room where this same Mr. Buell spoke the words, "O, that we, who are the children of God, should be cold and lifeless in religion!" This one sentence had such an impact on Sarah that she "felt such a sense of the deep ingratitude manifested by the children of God" that she felt very weak and sank to the floor. She was helped onto a chair, whereupon she conveyed to the guests the feelings she had of Christ's grace toward her, of her complete confidence in His having saved her from hell, of the importance of giving everything up to God, and of the peace and joy that followed such. After which, writes Sarah:

> Mr. Buell then read a melting hymn of Dr. Watts', concerning the loveliness of Christ, the enjoyments and employments of Heaven, and the Christian's earnest desire of heavenly things; and the truth and reality of the things mentioned in the hymn, made so strong an impression on my mind, and my soul was drawn so powerfully towards Christ and Heaven, that I leaped unconsciously from my chair. I seemed to be drawn upwards, soul and body, from the earth towards Heaven; and it appeared to me that I must naturally and necessarily ascend thither. These feelings continued while the hymn was reading, and during the prayer of Mr. Christophers, which followed.

It would be easy to reduce Sarah's experiences to those of an overly emotional woman, but for a couple of things. First, throughout her writing, Sarah mentions going about her duties at home while in these elevated states. At times, she was so overcome by the sweetness of what Christ did for her on the Cross that she felt weakened to the point of having difficulty in carrying out her tasks, but she was fully conscious nonetheless. That her rational, logical husband used Sarah's experiences to illustrate true piety and as a contrast to much of the "enthusiastic" nonsense going on during the revivals speaks strongly for Sarah's emotional stability.

The Revivals

1 John 4:1
Beloved, believe not every spirit, but try the spirits whether they are of God: because many false prophets are gone out into the world.

Growing up with a grandfather and a father famous for their revival preaching, Edwards felt a profound joy at the first stirrings of revival under his own preaching. He embraced every shake, shimmy, and shout, initially believing them to be signs of God at work. But appearances can be deceiving and Edwards, not a man to be blinded by emotion—even his own emotion—followed the biblical admonition to test all things against Scripture. He analyzed the proceedings of the revivals using the Bible as his guide and standard of truth and reformed his opinion of the outward signs occurring while the revivals were in full swing.

Edwards came to realize that loud outcries, tears, and fainting do not make an individual a true follower of Christ. The Bible says that we are all sinners: "For all have sinned, and come short of the glory of God" (Romans 3:23) and that to be a Christian, a man must first realize he is a sinner and then confess his sins to God—repent, as Mark 1:15 says, "repent ye and believe the Gospel." That is, we must turn away from and discontinue our sins and follow Christ—be born again. As Jesus Himself said in John 3:3, "Except a man be born again, he cannot see the kingdom of God."

Matthew 7:22-23
Many will say to me in that day, Lord, Lord, have we not prophesied in thy name? and in thy name have cast out devils? and in thy name done many wonderful works? And then will I profess unto them, I never knew you: depart from me, ye that work iniquity.

Edwards determined that the actions and proclamations during the periods of revival were not proof of salvation—in fact, that much of it was unbiblical and even the work of Satan. He watched for evidence of lasting changes in the people, concluding that only some of those making professions of faith were actually converted. Yet, with his typical logic, sound biblical foundation, and inclination toward a fine balance of reason and sentiment, Edwards knew that believing God was not simply an intellectual assent to what the Bible teaches; were the heart not engaged, the man was not saved.

Edwards wrestled with how to discern the Spirit of God and how to know true piety from its counterfeit. He observed the commotions of the revivals, and compared them to the experiences of his pious wife. He came back to these fundamental questions time and again in his treatises, with the culminating work being his *Treatise Concerning Religious Affections,* written in 1746. Though he defended the revivals, in "Religious Affections," he wrote,

> Thus the children of God are led by the Spirit of God in judging of actions themselves, and in their meditations upon, and judging of, and applying the rules of God's holy Word: and so God teaches them His statutes, and causes them to understand the way of His precepts; which the Psalmist so often prays for.
>
> But this leading of the Spirit is a thing exceeding diverse from that which some call so; which consists not in teaching them God's statutes and precepts, that He has already given; but in giving them new precepts, by immediate inward speech or suggestion; and has in it no tasting the true excellency of things, or judging or discerning the nature of things at all.

Backing the revivals as acts of the Holy Spirit, Edwards nonetheless cautioned against much of the carryings on. "Enthusiasm" was one such error for which he openly rebuked people. In "Some Thoughts Concerning the Present Revival of Religion in New England" (1743), he criticized the "notion that 'tis God's manner now in these days to guide His saints . . . by inspiration, or immediate revelation; and to make known to them what shall come to pass hereafter, or what it is His will that they should do, by impressions that He by His Spirit makes upon their minds." These words defined enthusiasm, which Edwards vigorously fought as unbiblical and even a danger to truth. He wrote that "this error will defend and support all errors," recognizing that an individual who believed he was "guided by immediate direction from Heaven," would not listen to reason—even were that reason to come from the Bible itself. Knowing that such people would not likely heed his warnings, he rebuked and exhorted, using Scripture to back his position. This is a perfect portrayal of the austere Jonathan Edwards, the man who preached fire and brimstone to young children, and who, by all appearances, seemed to prefer books to people and yet was perhaps the greatest supporter of the revivals, seeing in them the visible hand of God in New England.

For the sake of those who opposed the revivals, Edwards added to his book *Some Thoughts* the account of his devout yet sensible wife's rapturous transports, removing her name, gender, and all other identifying marks and referring to her as "the person." In his impersonal description of her experience, he let the reader know that "the person" was not a recent convert, nor a convert of any of the Northampton revivals, but a Christian mature both in faith and in age. He made it clear that nothing in "the person's" experience involved superstition, revelation, delusion, fancy, or despondency, and clarified the fact that "this person" was of sober mind and reason and lived out an obedience to God. He pointed out that the individual spent their ecstatic days "eating for God, and working for God, and sleeping for God, and bearing pain and trouble for God, and doing all as the service of love, and so doing it with a continual, uninterrupted cheerfulness, peace, and joy."

He wrote sixteen pages detailing Sarah's sound character and mind and her ecstatic experience of God before unleashing his opinion of the revivals through his pen.

Three years later, in *Religious Affections,* Edwards both spoke against the extreme intellectualism that dismissed the revivals out of hand, and had more very strong words against the excesses of the Great Awakening, proposing that much of the excesses were likely carried out by people who were not emotionally stable and therefore easily persuaded to follow the influences of Satan:

> And this seems to be the reason why persons that are under the disease of melancholy, are commonly so visibly and remarkably subject to the suggestions and temptations of Satan: that being a disease which peculiarly affects the animal spirits, and is attended with weakness of that part of the body which is the fountain of the animal spirits, even the brain, which is, as it were, the seat of the phantasy. 'Tis by impressions made on the brain that any ideas are excited in the mind, by the motion of the animal spirits, or any changes made in the body. The brain being thus weakened and diseased, 'tis less under the command of the higher faculties of the soul, and yields the more easily to extrinsic impressions, and is overpowered by the disordered motions of the animal spirits; and so the devil has greater advantage to affect the mind, by working on the imagination. And thus Satan, when he casts in those horrid suggestions into the minds of many melancholy persons, in which they have no hand themselves, he does it by exciting imaginary ideas, either of some dreadful words or sentences, or other horrid outward ideas. And when he tempts other persons who are not melancholy, he does it by presenting to the imagination, in a lively and alluring manner, the objects of their lusts, or by exciting ideas of words, and so by them exciting thoughts; or by promoting an imagination of outward actions, events, circumstances,

etc. Innumerable are the ways by which the mind might be led on to all kind of evil thoughts, by exciting external ideas in the imagination. If persons keep no guard at these avenues of Satan, by which he has access to the soul, to tempt and delude it, they will be likely to have enough of him. And especially, if instead of guarding against him, they lay themselves open to him, and seek and invite him, because he appears as an angel of light, and counterfeits the illuminations and graces of the Spirit of God, by inward whispers, and immediate suggestions of facts and events, pleasant voices, beautiful images, and other impressions on the imagination. There are many who are deluded by such things, and are lifted up with them, and seek after them, that have a continued course of them, and can have them almost when they will; and especially when their pride and vainglory has most occasion for them, to make a show of them before company. 'Tis with them, something as 'tis with those who are the professors of the art of telling where lost things are to be found, by impressions made on their imaginations; they laying themselves open to the devil, he is always at hand to give them the desired impression.

Before I finish what I would say on this head of imaginations, counterfeiting spiritual light, and affections arising from them, I would renewedly (to prevent misunderstanding of what has been said) desire it may be observed, that I am far from determining that no affections are spiritual which are attended with imaginary ideas.

When the mind is much engaged, and the thoughts intense, oftentimes the imagination is more strong, and the outward idea more lively; especially in persons of some constitutions of body. But there is a great difference between these two things, viz. *lively imaginations arising*

> *from strong affections,* and *strong affections arising from lively imaginations*. The former may be, and doubtless often is, in case of truly gracious affections. The affections don't arise from the imagination, nor have any dependence upon it; but on the contrary, the imagination is only the accidental effect, or consequent of the affection, through the infirmity of human nature. But when the latter is the case, as it often is, that the affection arises from imagination, and is built upon it, as its foundation, instead of a spiritual illumination or discovery; then is the affection, however elevated, worthless and vain. And this is the drift of what has been now said, of impressions on the imagination.

Scripture was Edwards' standard; everything he wrote and did, stemmed from his belief in the Bible as God's Word and so as truth. Though he denounced much of the behaviors that attended the revivals, Edwards saw in some people changes that happened outside the excesses of the revivals and that lasted over time. He compared these results to Scripture, and, finding such changes biblical, he stood firm as a supporter of the revivals.

A Third Generation Revival Preacher

Edwards's preaching incited both the lesser revivals of 1734-1735 and the explosive beginnings of the "Great Awakening"—a revival that spread like wildfire through the

American Colonies of the 1740s. We might think that such a preacher was fiery and passionate, yet Edwards preached not with fervor and agitation, but with solemnity, knowing himself to be in the presence of God. He delivered even his imprecatory sermons with a low and sensible voice and used a natural delivery, his conviction being that any effects on his hearers came not from oratorical devices, but from the force of the truth he declared; to Edwards, the weight of a sermon was in the truth it laid bare, not in the emotional antics of the preacher. Even his now famous *Sinners in the Hands of an Angry God,* with its merciless depiction of hell, was preached in a moderate voice and with great earnestness by the man known for his phenomenal intellect and calm reason, which must have amplified the terror of his listeners.

Edwards did not wish for souls to perish in hell, and this was one of the forces that drove him through life. This highly logical man, devoted to Christ as he was, would preach hell's fire and damnation even to young children and was even accused of frightening innocent children, despite his calm delivery. He endured the accusations for the sake of the children's souls, as he did not believe children were innocent. He drilled his own children on the Westminster Shorter Catechism, convinced that even children need to hear God's truth, presented plainly and clearly. Not known for his tact, yet driven by his missionary spirit to see people saved from hell, Edwards even used the occasions of children's deaths to deliver his eternal damnation sermons to children—and this included the death of his own little girl. This is not to say his sermons were solely focused on hell; the beauties of Christ shine through Edwards's messages.

Jonathan Edwards the Missionary

After more than twenty years of service as assistant pastor and then sole pastor of the Congregational Church of Northampton, a controversy arose in Jonathan Edwards's pastorate. It was 1748. An undertow of a party spirit—social and political efforts at work in the town—probably helped drag Edwards under, but the official reason for the contention began half a century earlier, with Edwards's grandfather. The Reverend Solomon Stoddard believed that communion—the serving of the bread and wine to the faithful—could be used by God in the conversion of the unrepentant. Near the beginning of the century, he had made the decision to serve communion even to those who had not made a profession of faith in Christ. As long as an individual affirmed intellectually the essential doctrines of the faith and strove to live a decent, upstanding life—though not professing repentance or faith in Christ—he or she was allowed to partake of the Lord's Supper. Jonathan Edwards was convinced that this practice was unscriptural. As time wore on, his conviction deepened and in December of 1748, Edwards stood up for his conviction, publicly opposing his grandfather's views and the church's half-century long tradition. He proclaimed that only those who professed to be regenerate would be allowed to approach the Lord's Table. This did not go over well with his congregation. A vote was taken as to Edwards's suitability for the position of pastor. Some 230 of his own congregation voted him out, while he claims only 23 stood by his side.

On June 22, 1750, the great revival preacher Jonathan Edwards was dismissed from his pastorate. And so began the period in which Edwards penned some of his greatest works while acting as a missionary on the frontier of colonial America.

Jonathan Edwards is remembered by secular and religious scholars alike for his sharp, rational mind, his prolific writings, and his adherence to God's Word, but his involvement with missions is generally relegated to barely more than a footnote describing his stint at the Indian mission in Stockbridge, Massachusetts, where he is portrayed as being holed up in his study for the better part of his seven years there.

Edwards did not actively seek to become a missionary, yet we see in him the heart of a missionary, nurtured from his early childhood. Edwards inherited his grandfather Solomon Stoddard's belief that the colonial wars and other trials and tribulations were punishments from God, meted out for the colony's having abandoned their commitment in the Massachusetts Bay charter of 1629 to share the gospel with the Indians and train them up spiritually. And when the Massachusetts government wanted to purchase land from the Housatonic-Mohican Indians for an English settlement, Edwards's uncle, John Stoddard, son of the Reverend Solomon Stoddard, played a large part in the negotiations. Ten years later, John Stoddard was one of the founders of the Indian mission in Stockbridge. The Reverend Stephen Williams, Edwards's relative who was captured as a child in 1704 during an Indian raid on Deerfield, advocated for the Housatonic mission. This family of Puritans took God's Word seriously, right down to sharing the gospel with groups of people they deemed savages and without so much as a spark of God's truth.

The first time Jonathan Edwards preached in Stockbridge was in October of 1750, some four months after losing his position at the Congregational Church, but he was not officially established there until nearly a year later, on August 8, 1751. About the time Edwards's own congregation ousted him, the Reverend John Sergeant of the Stockbridge mission passed away. When Edwards was considered as a replacement for Sergeant, Ephraim Williams, Jr., a resident of Stockbridge—and one of Edwards's relatives—balked at the idea. He protested that Jonathan Edwards was not only too old to learn the Indians' language, but he was unsocial and tactless. It was all true. Williams was perturbed that "a head so full of divinity should be so empty of politics." Williams' practical side finally acquiesced, knowing property values would rise, should Edwards move to Stockbridge.

While pastor to the small English congregation at Stockbridge and missionary to 150 Indian families, Edwards was notorious for spending a great deal of time secluded in his study. At that time in history, the Colonials in America had rather low opinions of the Indians, their culture, and their religion. Even Edwards, who found tiny sparks of God's truth in Islam, Judaism, and various Chinese religions, could find no such spark in the religion of the Stockbridge Indians. To his credit, unlike many white men, who viewed the Indians as a sub-human species, Edwards warmed to the people and saw them as men created in the image of God. He fully believed that some among them were God's elect, and he let them all know that he did not consider the whites to be any better than they were.

Williams was right about Edwards not learning the Indian languages, but despite this, Edwards managed to win the trust and respect of the natives of Stockbridge.

During the time Edwards remained sequestered in his study, he wrote a large number of sermons and innumerable letters to Boston, to the mission's administrators, doing all he could to protect the Indians' interests, as well as justifying the way he managed the mission.

A large part of Jonathan Edwards's time in Stockbridge was used to write many of his major works, including his prodigious *Freedom of the Will* (1754), which is considered among one of the five hundred most important works in American history. Although a blow for Edwards, his dismissal from his pastorate allowed him the time to write some of Christendom's finest treatises.

Not compromising on his belief that the Indians should learn English, he nonetheless availed himself of the aid of an interpreter, John Wauwaumpequunaunt. In the more than 200 manuscript sermons that survive today, we see that Edwards preached regularly to the Indians, standing firm on his Calvinist doctrine. He taught them that Christ died for the elect, who would comprise some people from *all* nations, and encouraged them by reminding them that wealth and power are not signs of election.

Despite the years Edwards spent sharing the Gospel with the Indians of Stockbridge, the greatest impact he had as a missionary came in 1749, when he published the journal of the missionary David Brainerd. First printed two years after the young missionary died of tuberculosis (with Jonathan Edwards's daughter at his side), the journal was popular from the start. Over 250 years later, *The Life of David Brainerd* is still encouraging missionaries worldwide. To this effect, Edwards's impact on the mission field is among the greatest of any man.

Edwards's missionary heart can also be seen in his preaching that led to the revivals and underpinned the Great Awakening. Jonathan Edwards, like pastors today, was a missionary to his town and his congregation.

Revival of a Puritan Legacy

Jonathan Edwards, as a man of great intellect and spiritual integrity, was many things: a philosopher so highly thought of by the secular humanists that they longed for the day he would give up his faith and join them; a pastor to young and old alike; an influential theologian; and a preacher whose calm yet truthful preaching sparked the fires of the lesser revivals and the Great Awakening.

Edwards's legacy has survived going on three centuries and, though it faded for a time, is once again growing strong. Jonathan Edwards, a Christian of backbone and conviction, of soaring intellect and spiritual sweetness, is very much a man after the heart of modern-day Christians.

To God be the glory in all things; Jonathan Edwards would agree.

Illustration Portfolio

JONATHAN EDWARDS
1703-1758

Jonathan Edwards grew up in a large family in East Windsor, Connecticut. He enjoyed the Puritan life of the early American era.

For nearly a quarter of a century, Jonathan Edwards ministered at this church in Northampton, Massachusetts, home to one of the most powerful revivals in American history.

George Whitefield, who was also part of The Great Awakening, was a close friend to Jonathan Edwards.

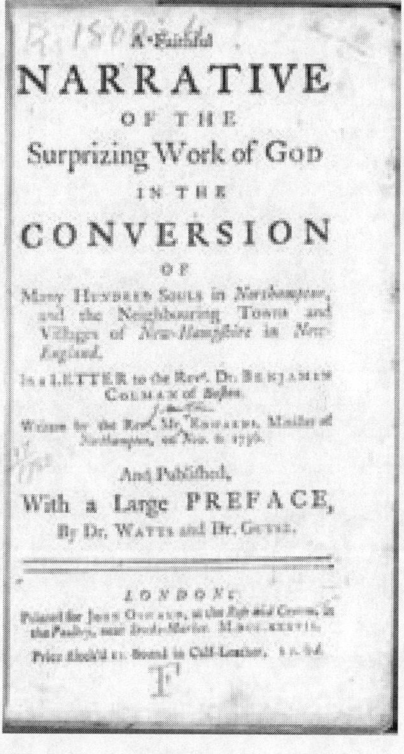

A Faithful
NARRATIVE
OF THE
Surprizing Work of GOD
IN THE
CONVERSION
OF
Many Hundred Souls in Northampton, and the Neighbouring Towns and Villages of New-Hampshire in New-England.

In a LETTER to the Revd. Dr. BENJAMIN COLMAN of Boston.

Written by the Revd. Mr. EDWARDS, Minister of Northampton, on Nov. 6. 1736.

And Published,
With a Large PREFACE,
By Dr. WATTS and Dr. GUYSE.

LONDON:
Printed for JOHN OSWALD, at the Rose and Crown, in the Poultry, near Stocks-Market. M.DCC.XXXVII.
Price Stitch'd 1s. Bound in Calf-Leather, 1s. 6d.

In A Faithful Narrative of the Surprising Work of God, Edwards gave his account of the local revival in Northampton. It would be several years before the fires of The Great Awakening burst forth throughout New England and Europe.

In 1747, Edwards came to know David Brainerd, an evangelist who worked among the Indians. Upon his dismissal from Northampton, Edwards spent six years ministering among the Indians and settlers in the outpost of Stockbridge.

In 1757, Edwards accepted the position of president of the College of New Jersey, which later became Princeton University.

Aaron Burr, Edwards' son-in-law, was President of the College of New Jersey until his death in 1757.

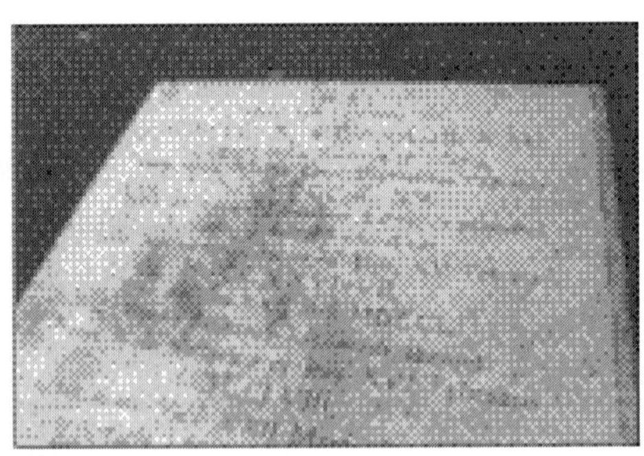

Jonathan Edwards died March 22, 1758, as the result of an allergic reaction to a smallpox vaccination.

MOODY GOLD

Compiled by Ray Comfort

The Old Judge Converted

I remember, as I was coming out of the daily prayer meeting in one of our American cities a few years ago, a lady said she wished to speak to me; her voice trembled with emotion, and I saw at once that she was heavily burdened by something or other. She said she had long been praying for her husband, and she wanted to know if I would go to see him; she thought it might do him some good. What is his name? "Judge _____," and she mentioned one of the most eminent politicians in the State.

"I have heard of him," I said; "I am afraid I need not go; he is a booked infidel; I cannot argue with him."

"That is not what he wants," said the lady. "He has had too much argument already. Go and speak to him about his soul." I said I would, although I was not very hopeful. I went to his house, was admitted to his room, and introduced myself as having come to speak to him about salvation.

"Then you have come on a very foolish errand," said he; "there's no use in attacking me, I tell you that. I am proof against all these things, I don't believe in them."

Well, I saw it was no use arguing with him; so I said, "I'll pray for you, and I want you to promise me that when you are converted you'll let me know."

"Oh, yes, I'll let you know," he said in a tone of sarcasm. "Oh, yes, I'll let you know when I'm converted!" I left him, but I continued to pray for him.

Some time subsequently I heard that the old judge was converted. I was again preaching in that city a while after that, and when I had done talking the judge himself came to me, and said: "I promised I'd let you know when I was converted; I have come to tell you of it. Have you not heard of it?"

"Yes; but I would like to hear from you how it happened."

"Well," said the judge, "one night, some time after you called on me, my wife had gone to the meeting; there was no one in the house but the servants. I sat by the drawingroom fire, and I began to think: Suppose my wife is right, that there is a heaven and a hell; and suppose she is on the right way to heaven, where am I going? I just dismissed the thought. But a second thought came: Surely He who created me is able to teach me. Yes, I thought, that is so. Then why not ask Him? I struggled against it, but at last, though I was too proud to get down on my knees, I just said, 'Father, all is dark; Thou who created me canst teach me.'

"Somehow, the more I prayed the worse I felt. I was very sad. I did not wish my wife to come home and find me thus, so I slipped away to bed, and when she came into the room

I pretended to be asleep. She got down on her knees and prayed. I knew she was praying for me, and that for many long years she had been doing so. I felt as if I could have jumped up and knelt beside her; but no, my proud heart would not let me, so I lay still, pretending to be asleep. But I didn't sleep that night. I soon changed my prayer; it was now, 'O God, save me; take away this terrible burden.'

"I didn't believe in Christ even yet. I thought I'd go right straight to the Father Himself. But the more I prayed I only became the more miserable; my burden grew heavier. The next morning I did not wish to see my wife, so I said 'I am not well, and wouldn't wait for breakfast.' I went to the office, and when the boy came I sent him home for a holiday. When the clerks came I told them they might go for the day. I closed the office doors: I wanted to be alone with God. I was almost frantic in my agony of heart. I cried to God to take away this load of sin. At last I fell on my knees, and cried, 'For Jesus Christ's sake take away this load of sin.' At length I went to my wife's pastor, who had been praying with her for my conversion for years, and the same minister who had prayed with my mother before she died. As I walked down the street the verse that my mother had taught me came into my mind, 'Whatsoever things ye desire, when ye pray, believe that ye receive them, and ye shall have them.'

"Well, I thought, I have asked God, and here I am going to ask a man. I won't go. I believe I am a Christian. I turned and went home. I met my wife in the hall as I entered. I caught her hand, and said, 'I am a Christian now.' She turned quite pale; she had been praying for twenty-one years for me, and yet she could not believe the answer had come. We went into our room, and knelt down by the very bedside where she had so often knelt to pray for her husband. There we erected our family altar; and for the first time our voices mingled in prayer. And I can only say that the last three months have been the happiest months ever I spent in my life."

Since then that judge has lived a consistent Christian life; and all because he came to God, asking for guidance.
(From *Christ All in All*: D.L. Moody)

The Qualifications for Soul Winning

Away in the United States, a young lady was sent to a boarding school, and was there led to Christ; not only so, but taught that she ought to work for Him. By-and-by she goes home, and now she seeks, in one way and another, to work for Him, but without finding how. She asks for a class in her church Sunday school, but the superintendent is obliged to tell her that he has already more than enough teachers. One day, going along the street, she sees a little boy struck by his companion, and crying bitterly. She goes up and speaks to him; asks him what the trouble is? The boy thinks she is mocking him, and replies sullenly. She speaks kindly, tries to persuade him to go to Sunday school. He does not want to learn. She coaxes him to come and hear her and the rest singing there; and so the next Sunday he comes with her. She gets a corner seat in the school of well dressed scholars for herself and her charge. He sits and listens, full of wonder. On going home, he tells his mother he has been among the angels. At first at a loss, she becomes angry, when a question

or two brings out that he has been to a Protestant Sunday school; and the father, on coming home, forbids his going back, on pain of flogging. Next Sunday, however, he goes, and is flogged, and so again, and yet again, till one Sunday, he begs to be flogged before going, that he may not be kept thinking of it all the time. The father relents a little, and promises him a holiday every Saturday afternoon, if he will not go to Sunday school. The lad agrees, sees his teacher, who offers to teach him then. How many wealthy young folks would give up their Saturdays to train one poor ragged urchin in the way of salvation? Some time after, at his work, the lad is on one of the railway cars. The train starts suddenly; he slips through, and the wheels pass over his legs; he asks the doctor if he will live to get home; it is impossible. "Then," says he, "tell father and mother that I am going to Heaven, and want to meet them there." Will the work she did seem little now to the young lady? Or is it nothing that even one thus grateful waits her yonder?
(Sermon delivered by Dwight L. Moody in Dr. Bonar's church, Edinburgh, Scotland, 7th December, 1873.)

The Ten Commandments

An Infidel's Testimony

It is related of a clever infidel that he sought an acquaintance with the truths of the Bible, and began to read at the books of Moses. He had been in the habit of sneering at the Bible, and in order to be able to refute arguments brought by Christian men, he made up his mind, as he knew nothing about it, to read the Bible and get some idea of its contents. After he had reached the Ten Commandments, he said to a friend:

"I will tell you what I used to think. I supposed that Moses was the leader of a horde of bandits; that, having a strong mind, he acquired great influence over a superstitious people; and that on Mount Sinai he played off some sort of fireworks to the amazement of his ignorant followers, who imagined in their fear and superstition that the exhibition was supernatural. I have been looking into the nature of that Law. I have been trying to see whether I could add anything to it, or take anything from it, so as to make it better. Sir, I cannot! It is perfect!

"The first Commandment directs us to make the Creator the object of our supreme love and reverence. That is right. If He be our Creator, Preserver, and supreme Benefactor, we ought to treat Him, and none other, as such. The second forbids idolatry. That certainly is right. The third forbids profanity. The fourth fixes a time for religious worship. If there be a God, He ought surely to be worshipped. It is suitable that there should be an outward homage significant of our inward regard. If God be worshipped, it is proper that some time should be set apart for that purpose, when all may worship Him harmoniously, and without interruption. One day in seven is certainly not too much, and I do not know that it is too little.

"The fifth Commandment defines the peculiar duties arising from family relations. Injuries to our neighbor are then classified by the moral Law. They are divided into offenses against life, chastity, property, and character; and I notice that the greatest offense in each class is expressly forbidden. Thus the greatest injury to life is murder; to chastity, adultery; to property, theft; to character, perjury. Now the greatest offense must include the least of the same kind. Murder must include the least of the same kind. Murder must include every injury to life; adultery every injury to purity, and so of the rest. And the moral code is closed and perfected by a command forbidding every improper desire in regard to our neighbors. "I have been thinking. Where did Moses get that Law? I have read history. The Egyptians and the adjacent nations were idolaters; so were the Greeks and Romans; and the wisest or best Greeks or Romans never gave a code of morals like this. Where did Moses obtain that Law, which surpasses the wisdom and philosophy of the most enlightened ages? He lived at a period comparatively barbarous; but he has given a Law in which the learning and sagacity of all subsequent time can detect no flaw. Where did he obtain it? He could not have soared so far above his age as to have devised it himself. I am satisfied where he obtained it. It came down from heaven. It has convinced me of the truth of the religion of the Bible."

The former infidel remained to his death a firm believer in the truth of Christianity.

The Ten Commandments Continued

But though there is far too much of this frivolous, familiar use of God's name, the Commandment is broken a great deal more by profanity. Taking the name of God in vain is blasphemy. Is there a swearing man who reads this? What would you do if you were put into the balances of the sanctuary, if you had to step in opposite to this Third Commandment? Think a moment, have you been taking God's name in vain today? I do not believe men would ever have been guilty of swearing unless God had forbidden it. They do not swear by their friends, their fathers or mothers, their wives or children. They want to show how they despise God's Law.

A great many men think there is nothing in swearing. Bear in mind that God sees something wrong in it, and He says He will not hold men guiltless, even though society does.

I met a man sometime ago who told me he had never sinned in his life. He was the first perfect man I had ever met. I thought I would question him, and began to measure him by the Law. I asked him: "Do you ever get angry?"

"Well," he said, "sometimes I do; but I have a right to do so. It is righteous indignation."

"Do you swear when you get angry?"

He admitted he did sometimes.

"Then," I asked, "are you ready to meet God?"

"Yes," he replied, "because I never mean anything when I swear."

Suppose I steal a man's watch and he comes after me. "Yes," I say, "I stole your watch and pawned it, but I did not mean anything by it. I pawned it and spent the money, but I did nor mean anything by it."

You would smile at and deride such a statement.

Ah, friends! You cannot trifle with God in that way. Even if you swear without meaning it, it is forbidden by God. Christ said: "Every idle word that men shall speak, they shall give an account thereof in the day of judgment; for by thy words thou shalt be justified, and by thy words thou shalt be condemned" (Matthew 12:36, 37). You will be held accountable whether your words are idle or blasphemous.

More Insight from The Ten Commandments

When I was out west about thirty years ago, I was preaching one day in the open air, when a man drove up in a fine carriage, and after listening a little while to what I was saying, he put the whip to his fine looking steed, and away he went, I never expected to see him again, but the next night he came back, and he kept on coming regularly night after night.

I noticed that his forehead itched—you have noticed people who keep putting their hands to their foreheads?—he didn't want any one to see him shedding tears—of course not! It is not a manly thing to shed tears in a religious meeting, of course!

After the meeting I said to a gentleman: "Who is that man who drives up here every night? Is he interested?"

"Interested! I should think not! You should have heard the way he talked about you today."

"Well," I said, "that is a sign he is interested."

If no man ever has anything to say against you, your Christianity isn't worth much. Men said of the Master, "He has a devil," and Jesus said that if they had called the master of the house Beelzebub, how much more them of his household. I asked where this man lived, but my friend told me not to go to see him, for he would only curse me. I said: "It takes God to curse a man; man can only bring curses on his own head." I found out where he lived and went to see him. He was the wealthiest man within a hundred miles of that place, and had a wife and seven beautiful children. Just as I got to his gate I saw him coming out of the front door. I stepped up to him and said: "This is Mr. _______, I believe?"

He said, "Yes, sir; that is my name." Then he straightened up and asked, "What do you want?"

"Well," I said, "I would like to ask you a question, if you won't be angry."

"Well, what is it?"

"I am told that God has blessed you above all men in this part of the country; that He has given you wealth, a beautiful Christian wife, and seven lovely children. I do not know if it is true, but I hear that all He gets in return is cursing and blasphemy"

He said, "Come in; come in." I went in.

"Now," he said, "what you said out there is true. If any man has a fine wife I am the man, and I have a lovely family of children, and God has been good to me. But do you know, we had company here the other night, and I cursed my wife at the table and did not know it till after the company had gone. I never felt so mean and contemptible in my life as when my wife told me of it. She said she wanted the floor to open and let her down out of her seat. If I have tried once, I have tried a hundred times to stop swearing. You preachers don't know anything about it."

"Yes," I said, "I know all about it; I have been a drummer."

"But," he said, "you don't know anything about a businessman's troubles. When he is harassed and tormented the whole time, he can't help swearing."
"Oh, yes," I said, "he can. I know something about it. I used to swear myself."
"What! You used to swear?" he asked; "how did you stop?"

"I never stopped."

"Why, you don't swear now, do you?"

"No; I have not sworn for years."

"How did you stop?"

"I never stopped. It stopped itself."

He said, "I don't understand this."

"No," I said, "I know you don't. But I came up to talk to you, so that you will never want to swear as long as you live."

I began to tell him about Christ in the heart; how that would take the temptation to swear out of a man.

"Well," he said, "how am I to get Christ?"

"Get right down here and tell Him what you want."

"But," he said, "I was never on my knees in my life. I have been cursing all the day, and I don't know how to pray or what to pray for."

"Well," I said, "it is mortifying to have to call on God for mercy when you have never used His name except in oaths; but He will not turn you away. Ask God to forgive you if you want to be forgiven."

Then the man got down and prayed—only a few sentences, but thank God, it is the short prayers, after all, which bring the quickest answers. After he prayed he got up and said: "What shall I do now?"

I said, "Go down to the church and tell the people there that you want to be an out-and-out Christian."

"I cannot do that," he said; "I never go to church except to some funeral."

"Then it is high time for you to go for something else," I said. After a while he promised to go, but did not know what the people would say. At the next church prayer meeting, the man was there, and I sat right in front of him. He stood up and put his hands on the settee, and he trembled so much that I could feel the settee shake. He said:

"My friends, you know all about me. If God can save a wretch like me, I want to have you pray for my salvation."

That was thirty odd years ago. Sometime ago I was back in that town, and did not see him; but when I was in California, a man asked me to take dinner with him. I told him that I could not do so, for I had another engagement. Then he asked if I remembered him, and told me his name. "Oh," I said, "tell me, have you ever sworn since that night you knelt in your drawing room, and asked God to forgive you?"

"No," he replied, "I have never had a desire to swear since then. It was all taken away."

He was not only converted, but became an earnest, active Christian, and all these years has been serving God. That is what will take place when a man is born of the divine nature.
(*The Ten Commandments:* A sermon delivered by D.L. Moody)

May God give us more testimonies like this. Things like this delight me and bring me to tears. God bless D. L. Moody for his boldness, and may He make us just as bold. If you need help in this area, feel free to listen to free audios on www.livingwaters.com ~ Ray Comfort

Hell

I remember a few years ago, while the Spirit of God was working in my church, I closed the meeting one night by asking any that would like to become Christians to rise, and to my great joy, a man arose who had been anxious for some time. I went up to him and took him by the hand and shook it, and said, "I am glad to see you get up. You are coming out for the Lord now in earnest, are you not?"

"Yes," said he, "I think so. That is, there is only one thing in my way."

"What's that?" said I.

"Well," said he, "I lack moral courage. I confess to you that if such a man [naming a friend of his] had been here tonight I should not have risen. He would laugh at me if he knew of this, and I don't believe I have the courage to tell him."

"But," said I, "You have got to come out boldly for the Lord if you come out at all."

While I talked with him he was trembling from head to foot, and I believe the Spirit was striving earnestly with him. He came back the next night, and the next, and the next; the Spirit of God strove with him for weeks; it seemed as if he came to the very threshold of Heaven, and was almost stepping over into the blessed world. I never could find out any reason for his hesitation, except that he feared his old companions would laugh at him.

At last the Spirit of God seemed to leave him; conviction was gone. Six months from that time I got a message from him that he was sick and wanted to see me. I went to him in great haste. He was very sick, and thought he was dying. He asked me if there was any hope. Yes, I told him, God had sent Christ to save him; and I prayed with him.

Contrary to all expectations he recovered. One day I went down to see him. It was a bright, beautiful day, and he was sitting out in front of his house.

"You are coming out for God now, aren't you? You will be well enough soon to come back to our meetings again."

"Mr. Moody," said he, "I have made up my mind to become a Christian. My mind is fully made up to that, but I won't be one just now. I am going to Michigan to buy a farm and settle down, and then I will become a Christian."
"But you don't know yet that you will get well."

"O," said he, "I shall be perfectly well in a few days. I have got a new lease of life."

I pleaded with him, and tried every way to get him to take his stand. At last he said, "Mr. Moody, I can't be a Christian in

Chicago. When I get away from Chicago, and get to Michigan, away from my friends and acquaintances who laugh at me, I will be ready to go to Christ."

"If God has not grace enough to save you in Chicago, he has not in Michigan" I answered.

At last he got a little irritated and said, "Mr. Moody, I'll take the risk," and so I left him.

I well remember the day of the week, Thursday, about noon, just one week from that very day, when I was sent for by his wife to come in great haste. I hurried there at once. His poor wife met me at the door, and I asked her what was the matter. "My husband," she said, "has had a relapse; I have just had a council of physicians here, and they have all given him up to die."

"Does he want to see me?" I asked.

"No."

"Then why did you send for me?"

"I cannot bear to see him die in this terrible state of mind." "What does he say?" I asked.

"He says his damnation is sealed, and he will be in hell in a little while."

I went in, and he at once fixed his eyes upon me. I called him by name, but he was silent. I went around to the foot of the bed, and looked in his face and said, "Won't you speak to me?", and at last he fixed that terrible deathly look upon me and said:

"Mr. Moody, you need not talk to me any more. It is too late. You can talk to my wife and children; pray for them; but my heart is as hard as the iron in that stove there. My damnation is sealed, and I shall be in hell in a little while."

I tried to tell him of Jesus' love and God's forgiveness, but he said, "Mr. Moody, I tell you there is no hope for me." And as I fell on my knees, he said, "You need not pray for me. My wife will soon be left a widow and my children will be fatherless; they need your prayers, but you need not pray for me."

I tried to pray, but it seemed as if my prayers didn't go higher than my head, and as if Heaven above me was like brass. The next day, his wife told me, he lingered until the sun went down, and from noon until he died all he was heard to say was, "The harvest is past, the summer is ended, and I am not saved." After lingering along for an hour he would say again those awful words, and just as he was expiring his wife noticed his lips quiver, and that he was trying to say something, and as she bent over him she heard him mutter, "The harvest is past, the summer is ended, and I am not saved." He lived a Christless life, he died a Christless death —we wrapped him in a Christless shroud, and bore him away to a Christless grave.

Are there some here that are almost persuaded to be Christians? Take my advice and don't let any thing keep you away. Fly to the arms of Jesus this hour. You can be saved if you will.
(Hell: A sermon by D.L. Moody)

Never be afraid to put the fear of God in those who prefer man's approval to God's. Open up the Commandments and speak plainly about the justice of death and hell. There is an insanity that blinds us to the reality of our personal demise. We think that death is something that happens to other people. Speak of its immanence for every one of us, and pray that God makes your words come alive. ~ Ray Comfort

Heaven—Its Hope

In England I was told of a lady who had been bedridden for years. She was one of those saints that God polishes up for the kingdom; for I believe that there are a good many saints in this world that we never hear about; we never see their names heralded through the press; they live very near the Master; they live very near Heaven; and I think it takes a great deal more grace to suffer God's will than it does to do God's will; and if a person lies on a bed of sickness, and suffers cheerfully, it is just as acceptable to God as if they went out and worked in his vineyard.

I am sure he means that they rejoice in their suffering. A Christian should give thanks for and in everything. See Romans 8:28. ~ Ray Comfort

Now, it was one of those saints, and a lady, who said that for a long time she used to have a great deal of pleasure in watching a bird that came to make its nest near her window. One year it came to make its nest, and it began to make it so low she was afraid something would happen to the young; and every day that she saw that bird busy at work making its nest, she kept saying, "O bird, build higher!" She could see that the bird was going to come to grief and disappointment. At last the bird got its nest done, and laid its eggs and hatched its young; and every morning the lady looked out to see if the nest was there, and she saw the old bird bringing food for the little ones, and she took a great deal of pleasure in looking at it. But one morning she woke up and she looked out and she saw nothing but feathers scattered all around, and she said, "Ah, the cat has got the old bird and all its young." It would have been a mercy to have torn that nest down. That is what God does for us very often just snatches things away before it is to late. Now, I think that is what we want to say to church people that if you build for time you will be disappointed. God says: Build up yonder. It is a good deal better to have life in Christ and God than any where else.
(*Heaven—Its Hope:* A sermon by D.L. Moody)

Lost and Found

While in Philadelphia a man with his wife came to our meetings. When he left the service, he wouldn't speak to his wife. She thought it was very strange but said nothing and went to bed thinking that in the morning he would be all right.

At breakfast, however, he would not speak a word. Well, she thought this strange, but she was sure he would have gotten over whatever was wrong with him by dinner.
The dinner hour arrived, and it passed without his saying a word.

At supper not a word escaped him, and he would not go with her to the meeting. Every day for a whole week the same thing went on.

But at the end of the week he could not stand it any longer, and he said to his wife, "Why did you write Mr. Moody and tell him all about me?"

"I never wrote to Mr. Moody in my life," said the wife.
"You did," he answered.

"You're mistaken. Why do you think that?"

"Well, then, I wronged you; but when I saw Mr. Moody picking me out among all those people and telling all about me, I was sure you must have written him."

It was the Son of Man seeking for him, my friends. And I hope there will be one here tonight who will feel that I am talking personally to him. May you feel that you are lost and that the Lord is seeking for you. When you feel this, it is an invitation for you to be saved.

I was in an infirmary not long since where a mother brought a little child in. She said, "Doctor, my little child's eyes have not been opened for several days, and I would like you to do something for them."

The doctor got some ointment and put it first on one, then on the other, and pulled them open. "Your child is blind," said the doctor. "He will never be able to see."

At first the mother couldn't take it in, but after a little she cast an appealing look upon that physician, and in a voice full of emotion, said, "Doctor, you don't mean to say that my child will never see again?"

"Your child has lost his sight, and he will never see again," replied the doctor.

That mother gave a scream and drew that child to her bosom. "O my darling child," sobbed the woman, "are you never to see the mother who gave you birth? never to see the world again?"

I could not keep back the tears when I saw the terrible agony of that woman when she realized the misfortune that had come upon her child.

A terrible calamity, to grope in total darkness through the world, never to look upon the bright sky, the green fields; never to see the faces of loved ones; but what was it in comparison to the loss of a soul? I would rather have my eyes plucked out of my head and go down to my grave in total blindness than lose my soul.

There is a very good story told of Rowland Hill and Lady Ann Erskine. You have seen it, perhaps, in print.

While he was preaching in a park in London to a large assemblage, she was passing in her carriage. She asked her footman when she saw Rowland Hill in the midst of the people: "Who is that man?"

"That is Rowland Hill, my lady."

She had heard a good deal about the man and thought she would like to see him, so she directed her coachman to drive near the platform. When the carriage came near, Rowland Hill saw the insignia of nobility and asked who that noble lady was. Upon being told, he said, "Stop, my friends, I have something to sell."

The idea of the preacher's becoming suddenly an auctioneer made the people wonder; but in the midst of a dead silence he said:

"I have more than a title to sell; I have more than the crown of Europe to sell—it is the soul of Lady Ann Erskine. Is there anyone here who bids for it? Yes, I hear a bid. Satan, Satan, what will you give?"

"I will give pleasure, honor, riches—yea, I will give the whole world for her soul."

"Do you hear another bid? Is there any other one? Do I hear another bid? Ah, I thought so; I hear another bid. The Lord Jesus Christ, what will You give for this soul?"

"I will give peace, joy, comfort that the world knows not of—yea, I will give eternal life."

"Lady Ann Erskine, you have heard the two bidders for your soul. Which will you accept?"
She ordered the door of her carriage to be opened. Then she came weeping from it and accepted the Lord Jesus Christ.

He, the great and mighty Savior, is a bidder for your soul tonight. He offers you riches and comfort, joy and peace here and eternal life hereafter, while Satan offers you what he cannot give.

Poor lost soul, which will you have? Christ will ransom your soul if you put your burden upon Him.
(*Lost and Found:* A sermon by D.L. Moody)

Repentance

My sister, I remember, told me her little boy said something naughty one morning, when his father said to him, "Sammy, go and ask your mother's forgiveness."
"I won't," replied the child.

"If you don't ask your mother's forgiveness I'll put you to bed." It was early in the morning, before he went to business, and the boy didn't think he would do it. He said "I won't" again. They undressed him and put him to bed.

The father came home at noon expecting to find his boy playing about the house. He didn't see him about, and asked his wife where he was. "In bed still." So he went up to the room, and sat down by the bed, and said: "Sammy, I want you to ask your mother's forgiveness." But the answer was "No." The father coaxed and begged, but could not induce the child to ask forgiveness. The father went away, expecting certainly that when he came home that night the child would have got all over it. At night, however, when he got home he found the little fellow still in bed. He had lain there all day. He went to him and tried to get him to go to his mother, but it was no use. His mother went and was equally unsuccessful.

That father and mother could not sleep any that night. They expected every moment to hear the knock at their door by their little son. Now they wanted to forgive the boy. My sister told me it was just as if death had come into their home. She never passed through such a night. In the morning she went to him and said: "Now, Sammy, you are going to ask my forgiveness?" but the boy turned his face to the wall and wouldn't speak.

The father came home at noon and the boy was as stubborn as ever. It looked as though the child was going to conquer. It was for the good of the boy that they didn't want to give him his own way. It is a great deal better for us to submit to God than have our own way. Our own way will lead us to ruin; God's way leads to life everlasting. The father went off to his office, and that afternoon my sister went in to her son about four o'clock and began to reason with him, and, after talking for some time, she said, "Now, Sammy, say, 'Mother.'" "Mother," said the boy. "Now say 'for.'" "For." "Now just say 'give.'" And the boy repeated, "Give." "Me," said the mother. "Me," and the little fellow fairly leaped out of bed. "I have said it," he cried; "take me down to papa, so that I can say it to him."

Oh, sinner, go to Him and ask His forgiveness. This is repentance. It is coming in with a broken heart and asking the King of Heaven to forgive you. Don't say you can't. It is a lie. It is your stubborn will—it is your stubborn heart.
(*Repentance:* A sermon by D.L. Moody)

R. A. Torrey: Moody's Best Friend

Dr. R. A. Torrey was probably Moody's closest associate and friend. Dr. Torrey was the first superintendent of the Moody Bible Institute and set up a curriculum for that Bible Institute which has been a pattern for others like it. When Moody died, Torrey soon took worldwide lead in great citywide campaigns in Australia, England and the United States. In 1923, Dr. Torrey was asked to speak at a great memorial service on "Why God Used D. L. Moody," and this is that remarkable address about that amazing man, probably the greatest man of his generation, as Dr. Torrey said:

Eighty-six years ago (February 5, 1837), there was born of poor parents in a humble farmhouse in Northfield, Massachusetts, a little baby who was to become the greatest man, as I believe, of his generation or of his century—Dwight L. Moody. After our great generals, great statesmen, great scientists and great men of letters have passed away and been forgotten, and their work and its helpful influence has come to an end, the work of D. L. Moody will go on, and its saving influence continue and increase, bringing blessing not only to every state in the Union but to every nation on Earth. Yes, it will continue throughout the ages of eternity.

My subject is "Why God Used D. L. Moody," and I can think of no subject upon which I would rather speak. For I shall not seek to glorify Mr. Moody, but the God who by His grace, His entirely unmerited favor, used him so mightily, and the Christ who saved him by His atoning death and resurrection life, and the Holy Spirit who lived in him and wrought through him and who alone made him the mighty power that he was to this world.

Furthermore, I hope to make it clear that the God who used D. L. Moody in his day is just as ready to use you and me, in this day, if we, on our part, do what D. L. Moody did, which was what made it possible for God to so abundantly use him.

He Was a Fully Surrendered Man

The whole secret of why D. L. Moody was such a mightily used man you will find in Psalm 62:11: "God hath spoken once; twice have I heard this; that POWER BELONGETH UNTO GOD." I am glad it does. If D. L. Moody had any power, and he had great power, he got it from God.

The first thing that accounts for God's using D. L. Moody so mightily was that he was a fully surrendered man. Every ounce of that two hundred and eighty pound body of his belonged to God; everything he was and everything he had, belonged wholly to God. Now, I am not saying that Mr. Moody was perfect; he was not. If I attempted to, I presume I could point out some defects in his character. It does not occur to me at this moment what they were; but I am confident that I could think of some, if I tried real hard.

The first month I was in Chicago, we were having a talk about something upon which we very widely differed, and Mr. Moody turned to me very frankly and very kindly and said in defense of his own position: "Torrey, if I believed that God wanted me to jump out of that window, I would jump." I believe he would. If he thought God wanted him to do anything, he would do it. He belonged wholly, unreservedly, unqualifiedly, entirely, to God.

Henry Varley, a very intimate friend of Mr. Moody in the earlier days of his work, loved to tell how he once said to him: "It remains to be seen what God will do with a man who gives himself up wholly to Him." I am told that when Mr. Henry Varley said that, Mr. Moody said to himself: "Well, I will be that man." And I, for my part, do not think "it remains to be seen" what God will do with a man who gives himself up wholly to Him. I think it has been seen already in D. L. Moody. There are thousands and tens of thousands of men and women in Christian work, brilliant men and women, rarely gifted men and women, men and women who are making great sacrifices, men and women who have put all conscious sin out of their lives, yet who, nevertheless, have stopped short of absolute surrender to God, and therefore have stopped short of fullness of power. But Mr. Moody did not stop short of absolute surrender to God; he was a wholly surrendered man, and if you and I are to be used, you and I must be wholly surrendered men and women.

He Was a Man of Prayer

The second secret of the great power exhibited in Mr. Moody's life was that Mr. Moody was in the deepest and most meaningful sense a man of prayer. People oftentimes say to me: "Well, I went many miles to see and to hear D. L. Moody, and he certainly was a wonderful preacher." Yes, D. L. Moody certainly was a wonderful preacher; taking it all in all, the most wonderful preacher I have ever heard, and it was a great privilege to hear him preach as he alone could preach; but out of a very intimate acquaintance with him I wish to testify that he was a far greater pray-er than he was preacher. Time and time again, he was confronted by obstacles that seemed insurmountable, but he always knew the way to surmount and to overcome all difficulties. He knew the way to bring to pass anything that needed to be brought to pass. He knew and believed in the deepest depths of his soul that "nothing was too hard for the Lord" and that prayer could do anything that God could do.

Oftentimes Mr. Moody would write me when he was about to undertake some new work, saying: "I am beginning work in such and such a place on such and such a day; I wish you would get the students together for a day of fasting and prayer." And often I have taken those letters and read them to the students in the lecture room and said: "Mr. Moody wants us to have a day of fasting and prayer, first for God's blessing on our own souls and work, and then for God's blessing on him and his work." Often we were gathered in the lecture room far into the night—sometimes till one, two, three, four or even five o'clock in the morning, crying to God, just because Mr. Moody urged us to wait upon God until we received His blessing. How many men and women I have known whose lives and characters have been transformed by those nights of prayer and who have wrought mighty things in many lands because of those nights of prayer!

One day Mr. Moody drove up to my house at Northfield and said: "Torrey, I want you to take a ride with me." I got into the carriage, and we drove out toward Lover's Lane, talking about some great and unexpected difficulties that had arisen in regard to the work in Northfield and Chicago, and in connection with other work that was very dear to him. As we drove along, some black storm clouds lay ahead of us, and then suddenly, as we were talking, it began to rain. He drove the horse into a shed near the entrance to Lover's Lane to shelter the horse, and then laid the reins upon the dashboard and said: "Torrey, pray;" and then, as best I could, I prayed, while he in his heart joined me in prayer. And when my voice was silent he began to pray. Oh, I wish you could have heard that prayer! I shall never forget it, so simple, so trustful, so definite and so direct and so mighty.

When the storm was over and we drove back to town, the obstacles had been surmounted, and the work of the schools, and other work that was threatened, went on as it had never gone on before, and it has gone on until this day. As we drove back, Mr. Moody said to me: "Torrey, we will let the other men do the talking and the criticizing, and we will stick to the work that God has given us to do, and let Him take care of the difficulties and answer the criticisms."

On one occasion Mr. Moody said to me in Chicago: "I have just found, to my surprise, that we are twenty thousand dollars behind in our finances for the work here and in Northfield, and we must have that twenty thousand dollars, and I am going to get it by prayer." He did not tell a soul who had the ability to give a penny of the twenty thousand dollars' deficit, but looked right to God and said: "I need twenty thousand dollars for my work; send me that money in such a way that I will know it comes straight from Thee." And God heard that prayer. The money came in such a way that it was clear that it came from God in direct answer to prayer.

He Was a Deep Student of the Word

The third secret of Mr. Moody's power, or the third reason why God used D. L. Moody, was because he was a deep and practical student of the Word of God. Nowadays it is often said of D. L. Moody that he was not a student. I wish to say that he was a student; most emphatically he was a student. He was not a student of psychology; he was not a student of anthropology—I am very sure he would not have known what that word meant; he was not a student of biology; he was not a student of philosophy; he was not even a student of theology, in the technical sense of the term; but he was a student, a profound and practical student of the one Book that is more worth studying than all other books in the world put together; he was a student of the Bible.

Every day of his life, I have reason for believing, he arose very early in the morning to study the Word of God, way down to the close of his life. Mr. Moody used to rise about four o'clock in the morning to study the Bible. He would say to me: "If I am going to get in any study, I have got to get up before the other folks get up;" and he would shut himself up in a remote room in his house, alone with his God and his Bible.

I shall never forget the first night I spent in his home. He had invited me to take the superintendency of the Bible Institute. and I had already begun my work; I was on my way to some city in the East to preside at the International Christian Workers' Convention. He wrote me saying: "Just as soon as the Convention is over, come up to Northfield." He learned when I was likely to arrive and drove over to South Vernon to meet me.

That night he had all the teachers from the Mount Hermon School and from the Northfield Seminary come together at the house to meet me, and to talk over the problems of the two schools. We talked together far on into the night, and then, after the principals and teachers of the schools had gone home, Mr. Moody and I talked together about the problems a while longer. It was very late when I got to bed that night, but very early the next morning, about five o'clock, I heard a gentle tap on my door. Then I heard Mr. Moody's voice whispering: "Torrey, are you up?" I happened to be; I do not always get up at that early hour but I happened to be up that particular morning. He said: "I want you to go somewhere with me," and I went down with him. Then I found out that he had already been up an hour or two in his room studying the Word of God.

It was largely because of his thorough knowledge of the Bible, and his practical knowledge of the Bible, that Mr. Moody drew such immense crowds. On "Chicago Day," in October, 1893, none of the theaters of Chicago dared to open because it was expected that everybody in Chicago would go on that day to the World's Fair; and, in point of fact, something like four hundred thousand people did pass through the gates of the Fair that day. Everybody in Chicago was expected to be at that end of the city on that day. But Mr. Moody said to me: "Torrey, engage the Central Music Hall and announce meetings from nine o'clock in the morning till six o'clock at night."

"Why," I replied, "Mr. Moody, nobody will be at this end of Chicago on that day; not even the theaters dare to open; everybody is going down to Jackson Park to the Fair; we cannot get anybody out on this day."

Mr. Moody replied: "You do as you are told;" and I did as I was told and engaged the Central Music Hall for continuous meetings from nine o'clock in the morning till six o'clock at night. But I did it with a heavy heart; I thought there would be poor audiences. I was on the program at noon that day. Being very busy in my office about the details of the campaign, I did not reach the Central Music Hall till almost noon. I thought I would have no trouble in getting in. But when I got almost to the Hall I found to my amazement that not only was it packed but the vestibule was packed and the steps were packed, and there was no getting anywhere near the door; and if I had not gone round and climbed in a back window they would have lost their speaker for that hour. But that would not have been of much importance, for the crowds had not gathered to hear me; it was the magic of Mr. Moody's name that had drawn them. And why did they long to hear Mr. Moody? Because they knew that while he was not versed in many of the philosophies and fads and fancies of the day, he did know the one Book that this old world most longs to know —the Bible.

During all the months of the World's Fair in Chicago, no one could draw such crowds as Mr. Moody. Judging by the papers, one would have thought that the great religious event in Chicago at that time was the World's Congress of Religions. One very gifted man of letters in the East was invited to speak at this Congress. He saw in this invitation the opportunity of his life and prepared his paper, the exact title of which I do not now recall, but it was something along the line of "New Light on the Old Doctrines." He prepared the paper with great care, and then sent it around to his most trusted and gifted friends for criticisms. These men sent it back to him with such recommendations as they had to suggest. Then he rewrote the paper, incorporating as many of the suggestions and criticisms as seemed wise. Then he sent it around for further criticisms. Then he wrote the paper a third time, and had it, as he trusted, perfect. He went on to Chicago to meet this coveted opportunity of speaking at the World's Congress of Religions.

It was at eleven o'clock on a Saturday morning (if I remember correctly) that he was to speak. He stood outside the door of the platform waiting for the great moment to arrive, and as the clock struck eleven he walked on to the platform to face a magnificent audience of eleven women and two men! But there was not a building anywhere in Chicago that would accommodate the very same day the crowds that would flock to hear Mr. Moody at any hour of the day or night.

He Was a Humble Man

The fourth reason why God continuously, through so many years, used D.L. Moody was because he was a humble man. I think D. L. Moody was the humblest man I ever knew in all my life. He loved to quote the words of another; "Faith gets the most; love works the most; but humility keeps the most." He himself had the humility that keeps everything it gets. As I have already said, he was the most humble man I ever knew, i.e., the most humble man when we bear in mind the great things that he did, and the praise that was lavished upon him. Oh, how he loved to put himself in the background and put other men in the foreground. How often he would stand on a platform with some of us little fellows seated behind him and as he spoke he would say: "There are better men coming after me." As he said it, he would point back over his shoulder with his thumb to the "little fellows." I do not know how he could believe it, but he really did believe that the others that were coming after him were really better than he was. He made no pretense to a humility he did not possess. In his heart of hearts he constantly underestimated himself, and overestimated others. He really believed that God would use other men in a larger measure than he had been used. Mr. Moody loved to keep himself in the background. At his conventions at Northfield, or anywhere else, he would push the other men to the front and, if he could, have them do all the preaching—McGregor, Campbell Morgan, Andrew Murray, and the rest of them. The only way we could get him to take any part in the program was to get up in the convention and move that we hear D. L. Moody at the next meeting. He continually put himself out of sight.

God used D. L. Moody, I think, beyond any man of his day; but it made no difference how much God used him, he never was puffed up.

One day, speaking to me of a great New York preacher, now dead, Mr. Moody said: "He once did a very foolish thing, the most foolish thing that I ever knew a man, ordinarily so wise as he was, to do. He came up to me at the close of a little talk I had given and said: 'Young man, you have made a great address tonight.'" Then Mr. Moody continued: "How foolish of him to have said that! It almost turned my head." But, thank God, it did not turn his head, and even when pretty much all the ministers in England, Scotland, and Ireland, and many of the English bishops were ready to follow D. L. Moody wherever he led, even then it never turned his head one bit. He would get down on his face before God, knowing he was human, and ask God to empty him of all self-sufficiency. And God did.

His Freedom From Love of Money

The fifth secret of D. L. Moody's continual power and usefulness was his entire freedom from the love of money. Mr. Moody might have been a wealthy man, but money had no charms for him. He loved to gather money for God's work; he refused to accumulate money for himself. He told me during the World's Fair that if he had taken, for himself, the royalties on the hymnbooks which he had published, they would have amounted, at that time, to a million dollars. But Mr. Moody refused to touch the money. He had a perfect right to take it, for he was responsible for the publication of the books and it was his money that went into the publication of the first of them.

Mr. Sankey had some hymns that he had taken with him to England and he wished to have them published. He went to a publisher (I think Morgan & Scott) and they declined to publish them, because, as they said, Philip Phillips had recently been over and published a hymnbook, and it had not done well. However, Mr. Moody had a little money, and he said that he would put it into the publication of these hymns in cheap form; and he did. The hymns had a most remarkable and unexpected sale; they were then published in book form and large profits accrued. The financial results were offered to Mr. Moody, but he refused to touch them. "But," it was urged on him, "the money belongs to you;" but he would not touch it.

In a certain city to which Mr. Moody went in the latter years of his life, and where I went with him, it was publicly announced that Mr. Moody would accept no money whatever for his services. Now, in point of fact, Mr. Moody was dependent, in a measure, upon what was given him at various services; but when this announcement was made, Mr. Moody said nothing, and left that city without a penny's compensation for the hard work he did there; and, I think, he paid his own hotel bill. And yet a minister in that very city came out with an article in a paper, which I read, in which he told a fairy tale of the financial demands that Mr. Moody made upon them, which story I knew personally to be absolutely untrue. Millions of dollars passed into Mr. Moody hands, but they passed through; they did not stick to his fingers.

His Consuming Passion for the Salvation of the Lost

The sixth reason why God used D. L. Moody was because of his consuming passion for the salvation of the lost. Mr. Moody made the resolution, shortly after he himself was saved, that he would never let twenty-four hours pass over his head without speaking to at least one person about his soul. His was a very busy life, and sometimes he would forget his resolution until the last hour, and sometimes he would get out of bed, dress, go out and talk to someone about his soul in order that he might not let one day pass without having definitely told at least one of his fellow mortals about his need and the Savior who could meet it.

One night Mr. Moody was going home from his place of business. It was very late, and it suddenly occurred to him that he had not spoken to one single person that day about accepting Christ. He said to himself: "Here's a day lost. I have not spoken to anyone today, and I shall not see anybody at this late hour." But as he walked up the street he saw a man standing under a lamppost. The man was a perfect stranger to him, though it turned out afterwards the man knew who Mr. Moody was. He stepped up to this stranger and said: "Are you a Christian?"

The man replied: "That is none of your business, whether I am a Christian or not. If you were not a sort of a preacher I would knock you into the gutter for your impertinence."

Mr. Moody said a few earnest words and passed on. The next day that man called upon one of Mr. Moody's prominent business friends and said to him: "That man Moody of yours over on the North Side is doing more harm than he is good. He has got zeal without knowledge. He stepped up to me last night, a perfect stranger, and insulted me. He asked me if I were a Christian, and I told him it was none of his business and if he were not a sort of a preacher I would knock him into the gutter for his impertinence. He is doing more harm than he is good. He has got zeal without knowledge."

Mr. Moody's friend sent for him and said: "Moody, you are doing more harm than you are good; you've got zeal without knowledge: you insulted a friend of mine on the street last night. You went up to him, a perfect stranger, and asked him if he were a Christian, and he tells me if you had not been a sort of a preacher he would have knocked you into the gutter for your impertinence. You are doing more harm than you are good; you have got zeal without knowledge.

Mr. Moody went out of that man's office somewhat crestfallen. He wondered if he were not doing more harm than he was good, if he really had zeal without knowledge.

Weeks passed by. One night Mr. Moody was in bed when he heard a tremendous pounding at his front door. He jumped out of bed and rushed to the door. He thought the house was on fire. He thought the man would break down the door. He opened the door and there stood this man. He said: "Mr. Moody, I have not had a good night's sleep since that night you spoke to me under the lamppost, and I have come around at this unearthly hour of the night for you to tell me what I have to do to be saved." Mr. Moody took him in and told him what to do to be saved. Then he accepted Christ, and when the Civil War broke out, he went to the front and laid down his life fighting for his country.

Another night, Mr. Moody got home and had gone to bed before it occurred to him that he had not spoken to a soul that day about accepting Christ. "Well," he said to himself, "it is no good getting up now; there will be nobody on the street at this hour of the night." But he got up, dressed and went to the front door. It was pouring rain. "Oh," he said, "there will be no one out in this pouring rain.
Just then he heard the patter of a man's feet as he came down the street, holding an umbrella over his head. Then Mr. Moody darted out and rushed up to the man and said: "May I share the shelter of your umbrella?" "Certainly," the man replied. Then Mr. Moody said: "Have you any shelter in the time of storm?" and preached Jesus to him. Oh, men and women, if we were as full of zeal for the salvation of souls as that, how

long would it be before the whole country would be shaken by the power of a mighty, God-sent meeting?

One day in Chicago—the day after the elder Carter Harrison was shot, when his body was lying in state in the City Hall—Mr. Moody and I were riding up Randolph Street together in a streetcar right alongside of the City Hall. The car could scarcely get through because of the enormous crowds waiting to get in and view the body of Mayor Harrison. As the car tried to push its way through the crowd, Mr. Moody turned to me and said: "Torrey, what does this mean?"

"Why," I said, "Carter Harrison's body lies there in the City Hall, and these crowds are waiting to see it."

Then he said: "This will never do, to let these crowds get away from us without preaching to them; we must talk to them. You go and hire Hooley's Opera House (which was just opposite the City Hall) for the whole day." I did so. The meetings began at nine o'clock in the morning, and we had one continuous service from that hour until six in the evening, to reach those crowds.

Mr. Moody was a man on fire for God. Not only was he always "on the job" himself, but he was always getting others to work as well. He once invited me down to Northfield to spend a month there with the schools, speaking first to one school and then crossing the river to the other. I was obliged to use the ferry a great deal; it was before the present bridge was built at that point.

One day he said to me: "Torrey, did you know that that ferryman that ferries you across every day was unconverted?" He did not tell me to speak to him, but I knew what he meant.

When some days later it was told him that the ferryman was saved, he was exceedingly happy.

Once, when walking down a certain street in Chicago, Mr. Moody stepped up to a man, a perfect stranger to him, and said: "Sir, are you a Christian?" "You mind your own business," was the reply. Mr. Moody replied: "This is my business." The man said, "Well, then, you must be Moody." Out in Chicago they used to call him in those early days "Crazy Moody," because day and night he was speaking to everybody he got a chance to speak to about being saved. One time he was going to Milwaukee, and in the seat that he had chosen sat a traveling man. Mr. Moody sat down beside him and immediately began to talk with him. "Where are you going?" Mr. Moody asked. When told the name of the town he said: "We will soon be there; we'll have to get down to business at once. Are you saved?" The man said that he was not, and Mr. Moody took out his Bible and there on the train showed him the way of salvation. Then he said: "Now, you must take Christ." The man did; he was converted right there on the train.

Most of you have heard, I presume, the story President Wilson used to tell about D. L. Moody. Ex-President Wilson said that he once went into a barber shop and took a chair next to the one in which D. L. Moody was sitting, though he did not know that Mr. Moody was there. He had not been in the chair very long before, as ex-President Wilson phrased it, he "knew there was a personality in the other chair," and he began to listen to the conversation going on; he heard Mr. Moody tell the barber about the Way of Life, and President Wilson said, "I have never forgotten that scene to this day." When Mr. Moody was gone, he asked the barber who he was; when he was told that it was D. L. Moody, President Wilson said: "It made an impression upon me I have not yet forgotten."

On one occasion in Chicago Mr. Moody saw a little girl standing on the street with a pail in her hand. He went up to her and invited her to his Sunday school, telling her what a pleasant place it was. She promised to go the following Sunday, but she did not do so. Mr. Moody watched for her for weeks, and then one day he saw her on the street again, at some distance from him. He started toward her, but she saw him, too, and started to run away. Mr. Moody followed her. Down she went one street, Mr. Moody after her; up she went another street, Mr. Moody after her, through an alley, Mr. Moody still following; out on another street, Mr. Moody after her; then she dashed into a saloon and Mr. Moody dashed after her. She ran out the back door and up a flight of stairs, Mr. Moody still following; she dashed into a room, Mr. Moody following; she threw herself under the bed and Mr. Moody reached under the bed and pulled her out by the foot, and led her to Christ. He found that her mother was a widow who had once seen better circumstances, but had gone down until now she was living over this saloon. She had several children. Mr. Moody led the mother and all the family to Christ. Several of the children were prominent members of the Moody Church until they moved away, and afterwards became prominent in churches elsewhere. This particular child, whom he pulled from underneath the bed, was, when I was the pastor of the Moody Church, the wife of one of the most prominent officers in the church.

Only two or three years ago, as I came out of a ticket office in Memphis, Tennessee, a fine looking young man followed me. He said: “Are you not Dr. Torrey?” I said, “Yes.” He said: “I am so and so.” He was the son of this woman. He was then a traveling man, and an officer in the church where he lived. When Mr. Moody pulled that little child out from under the bed by the foot, he was pulling a whole family into the Kingdom of God, and eternity alone will reveal how many succeeding generations he was pulling into the Kingdom of God.

D.L. Moody's consuming passion for souls was not for the souls of those who would be helpful to him in building up his work here or elsewhere; his love for souls knew no class limitations. He was no respecter of persons; it might be an earl or a duke or it might be an ignorant colored boy on the street; it was all the same to him; there was a soul to save and he did what lay in his power to save that soul.

A friend once told me that the first time he ever heard of Mr. Moody was when Mr. Reynolds of Peoria told him that he once found Mr. Moody sitting in one of the squatters' shanties that used to be in that part of the city toward the lake, which was then called, "The Sands," with a black boy on his knee, a tallow candle in one hand and a Bible in the other, and Mr. Moody was spelling out the words (for at that time the boy could not read very well) of certain verses of Scripture, in an attempt to lead that ignorant black boy to Christ.
(From http://www.whatsaiththescripture.com/Voice/Why.God.Used.D.L.Moody.html)

D.L. Moody Quotes

"We are told to let our light shine, and if it does, we won't need to tell anybody it does. Lighthouses don't fire cannons to call attention to their shining—they just shine."

"There are many of us that are willing to do great things for the Lord, but few of us are willing to do little things

---

This is the key to having God open doors of opportunity. If you want to preach to large crowds, prove yourself at one-to-one. Wash the saints' feet. Be a servant. Love the lost. — *Ray Comfort*

"Either these [unsaved] people are to be evangelized, or the leaven of communism and infidelity will assume such enormous proportions that it will break you in a reign of terror such as this country has never known."

"Some day you will read in the papers that D.L. Moody of East Northfield, is dead. Don't you believe a word of it! At that moment I shall be more alive than I am now; I shall have gone up higher, that is all, out of this old clay tenement into a house that is immortal—a body that death cannot touch, that sin cannot taint; a body fashioned like unto His glorious body."

"I was born of the flesh in 1837. I was born of the Spirit in 1856. That which is born of the flesh may die. That which is born of the Spirit will live forever."

"Henry Varley, a very intimate friend of Mr. Moody in the earlier days of his work, loved to tell how he once said to him: "*It remains to be seen what God will do with a man who gives himself up wholly unto Him.*" When Mr. Henry Varley said that Mr. Moody said to himself: "*Well I will be that man.*"

"There's no better book with which to defend the Bible than the Bible itself."

"There are many of us that are willing to do great things for the Lord, but few of us are willing to do little things."

"A rule I have had for years is: to treat the Lord Jesus Christ as a personal friend. His is not a creed, a mere doctrine, but it is He himself we have."

"Where one man reads the Bible, a hundred read you and me."

"We talk about Heaven being so far away. It is within speaking distance to those who belong there. Heaven is a prepared place for a prepared people."

"I know the Bible is inspired because it inspires me"

"God never made a promise that was too good to be true."

"Death may be the King of terrors, but Jesus is the King of kings!"

"A man ought to live so that everybody knows he is a Christian—and most of all, his family ought to know."
"Character is what a man is in the dark."

It is also what we do in the darkness of the imagination. The essence of a godly character is the fear of the Lord.
— Ray Comfort

"God doesn't seek for golden vessels, and does not ask for silver ones, but He must have clean ones."

"The Bible will keep you from sin, or sin will keep you from the Bible."

"It is a masterpiece of the devil to make us believe that children cannot understand religion. Would Christ have made a child the standard of faith if He had known that it was not capable of understanding His words?"
Either these [unsaved] people are to be evangelized, or the leaven of communism and infidelity will assume such enormous proportions that it will break you in a reign of terror such as this country has never known."

"Church attendance is as vital to a disciple as a transfusion of rich, healthy blood to a sick man."

"Preparation for old age should begin not later than one's teens. A life which is empty of purpose until sixty-five will not suddenly become filled on retirement."

"Where I was born and where and how I have lived is unimportant. It is what I have done with where I have been that should be of interest."

"Never think that Jesus commanded a trifle, nor dare to trifle with anything He has commanded."

"Give me a man who says this one thing I do, and not those fifty things I dabble in."

"No man can resolve himself into Heaven."

The Gospel Awakening

Is it well to number converts? Elijah got into trouble by trying to number Israel. It is best to let, the Lord keep the record. It makes me creep all over to hear a man tell how many he has converted. It is best not to triumph.

This is a wonderful quote. I am always amazed at how many evangelists and preachers seem to have access to the Book of Life. Such numbering reveals a lack of understanding to the nature of true and false conversion. Make sure you freely listen to "True and False Conversion" on www.livingwaters.com — Ray Comfort

Is there any danger starting men into the work too young? There is a good deal of danger, in not starting them to work soon enough. Pitt was in Parliament at 21 and was Prime Minister at 32. Napoleon was young and Alexander had conquered the world at 32. There is danger sometimes in flattering young men who are at work for Christ. Spiritual pride is a very great injury. The young men in Chicago could be used to good advantage. They could go out and talk seven nights in the week while the minister preached but one. And these young men could reach men who could not be approached by anybody else.

Do you believe in open-air preaching? Yes; but not every man who can talk is fit to preach to open-air audiences. It needs a peculiar talent to go there. He wants to have tact, to know how to get along with these people. These meetings were attended by shrewd men, infidels and skeptics, and they were always ready to trip up the preacher. The man preaching to open-air audiences should not allow himself to be drawn into controversy.

The Qualifications for Soul-Winning

God had no children too weak, but a great many too strong to make use of. God stands in no need of our strength or wisdom, but of our ignorance, of our weakness; let us but give these to Him, and He can make use of us in winning souls. Now we all want to shine; the mother wishes it for her boy, when she sends him to school, the father for his lad, when he goes off to college; and here God tells us who are to shine—not statesmen, or warriors, or such like, that shine but for a season, but such as will shine forever and ever; those, namely, who win souls to Christ; the little boy even who persuades one to come to Christ.

Paul counts up five things (1 Corinthians 1:27-9) that God makes use of: the weak things, the foolish things, the base things, the despised things, and the things which are not, and for this purpose—that no flesh might glory in His sight—all five being just such as we should despise. He can and will use us, just when we are willing to be humble for Christ's sake, and so for six thousand years God has been teaching men; so with an ass's jawbone Samson slew his thousands (Judges 15:15), so at the blowing of rams' horns the walls of Jericho fell (Joshua 6:20). Let God work in His own way, and with His own instruments; let us all rejoice that He should, and let us too get into the position in which God can use us. A man who has found out what his true work is—winning souls to Christ—and does it, such is the happiest man. Not the richest are these, least of all those who have just got converted for themselves, and into the Church, lost what pleasure the world could give and found none other. Job's captivity turned away when he began praying for his friends; and so will all who thus work for others shine not in heaven alone and hereafter, but here as well, and now.

I am often saddened that some pastors don't cultivate and encourage those who care about the lost. Those who do so are the life of their church. — *Ray Comfort*

But you say "I haven't got the ability." Well, God doesn't call you to do Dr. Bonar's work, or Dr. Duff's work, else He had given you their ability, their talent. The word is, "To every man his work." I have a work to do, laid out for me in the secret counsels of eternity; no other can do it. If I neglect it, it is not true that some other will do it; it will remain undone. And if, for the work laid upon us, we feel we have not the ability or talent necessary, then we have a throne of grace; and God never sends, unless that He is willing to give the strength and wisdom. The instruments He often uses may seem all unlikely, yet when did they fail? When once? And why not? Because He had fitted them out as well. He sent Moses to Egypt to deliver His people—not an eloquent, but a stuttering man. He refuses a while, at last he went; and no man once sent by God ever did break down.

We must be ready to *do little things* for God; many are willing to do the great things. I dare say hundreds would have been ready to occupy this pulpit today. How many of them would be as willing to teach a dirty class in the ragged school?

> *Many years ago, in between my times of teaching at a large Bible school in Dallas, TX, I would make my way to the kitchen and help the students wash and dry the dishes. I was amazed that other students heard rumors that I was helping do dishes and would show up just to stare. This shouldn't have been an unusual occurrence. All of us should be servants.* — *Ray Comfort*

I remember, one afternoon I was preaching, observing a young lady from the house I was staying at, in the audience. I had heard she taught in the Sabbath school, which I knew was at the same hour; and so I asked her, after service, how she came to be there?

"Oh," said she, "my class is but five little boys, and I thought it did not matter for them." And yet among these there might have been, who knows, a Luther or a Knox, the beginning of a stream of blessing, that would have gone on widening and ever widening; and besides, one soul is worth all the kingdoms of the earth.

Another thing we want is, to be *of good courage.* Three or four times this comes out in the first chapter of Joshua; and I have observed that God never uses a man that is always looking on the dark side of things: what we do for Him let us do cheerfully, not because it is our duty—not that we should sweep away the word—but because it is our privilege. What would my wife or children say if I spoke of loving them because it was my *duty* to do so? And my mother, if I go to see her once a year, and were to say, "Mother, I am come all this way to discharge what I feel to be my duty in visiting you;" might she not rightly reply, "My son, if this is all that has brought you, you might have spared coming at all!" and go on in brokenhearted sorrow to the grave?

A London minister, a friend of mine, lately pointed out a family of seven, all of whom he was just receiving into the Church. Their story was this: going to church, he had to pass by a window, looking up at which one day, he saw a baby looking out; he smiled; the baby smiled again. Next time he passes he looks up again, smiles, and the baby smiles back. A third time going by, he looks up, and seeing the baby, throws it a kiss, which the baby returns to him. Time after time he has to pass the window, and now cannot refrain from looking up each time, and each time there are more faces to receive his smiling greeting, till by-and-by he sees the whole family grouped at the window—father, mother, and all.

The father conjectures the happy, smiling stranger must be a minister, and so, next Sunday morning, after they have received at the window the usual greeting, two of the children, ready dressed, are sent out to follow him. They enter his church, hear him preach, and carry back to their parents the report that they never heard such preaching; and what preaching could equal that of one who had so smiled on them? Soon the rest come to the church, too, and are brought in—all by a smile.

Let us not go about, hanging our heads like a bulrush; if Christ gives joy, let us live it! The whole world is in all matters for the very best thing—you always want to get the best possible thing for your money. Let us show, then, that our religion is the very best thing. Men with long, gloomy faces are never wise in the winning of souls.
(*The Qualifications for Soul-Winning:* A Sermon delivered by Dwight L. Moody in Dr. Bonar's church, Edinburgh, Scotland, 7th December, 1873.)

Repentance

There is a good deal of trouble among people about what repentance really is. If you ask people what it is, they will tell you "It is feeling sorry." If you ask a man if he repents, he will tell you, "Oh, yes; I generally feel sorry for my sins." That is not repentance. It is something more than feeling sorry. Repentance is turning right about and forsaking sin.

Repentance can't save us. Muslims repent. That's the basis of their hope of salvation. The same with many unsaved Catholics. They trust that their repentance is enough. But no good judge would let a devious criminal go simply because he said that he had turned from his crimes. The only thing that can save us is God's free grace; and we receive that through faith in Jesus. Salvation is by grace through faith (see Ephesians 2:8-9). The way to partake of the grace of God, is through repentance ("repentance unto life"). But it's very clear from Scripture that repentance doesn't save us. If it did, we wouldn't need a Savior. We preach free grace, through faith. Paul said of his own ministry that he spent his time "testifying both to the Jews, and also to the Greeks, repentance toward God, and faith toward our Lord Jesus Christ" *(Acts 20:21, italics added). However, if someone says that they are saved, and they continue to willfully sin "after the flesh," they shouldn't have assurance of salvation. They are deceived. 1 John 3:7-9 makes that clear: "Little children, let no man deceive you: he that doeth righteousness is righteous, even as he is righteous. He that committeth sin is of the devil; for the devil sinneth from the beginning. For this purpose the Son of God was manifested, that he might destroy the works of the devil. Whosoever is born of God doth not commit sin; for his seed remaineth in him: and he cannot sin, because he is born of God." Anyone who has tasted of the grace of God continually turns from sin. His repentance is perpetual. If he doesn't turn from sin, he is a hypocrite, deceives himself, and will be one of those mentioned in Matthew 7:21-24 who cry "Lord, Lord." Our churches are filled with these false converts who think that there is a category for the "sinning" Christian. It's not in Scripture. Such a "category" comes from a lack of understanding of the reality of the spurious convert. However, if someone is a good soil hearer (genuine convert), he will put his hand to the plow and not look back, because he is "fit" for the Kingdom (see Luke 9:62).* ⁓ *Ray Comfort*

You will find men sorry for their misdeeds. Cain, no doubt, was sorry, but that was not true repentance. There is no cry recorded in the Scriptures as coming from him, "O my God, O my God, forgive me." There was no repentance in his only feeling sorry. Look at Judas. There is no sign that he turned to God—no sign that he came to Christ asking forgiveness. Yet, probably, he felt sorry. He was, very likely, filled with remorse and despair; but he didn't repent. Repentance is turning to

Him who loved us and gave himself for us.

Now, we read in Scripture that God deals with us as a father deals with a son. Fathers and mothers, you who have children, let me ask by way of illustration, suppose you go home, and you find that while you have been here your boy has gone to your private drawer and stolen $5 of your money. You go to him and say: "John, did you take that money?" "Yes, father, I took that money," he replies. When you hear him saying this without any apparent regret you won't forgive him. You want to get at his conscience; you know it would do him an injury to forgive him unless he confesses his wrong.

Suppose he won't do it. "Yes," he says, "I stole your money, but I don't think I've done wrong." The mother cannot, the father cannot forgive him, unless he sees he has done wrong and wants forgiveness.

That's the trouble with the sinners in Chicago. They've turned against God, broken His commandments, trampled His Law under their feet, and their sins hang upon them; until they show signs of repentance their sin will remain. But the moment they see their iniquity and come to God, forgiveness will be given them and their iniquity will be taken out of their way.

No unrepentant sinner will ever get into Heaven, unless they forsake their sin they cannot enter there. The Law of God is very plain on this point: "Except a man repent." That's the language of Scripture. And when this is so plainly set down, why is it that men fold their arms and say, "God will take me into Heaven anyway."

Make sure you listen to "Hell's Best Kept Secret" on www.livingwaters.com ⁓ *Ray Comfort*

Suppose a governor elected today comes into office in a few months, and he finds a great number of criminals in prison, and he goes and says: "I feel for those prisoners. They cannot stay in jail any longer." Suppose some murders have been committed, and he says: "I am tender hearted, I can't punish those men." and he opens the prison door and lets them all out. How long would that governor be in his position? These very men who are depending on the mercy of God would be the first to raise their voice against that governor. These men would say, "These murders must be punished or society will be imperiled; life will not be safe;" and yet they believe in the mercy of God whether they repent or not. My dear friends, don't go on under that delusion; it is a snare of the Devil. I tell you the Word of God is true, and it tells us "Except a man repent" there is not one ray of hope held out. May the Spirit of God open your eyes tonight and show you the truth—let it go into your hearts. Let the wicked forsake his way and the unrighteous his thoughts.

True repentance is the Holy Ghost showing sinners their sin.

It is impossible for a man to live without sinning, there are so many things, to draw away the heart and affections of men from God. I feel as if I ought to be repenting all the time. Is there a man here who can say honestly, "I have not got a sin that I need ask forgiveness for, I haven't one thing to repent of"? Some men seem to think that God has got ten different Laws for each of those Ten Commandments, but if you have been guilty of breaking one you are guilty of breaking all. If a man steals $5 and another steals $500, the one is as guilty of theft as the other. A man who has broken one Commandment of God is as guilty as he who has broken ten. If a man doesn't feel this, and come to Him repentant and turn his face from sin toward God there is not a ray of hope. Nowhere can you find one ray from Genesis to Revelation. Don't go out of this Tabernacle saying, "I have nothing to repent."

When a man turns to God he is made a new creature—a new man. His impulses all the time are guided by love. He loves his enemies and tries to repair all wrong he has done. This is a true sign of conversion. If this sign is not apparent his conversion has never got from his head to his heart. We must be born of the Spirit, hearts must be regenerated—born again. When a man repents, and turns to the God of Heaven, then the work is deep and thorough.

Suppose I was called to New York tonight and went down to the Illinois Central Depot to catch the ten o'clock train. I go on the train, and a friend should see me and say, "You are on the wrong train for New York. You are on the Burlington train." "Oh, no," I say, "you are wrong; I asked someone and he told me this was the right train."

"Why," this friend replies, "I've been in Chicago for twenty years, and know that you are on the wrong train," and the man talks, and at last convinces me, but I sit still, although I believe I am in the wrong train for New York, and I go on to Burlington. If you don't get off the wrong train and get on the right one you will not reach Heaven. If you have not repented, seize your baggage tonight and go to the other train.

If a man is not repentant his face is turned away from God, and the moment his face is turned toward God peace and joy follow.

When I was a little boy I remember I tried to catch my shadow. I don't know if you were ever so foolish: but I remember running after it and trying to get ahead of it. I could not see why the shadow always kept ahead of me. Once I happened to be racing with my face to the sun, and I looked over my head and saw my shadow coming back of me, and it kept behind me all the way. It is the same with the Sun of Righteousness, peace and joy will go with you while you go with your face toward Him, and these people who are getting at the back of the Sun are in darkness all the time. Turn to the light of God and the reflection will flash in your heart.

Look at that beautiful steamer Atlantic. There she is in the bay groping her way along a rocky coast. The captain don't know, as his vessel plows through that ocean, that in a few moments it will strike a rock and hundreds of those on board will perish in a watery grave. If he knew, in a minute he could strike a bell and the steamer would be turned from that rock and the people would be saved. The vessel has struck, but he knows now too late. You have time now. In five minutes, for all you and I know, you may be in eternity. God hangs a mist over our eyes as to our summons. So now God calls: Now everyone repent, and all your sins will be taken from you. I

have come in the name of the Master to ask you to turn to God now. May God help you to turn and live.
(Repentance: A sermon by D.L. Moody)

More on The Ten Commandments

I can imagine someone saying, "I won't be weighed by that Law. I don't believe in it." Now men may cavil as much as they like about other parts of the Bible, but I have never met an honest man that found fault with the Ten Commandments. Infidels may mock the Lawgiver and reject Him who has delivered us from the curse of the Law, but they can't help admitting that the commandments are right. Renan said that they are for all nations, and will remain the commandments of God during all the centuries.

If God created this world, He must make some laws to govern it. In order to make life safe we must have good laws; there is not a country the sun shines upon that does not possess laws. Now this is God's Law. It has come from on high, and infidels and skeptics have to admit that it is pure. Legislatures nearly all over the world adopt it as the foundation of their legal systems. "The Law of the LORD is perfect, converting the soul: the testimony of the Lord is sure, making wise the simple: the statutes of the Lord are right, rejoicing the heart: the commandment of the Lord is pure, enlightening the eyes (Psalm 19:7-8). Now the question for you and me is: Are we keeping these Commandments? Have we fulfilled all the requirements of the Law? If God made us, as we know He did, He had a right to make that Law; and if we don't use it aright it would have been better for us if we had never had it, for it will condemn us. We shall be found wanting. The Law is all right, but are we right.

I tell you that a man who does evil in these gospel days is far worse than that king. We live in a land of Bibles. You can get the New Testament for a nickel, and if you haven't got a nickel, you can get it for nothing. Many societies will be glad to give it to you free. We live in the full blaze of Calvary. Let us imagine that now, while I am preaching, down come some balances from the throne of God. They are fastened to the very throne itself. It is a throne of equity, of justice. You and I must be weighed. I venture to say this would be a very solemn audience. There would be no tiring There would be no indifference. No one would be thoughtless. Some people have their own balances. A great many are making balances to be weighed in. But after all we must be weighed in God's balances, the balances of the sanctuary. It is a favorite thing with infidels to set their own standard, to measure themselves by other people. But that will not do in the Day of Judgment. Now we will use God's Law as a balance weight. When men find fault with the lives of professing Christians, it is a tribute to the Law of God.

If it were known that God himself were going to speak once again to man, what eagerness and excitement there would be! For nearly nineteen hundred years He has been silent. No inspired message has been added to the Bible for nearly nineteen hundred years. How eagerly all men would listen if God should speak once more. Yet men forget that the Bible is God's own Word, and that it is as truly His message today as when it was delivered of old. The Law that was given at

Sinai has lost none of its solemnity. Time cannot wear out its authority or the fact of its authorship.

We call it the "Mosaic" Law, but it has been well said that the Commandments did not originate with Moses, nor were they done away with when the Mosaic Law was fulfilled in Christ, and many of its ceremonies and regulations abolished. We can find no trace of the existence of any lawmaking body in those early times, no parliament, or congress that built up a system of laws. It has come down to us complete and finished, and the only satisfactory account is that which tells us that God himself wrote the Commandments on tables of stone. The conviction deepens in me with the years that the old truths of the Bible must be stated and restated in the plainest possible language.

The people must be made to understand that the Ten Commandments are still binding, and that there is a penalty attached to their violation.

Now, my friend, are you ready to be weighed by this Law of God? A great many people say that if they keep the Commandments they do not need to be forgiven and saved through Christ. But have you kept them? I will admit that if you perfectly keep the Commandments, you do not need to be saved by Christ; but is there a man in the wide world who can truly say that he has done this? Young lady, can you say: "I am ready to be weighed by the Law? Can you, young man? Will you step into the scales and be weighed one by one by the Ten Commandments? Now face these Ten Commandments honestly and prayerfully. See if your life is right, and if you are treating God fairly. God's statutes are just, are they not? If they are right, let us see if we are right. Let us get alone with God and read His Law—read it carefully and prayerfully, and ask Him to forgive us our sin and what He would have us to do.

The First Commandment, Thou shalt have no other gods before Me. My friend, are you ready to be weighed against this Commandment? Have you fulfilled, or are you willing to fulfill all the requirements of this Law? Put it into one of the scales, and step into the other. Is your heart set upon God alone? Have you no other God? Do you love Him above father or mother, the wife of your bosom, your children, home or land, wealth or pleasure? If men were true to this commandment, obedience to the remaining nine would follow naturally. It is because they are unsound in this that they break the others. Philosophers are agreed that even the most primitive races of mankind reach out beyond the world of matter to a superior Being. It is as natural for man to feel after God as it is for the ivy to feel after a support. Hunger and thirst drive man to seek for food, and there is a hunger of the soul that needs satisfying, too. Man does not need to be commanded to worship, as there is not a race so high or so low in the scale of civilization but has some kind of god. What he needs is to be directed aright. This is what the first commandment is for. Before we can worship intelligently, we must know what or whom to worship. God does not leave us in ignorance. When Paul went to Athens, he found an altar dedicated to "The Unknown God," and he proceeded to tell of Him whom we worship. When God gave the commandments to Moses, He commenced with a declaration of His own character, and demanded exclusive recognition. "I am the LORD thy God, which have brought thee out of the land of Egypt, out of the house of bondage. Thou shalt have no other gods before me" (Exodus 20:2-3).

Someone asked an Arab: "How do you know that there is a God?" "How do I know whether a man or a camel passed my tent last night?" he replied. God's footprints in nature and in our own experience are the best evidence of His existence and character.

If He created us, He certainly ought to have our homage. Is it not right that He should have the first and only place in our affections?

There are very few who in their hearts do not believe in God, but what they will not do is give Him exclusive right of way. Missionaries tell us that they could easily get converts if they did not require them to be baptized, thus publicly renouncing their idols. Many a person in our land would become a Christian if the gate was not so strait. Christianity is too strict for them. They are not ready to promise full allegiance to God alone. Many a professing Christian is a stumbling block because his worship is divided. On Sunday he worships God; on weekdays God has little or no place in his thoughts.

You don't have to go to heathen lands today to find false gods. America is full of them. Whatever you make most of is your god. Whatever you love more than God is your idol. A man may make a god of himself, of a child, of a mother, of some precious gift that God has bestowed upon him. He may forget the Giver and let his heart go out in adoration toward the gift. Many make a god of pleasure; that is what their hearts are set on. Many make a god of pleasure; that is what their hearts are set on. With many it is the god of money. But all false gods are not as gross as these. There is the atheist. He says that he does not believe in God; he denies His existence, but he can't help setting up some other god in His place. Voltaire said, "If there were no God, it would be necessary to invent one." So the atheist speaks of the Great Unknown, the First Cause, the Infinite Mind, etc. Then there is the deist. He is a man who believes in one God who caused all things; but he doesn't believe in revelation. He only accepts such truths as can be discovered by reason. He doesn't believe in

Jesus Christ, or in the inspiration of the Bible. Then there is the pantheist, who says: "I believe that the whole universe is God. He is in the air, the water, the sun, the stars" the liar and the thief included.

When I was settled in Chicago, I used to be called out to attend many funerals. I would inquire what the man was in his belief. If I found out he was an atheist, or a deist, or a pantheist, when I went to the funeral and in the presence of his friends and said one word about that man's doctrine, they would feel insulted. Why is it that in a trying hour, when they have been talking all the time against God–why is it that in the darkness of affliction they call in believers in that God to administer consolation? Why doesn't the atheist preach no hereafter, no heaven, no God in the hour of affliction?

Some years ago I went into a man's house, and when I commenced to talk about religion he turned to his daughter and said: "You had better leave the room. I want to say a few words to Mr. Moody." When she had gone, he opened a perfect torrent of infidelity upon me. "Why did you send your daughter out of the room before you said this?" I asked. "Well," he replied, "I did not think it would do her any good to hear what I said." Is his rock as our Rock? Would he have sent his daughter out if he really believed what he said?

God will not accept a divided heart. He must be absolute monarch. There is not room in your heart for two thrones. Christ said: "No man can serve two masters: for either he will hate the one, and love the other; or else he will hold to the one, and despise the other. Ye cannot serve God and mammon" (Matthew 6: 24). Mark you, He did not say, "No man shall serve ... Ye shall not serve" but "No man can serve ... Ye cannot serve." That means more than a command; it means that you cannot mix the worship of the true God with the worship of another god any more than you can mix oil and water. It cannot be done. There is not room for any other throne in the heart if Christ is there. If worldliness should come in, godliness would go out.

When God said, "I will not hold him guiltless that takes my name in vain," He meant what He said, and I don't believe anyone can be a true child of God who takes the name of God in vain. What is the grace of God for, if it is not to give me control of my temper so that I shall not lose control and bring down the curse of God upon myself? When a man is born of God, God takes the "swear" out of him. Make the fountain good, and the stream will be good. Let the heart be right; then the language will be right; the whole life will be right. But no man can serve God and keep His Law until he is born of God. There we see the necessity of the new birth. To take God's name "in vain" means either (1) lightly, without thinking, flippantly; or (2) profanely, deceitfully.

I think it is shocking to use God's name with so little reverence as is common nowadays, even among professing Christians. We are told that the Jews held it so sacred that the covenant name of God was never mentioned amongst them except once a year by the high priest on the Day of Atonement, when he went into the holy of holies. What a contrast that is to the familiar use Christians make of it in public and private worship! We are apt to rush into God's presence and rush out again without any real sense of the reverence and awe that is due Him. We forget that we are on holy ground.

Do you know how often the word "reverend" occurs in the Bible? Only once. And what is it used in connection with? God's name. Psalm 111:9: "holy and reverend is his name." The habit of swearing is condemned by all sensible persons. It has been called "the most gratuitous of all sin," because no one gains by it; it is "not only sinful, but useless." An old writer said that when the accusing angel, who records men's words, flies up to heaven with an oath, he blushes as he hands it in.

When a man blasphemes, he shows an utter contempt for God. I was in the army during the war, and heard men cursing and swearing. Some godly woman would pass along the ranks looking for her wounded son, and not an oath would be heard. They would not swear before their mothers, or their wives, or their sisters; they had more respect for them than they had for God!

Men often ask: "How can I keep from swearing?" I will tell you. If God puts His love into your heart, you will have no desire to curse Him.

If you give up the Sabbath the church goes; if you give up the church the home goes; and if the home goes the nation goes. That is the direction in which we are traveling.

No man enjoys idleness for any length of time. When one goes on a vacation, one does not lie around doing nothing all that time. Hard work at tennis, hunting, and other pursuits fills the hours. A healthy mind must find something to do.

Young man, young woman, how do you treat your parents? Tell me that, and I will tell you how you are going to get on in life. When I hear a young man speaking contemptuously of his grey-haired father or mother, I say he has sunk very low indeed. When I see a young man as polite as any gentleman can be when he is out in society, but who snaps at his mother and speaks unkindly to his father, I would not give the snap of my finger for his religion. If there is any man or woman on earth that ought to be treated kindly and tenderly, it is that loving mother or that loving father. If they cannot have your regard through life, what reward are they to have for all their care and anxiety? Think how they loved you and provided for you in your early days.

When I was in England, I read of a man who professed to be a Christian, who was brought before the magistrate for not supporting his aged father. He had let him go to the workhouse. My friends, I'd rather be content with a crust of bread and a drink of water than let my father or mother go to the workhouse. The idea of a professing Christian doing such a thing! God have mercy on such a godless Christianity as that! It is a withered up thing, and the breath of heaven will drive it away. Don't profess to love God and do a thing like that.

Come, now, are you ready to be weighed? If you have been dishonoring your father and mother, step into the scales and see how quickly you will be found wanting. See how quickly you will strike the beam. I don't know any man who is much lighter than one who treats his parents with contempt. Do you disobey them just as much as you dare? Do you try to deceive them? Do you call them old-fashioned, and sneer at their advice? How do you treat that venerable father and praying mother? You may be a professing Christian, but I wouldn't give much for your religion unless it gets into your life and teaches you how to live. I wouldn't give a snap of my finger for a religion that doesn't begin at home and regulate your conduct toward your parents.

I used to say: "What is the use of taking up a Law like this in an audience where, probably, there isn't a man who ever thought of, or ever will commit, murder?" But as one gets on in years, he sees many a murder that is not outright killing. I need not kill a person to be a murderer. If I get so angry that

I wish a man dead, I am a murderer in God's sight. God looks at the heart and says he that hateth his brother is a murderer. Lust is the Devil's counterfeit of love. There is nothing more beautiful on earth than a pure love, and there is nothing so blighting as lust. J do not know of a quicker, shorter way down to hell than by adultery and the kindred sins condemned by this commandment. The Bible says that with the heart man believeth unto righteousness, but "whoredom and wine and new wine take away the heart" (Hosea 4: 11). Lust will drive all natural affection out of a man's heart. For the sake of some vile harlot he will trample on the feelings and entreaties of a sainted mother and beautiful wife and godly sister.

Young man, are you leading an impure life? Suppose God's scales should drop down before you, what would you do? Are you fit for the kingdom of heaven? May God show us what a fearful sin it is! The idea of making light of it! I do not know of any sin that will make a man run down to ruin more quickly. I am appalled when I think of what is going on in the world; of so many young men living impure lives, and talking about the virtue of women as if it didn't amount to anything. This sin is coming in upon us like a hood at the present day. In every city there is an army of prostitutes. Young men by hundreds are being utterly ruined by this accursed sin.

Young man, young woman, are you guilty, even in thought? Bear in mind what Christ said: "Ye have heard that it was said by them of old time, Thou shalt not commit adultery: but I say unto you, That whosoever looketh on a woman to lust after her has committed adultery with her already in his heart" (Matthew 5: 27-28).

How many would repent but that they are tied hand and foot, and some vile harlot whose feet are fastened in hell, clings to him and says: "If you give me up, I will expose you!" Can you step on the scales and take that harlot with you? If you are guilty of this awful sin, escape for your life. Hear God's voice while there is yet time. Confess your sin to Him. Ask Him to snap the fetters that bind you. Ask Him to give you victory over your passions. If your right eye offends, pluck it out. If your right hand offends, cut it off. Shake yourself like Samson, and say: "By the grace of God I will not go down to an adulterer's grave."

There is hope for you, adulterer. There is hope for you, adulteress. God will not turn you away if you truly repent. No matter how low down in vice and misery you may have sunk, you may be washed, you may be sanctified, you may be justified in the name of the Lord Jesus, and by the Spirit of our God. Remember what Christ said to that woman which was a sinner, "Thy sins are forgiven ... thy faith hath saved thee; go in peace" (Luke 7:47-50); and to that woman that was taken in adultery, "Go, and sin no more" (John 8:11).

The story is told that one of Queen Victoria's diamonds valued at six-hundred thousand dollars was stolen from a jeweler's window, to whom it had been given to set. A few months afterward a miserable man died a miserable death in a poor lodging house. In his pocket was found the diamond and a letter telling how he had not dared to sell it lest it lead to his discovery and imprisonment. It never brought him anything but anxiety and pain. Everything you steal is a curse to you in that way. The sin overreaches itself. A man who takes money that does not belong to him never gets any lasting comfort. He has no real pleasure, for he has a guilty conscience.

We have got nowadays so that we divide lies into white lies and black lies, society lies, business lies, etc. The Word of God knows no such letting down of the standard. A lie is a lie, no matter what are the circumstances under which it is uttered, or by whom.

The greatest dupe the devil has in the world is the hypocrite; but the next greatest is the covetous man, "for a man's life consisteth not in the abundance of the things which he possesseth" (Luke 12:15).

These Ten Commandments are not ten different Laws; they are one law. If I am being held up in the air by a chain with ten links and I break one of them, down I come, just as surely as if I break the whole ten. If I am forbidden to go out of an enclosure, it makes no difference at what point I break through the fence. "Whosoever shall keep the whole Law, and yet offend in one point, he is guilty of all" (James 2: 10). The golden chain of obedience is broken if one link is missing.

For fifteen hundred years man was under the Law, and no one was equal to it. Christ came and showed that the commandments went beyond the mere letter; and can anyone since say that he has been able to keep them in his own strength? As the plummet is held up, we see how much we are out of the perpendicular. As we measure ourselves by that holy standard, we find how much we are lacking. As a child said, when reproved by her mother and told that she ought to do right: "How can I do right when there is no right in me?" "All have sinned and come short of the glory of God" (Romans 3:23), "There is none righteous, no, not one" (Romans 3:10). The moral man is as guilty as the rest. His morality cannot save him. "Except ye repent, ye shall all likewise perish" (Luke 13:3, 5). "Except ye be converted, and become as little children, ye shall not enter into the kingdom of heaven" (Matthew 18:3). I have often heard good people say that our meetings were doing good, they were reaching the drunkards, and gamblers, and harlots; but they never realized that they needed the grace of God for themselves.

Nicodemus was probably one of the most moral men of his day. He was a teacher of the Law. Yet Christ said to him: "Except a man be born again, he cannot see the kingdom of God." It is much easier to reach thieves and drunkards and vagabonds than self-righteous Pharisees. You do not have to preach to those men for weeks and months to convince them that they are sinners. When a man learns that he has need of God and that he is a sinner, it is very easy to reach him. But the self-righteous Pharisee needs salvation as much as any drunkard that walks the streets.

I read of a minister traveling in the South who obtained permission to preach in the local jail. A son of his host went with him. On the way back the young man who was not a Christian, said to the minister: "I hope some of the convicts were impressed. Such a sermon as that ought to do them good."

"Did it do you good?" the minister asked. "Oh, you were preaching to the convicts," the young man answered. The minister shook his head and said: "I preached Christ, and you need Him as much as they." If you do not repent of your sins and ask Him for mercy, there is no hope for you.

I can imagine that you are saying to yourself, "If we are to be judged by these Laws, how are we going to be saved? Nearly every one of them has been broken by us—in spirit, if not in letter."

I almost hear you say: "I wonder if Mr. Moody is ready to be weighed. Would he like to put those tests to himself?" With all humility I reply that if God commanded me to step into the scales now, I am ready. "What!" you say, "haven't you broken the Law?"

Yes, I have. I was a sinner before God, the same as you; but forty years ago I pled guilty at His bar. I cried for mercy, and He forgave me. If I step into the scales, the Son of God has promised to be with me. I would not dare to step in without Him. If I did, how quickly the scales would fly up! Christ kept the Law. If He had ever broken it, He would have to die for himself; but because He was a Lamb without spot or blemish, His atoning death is efficacious for you and me. He had no sin of His own to atone for, and so God accepted His sacrifice. Christ is the end of the Law for righteousness to everyone that believeth. We are righteous in God's sight, because the righteousness of God which is by faith in Jesus Christ is unto all and upon all them that believe. If we had to live forever with our sins in the handwriting of God on the wall, it would be hell on Earth. But thank God for the gospel we preach! If we repent, our sins will all be blotted out. "You, being dead in your sins ... hath he quickened together with him, having forgiven you all trespasses; blotting out the handwriting of ordinances that was against us, which was contrary to us, and took it out of the way, nailing it to his Cross" (Colossians 2:13-14)."

(*More on The Ten Commandments* by D.L. Moody)

Christ All in All

"Whosoever will, let him take the water of life freely." That is the message for the sinner. I am sent to preach the gospel to all.

Supposing I saw a man tumble into a river, and I were to jump in and rescue him, I should be a savior to him—I should have saved him. But when I brought the man ashore, I should probably leave him, and do nothing further. But the Lord does more. He not only saves us, but He redeems us—that is, buys us back. He ransoms us from the power of sin, as if I should promise to watch over that rescued man for ever, and see that he did not again fall into the water. The Lord not only saves us from spiritual death, but He redeems us for ever that death can never touch us.

In Isaiah 49:24, we read: "Shall the prey be taken from the mighty, or the Lawful captive delivered? But thus saith the Lord, Even the captives of the mighty shall be taken away, and the prey of the terrible shall be delivered: for I will contend with him that contendeth with thee, and I will save thy children."

I will save him; I will deliver him. The children of Israel were saved from the cruel bondage of Egypt, they were led out of the land of Goshen; but still they were not fully delivered. The great host of the Egyptians was thundering behind them. It was not till they had passed safely through the Red Sea, which closing behind them, swallowed up the host of the enemy. It was not till then that they were free, that they were delivered. And similarly in our times of danger we shall find it to be true of Christ, "He delivered my soul;" and again in Job

33:24-28, "Then He is gracious unto him, and saith, Deliver him from going down to the pit: I have found a ransom. His flesh shall be fresher than a child's: he shall return to the days of his youth: he shall pray unto God, and He will be favorable unto him: and he shall see His face with joy: for He will render unto man His righteousness. He will deliver his soul from going into the pit, and his life shall see the light." Here we have the saving, the redeeming, the deliverance from the pit. Man is fallen into the deep pit, he is kept there a lawful captive by one who is mighty. If he is to be brought back from the darkness of the pit to see the light, then we must have a ransom. Here God comes forward, and says, "I have found a ransom." Christ is the ransom, and He will deliver us. Sound out the cry, "Christ is our deliverer." He is mighty to save, He is able to deliver.

"Bread of heaven, Feed me till I want no more." Yes, that is the true prayer of the bewildered sinner. God is able, and still more, He is willing, to lead us, and to feed us. "Thou gavest them bread from heaven for their hunger, and broughtest forth water for them out of the rock for their thirst" (Nehemiah 9:15).

May God help His own people to shine brightly, to flash out of darkness, that men may take knowledge of us that we have been with Jesus. But remember, the world hates the light. Christ was the light of the world, and the world sought to extinguish it at Calvary. Now He has left His people to shine. "Ye are the light of the world." He has left us here to shine. He means us to be "living epistles, known and read of all men." The world is certain to watch, and to read you and me. If we are inconsistent, then you may be sure the world will take occasion to stumble at us. The world finds plenty of difficulties on the way; let us see that we Christians do not add more stumbling blocks by our un-Christlike walk. God help us to keep our lights burning clear and brilliant!

Out West a friend of mine was walking along one of the streets one dark night, and saw approaching him a man with a lantern. As he came up close to him he noticed by the bright light that the man had no eyes. He went past, but the thought struck him, "Surely that man is blind." He turned round, and said, "My friend, are you not blind?" "Yes." "Then what have you got the lantern for?" "I carry the lantern that people may not stumble over me, of course," said the blind man. Let us take a lesson from that blind man, and hold up our light, burning with the clear radiance of heaven, that men may not stumble over us.

I remember during the American war I was in a prayer meeting. We were all very dark and gloomy. Things had been going against us for some time. At last an old man got up, and said, "What is the matter with us, that we are downhearted and sad? It is simply our lack of faith. Moses, Joshua, and David were men strong in faith. They believed, and therefore God honored them. Whence comes our want of faith? God is not dead. He is as powerful, as willing, to help today as ever He was. Why, then, are we not full of faith in Him? It is God dishonoring to forget that He still has power, although our armies are defeated, and all seems dark and gloomy.

I will tell you what happened to me some time ago when I was out West. I wanted to reach the summit of one of the Western mountains. I had been told that sunrise was very beautiful when seen from the summit. We got up to the halfway house one afternoon, where we were to rest till midnight, and then set out for the top. Soon a little party of us started with a good guide. Before a great while it began to rain, and then it became a regular storm of thunder and lightning. I thought there was little use in going on, and said to the guide, "Guess we'd better turn back; we won't see anything this morning, with all these clouds."

"Oh," said the guide, "I expect we'll soon get through these clouds, and get above them, and then we'll have a glorious view."

So we went on, whilst the thunders were rumbling right about our ears. But soon we began to get above the thunder-cloud; the air was quite clear, and when the sun rose we had a splendid view of his rays as they tinged the hilltops; and then, as the glorious sunshine began to break on where we stood, we could see the dark cloud far beneath our mountain height. That's what God's people want—to get into the clear air above the stormy clouds, and to CLIMB HIGHER away up to the mountain peak. There you'll catch the first rays from the Sun of Righteousness far above the clouds and mists.
Some of you may be in great darkness and gloom; but fear not, climb higher, get nearer to the Master, and soon you'll catch His bright rays on your own soul, and they will sprinkle back upon others.

What a wonderful thing to have a teacher sent from heaven. "If any man lack wisdom, let him ask of God, that giveth to all men liberally, and upbraideth not; and it shall be given him" (James 1:5).

"If any lack wisdom": I am afraid there are a great many of us who lack wisdom, and even the best of us at times will be in perplexity. There are moments in the life of us all when we seem in a fix; we just stand still, and say, "What shall I do? I don't know what is the best way." Oh, leave it with God, He will himself be our teacher! "Come unto me, all ye that labor and are heavy laden, and I will give you rest. Take my yoke upon you, and learn of me." Here is a wonderful teacher. He has had a school for many thousand years; He has had the best men in His school; but still there's room for another scholar there. His college is not too full yet, and the teacher is the One sent from heaven.

Anxious sinner, seek the good teacher, as Nicodemus did: "Master, we know thou art a teacher sent from God." If you seek Him thus He will direct you. He will keep you, and lead you into green pastures and by the still waters. I met a woman the other day who was full of infidel doubts and fancies. She could not believe. Reading for some time infidel works had thrown a dark and gloomy pall over her mind. It made me sad to see her in such a case. Some of you may be like her. I wish you would take Christ as your teacher, and then all darkness would flee away. Christ is able to teach us. See how He taught the disciples. He never wearied of their learning from Him. So He will teach us if we will only listen to Him.

If time permitted, I should like to take up the subject of Christ as our Justification, our Wisdom, our Righteousness, the Friend that sticketh closer than a brother; but it would take a whole eternity to tell what Christ is to His people and what He does for them. I remember when I was preaching on this subject in Scotland; after I was done, I said to a man that I was sorry I could not finish the subject for want of time. "Finish the subject?" said the Scotchman, "Why, that would require all eternity, and even then it would not be complete; it will be the occupation of heaven."

On one occasion ... a woman came forward and said, "Oh, Mr. Moody, it's all very well for you to talk like that, about a light heart. But you are a young man, and if you had a heavy burden like me you would talk differently. I could not talk in that way, my burden is too great."

I replied, "But it's not too great for Jesus." "Oh," she said, "I cannot cast it on Him." "Why not? surely it is not too great for Him. It is not that He is feeble. But it is because you will not leave it to Him. You're like many others. They will not leave it with Him. They go about hugging their burden, and yet crying out against it. What the Lord wants is, you to leave it with Him, to let Him carry it for you. Then you will have a light heart, sorrow will flee away, and there will be no more sighing. What is your burden, my friend, that you cannot leave with Christ?"

She replied, "I have a son who is a wanderer on the face of the earth. None but God knows where he is." "Cannot Christ find him, and bring him back?" "I suppose He can." "Then go and tell Jesus, and ask Him to forgive you for doubting His power and willingness; you have no right to mistrust Him." She went away much comforted, and I believe she ultimately had her wandering boy restored to her!
(*Christ All in All:* A sermon by D.L. Moody)

A Mother's Prayer Answered

A faithful father and mother in our country—whose eldest son had gone to Chicago to a situation—[and] a neighbor of theirs [that] was in the city on some business, met the young man reeling along the streets drunk. He thought, "How am I to tell his parents?"

When he returned to his village, he went and called out the father, and told him. It was a terrible blow to that father, but he said nothing to the mother till the little ones had all gone to rest, the servants had retired, and all was quiet in that little farm on the Western prairies. They drew up their chairs to the little drawing room table, and then he told her the sad news. "Our boy has been seen drunk on the streets of Chicago—drunk." Ah, that mother was sorely hurt; they did not sleep much that night, but spent the hours in fervent prayers for their boy.

About daybreak the mother felt an inward conviction that all would be well. She told the father she had cast it on the Lord, had left her son with Jesus, and she felt He would save him. One week from that time the young man left Chicago, took a journey of three hundred miles into the country, and when he reached his home, he walked in and said, "Mother, I've come home to ask you to pray for me." Ah, her prayer had reached heaven; she had cast her burden on Jesus, and He had borne it for her. He took the burden, presented her prayer sprinkled with the atoning blood, and got it answered. In two days that young man returned to Chicago rejoicing in the Savior.

What a wonderful thing it is to have Christ as our burden bearer! How easy, how light do our cares become when cast upon Him!

Does God Answer Prayer?

We cannot but notice that every man of God spoken of in the Bible was a man of *prayer.* You have therefore very good authority and encouragement for asking God to hear your prayers, and for praying on behalf of others, as we are daily requested to do. Many are surprised at these requests. But many mothers and fathers are rejoicing that they sent them in. The prayers offered up here have been answered, and their children have been saved.

Last night I was more confirmed in my views regarding the power of *prayer* than ever. "This is all excitement," some say; "it is got up by earnest appeals that work on the feelings of people, and move their impulses, making them uneasy and anxious."

Now, for example, there was nothing said last night to speak of, and I never was more disgusted with myself than I was on Sunday night. It seemed as if I could not preach the gospel, as if my tongue would not speak. But still the number of inquirers was extraordinary. Last night, when there was no speaking at all, and when I just came in and asked that any inquirers might follow me into the moderator's room, taking a few with me, and expecting to come in and ask out a few more when I had seen these, the number was so great that came out without solicitation that I did not need to return. I saw over a hundred inquirers last night, and there were from fifty to seventy that I had to close the door on, being unable to see them.

A great many who have not been at the meetings at all, have been converted in their own homes. God is working, not we. Oh! that we would keep ourselves down in the dust, and every one of us get out of the way, and let God work. It would be so easy for Him to go into every dwelling in Edinburgh, and convict and convert ten thousand souls.

Look at the 6th verse of the 4th chapter of Philippians. "Be careful for nothing, but in everything"—mark that—"by prayer and supplication, with thanksgiving, let your requests be made known unto God." He doesn't say He will answer all, but He says, "And the peace of God, which passeth all understanding, shall keep your hearts and minds through Jesus Christ." He tells us to make our wants known; to make our requests known to Him by prayer and supplication. It is right to come and make our requests known. He has told us to come and pray for the conversion of souls.

Turn to the 20th chapter of 2nd Chronicles. There we read that the Moabites, the Ammonites, and others coming against Jehoshaphat, he was afraid, "and set himself to seek the Lord," and that afterwards Judah "gathered themselves together to ask help of the Lord." That is what we want—to seek the Lord not only here in the public assembly, but alone. If you have got an unconverted friend and are anxious that he should be saved, go and tell it privately to Jesus, and if a blessing does not come, like Jehoshaphat, spend a few days in fasting, and prayer, and humiliation.

When I go into the streets and see the terrible wickedness, and blasphemy, and drunkenness that is in them, it seems dark, but I look up and think that God can repel those dark waves of sin and iniquity. Let us pray that God will bless this land of Scotland, bless and save all the people in it. It would be a great thing for us, but very little for God. May God give us faith!
(*Does God Answer Prayer?* A sermon by D.L. Moody)

Enduement For Service

When the disciples were about to begin their great work, our Lord said: "Ye shall receive power, after that the Holy Ghost is come upon you." How many, do you suppose, would have been converted on the day of Pentecost if Peter had gone and preached without this power? Not one. The disciples were commissioned to go and preach, but they were to wait till they were recommissioned and endued with power by the Holy Ghost. "Ye shall receive power, after that the Holy Ghost is come upon you: and ye shall be witnesses unto Me, both in Jerusalem, and in all Judea, and in Samaria, and unto the uttermost part of the earth." How quickly this whole world would be reached if we were just looking to God for this same Apostolic power!

There was a time when I thought the raising of Lazarus was the greatest work ever done on this earth. But I think the conversion of those 3,000 Jews on the day of Pentecost was more wonderful still. Those hard-hearted Jews were full of hatred and unbelief; many, no doubt, were the same men who murdered Christ. And yet they were swept down by the mighty power of the Spirit. We have got the same obstacles to contend with as the apostles had. Our gospel that we are preaching is a supernatural gospel, and we have got to have supernatural power to preach it.

Notice that those who are filled with the Holy Ghost immediately begin to testify of Jesus Christ. Elisabeth, when visited by the Virgin, was "filled with the Holy Ghost," and spoke of the coming Lord. Zacharias also was "filled with the Holy Ghost," and quoted Scripture in reference to the Messiah. Stephen was "filled with the Spirit," and received such unction that the men of the synagogue "were not able to resist the wisdom and the spirit by which he spake." He was able to stand before the whole Sanhedrim, and the power of God was on him in a wonderful degree while he testified of Christ.

When Peter was "filled with the Spirit" he went out to preach Christ—he couldn't help it. All through the New Testament we are told that the apostles were again and again filled with the Spirit. And as they preached "much people were added to the church." That always follows. There will be conversions breaking out in all the churches if we are filled with the Spirit. Let us pray that we may receive power for service. Let us not be satisfied with only the power by which we are "sealed unto the day of redemption;" but let us pray that we may be baptized with that power from on high by which we can do great things for the Master.

It is important to know whether the work we are doing is the work God would have us do. I remember that one time when Dr. Kirk came to Chicago, his old power came back upon him, and he just shook that city as I had never seen it shaken. I suppose if he had stayed, there would have been thousands and thousands converted. The mayor of the city and the leading men all came to hear him, and they said: "If we could have that kind of preaching we would be glad to hear it." But he went back to his pastoral work. I believe that man was meant for an evangelist; yet he went back to visit the widow and the fatherless. That was an important work, but others could have done it. Some men are gifted one way and some another. One man has got gifts as a pastor, and another has got gifts as an evangelist, while another is specially qualified to stir up Christians. Let every one ask, "Am I in the right place? Am I where God wants me to be?" If we would do that, it might break up a good many pastorates. Are you ready—ready to cut the tie?

When I was in Chicago I used to take a circuit out in the country, and preach during the week evenings; but I think I made a great mistake in binding myself too closely to my regular work. There was time after time when there would be a hundred inquirers in the country, and yet I would hurry away so as to preach in my own place in the city on Sunday night, and then perhaps only find myself beating against the air. Let us be ready to go anywhere—to go wherever the Master calls.

Just say: "Here I am, Lord. Send me where you please —only give me souls. Give me power to win souls for Jesus Christ." When that is the uppermost thought in our hearts He won't disappoint us. "He that spared not His own Son, but delivered Him up for us all, how shall He not with Him also freely give us all things." If He gave us His Son, will He withhold the Spirit? "Herein is My Father glorified, that ye bear much fruit." Are you toiling all night and catching nothing? Cast the net on the right side. Come, my friend, are you ready to go anywhere? Can you say: "Lord, send me to whom you will —only send me. Let that power come upon me, that I may win souls for Jesus Christ?" May we have no will but God's sweet will. Oh, that our wills may be swallowed up in God's will.
(*Enduement For Service:* A sermon by D.L. Moody)

Tomorrow May Be Too Late

I have learned that when anyone becomes in earnest about his soul's salvation and he begins to seek God, it does not take long for an anxious sinner to meet an anxious Saviour. "Ye shall seek me, and find me, when ye shall search for me with all your heart" (Jeremiah 29:13). Those who seek for Him with all their hearts, find Christ.

I believe the reason why so few find Christ is that they do not search for Him with all their hearts; they are not terribly in earnest about their souls' salvation.

Everything God has done proves that He is in earnest about the salvation of men's souls. He has proved it by giving His only Son to die for us. The Son of God was in earnest when He died. What is Calvary but a proof of that? And the Lord wants us to be in earnest when it comes to this great question of the soul's salvation. I never saw men seeking Him with all their hearts but they soon found Him.

It was quite refreshing one night to find in the inquiry room a young man who thought he was not worth saving, he was so vile and wicked. There was hope for him because he was so desperately in earnest about his soul. He thought he was worthless. He had a sight of himself in God's looking glass and had a very poor opinion of himself. One can always tell when a man is a great way from God, for he is always talking about himself, and how good he is. But the moment he sees God by the eye of faith, he is down on his knees, and, like Job, he cries, "Behold, I am vile." All his goodness flees away.

When men earnestly seek the Lord and are in earnest about their salvation, they will soon find Christ. You do not need to go up to the heights to bring Him down, or down to the depths to bring Him up, or go off to some distant city to find Him. This day He is near to every one of us.

I once heard someone in the inquiry room telling a young person to go home and seek Christ in his closet. I would not dare tell anyone to do that. He might be dead before he got home. If I read my Bible correctly, the man who preaches the gospel will not tell me to seek Christ tomorrow or an hour hence, but now. He is near to every one of us this minute to save.

Suppose I should say I have lost a very valuable diamond here worth $100,000. I had it in my pocket when I came into the hall, and when I was done preaching, it was not in my pocket but in the hall somewhere. Suppose I should say that anyone who finds it could have it. How earnest you would all become! You would not get very much of my sermon for thinking of the diamond. I do not believe the police could get you out of this hall. The idea of finding a diamond worth $100,000! If I could only find it, it would lift me out of poverty at once, and I would be independent for the rest of my days! Oh, how soon everybody would become terribly in earnest! I would to God I could get men to seek for Christ in the same way. I have something worth more than a diamond to offer you. Is not salvation—eternal life—worth more than all the diamonds in the world?

People seem to forget that there is no door out of hell. If they enter there, they must remain there age after age. Millions on millions of years will roll on, but there is no door, no escape out of hell.

People talk about our being earnest and fanatical—about our being on fire. Would to God the church were on fire! This world would soon shake to its foundation. May God wake up a slumbering church! What we want you to do is not to shout "amen" and clap your hands. The deepest and quietest waters very often run swiftest. We want you to go right to work; there will be a chance for you to shout by and by. Go and speak to your neighbor and tell him of Christ and Heaven. You need not go far before you will find someone passing down to the darkness of eternal death. Haste to his rescue! We want you to go right to work; there will be a chance for you to shout by and by. Go and speak to your neighbor and tell him of Christ and Heaven. You need not go far before you will find someone passing down to the darkness of eternal death. Haste to his rescue! What we want to see is people really wishing to become Christians, those who are in dead earnest about it. The idea of hearing one say in answer to the question, "Do you want to become a Christian?" "Well, I would not mind"! My friend, you will never get into the Kingdom of God until you change your language. Men should be crying from the depths of their hearts, "I want to be saved!" When men seek Christ as they do wealth, they will soon find Him. To be sure, the world will raise a cry that they are excited. Let cotton go up ten or fifteen percent before tomorrow morning, and you will see how quickly the merchants will get excited! And the papers won't cry it down either. They say it is healthy excitement; commerce is getting on. But when you begin to get excited about your soul and are in earnest, then they raise the cry, "Oh, they are getting excited; most unhealthy state of things." Yet they don't talk nor write about men hastening down to death by the thousands.

There is the poor drunkard—look at him! Hear the piercing cry going up to Heaven? Yet the Church of God slumbers and sleeps. Here and there is an inquirer, yet they go into the inquiry room as if they were half asleep. When will men seek for Christ as they seek for wealth, or as they seek for honor? There is a story told of a vessel that was wrecked and was going down at sea. There were not enough lifeboats to take all on board. When the vessel went down, some of the lifeboats were near the vessel. A man swam from the wreck to one of the boats, but they had no room to take him on. When they refused, he seized hold of the boat with his right hand, but they took a sword and cut off his fingers. When he had lost the fingers of his right hand, the man was so earnest to save his life that he seized the boat with his left hand. They cut off the fingers of that hand too. Then the man swam up and seized the boat with his teeth. Now they had compassion on him and relented. They could not cut off his head, so they took him in, and the man's life was saved. Why? Because he was in earnest. Why not seek your soul's salvation as that man sought to save his life?

Will there ever be a better time for the old man whose locks are growing gray, whose eyes are growing dim, and who is hastening to the grave? Is not this the very best time for him? "Seek ye the Lord while he may be found."

There is a man in the middle of life. Is this not the best time for him to seek the Kingdom of God? Will he ever have a better opportunity? Will Christ ever be more willing to save than now? He says, "Come; for all things are now ready"—not "going to be," but "are now ready."

There is a young man. My friend, is it not the best time for you to seek the Kingdom of God? Seek the Lord; you can find Him now. Can you say that you will find Him tomorrow? Young man, you know not what tomorrow may bring forth. Do you know that every time the clock ticks, a soul passes away? Is not this the best time for you to seek the Kingdom of God? My boy, the Lord wants you. Seek first the Kingdom of God, and seek Him while He may be found.

At Dublin a young man found Christ. He went home and lived so godly and so Christlike a life that two of his brothers could not understand what had wrought the change in him. They left Dublin and followed us to Sheffield, and there found Christ. They were in earnest. But, thanks be to God, Christ can be found now. I firmly believe every reader can find Christ now, if you will seek for Him with all your heart. He says, "Call upon me."

Men are pretty near the kingdom of God when they do not see anything good in themselves.

At the Fulton Street prayer meeting a man came in, and this was his story. He had a mother who prayed for him—he was a wild, reckless prodigal. Some time after his mother's death he began to be troubled. He thought he ought to get into new company and leave his old companions, so he said he would go and join a secret society. He thought he would join the Odd Fellows. They made inquiry about him, and when they found he was a drunken sailor, they blackballed him. They would not have him. He went to the Freemasons. He had nobody to recommend him. When they inquired and found there was no good in his character, they blackballed him. They didn't want him. One day someone handed him a little notice in the street about the prayer meeting. He went. He heard that Christ had come to save sinners. He believed Him; he took Him at His word; and, in reporting the matter, he said he "came to Christ without a character, and Christ hadn't blackballed him."

Are you without a character, with nobody to say a good word for you? I bring you good news. Call on the Son of God, and He will hear you.

Let us be in earnest about the salvation of our children and friends. Warn that young lady. Yes, Mother, speak to that daughter. Father, speak to that child. Wife, speak to your unconverted husband. Husband, speak to your unconverted wife. Do not let anyone say, "Nobody cares for my soul." I never saw parents burdened for their children but that the children soon became anxious to be saved.

Every true friend, if you could get his advice, would tell you to be saved now. Ask your minister, "Had I better seek the Kingdom of God now?" What will he tell you? "By all means, don't put it off another minute." Ask your godly, praying mother, "Is it best to seek the Kingdom of God now?" Will she say, "Put it off one week, or a month"? There is not a Christian mother in this land who would say that. I doubt if there is even an unconverted mother whose advice would be to put off becoming a Christian. Ask that praying sister of yours, that praying brother, any friend you have, whether it is not the very best thing you can do. And then cry to Heaven and ask Him who is sitting at the right hand of God, and who loves you more than your father or your mother or anyone on Earth—who loves you so much that He gave Himself for you—ask Him what He will have you do, and hear His voice from the throne, "Seek ye first the Kingdom of God." And then shout down to the infernal regions, and ask those down there. What will they say? "Send someone to my father's house, for

I have five brethren, that he may testify unto them, lest they also come into this place." Heaven, Earth, and Hell unite in this one thing: "Seek ye first the Kingdom of God." Don't put it off. Call upon Him while He is near. And if you call upon Him in earnest, He will hear that call
I have no doubt that those who would not pray when the ark was being built, prayed when the Flood came; but their prayer was not answered. I have no doubt that when Lot went out of Sodom, Sodom cried to God; but it was too late, and God's judgment swept them from the earth. My friend, it is not too late now, but it may be at twelve o'clock tonight. I cannot find any place in the Bible where it says you may call tomorrow. I am not justified in saying that. "Behold, NOW is the accepted time; behold, NOW is the day of salvation."
(Tomorrow May Be Too Late: A sermon by D.L. Moody)

Heaven—Its Hope

Men's ideas differ about the extent that human skill can go; but the reason why we believe the Bible is inspired, is so simple that the humblest child of God can comprehend it. If the proof of its divine origin lay in its wisdom alone, a simple and uneducated man might not be able to believe it. We believe it is inspired, because there is nothing in it that could not have come from God. God is wise, and God is good. There is nothing in the Bible that is not wise, and there is nothing in it that is not good.

If the Bible had anything in it that was opposed to reason, or to our sense of right, then, perhaps, we might think that it was like all the books in the world that are written merely by men. Books that are just human books—like merely human lives—have in them a great deal that is foolish and a great deal that is wrong. The life of Christ alone was perfect, being both human and divine. Not one of the other volumes, like the Koran, that claim divinity of origin, agree with common sense. There is nothing at all in the Bible that does not conform to common sense. What it tells us about the world having been destroyed by a deluge, and Noah and his family alone being saved, is no more wonderful than what is being taught in the schools—that all of the earth we see now, and everything upon it came out of a ball of fire. It is a great deal easier to believe that man was made after the image of God than it is to believe, as some young men and women are being taught now, that he was once a monkey.

What the Bible tells about Heaven is not half so strategic as what Professor Proctor tells about the hosts of stars that are beyond the range of any telescope, yet people very often think that science is all fact, and that religion is only fancy. A great many persons who think that Jupiter and many more of the stars around us are inhabited, cannot bring themselves to believe that there is a life beyond this earth for immortal souls. The true Christian puts faith before reason, and believes that reason always goes wrong when faith is set aside. If people would but read their Bibles more, and study what there is to be found there about Heaven, they would not be as worldly minded as they are. They would not have their hearts set upon things down here, but would seek the imperishable things above.

It seems perfectly reasonable that God should have given us a glimpse of the future, for we are constantly losing some of our friends by death, and the first thought that comes to us is, "Where have they gone?" When a loved one is taken away from us, how that thought comes up before us! How we wonder if we will ever see them again, and where and when it will be! Then it is that we turn to this blessed Book, for there is no other book in all the world that can give us the slightest comfort; no other book that can tell us where the loved ones have gone.

There are men who say that there is no Heaven. I was once talking with a man who said he thought there was nothing to justify us in believing in any other Heaven than we know here on Earth. If this is Heaven, it is a very strange one—this world of sickness, and sorrow, and sin. I pity from the depths of my heart the man or woman who has that idea. This world that so many think is Heaven, is the home of sin, a hospital of sorrow, a place that has nothing in it to satisfy the soul. Men go all over it and then want to get out of it. The more one sees of the world the less they think of it. People soon grow tired of the best pleasures it has to offer. Some one has said that the world is a stormy sea, whose every wave is strewed with the wrecks of mortals that perish in it. Every time we breathe, someone is dying. We all know that we are going to stay here but a very little while. Our life is but a vapor. It is just a mere shadow. We meet one another, as someone has said, salute one another, and pass on and are gone.

The longest time man has to live, has no more proportion to eternity than a drop of dew has to the ocean.

I do not think that it is wrong for us to think and talk about Heaven. I would like to locate Heaven and find out all I can about it. I expect to live there through all eternity. If I was going to dwell in any place in this country, if I was going to make it my home, I would want to inquire about the place, about its climate, about the neighbors I would have, and about everything in fact, that I could learn concerning it. If any of you were going to emigrate, that would be the way you would feel.

Well, we are all going to emigrate in a very little while to a country that is very far away. We are going to spend eternity in another world—a grand and glorious world where God reigns. Is it right and natural, then, that we should look and listen and try to find out who is already there, and what is the route to take?

Soon after I was converted, an infidel asked me one day why I looked up when I prayed. He said that Heaven was no more above as than below us; that Heaven was everywhere. Well, I was greatly bewildered, and the next time I prayed, it seemed almost as if I was praying into the air. Since then I have become better acquainted with the Bible, and I have come to see that Heaven is above us; that it is upward and not downward. The Spirit of God is everywhere, but God is in Heaven, and Heaven is above our heads. It does not matter what part of the globe we may stand upon, Heaven, is above us.

Look at the cities of the past. There is Babylon. It was founded by a woman named Semiramis, who had two millions of men at work for years building it. It is nothing but dust now. Nearly a thousand years ago, some historian wrote that the ruins of Nebuchadnezzar's palace were still standing, but men were afraid to go near them because they were full of scorpions and snakes. That's the sort of ruin that greatness often comes to in our own day.

When I was in Dublin, they were telling me about a father who had lost a little boy, and he had not thought about the future, he bad been so entirely taken up with this world and its affairs; but when that little boy—his only child—died, that father's heart was broken, and every night when he got home from work, they would find him with his tallow candle and his Bible in his room. He was hunting up all that he could find there about Heaven. Someone asked him what he was doing, and he said he was trying to find out where his child had gone, and I think he was a reasonable man.

My friends, let us believe this good old Book, that Heaven is not a myth, and let us be prepared to follow the dear ones who have gone before. There, and there alone, can we find the peace we seek for.

What has been, and is now, one of the strongest feelings in the human heart? Is it not to find some better place, some lovelier spot, than we have now? It is for this that men are seeking everywhere; and yet, they can have it, if they will; but instead of looking down, they must look up to find it. As men grow in knowledge, they vie with each other more and more to make their homes attractive, but the brightest home on Earth is but an empty barn compared with the mansions that are in the skies.

You know, when a man is going up in a balloon, he takes in sand as a ballast, and when he wants to mount a little higher, he throws out a little of the ballast, and then he will mount a little higher; he throws out a little more ballast, and he mounts still higher; and the higher he gets the more he throws out, and so the nearer we get to God the more we have to throw out of the things of this world. Let go of them; do not let us first set our hearts and affections on them, but do what the Master tells us: Lay up for ourselves treasures in heaven. (*Tomorrow May Be Too Late:* A sermon by D.L. Moody)

Hell

A man came to me the other day and said: "I like your preaching. You don't preach hell, and I suppose you don't believe in one."

Now I don't want any one to rise up in the Judgment and say that I was not a faithful preacher of the Word of God. It is my duty to preach God's Word just as He gives it to me. I have no right to pick out a text here and there, and say, "I don't believe that." If I throw out one text I must throw out all, for in the same Bible I read of rewards and punishments, Heaven and hell. No one ever drew such a picture of hell as the Son of God. No one could do it, for He alone knew what the future would be. He didn't keep back this doctrine of retribution, but preached it out plainly; preached it, too, with pure love, just as a mother would warn her son of the end of his course of sin.

We won't need any one to condemn us at the bar of God; it will be our own conscience that will come up as a witness against us. God won't condemn us at His bar; we shall condemn ourselves. Memory is God's officer, and when He shall touch these secret springs and say, "Son, daughter, remember"—then tramp, tramp, tramp will come before us, in a long procession, all the sins we have ever committed.

I have been twice in the jaws of death. Once I was drowning and was about to sink, when I was rescued. In the twinkling of an eye everything I had said, done, or thought of flashed across my mind. I do not understand how everything in a man's life can be crowded into his recollection in an instant of time, but it all flashed through my mind at once.

Another time I was caught in the Clark Street bridge and thought I was dying. Then memory seemed to bring all my life back to me again. It is just so that all things we think we have forgotten will come back by and by. It is only a question of time. We shall hear the words, "Son, remember," and it is a good deal better to remember our sins now, and be saved from them, than to put off repentance till it is too late to do any good.

You laugh at the Bible; but how many there are in that lost world today who would give countless treasures if they had the blessed Bible there! You may make sport of Ministers, but bear in mind there will be no preaching of the Gospel there. Here they are God's messengers to you—loving friends that look after your soul. You may have some friends praying for your salvation today; but remember, you will not have one in that lost world. There will be no one to come and put his hand on your shoulder and weep over you there and invite you to come to Christ. There are some people who ridicule these meetings, but remember, there will be no meetings in hell.

A good man was one day passing a saloon as a young man was coming out, and thinking to make sport of him he called out, "Deacon, how far is it to hell?" The deacon gave no answer, but after riding a few rods he turned to look after the scoffer, and found that his horse had thrown him to the ground and broken his neck. I tell you, my friends, I would sooner give that right hand than to trifle with eternal things. (*Hell:* A sermon by D.L. Moody)

Lost and Found

You might have had a tract presented to you. You might have turned it off. It might have been headed with our same text. That was the Son of God seeking for your soul. He has used a four-page tract—sometimes just one page—to seek to convert a man.

When I was taking my family south last summer, I heard of a man who would not go to church but would go to a theater. He was a hard case—a drinking, swearing, gambling man. He heard that a minister was going to preach in a theater, so he went. When he heard the preacher, the man was convinced that he was preaching at him. He went out swearing and stamping. He told all the people outside that he had been insulted by the minister and intended to wait for him and give him a good licking.

When the minister came out, he was seized by the collar. The man greeted him by saying, "Sir, you have insulted me!" "I don't know you, sir," said the minister.

"Why," replied the man, "you have picked me out among all those people and told them all about me." It was the Spirit of God seeking him, and the result was that the Spirit got hold of him.

You pity men who have lost wealth; you pity men who suffered loss in the Chicago fire; you pity men who, once wealthy, are now almost starving. Such things naturally excite our sympathy. But what is all this loss of wealth to the loss of the soul? You pity men who once occupied a great position in the world and who are now reduced to beggary. But what is the loss of position in comparison to the loss of the soul? If a man loses wealth, character, reputation, he may gain it again; but oh, if he loses his soul, he can never regain it. In my native town one afternoon a man went out to see to his stock. Seven o'clock came, and he did not return; eight o'clock came, and there was no sign of him; nine o'clock came, and still he did not come. It was a dark night. The news spread through the streets that the man must have been killed. When the news was flashed, people did not fold their arms and say they would wait till daylight to seek for him. The old and the young men saddled their horses instantly, lighted their torches, and went forth into the darkness to find the lost one. They found him in the pasture, dead. They brought him into the little village. I never saw a community so excited and so grieved. But what was that—the cutting from a man's life of say twenty years—to the loss of a soul?"

Is there a poor drunkard here tonight who wants to come? Christ can save a drunkard just as easily as I can turn my hand. He can turn that cup of liquor from you as easily as you turn to it now.

There was among those who came to our meetings in New York a man who came every night but never seemed to get any light, never seemed to come any nearer God. I almost got tired of speaking with him. But one night when some young men were giving their experiences, he got up. I wondered why, because the very last time I spoke to him he seemed more hopeless than ever. He got up and told how he had become a Christian. He said one day he was walking down Broadway and the street was crowded with people and carriages and horses. This thought came to him: If I only gave my consent, the Lord would save me. He said he gave it at once and he was accepted. (He was one of the most hopeless cases in the city.) (*Lost and Found:* A sermon by D.L. Moody)

Emma Revell Moody (D.L. Moody's wife)

Born in London in 1842, her family immigrated to Chicago in 1849 when she was only seven. After graduating from high school, she taught briefly, and on August 28, 1862 she married Moody. The Lord blessed them with several children—a daughter, Emma Reynolds Moody, and two sons, William Revell And Paul Dwight Moody. Emma served with her husband in Sunday school work, evangelistic campaigns, and took care of much of his correspondence. She died in 1903.

D.L. Moody's Early life

D.L. Moody was of old New England Puritan stock. For seven generations, or two hundred years, his ancestors lived the quiet lives of farmers in the Connecticut Valley. Moody inherited the vigorous constitution and hardy common sense of the typical New Englander. He was the sixth child in a family of nine children, and was born in 1837, in the town of Northfield, Massachusetts. His home town was always very dear to him, and it was one of the greatest pleasures of his life to return to it after a long and arduous evangelistic campaign. Moody's father, a small farmer and stone mason, was an alcoholic and died at the early age of forty-one, when Moody was only four years old. He left his widow (who was pregnant with Moody's twin brother and sister) in poverty with a mortgage on the home and seven children to support. The creditors seized everything they could, even to the firewood, and the children had to stay in bed until school time to keep warm. A brother of the widowed mother then came to their rescue and helped to relieve their immediate needs. In their extremity Rev. Mr. Everett, the Unitarian minister, was very kind to them, and all the Moody children became members of his Sunday school, and were enlisted as workers to bring in other children.

It was here, therefore, that young Moody began his successful career as a Sunday school worker. Moody's mother had sought to bring up her children as a Christian mother should and Moody never wandered into gross sins as so many young men have done. Lying, complaining, breaking promises, or talking evil about others, was never allowed in the home. One evening when the children had little to eat, they divided their scant supply with a beggar. When Moody was eight years of age, he and an elder brother were crossing the river in a skiff with a boatman who was too drunk to row the boat, and who would not let them touch the oars. They were drifting with the current, but Moody urged his brother to trust in the Lord, and they came safely to land. Moody was mischievous but not wicked as a boy. The Moody family was so poor that the boys would carry their shoes and stockings in their hands on their way to church, to save them from wear, and when in sight of the church would put them on. Moody thought it hard, after working all week, to have to go to church and listen to a sermon he did not understand. In one instance, the preacher had to send someone to the gallery to awaken him. But he got in such a habit of going that he could not stay away, and he afterwards said that he thanked his mother for making him go when he did not feel like going.

At ten years of age, Moody left home in company with another brother to work at a place about thirteen miles away. This nearly broke his mother's heart, as she had striven so hard to keep the family together. He was fondly attached to his mother and sorrowed over leaving her. When he arrived at the new place an aged man gave him a penny and bade him trust the Lord. "That old man's blessing has followed me for fifty years," said Moody. While working there, he received cornmeal porridge and milk, three times a day. He complained to his mother, but when she found out that he had all he wanted to eat, she sent him back. Even during this time, she continued to send them to church. His oldest brother ran away and was not heard from by the family until many years later. Moody didn't attend school beyond the fifth grade; he couldn't spell, and his grammar was awful. His manners were often brash and crude, and he never became an ordained minister. Once, before his conversion, he so outraged an Italian shoe salesmen with a prank, that the man chased him with a sharp knife, clearly intending to kill him. Yet, Dwight L. Moody was used by God to lead thousands of people to Christ.

> *This is the wonderful thing about the life of D. L. Moody. Spurgeon was eloquent. George Whitefield was brilliant. John Wesley was also brilliant. Moody is someone you and I can not only identify with, but take strong consolation from the fact that God can use anyone for His purposes. In fact, it seems from Scripture that God passes over the eloquent and the brilliant and uses shepherd boys from nowhere to fulfill His purposes.* — *Ray Comfort*

At seventeen years of age, Moody, tired of farm life and ambitious to work his way upward in the world, decided to go to Boston. He arrived there without any money, and tried in vain to find work until he was almost in despair and felt all alone in the big city. His uncle took him on as a shoe salesman—on condition that he be obedient and that he attend Mt. Vernon Congregational Church where Dr. Edward Norris Kirk was pastor. He succeeded well as a salesman, and over the next eleven months, Moody listened to sermon after sermon from Kirk. The church itself had been formed twelve years earlier by Bostonians unhappy with the rigid doctrinal exclusiveness of another large city church. Pastor Kirk emphasized the sinfulness of man and man's inability to save himself. He spoke of Christ's death on the Cross for all mankind, of Christ's resurrection from the dead, and of Christ's desire to be the friend of each one who trusted Him. On the other hand, the minister issued dire warnings to all who refused so great a salvation, and he verbally assaulted those who failed to do so.

The biblical way to convince any sinner of his inability to save himself is to put him up the river Niagara, without a paddle. Reveal the holiness of God and the sinfulness of man by preaching the moral Law. Show that God sees the thought life, considers lust to be adultery (Matthew 5:27-28) and hatred to be murder.
— Ray Comfort

Moody's upbringing in the Unitarian church taught him that Christ was not fully divine and did not emphasize human need for salvation from sins. Now, listening to Kirk, Moody heard about those things. Having but little schooling, he took but little part in the discussions in the class in Sunday school, but gradually became deeply interested in the study of the Bible, and finally took part in the discussions in the class. Pastor Kirk's messages and his Sunday school teacher Edward Kimball's teaching combined in Moody's mind, and he found himself caught up in a spiritual struggle. But he decided that he wanted to enjoy the pleasures of the world and wait to get saved until just before he died.

This is the attitude of most young men, but thanks to God and to the tenacious attitude of Edward Kimball, life didn't go the way Moody intended. May we be tenacious with the lost. We should only give up on someone when they stop breathing. No sooner.
— Ray Comfort

> Repeatedly stressing that the spiritual issue was one of choice and of yielding one's will to another, Kirk emphasized that this choice led to a life of faith. Young Moody sensed the minister was right, yet seemed unable to yield his will to God.

However, the kindness of Kimball, turned young Moody into his lifelong friend, and encouraged him to persist in his church attendance and regular Bible reading. Though Moody did try to read the Bible, he couldn't understand it. Kimball later stated, "I can truly say, and in saying it I magnify the infinite grace of God as bestowed upon him, that I have seen few persons whose minds were spiritually darker than was his when he came into my Sunday School class; and I think that the committee of the Mount Vernon Church seldom met an applicant for membership more unlikely ever to become a Christian of clear and decided views of gospel truth [the Lord], still less to fill any extended sphere of public usefulness."

Then in April, Mount Vernon Church held a meeting. And on Saturday, April 21, 1855, Edward Kimball resolutely decided to speak to his recalcitrant Sunday school pupil about his soul. Kimball came to the shoe store to ask Moody to commit his life to Christ. Arriving at the store, he found that Moody was in the back, wrapping shoes. He didn't want to embarrass him, however, and almost had decided to come back at a more convenient time. "I began to wonder whether I ought to go just then during business hours," he later reported. And I thought maybe my mission might embarrass the boy, that when I went away the other clerks might ask who I was, and when they learned might taunt Moody and ask if I was trying to make a good boy out of him. Then, I decided to make a dash for it and have it over at once."

Going over to Moody in the back of the shoe store, "I placed my hand on his shoulder, leaned over, and placed my foot on a shoe box." Kimball looked into Moody's eyes and "asked him to come to Christ, who loved him and who wanted his love and should have it." Moody's struggle came to a head, and he surrendered his will to God's will and came to Christ through Kimball's invitation.

"My plea was a very weak one," Kimball observed later, "but I was sincere." He also realized, "The young man was just ready for the light that broke upon him. For there, at once, in the back of that shoe store in Boston, Dwight gave himself and his life to Christ."

The following morning as he left his room, Moody's joy knew no bounds. The wide grin on his face and the fresh sparkle in his big brown eyes reflected his newfound life in Christ. He sensed, "The old sun shone a good deal brighter then it ever had before—I felt that it was just smiling upon me; and as I walked out upon Boston Common and heard the birds singing in the trees, I thought they were all singing a song to me." As he marched along, it seemed all creation cheered him on his way, and he sensed that "I had not a bitter feeling against any man, and I was ready to take all men to heart" (Harvey, *Moody* 28-30).

It is often the way of God to open the heavens with a new convert, but then he is lead into the wilderness to be tempted by the devil. When I became a Christian I had never known joy like it. But then I went into a wilderness experience and had never known depression like it. The heat of the sun sure did make me send me roots down deep, and I have to say, "It was good for me that I was afflicted, that I might learn your statutes." — *Ray Comfort*

Moody's whole life was now changed, and became one of joyful Christian service. "Before my conversion," says he, "I worked towards the Cross, but since then I have worked from the Cross; then I worked to be saved, now I work because I am saved." Immediately he began sharing his faith with others, including his own family. They wanted nothing to do with his faith. "I will always be a Unitarian," his mother said. (However, she converted shortly before her death.)

Moody was now running over with zeal and love for the Master, but he did not seem to have received much help and encouragement from the conservative deacons and church members in the church which he was attending. In May 1855, he was denied church membership, because he was "not sufficiently instructed in Christian doctrine." Three of the committee who examined him were appointed to instruct him in the way of God more perfectly. When asked what Christ had done for him, the nervous boy replied that he wasn't aware of anything particular. Leaders felt that was an unacceptable answer, and he was not received as a church member until May 4, 1856.

Chicago and the Civil War

In September1856, Moody moved to Chicago, where he united with the Plymouth Congregational Church and became a very active Christian worker, putting his soul and energy into the work of winning men to Christ. He found a little mission Sunday school in Chicago where they had sixteen teachers and only twelve scholars. Here he applied to become a teacher. They consented on condition that he would find his own scholars. This just suited his taste, and the next Sunday he arrived with eighteen little hoodlums which he had gathered from the streets. He soon had the building crowded. The great meeting awakened by Finney spread to Chicago, and Moody was in his element. Meanwhile he was prospering in his business, and was so good a salesman of shoes that his employer sent him out as a commercial traveler.

In the spring of 1857, he began to minister to the welfare of the sailors in Chicago's port, then gamblers and thieves in the saloons. He had a passion for saving souls and determined never to let a day pass without telling someone the gospel of Jesus Christ. Often he irritated strangers on the street by asking them if they were Christians—but his pointed questioning stirred the consciences of many. God would use the converted shoe salesman to become the leading evangelist of his day.

A contemporary witness recalls these days

"The first meeting I ever saw him at was in a little old shanty that had been abandoned by a saloon-keeper. Mr. Moody had got the place to hold the meetings in at night. I went there a little late; and the first thing I saw was a man standing up with a few tallow candles around him, holding a negro boy, and trying to read to him the story of the Prodigal Son and a great many words he could not read out, and had to skip. I thought, 'If the Lord can ever use such an instrument as that for His honor and glory, it will astonish me.'"

His work led to the largest Sunday school of his time. As a result of his tireless labor, within a year the average attendance at his school was 650, while 60 volunteers from various churches served as teachers. In the fall of 1858, he began another mission school on a larger scale in another part of the city. The large hall was soon overcrowded. He then procured a larger hall, which afterward developed into one of the leading churches of Chicago. This big hall he soon had filled with street "gamins." The children loved him and crowded in by the hundreds and sang the hymns with great enjoyment. Moody also enticed them in with prizes, free pony rides, picnics, candies, and other things dear to the hearts of children. Scholars were allowed to transfer to any class they desired by simply notifying the superintendent; and this plan resulted in the survival of the fittest teachers. The school soon numbered 1,500. Moody decided to build a church and issued certificates on the "North Market Sabbath School Association; capital $10,000; 40,000 shares at 25 cents each." The Sunday school grew to such proportions that parents were drawn in, and then meetings were held almost every night in the week. Many prominent men assisted Moody in the Sunday school and in the meetings, but so much devolved on him that he had sometimes to be both janitor and superintendent. This practical training contributed much to his success as a preacher. Doubtless he needed such training, as at first he seemed to have spoken very awkwardly in public. When he first arose to speak in a prayer meeting one of the deacons assured him that, in his opinion, he would serve God best by keeping still. Another critic, who praised Moody for his zeal in filling the pews at Plymouth Church, said that he should realize his limitations and not attempt to speak in public. "You make too many mistakes in grammar," said he. "I know

I make mistakes," was the reply, "and I lack many things, but I'm doing the best I can with what I've got." He then paused, and looking at the man searchingly, inquired, in his own inimitable way, "Look, here, friend, you've got grammar enough—what are you doing with it for the Master?"

Mr. Moody's great Sunday school work was accomplished before he was more than twenty-three years of age. With all his work for Christ he had no thought of entering the ministry until he found that souls were being led to Christ through his efforts. He then decided to give up the business in which he had been engaged, and in which he had already made over $7,000, and devoted all his time to Christian work.

The growing Sunday school congregation needed a permanent home, so Moody started a church, the Illinois Street Church. It became so well known that the just-elected President Lincoln visited and spoke at a Sunday school meeting on November 25, 1860.

After the Civil War began in 1861, Moody was involved with the U.S. Christian Commission of the YMCA and paid nine visits to the battle-front, holding meetings and distributing gospels and tracts among the soldiers and prisoners of war quartered in Chicago and on many leading battlefields of the Southern States. He was present among the Union soldiers after the conflicts of Shiloh, Pittsburgh Landing, and Murfreesboro, and ultimately entered Richmond with the army of General Grant.

After the war, he returned to Chicago and again devoted himself to Sunday school and YMCA work. His Sunday school was so great a success that it made him famous all over the country. Inquiries concerning his methods of work came from all directions, and people traveled thousands of miles to learn them. He was called to many places to address Sunday school conventions and to help organize Sunday school work. Through his efforts, many Sunday schools were led to agree to use the same lessons each Sunday, and thus the International Sunday School lessons were started.

In 1867, Mr. Moody made up his mind to go to Great Britain and study the methods of Christian work employed in that country. He did so, accompanied by Mrs. Moody, who was suffering from asthma. He was particularly anxious to hear Spurgeon, the great English preacher, and George Muller, who had the large orphanages at Bristol. Moody was then unknown in England except to a few prominent Sunday school leaders, but he spoke a number of times in London and Bristol with good results.

It was during this first visit to Britain that Moody heard the words which set him hungering and thirsting after a deeper Christian experience and which marked a new era in his life. The words were spoken to him by Mr. Henry Varley, the well known evangelist, as they sat together on a seat in a public park in Dublin. The words were these: "The world has yet to see what God will do with and for and through and in and by the man who is fully consecrated to Him."

"He said *a man,*" thought Moody, "he did not say a *great* man, nor a *learned* man, nor a *smart* man, but simply *a man*. I am a man, and it lies with the man himself whether he will or will not make that entire and full consecration. I will try my utmost to be that man."

The words kept ringing in his mind, and burning their way into his soul until finally he was led into the deeper, richer, fuller experience for which his soul yearned. The impression the words made was deepened soon afterward by words spoken by Mr. Bewley, of Dublin, Ireland, to whom he was introduced by a friend.

"Is this young man all O and O?" asked Mr. Bewley. "What do you mean by 'O and O'?" said the friend. "Is he out and out for Christ?" was the reply. From that time forward Moody's desire to be "O and O" for Christ was supreme.

Moody returned home, and his hunger for a deeper spiritual experience was deepened by the preaching of Henry Moorehouse, the famous English boy preacher, who visited Moody's church in Chicago soon after Moody returned to the United States. For seven nights Moorehouse preached from the text, John 3:16, "For God so loved the world, that he gave his only begotten Son, that whosoever believeth in him should not perish, but have everlasting life." Every night he rose to a higher and higher plain of thought, beginning at Genesis and going through the Bible to Revelation, showing how much God loved the world. He pointed out how God loved the world so much that He sent patriarchs and prophets, and other holy men to plead with the people, and then He sent His only Son, and when they had killed Him, He sent the Holy Ghost.

In closing the seventh sermon from the text, he said: "My friends, for a whole week I have been trying to tell you how much God loves you, but I cannot do it with this poor stammering tongue. If I could borrow Jacob's ladder and climb up into Heaven and ask Gabriel, who stands in the presence of the Almighty, to tell me how much love the Father has for the world, all he could say would be, 'God so loved the world, that he gave his only begotten Son, that whosoever believeth in him should not perish, but have everlasting life.' "

Moody's heart melted within him as he listened to the young preacher describing the love of God for lost mankind. It gave him such a vision of the love of God as he had never seen before, and from that time forward Moody's preaching was of a more deeply spiritual character.

Moody had become one of the most prominent YMCA workers in the United States, and it was at a YMCA convention in Indianapolis, Indiana, in 1870, that he first met Ira David Sankey, who was destined to become his great singing partner. Moody was so impressed with his singing that he asked him to come with him and sing for him, and in Indianapolis they held their first meeting together, in the open air. Some months afterward, Sankey gave up his business and joined Mr. Moody in his work.

Moody continued to hunger for a deepening of his own spiritual life and experience. He had been greatly used of God, but felt that there were much greater things in store for him. The year 1871 was a critical one with him. He realized more and more how little he was fitted by personal acquirements for his work, and how much he needed to be qualified for service by the Holy Spirit's power.

This realization was deepened by conversations he had with two ladies who sat on the front pew in his church. He could see by the expressions on their faces that they were praying. At the close of the service they would say to him, "We have been praying for you."

"Why don't you pray for the people?" Mr. Moody would ask. "Because you need the power of the Spirit," was the reply. "I need the power! Why," said he, in relating the incident afterwards, "I thought I had power. I had the largest congregation in Chicago, and there were many conversions. I was in a sense satisfied. But right along those two godly women kept praying for me, and their earnest talk about anointing for special service set me thinking. I asked them to come and talk with me, and they poured out their hearts in prayer that I might receive the filling of the Holy Spirit. There came a great hunger into my soul. I did not know what it was. I began to cry out as I never did before. I really felt that I did not want to live if I could not have this power for service."

In October of 1871, the Great Chicago Fire destroyed Moody's church, home, and the dwellings of most of his members. His family had to flee for their lives, and, as Mr. Moody said, he saved nothing but his reputation and his Bible. "While Mr. Moody was in this mental and spiritual condition," said his son, "Chicago was laid in ashes. The great fire swept out of existence both Farwell Hall and Illinois Street Church. On Sunday night after the meeting, as Mr. Moody went homeward, he saw the glare of flames, and knew it meant ruin to Chicago. About one o'clock Farwell Hall was burned; and soon his church went down. Everything was scattered." Mr. Moody went East to New York City to collect funds for the sufferers from the Chicago fire, but his heart and soul were crying out for the power from on high. "My heart was not in the work of begging," says he. "I could not appeal. I was crying all the time that God would fill me with His Spirit. Well, one day, in the city of New York—oh, what a day!—I cannot describe it, I seldom refer to it; it is almost too sacred an experience to name. Paul had an experience of which he never spoke for fourteen years. I can only say that God revealed himself to me, and I had such an experience of His love that I had to ask Him to stay His hand. I went to preaching again. The sermons were not different; I did not present any new truths; and yet hundreds were converted. I would not now be placed back where I was before that blessed experience if you should give me all the world; it would be as the small dust of the balance." His soul was set on fire in such a way that his work would soon become a worldwide one.

His church was rebuilt within three months at a nearby location as the Chicago Avenue Church. Thousands of Sunday school scholars contributed five cents each to place a brick in the new edifice. His lay follower, William Eugene Blackstone was a prominent American Zionist.

In the years after the fire, Moody's wealthy Chicago supporter J. A. Farwell attempted to persuade him to make his permanent home in Chicago, offering to build Moody and his family a new house. But the now famous Moody, also sought by supporters in New York, Philadelphia, and elsewhere, chose the tranquil farm he had purchased next door to his birthplace in Northfield, Mass. He felt he could better recover from his lengthy and exhausting preaching trips in a rural setting.

Northfield became an important location in evangelical Christian history in the late 19th century as Moody organized summer conferences which were led and attended by prominent Christian preachers and evangelists from around the world. It was also in Northfield that Moody founded three schools which later merged into today's Northfield Mount Hermon School.

Great Britain

Desiring to learn more of the Scriptures from English Bible students, he visited England again in 1872. He did not expect to hold any meetings during this visit, but he accepted an invitation to preach at the Sunday morning and evening service at Arundel Square Congregational Church in the North part of London. In the evening, the power of the Spirit seemed to fall upon the congregation, and the inquiry room was crowded with persons seeking salvation. Next day he went to Dublin, Ireland, but an urgent telegram called him back to continue his meetings at the North London Church. He continued there for ten days and four hundred persons were added to the church.

He was invited to Dublin and Newcastle but decided not to go at that time, and he returned to the United States.

Next year, at the invitation of two English friends, he started for England, accompanied by Sankey. His English friends had promised funds for the visit, but the money did not come and Moody borrowed enough to enable him to go to England. On arriving there, he learned that both of his friends had died. No door seemed open for him. But before leaving the United States he had received a letter from the Secretary of the YMCA at York, England, inviting him to address the young men there if he ever came to England. He and Sankey went to York, and began a series of meetings there which lasted for five weeks. Interest gradually increased until the meeting places were crowded half an hour before the time of service, and many souls decided for Christ.

The evangelists went from York to Sunderland, where they had still greater meetings than in York. The largest halls in the city had to be secured for the services. Their next series of meetings was in Newcastle. Here the meetings were gigantic, special trains bringing people from surrounding cities and towns. Here the evangelists published their first hymn book entitled *Gospel Hymns, No. 1*, which was followed by Numbers 2, 3, 4, 5, and 6. The books soon became popular all over Britain and have been a means of blessing to multitudes throughout the world. They marked a new era in the history of the Christian church. The royalties on them were at first devoted to a number of benevolent purposes, but afterwards to the founding and carrying on of Moody's great Bible schools at Northfield.

Other great meetings were held in Liverpool and many other British cities, and finally in London. On several occasions Moody filled stadiums with seating from 2,000 to 4,000 to capacity. This turnout continued throughout 1874 and 1875, with crowds of even greater thousands at all of his meetings. Moody aided in the work of cross-cultural evangelism by promoting "The Wordless Book," a teaching tool that had been invented by Charles Spurgeon in 1866. In 1875 he added the fourth color—gold—to the design of the three-color evangelistic device to "represent Heaven." This "book" has been and is still used to teach uncounted thousands of illiterate people—young and old—around the globe about the gospel message.[2]

When the evangelists left Britain in 1875, the whole country had been stirred religiously as it had not been stirred since the days of Wesley and Whitefield. About 14,000 children attended the children's meeting in Liverpool. Over 600 ministers attended the closing services in London. Moody said that he had such a consciousness of the presence of God in the London meetings that "the people seemed as grasshoppers." Professor Henry Drummond said that Moody spoke to exactly "an acre of people" every meeting during his campaign in the East End of London.

On their return to the United States, Moody and Sankey held great meetings from Boston to New York, throughout New England and as far as San Francisco, and other West coast towns from Vancouver to San Diego. Crowds of 12,000 to 20,000 were just as common as in England. President Grant and some of his cabinet attended a meeting on January 19, 1876.

In 1881, they again visited Great Britain and conducted another gigantic evangelistic campaign. After these campaigns, Moody made repeated trips to Britain, and once he visited the Holy Land. He devoted much time to building up his great Bible schools at Northfield and in Chicago. During the World's Fair in Chicago, in 1893, he conducted great meetings in the largest halls in the city and in Forepaugh's Circus tent, with the assistance of famous preachers from all over the world. Millions heard the gospel preached during this campaign.

From the North of England the evangelists went to Scotland, and began a series of meetings in Edinburgh. Here they had one of the greatest series of meetings ever known in the world's history. No building was large enough to accommodate the immense throngs which flocked to their meetings. "Never, probably," says Professor Blaikie, "was Scotland so stirred; never was there so much expectation." During his visit to Scotland he was helped and encouraged by Andrew A. Bonar. The famous London Baptist preacher, Charles Spurgeon, invited him to speak and promoted him as well.

In 1883, Moody and Sankey visited Edinburgh and raised £10,000 for the building of a new home for the Carrubbers Close Mission. Moody later preached at the laying of the foundation stone for one of the few buildings on the Royal Mile which continues to be used for its original purpose and is now called the Carrubbers Christian Centre.

In Glasgow, Scotland, the evangelists had similar meetings to those at Edinburgh. At the closing service at the Crystal Palace, in the Botanic Gardens, the building was packed so tightly with people Moody could not enter, and there were still 20 to 30 thousand persons on the outside. Moody spoke to the great throng from the seat of a cab, and the choir led the singing from the roof of a nearby shed. When the Crystal Palace was filled with inquirers seeking salvation, there were still about 2,000 inquirers on the outside of the building. Moody probably addressed as many as 30,000 persons at one time in Edinburgh and as many as 40,000 in Glasgow.

D. L. Moody was undoubtedly one of the greatest evangelists of all time. The meetings held by Moody and Sankey were among the greatest the world has ever known. They were the means, under God, of arousing the church to new life and activity, and the means of sweeping tens of thousands of persons into the kingdom of God.

Moody's Influence in China and Sweden

Moody greatly influenced the cause of cross-cultural Christian missions after he met Hudson Taylor, the pioneer missionary to China. He actively supported the China Inland Mission and encouraged many of his congregation to volunteer for service overseas.

His influence was felt among Swedes despite the fact that he was of English heritage, had never visited Sweden or any Scandinavian country, and never spoke a word of the Swedish language. Nevertheless, he became a hero evangelist among Swedish Mission Friends in Sweden and the United States. News of Moody's large meeting campaigns in Great Britain from 1873–1875 traveled quickly to Sweden, making "Mr. Moody" a household name in homes of many Mission Friends. Moody's sermons published in Sweden were distributed in books, newspapers, and colporteur tracts, and led to the spread of Sweden's "Moody fever" from 1875–1880.

Moody's Death

Moody continued his evangelistic campaigns until his death in 1899. He preached his last sermon on November 16, 1899 in a gigantic hall in Kansas City, KS. While there, he was seized with heart trouble and returned home by train to Northfield. During the preceding several months, friends had observed he had added some thirty pounds to his already ample frame. Although his illness was never diagnosed, it has been speculated that he suffered congestive heart failure.

Among his last words were, "This is my triumph; this is my coronation day! I have been looking forward to it for years." This old world had lost its charm for him and for a long time he had been "homesick for Heaven."

His Last Moments and His Will

Another told how just before the last he said, "Can't a man die sitting up as well as lying down," and when the doctor said yes, they took him up and let him rest for a few moments in his chair, but it was only for a little while, and then they put him back again in his bed. It was the last time he was to rise, and he who told it said with a sob, "I cannot bring myself to realize that he has gone from us." Another told how, when he was aroused from his stupor and saw all his loved ones around him, he said in his old way, so characteristic of himself, "What's going on here," and when they told him that he had been worse for a little time, and that they had come to be with him, he closed his eyes and seemed to fall asleep again.

Still another told of the will he made, unlike any other will that any man had ever made. He gave the care of Mt. Hermon to his son, William R. Moody; the Northfield Young Ladies' School to the care of Paul, his son, a junior in Yale; the special oversight of the Bible Institute to Mrs. Fitt and her husband, Mr. A. P. Fitt, the latter having for years been Mr. Moody's closest and most confidential helper, particularly in the Bible Institute in Chicago and the Colportage Library work. The Northfield Training School was to be the care of Mr. Ambert G. Moody, his nephew. And when something was said about Mrs. Moody, he had said she was the mother of them all, and they must all care for her. An old friend gave the account of his words to his boys when he said, "I have always been an ambitious man, not ambitious to lay up money, but ambitious to leave you all work to be done, which is the greatest heritage one can leave to his children."[1]

A Triumphant Passing Away: More on Moody's Death

Still another gave the picture of his last hours. No more memorable sentences on one's deathbed have ever been spoken. It was just such a triumphant passing away as his dear friends would have wished. Where have you ever read better sayings than these?

"Is this dying? Why this is bliss. There is no valley. I have been within the gates. Earth is receding; Heaven is opening; God is calling; I must go."

And when he went away from them for a little time and came back, he said that he had seen his loved ones in Heaven, giving their names, and when it was suggested that he had been dreaming, he assured them it was not so, but that he had actually been within the gates of Heaven.

He died on December 22, surrounded by family. Already installed by Moody as leader of his Chicago Bible Institute, R. A. Torrey succeeded Moody as its president. Ten years after Moody's death, the Chicago Avenue Church was renamed The Moody Church in his honor, and the Chicago Bible Institute was likewise renamed Moody Bible Institute.

In this manner, his noble life went out, and though he is dead he continues to speak, and tens of thousands rise up to call him blessed. Such intimate associates as Mr. Ira D. Sankey, Mr. George C. Stebbins, Rev. George C. Neediham, Prof. W. W. White, Mr. William Phillips Hall, Mr. John R. Mott, Mr. Richard C. Morse, Rev. George A. Hall, and many others talked until the evening was gone, and then retired each to feel that his was a personal bereavement, because D. L. Moody was dead.

Moody's earthly remains were laid to rest on "Round Top," at his beloved Northfield. By his special request there were no emblems of mourning at his funeral services. It is estimated that no less than a hundred million people heard the gospel from his lips, and his schools are training many others to carry the glad tidings throughout the world.[1]

Words from those who were at Moody's Funeral

REV. A. T. PIERSON'S ADDRESS

"I want to say a word of Mr. Moody's entrance into Heaven. When he entered into Heaven there must have been an unusual commotion. I want to ask you today whether you can think of any other man of the last half-century whose coming so many souls would have welcomed at the gates of Heaven. It was a triumphal entrance into glory.

"No man 'who has been associated with him in Christian work has not seen that there is but one way to live, and that way to live wholly for God. The thing that D. L. Moody stood and will stand for centuries to come was his living only for God. He made mistakes, no doubt, and if any of us is without sin in this respect, we might cast a stone at him, but I am satisfied that the mistakes of D. L. Moody were the mistakes of a stream that overflowed its banks. It is a great deal better to be full and overflowing than to be empty and have nothing to overflow.

"I feel myself called today by the presence of God to give eye that what is left shall be consecrated more wholly to him. Mr. Moody, John Wanamaker, James Spurgeon (brother of Charles), and myself were born in the same year. Only two

1 Copied by Stephen Ross for WholesomeWords.org from Deeper Experiences of Famous Christians by J. Gilchrist Lawson. Anderson, Ind.: Warner Press, 1911.

of us are still alive. John Wanamaker, let us still live wholly for God."

DR. J. WILBUR CHAPMAN'S ADDRESS

"I cannot bring myself to feel this afternoon that this service is a reality. It seems to me that we must awake from some dream and see again the face of this dear man of God, which we have so many times seen. It is a new picture to me this afternoon. I never before saw Mr. Moody with his eyes closed. They were always open, and it seemed to me open not only to see where he could help others, but where he could help me. His hands were always outstretched to help others. I never came near him without his helping me."

At this point the sun came through a crack in a blind, and the rays fell directly on Mr. Moody's face, and nowhere else in the darkened church did a single beam of sunshine fall.

"The only thing that seems natural is the sunlight now on his face. There was always a halo around him. I can only give a slight tribute of the help he has done me, I can only especially dedicate myself to God, that I, with others, may preach the gospel he taught.

"When I was a student, Mr. Moody found me. I had no object in Christ. He pointed me to the hope in God; he saw my heart, and I saw his Saviour. I have had a definite life since then. When perplexities have arisen, from those lips came the words, 'Who are you doubting? If you believe in God's Word, who are you doubting?' I was a pastor, a preacher, without much result. One day Mr. Moody came to me, and, with one hand on my shoulder and the other on the open Word of God, he said: 'Young man, you had better get more of this into your life,' and when I became an evangelist myself, in perplexity I would still sit at his feet, and every perplexity would vanish just as mist before the rising sun. And, indeed, I never came without the desire to be a better man, and be more like him, as he was like Jesus Christ. If my own father were lying in the coffin I could not feel more the sense of loss."[2]

More on Moody's Life Plus His Conversion[3]

"I had never lost sight of Jesus Christ since the first night I met Him in the store in Boston. But for years I was only a nominal Christian, really believing that I could not work for God. No one had ever asked me to do anything."

> *This seems strange, in the light of the Great Commission of Mark 16:15. — Ray Comfort*

> "I went to Chicago, I hired five pews in a church, and used to go out on the street and pick up young men and fill these pews. I never spoke to those young men about their souls; that was the work of the elders, I thought. After working for some time like that, I started a mission Sabbath school. I thought numbers were everything, and so I worked for numbers. When the attendance ran below one thousand, it troubled me; and when it ran to twelve or fifteen hundred, I was elated. Still none were converted; there was no harvest. Then God opened my eyes.

"There was a class of young ladies in the school, who were, without exception, the most frivolous set of girls I ever met.

2 From The Life & Work of Dwight Lyman Moody by the Rev. Wilbur Chapman, D.D.

3 Taken from: http://www.chinstitute.org/DAILYF/2003/04/daily-04-21-2003.shtml. More Details on Moody's Conversion taken from: Harvey, Moody 28-30 Moody's own narrative taken from: The Life & Work of Dwight Lyman Moody by the Rev. Wilbur Chapman, D.D.

One Sunday the teacher was ill, and I took that class. They laughed in my face, and I felt like opening the door and telling them all to get out and never come back. That week the teacher of the class came into the place where I worked. He was pale, and looked very ill. 'What is the trouble?' I asked. ' I have had another hemorrhage of my lungs. The doctor says I cannot live on Lake Michigan, so I am going to New York State. I suppose I am going home to die.'

"He seemed greatly troubled, and when I asked him the reason, he replied: 'Well, I have never led any of my class to Christ. I really believe I have done the girls more harm than good.' I had never heard any one talk like that before, and it set me thinking. After a while I said: 'Suppose you go and tell them how you feel. I will go with you in a carriage, if you want to go.'

"He consented, and we started out together. It was one of the best journeys I ever had on earth. We went to the house of one of the girls, called for her, and the teacher talked to her about her soul. There was no laughing then! Tears stood in her eyes before long. After he had explained the way of life, he suggested that we have prayer. He asked me to pray. True, I had never done such a thing in my life as to pray God to convert a young lady there and then. But we prayed, and God answered our prayer. We went to other houses. He would go upstairs, and be all out of breath, and he would tell the girls what he had come for. It wasn't long before they broke down, and sought salvation. When his strength gave out, I took him back to his lodgings. The next day we went out again. At the end of ten days he came to the store with his face literally shining.

"'Mr. Moody,' he said, the last one of my class has yielded herself to Christ.' I tell you we had a time of rejoicing. He had to leave the next night, so I called his class together that night for a prayer meeting, and there God kindled a fire in my soul that has never gone out. The height of my ambition had been to be a successful merchant, and, if I had known that meeting was going to take that ambition out of me, I might not have gone. But how many times I have thanked God since for that meeting! The dying teacher sat in the midst of his class, and talked with them, and read the fourteenth chapter of John. We tried to sing 'Blest Be the Tie That Binds,' after which we knelt down to prayer. I was just rising from my knees, when one of the class began to pray for her dying teacher. Another prayed, and another, and before we rose, the whole class had prayed. As I went out I said to myself: 'O, God, let me die rather than lose the blessing I have received tonight!'

"The next morning I went to the depot to say good-bye to that teacher. Just before the train started, one of the class came, and before long, without any pre-arrangement, they were all there. What a meeting that was! We tried to sing, but we broke down. The last we saw of that dying teacher, he was standing on the platform of the car, his finger pointing upward, telling that class to meet him in Heaven."

Don't be fooled into thinking that this teacher gave these girls the "God has a wonderful plan for your life" or there's a "God-shaped hole in your heart" message. This was a man who was dying. Such an experience tends to sober us and make us think of the next life, rather than this one. Back in those days it was normal to speak to people about their sins by opening up the Ten Commandments and preaching the Cross. We must get into the mindset of that teacher. We are all dying men and women and we need to speak to sinners about their sin and eternity, rather than of how they can find fulfillment in this life. — Ray Comfort

"I didn't know what this was going to cost me. I was disqualified for business; it had become distasteful to me. I had got a taste of another world, and cared no more for making money. For some days after, the greatest struggle of my life took place. Should I give up business and give myself to Christian work, or should I not? I have never regretted my choice. O, the luxury of leading someone out of the darkness of this world into the glorious light and liberty of the gospel."[4] In a Moody Biography: "Moody did not have television, the Internet, radios, cable TV, fax machines, mp3 players, email, nor did he put out a national magazine. He did most of his preaching on foot and preached in the open air."

In P.B. Bliss' Biography: "Moody's modus operandi was to preach in the open air from the steps of the nearby courthouse for about thirty minutes and then to urge the crowd into his meeting. Bliss and his wife, having heard of Moody but never having heard him, out for a stroll before Sunday evening services, happened onto the outdoor preaching."[5]

The six o'clock meeting at Roundtop, known as the open air meeting, was largely attended, and to me exceedingly enjoyable. Mr. Moody sat beside me on the grass, and led in prayer just before the address. Elijah on Mount Carmel, pleading with his God was not nearer the heart of his Father in faith and acceptableness, I am sure, than he, as he led us all in prayer that beautiful evening. We had a fine meeting that night in the auditorium and several interesting addresses were made, after which, at Mr. Moody's kind invitation, we went to his house, where, in company with a number of others a social hour was much enjoyed.

4 From http://www.tjlbc.com/StreetQuotes.htm
5 Http://www.wholesomewords.org/biography/biomoody4.html

Mr. Moody was not easily discouraged, nor unduly elated. With all the activity of his great soul, there was still a calmness and courage characteristic of him that at once inspired hope, and kept us all at our best all the days and nights of toil. It was my privilege to be associated with him in the Central Palace Hall, in New York City, where thousands of people assembled every day to listen to his preaching. It was an unusual meeting in many respects, beginning in the early morning and continuing without intermission, throughout the day, until ten o'clock at night. There were many interesting conversions in those meetings, and the words which went abroad throughout the land must have accomplished great things. At the hotel, many of his co-workers were entertained, and the brief intervals of personal conversation were always heartily enjoyed. He would invite us to his room in the morning where, with Mrs. Moody and his daughter and others, he engaged in a daily worship before beginning the duties of the day. Handing me one of Henry Drummond's books one day with an inscription in his own hand to Mrs. Wharton, he turned the leaves rapidly and said, "Look at this," and showed me a paragraph where Drummond speaks of passing to the end of a journey of life, and then, "Isn't that good, Wharton—going to the Father, going to the Father." He has gone to the Father; he went before we wanted him to go, and as it seems to us the burning and shining light was consumed all too soon. Still the Father called, and when he went away, he said we must not call him back, and we will not. He cannot return to us, but we may go to him, and in that blessed land we shall meet to part no more. Thanks be unto God, who giveth us the victory through our Lord Jesus Christ. [6]

6 From http://www.biblebelievers.com/moody/33.html

Illustration Portfolio

DWIGHT LYMAN MOODY
1837–1899

Birthplace of D.L. Moody at Northfield, Mass.

D.L. Moody's Mother. From a portrait taken in 1867.

Dwight L. Moody at the time of leaving home for Boston.

D.L. Moody during early years in Chicago.

Mr. Moody at age 27: Sunday-school Worker.

Mr. and Mrs. D.L. Moody in 1864 and in 1869.

Home of D.L. Moody at Northfield.

Illinois Street Church, Chicago.
First building erected by Mr. Moody.
Scene of his efforts before the Chicago fire.

Moody's Tabernacle
First building erected after the Chicago fire. Occupied for two years.

Ira D. Sankey.

EXTERIOR OF OLD PENNSYLVANIA RAILROAD DEPOT, PHILADELPHIA.

INTERIOR OF OLD PENNSYLVANIA RAILROAD DEPOT, PHILADELPHIA.
SCENE OF THE GREAT MEETINGS IN PHILADELPHIA.

The "Hippodrome," New York

Interior View of the "Hippodrome."
During the New York Mission.

Ira S. Sankey (center) on the Porch of Betsy Moody Cottage at Northfield.

Delegates of the Y.M.C.A. assembled in convention at Northfield.

THE NORTHFIELD SEMINARY BUILDINGS, ON THE CONNECTICUT RIVER. MR. MOODY'S ENDURING MONUMENT.

Interior of the Moody Auditorium at Northfield.

Mr. Moody's study in his home at Northfield.

With Campers at Camp Northfield.

Mr. Moody hailing a friend.

Moody with Daughter and Granddaughter.

Mr. Moody as his townsfolk knew him.

Mr. and Mrs. Moody with Grandchildren.

ABSORBED IN HIS CORRESPONDENCE.

Mr. Moody as he appeared in 1886.

Bible used by Mr. Moody for many years.

SPURGEON GOLD

Compiled by Ray Comfort

Bridge-Logos
Alachua, Florida 32615

Foreword

by Rob Holm,
Great-great-great grandson
of Charles Haddon Spurgeon

As a very young child I distinctly remember my mother and me regularly reading together at the breakfast table—I would read the back of the cereal box and the four sides of the milk carton, and she would read her Bible and an old copy of Spurgeon's devotional, *Morning and Evening*. Occasionally she would say something like, "Charles Spurgeon was a very famous preacher in England a long time ago—he's related to us—he is your great, great, great, grandfather." I suppose I feigned interest in this fascinating tidbit of family history, and then continued reading my milk carton.

In 1965, at the age of 5, I "asked Jesus into my heart," but in 1997, I realized I had been a "false convert" for the intervening 32 years. A portion of 2 Corinthians 7:10 declares, "...godly sorrow worketh repentance to salvation." I never had a sorrow directed Godward because I never understood God's holiness and my sinfulness. Only after hearing *Hell's Best Kept Secret* did I realize that I had never repented of my sin—and repentance *must* precede faith (Acts 20:21). Spurgeon once said, "No man ever did come to Jesus Christ and receive Him until he had felt his need of a Savior: no sickness, no physician: no wound, no surgeon. No soul asks for pardon or obtains it till he has felt that sin is an evil for which pardon is necessary; that is to say, repentance always comes with faith." How could I repent of my sin if I didn't know what my sin was (Romans 7:7)? Upon hearing Ray Comfort's *Hell's Best Kept Secret*, the Holy Spirit of God used the Law of God to work in me repentance to salvation.

Immediately after I was saved, God began to prepare me for our present soul-winning ministry in many different ways. This included studying the life, writings, and sermons of my great-great-great grandfather, Charles Haddon Spurgeon. Some Christians have never heard of Charles Spurgeon, while others have researched the smallest details of his life, beliefs, and rich biblical insight. Many know more about Spurgeon than I ever will. Mr. Spurgeon was greatly used of the Lord during his relatively brief ministry, and many Christians in our day would do well to have even a *small* portion of the Holy Spirit power of this man of God.

Ray Comfort has brought together some of the best of Spurgeon, relating specifically to what was understandably my grandfather's greatest burden: the salvation of souls.

May the Lord bless your reading of this volume. May He give you deeper biblical insight and renewed zeal in the battle for lost souls, "...pulling them out of the fire..." (Jude 23).

The time is coming fast,
When all sinners breathe their last,
And the vapour of their life will be gone.

Will a stranger or a friend,
Come unto his journey's end,
Before you show God's grace to his soul? *

Rob and Karen Holm are soul-winners with Amazing Grace Mission (www.amazinggracemission.org), a small group of Christians who assist local churches in state and county fairs, farm shows, rodeos, and flea markets. Amazing Grace Mission operates in all 50 states and several foreign countries.

* From *Don't Let Another Get Away;* copyright 1998, by Rob and Karen Holm.

Preface

My original intention was to call this book *The Cream of Spurgeon*. However, that went sour when my publishers suggested *Spurgeon Gold*. Gold is far more appropriate for Spurgeon. It holds its market value. Heaven's everlasting streets are paved with it. While I am encouraged by the ministries of John Wesley, Whitefield, Edwards, and others, there is something especially awe-inspiring about Spurgeon's eloquence. It is said that the first time D. L. Moody heard him preach, he wept. Spurgeon was able to put into words what most only feel deep within our hearts. He had the ability to take the hammer of eloquence and nail a particular truth.

But is it right to esteem someone like this? To call him the *Prince of Preachers*?

In Hebrews 11, the Scripture makes a point of listing great heroes of the faith. Jesus esteemed John the Baptist, saying that there was none born of woman greater than John. So it is right to honor those who have gone before us—as the Scripture has said, "They being dead, yet speak." And *speak* Spurgeon does. It was said of Jesus, "Never a man spoke like this man," and although the *Prince of Preachers* could never be compared to the Son of God, it can rightly be said of him (when it comes to the sons of Adam), "Never a man spoke like this man." He was unique.

Intellectually, he was in the upper class of eloquence. He was akin to Shakespeare, who had a vocabulary of more than 23,000 words.[1] Spurgeon was eloquent, but not in a worldly sense. He had the ability of being able to pull back the veil of the eternal and give us a fleeting glance. Yet, look at his thoughts about his own preaching:

> It is a long time since I preached a sermon that I was satisfied with. I scarcely recollect ever having done so. You do not know, for you cannot hear my groanings when I go home, Sunday after Sunday, and wish that I could learn to preach somehow or other; wish that I could discover the way to touch your hearts and your consciences, for I seem to myself to be just like the fire when it wants stirring; the coals have got black when I want them to flame forth.

No doubt, such an attitude was the key to his being used by God. But you and I could easily fall back into the shadows of inability. Most of our attempts to communicate great spiritual truth are a weak candle next to the sun of His words. But rather than being discouraged, we should see him as a man gifted by the same God we serve. We should pray that He also gifts us with wisdom and words that express the gospel with greater clarity and greater effectiveness.

You will note that I have dared to put commentary to some of Spurgeon's words. This isn't because they needed a comment, but because I couldn't contain myself. Sometimes I gaze at a sunset and say nothing. I'm overwhelmed. Any talk would spoil the moment. But there are times when I have to say, "Incredible." So it is with Spurgeon's radiant eloquence. James Douglas wrote:

---

1. The average person has around 13,000 words.

> It was no trouble to him to clothe his thoughts, and to give them in doing so eloquent expression. Words trooped to his service as required, and the thought he had to enunciate shone forth clear as crystal. He was extempore in the true sense of the term, for his notes were but the barest bones of his thought. On the spot he mused and the fire burned. If the thought was sublime, he would give it sublime expression; if homely, he bedecked it accordingly. He had mental faculty far in excess of the average. He did with ease, and spontaneously, mental feats which men of name struggle in vain to accomplish. Besides, he had what every large brain has not, large method and power of concentration. He could grasp the bearings of a subject, hold this theme well in hand, and display his thought like troops in a tactical movement.[2]

I have often wondered what Spurgeon's voice was like, and found these words describing it:

> Everybody who tried to describe it spoke of it as "silvery." Both quality and ease were in its tones, comparable most of all to the clear voices of a company of choirboys. His first notes stilled the largest crowd, and his whisper, which could easily be heard over all the great tabernacle, thrilled his hearers. His modulation and compass, enunciation and emphasis were perfect. It was noted by a contemporary writer, "Mr. Spurgeon's voice ... was probably the finest voice that was ever heard in the pulpit."

I am often asked if there was one person who influenced my life and ministry, and without hesitation, I say, "Charles Spurgeon." There is good reason for this. It was a portion of

2. Douglas, *The Prince of Preachers*, pp. 86-87.

one of his sermons that I read way back in August of 1982, that sparked a teaching called *Hell's Best Kept Secret*. About twenty years after I first presented that teaching, I received a phone call from a man named Robert Holm. This gentleman claimed to be the great, great, great grandson of Spurgeon. I was skeptical. Very. He then said that he had come to Christ directly as a result of listening to *Hell's Best Kept Secret* and wanted to drop into our ministry for a few moments of fellowship. An hour or so later Mr. Holm showed up with a birth certificate and documentation proving indeed that he was a direct descendent of the great preacher. What a wonderful irony. God had used the very teaching that was sparked by Charles Spurgeon to save one of his descendents.

My research led me to examine a mountain of sermon information, where I found nugget after gold nugget. But I merely scraped the surface soil. Much of it could have been included in this book, but I reluctantly left it because I wanted to only include that which particularly advanced the evangelistic endeavor. As I read his words I sometimes wept, felt humbled, encouraged, and at times overwhelmed. I discovered sermons where the faithful pastor gently instructed his congregation on how to die. He spoke on every subject imaginable. But running through this wealth of wisdom was a simple crimson thread of the gospel of eternal salvation—that Christ came into this world to save sinners. He said of his ministry, "My main business is the saving of souls. This one thing I do."

I hope that this publication advances Spurgeon's main business; that its words will not just delight your taste buds. May they energize you to reach out to the lost. God forbid that they should add fat to the theological obesity of many. If you are tempted to *self* indulge on this feast of wisdom, please bear in mind that every person who heard his words live, is now dead. Every one of them. Faithful elders, godly deacons, fathers and mothers, and their precious children no doubt sat wide-eyed and feasted on the words of the great preacher. And they are all dead. Time will also take you and me into eternity. If we are trusting in Jesus Christ, we have a moral obligation to reach out to the unsaved while there is still time. This was Spurgeon's great passion, and I pray that it is yours. This gold is not meant to sit of the shelf of a rich man. If it does, then it becomes worthless. Its real value will be seen in its being spent on the cause of the Kingdom.

For this reason I thank God that you picked up this book.

Sincerely,

Ray Comfort

Some People's Eyes

I shall never forget one summer afternoon, when I was preaching in a village chapel about the joys of Heaven, that an elderly lady sitting on my right kept looking to me with intense delight. Some people's eyes greatly help the preacher. A telegraph goes on between us. She seemed to say to me, "Bless God for that. How I am enjoying it!" She kept drinking in the truth, and I poured out more and more precious things about the eternal kingdom and the sight of the Well Beloved, till I saw what I thought was a strange light pass over her face. I went on, and those eyes were still fixed on me. She sat still as a marble figure, and I stopped and said, "Friends, I think that yon sister over there is dead." They said that it was even so, and they bore her away. She had gone. While I was telling of Heaven, she had gone there; and I remember saying that I wished that it had been my case as well as hers. It was better not, perhaps, for many reasons; but oh, I did envy her! I am always looking for the day when I shall see her again. I shall know those eyes, I am sure I shall.

The Speed of Forgiveness

You can be forgiven all your sin in half the tick of a clock, and pass from death to life more swiftly than I can utter the words.

The Reason Sinners Live

Read the Ten Commandments, pause at each one, and confess that you have broken it in either thought or word or deed. Remember that by a glance, we may commit adultery; by a thought, we may be guilty of murder; by a desire, we may steal. Sin is any want of conformity to perfect holiness, and that want of conformity is justly chargeable upon every one of us. Yet the Lord does not, under the gospel dispensation, deal with us according to Law. He does not now sit on the throne of judgment, but He looks down upon us from the throne of grace. Not the iron rod, but the silver scepter, is held over us. The long-suffering of God rules the age, and Jesus the Mediator is the gracious Lord—lieutenant of the dispensation. Instead of destroying offending man from off the face of the earth, the Lord comes near to us in loving condescension, and pleads with us by His Spirit, saying, "You have sinned, but my Son has died. In Him, I am prepared to deal with you in a way of pure mercy and unmingled grace."

O sinner, the fact that you are alive proves that God is not dealing with you according to strict justice, but in patient forbearance; every moment you live is another instance of omnipotent long-suffering. It is the sacrifice of Christ that arrests the axe of justice, which else must execute you. The barren tree is spared because the great Dresser of the vineyard, who bled on Calvary, intercedes and cries, "Let it alone this year also." O my hearer, it is through the shedding of the blood and the mediatorial reign of the Lord Jesus that you are at this moment on praying ground and pleading terms with God! Apart from the blood of atonement, you would now be past hope, shut up forever in the place of doom. But see how the great Father bears with you! He stands prepared to hear your prayer, to accept your confession of sin, to honor your faith, and to save you from your sin through the sacrifice of his dear Son.

A Plea to the Lost

Remember, last of all, that the Law, which is so sharp and terrible to men when it only deals with them for their good, will, if you and I die without being brought to Christ, be much more terrible to us in eternity, when it deals with us in justice for our punishment. Then it will not be enshrined in the body of Moses, but, terrible to tell, it will be incarnate in the person of the Son of God sitting upon the throne. He will be at once the Lawgiver, the Judge, and the Savior; and you that have despised Him as the Savior will have to appear before Him as your Judge. No such judge as He, His justice will be clear and undiluted now that His mercy has been scorned. Oil is soft, but set it on fire, and see how it burns! Love is sweet, but curdle it to jealousy, and see how sour it is! If you turn the Lamb of Zion into the Lion of the tribe of Judah, beware, for He will tear you in pieces, and there shall be none to deliver. Rejected love will change its hand. The pierced hand was outstretched with invitations of mercy, but if these be rejected—O sirs, I am telling you solemn truth, and hear it, I pray you, ere I send you away—if from that hand that was pierced you will not take the perfect salvation, which He is prepared to give to all who confess their guilt, you will have to receive from that selfsame hand the blows of that iron rod, which shall break you into pieces as a potter's vessel. Fly now, and kiss the Son, lest He be angry, and you perish from the way while His wrath is kindled but a little. Blessed are all they that put their trust in Him! Amen.

It is amazing that we hesitate to talk about the wrath of God, for fear of making sinners feel fearful. The fear they feel this side of the grave will be nothing compared to the fear they feel when they stand before Almighty God. — *Ray Comfort*

No Sacrifice without Fire

Behold the altar, built of unhewn stones, and after God's own Law; behold the wood laid thereon; see the victim slain and the blood flowing; but you cannot make a sacrifice without fire—unless the fire from Heaven shall perfect the sacrificial preparations, all will be useless. Behold in the altar the figure of the man; he has faith, courage, love, and consecration, but if he lacks the fire of fervent zeal, his life will be a failure; he will remain an offering unconsumed, and consequently worthless and unaccepted. By this, indeed, may you know the genuine from the false when other things might raise a question: the false is like the altar of Baal whereon there is much wood and a well fed bullock, and around it are active genuflexions and vigorous ritualisms, but there is no true fire from Heaven; while the true is like the altar of Elijah, upon which, in answer to fervent prayers, the hallowed flames descend. One of the first requisites of an earnest, successful, soul-winning man must be zeal. As well a chariot without its steeds, a sun without its beams, a Heaven without its joy, as a man of God without zeal.

Hatred of Goodness

For which of his good works, for which of his generous words, for which of his holy deeds will they fasten His hands to the wood, and His feet to the tree? With unreasonable hatred, with senseless cruelty, they only answer to the question of Pilate, "Why, what evil has He done?" "Let Him be crucified! Let Him be crucified!" The true reason for their hate, no doubt, lay in the natural hatred of all men to perfect goodness. Man feels that the presence of goodness is a silent witness against his own sin, and therefore he longs to get rid of it. To be too holy in the judgment of men is a great crime, for it rebukes their sin. If the holy man has not the power of words, yet his life is one loud witness-bearing for God against the sins of his creatures.

The Christian's Relationship to the Law

And so when a man becomes a believer, he has come of age, and the schoolmaster's rule is over, he is no longer under his former tutors and governors, for his time of liberty appointed by the Father is come. He is not under the pedagogy of the Law any longer, for Christ's work has set Him entirely free therefrom. Certainly, a man sees the office of the Law as pedagogue ended when he ascertains that Christ has fulfilled it. I read the Ten Commandments and say, "These thundered at me and I trembled at them, but Christ has kept them, kept them for me. He was my representative in every act of His obedient life and death, and before God, it is as if I had kept the Law, and I stand accepted in the Beloved. When Jesus Christ is seen of God, God sees His people in Him, and they are justified through His righteousness, because they have faith in Him. "He that believeth in Him is not condemned." Oh, is it not a thousand mercies in one that the grand old cannons of the Law are no longer turned against us? Christ has either spiked them or else turned them on our enemies by fulfilling the Law so that they are on our side instead of against us.

A Plea to the Unsaved

There are some of you standing in these aisles and sitting in these pews, who I feel in my soul will never have another invitation, and if this be rejected today, I feel a solemn motion in my soul—I think it is of the Holy Ghost—that you will never hear another faithful sermon, but you shall go down to hell impenitent, unsaved, except you trust in Jesus *now*. I speak not as a man, but I speak as God's ambassador to your souls, and I command you, in God's name, trust Jesus, trust *now*. At your peril, reject the voice that speaks from Heaven, for "he that believeth not shall be damned." How shall you escape if you neglect so great salvation? When it comes right home to you, when it thrusts itself in your way, oh, if you will neglect it, how can you escape? With tears, I would invite you, and, if I could, would compel you to come in. Why will you not? O souls, if you will be damned, if you make up your mind that no mercy shall ever woo you, and no warnings shall ever move you, then, sirs, what chains of vengeance must you feel that slight these bonds of love. You have deserved the deepest hell, for you slight the joys above. God save you. He will save you, if you trust in Jesus. God help you to trust Him even now, for Jesus' sake. Amen.

The Instruction of Children

We testify that Christ is able to change man's nature, and then good fruits will come as a matter of course. But I am afraid that in many Sunday schools the children are taught a different doctrine, somewhat after this fashion: "Now, dear children, be very good, and obey your parents, and love Jesus, and you will be saved." That is not the gospel, and it is not true. Often do I hear it said, "*Love* Jesus, dear children." That is not the gospel. It is, "Trust Him"—"Believe." Not love, but faith is the saving grace, and that love of Jesus of a sentimental kind, which does not spring out of faith in Him, is a spurious emotion, a counterfeit of love, not at all the love of God, shed abroad in the heart by the Holy Spirit. The root of the matter is, "Believe in the Lord Jesus Christ and you shalt be saved;" and that is the gospel for a child of two years of age, and the gospel for a man of a hundred. There is only one gospel for all that are born on the face of the earth—"Believe in Jesus."

Finding the Right Church

If you wait for a perfect church, you must wait until you get to Heaven; and even if you could find a perfect assembly on earth, I am sure they would not admit you to their fellowship, for you are not perfect yourself. Find out those people who are nearest to the Scriptures, who hold the truth in doctrine and in ordinance, and are most like the apostolic church, and then cast in your lot with them, and you will be blessed in the deed

Prayer for the Unsaved

If you really desire that men should be saved, pray for them. It is an empty wish, a mere formality, if you do not turn it into prayer. Every loving desire for any man or woman should, by the believer, be taken before God in prayer. We cannot expect that God will save men unless His people pray for it. There must be travail before the birth, and there must be travail in prayer with God before we can expect that many will be born again into the church of God. Oh, for more prayer! Let us cry to God in secret, and in the family, and in all our assemblies, that God would save the sons of men.

Jesus of Nazareth

Commend me to a single sentence in the whole of Christ's teaching that would make a despot sit more steadfastly upon His throne. He never taught anarchy. Find, if you can, a single word that would make men burst the bonds of righteous fealty, and lead lawless lives. He taught no asceticism that would denude life of wholesome pleasure or healthful enjoyment. Far, far was He, on the other hand, from teaching any libertinism that would tolerate aught that is unclean, unchaste, and impure in word or deed. His teaching was for man—instructing him what was best for him to do, how it was best to do it, and what it was necessary for his own good that he should eschew and avoid. "Never man spake like this man!"

The Christian Attitude to the Law

If we are Christians, we delight in that Law, and we are not under it as a rule of condemnation and of judgment, but we rejoice to obey it. We could not suggest an alteration to it, which would be an improvement. The Ten Commandments are very simple, but absolutely perfect for the purpose for which they were intended. To add another to them or to take one away from them would be to spoil the whole. We "delight in the Law of God after the inward man." Whoever may be Antinomians, that is, those who are "against the Law," we are not to be numbered amongst them, for we can say, with Paul, "The Law is holy, and the commandment holy, and just, and good;" and though we are carnal, and often feel ourselves "sold under sin," yet we cannot find any fault with the Law. If eternal life could have come by any Law, it would have come by that Law; and even though that Law now can do nothing for us but condemn us, yet, as we hear its terrible sentence, we feel that the Law "is holy, and just, and good." We desire, then, to have even the moral Law in our hearts, and to have it written there, that none, of our steps may slide.

Judas Was a Preacher

Judas was *a preacher*; nay, he was a foremost preacher. "He obtained part of this ministry," said the Apostle Peter. He was not simply one of the seventy; he had been selected by the Lord Himself as one of the twelve, an honorable member of the college of the apostles. Doubtless, he had preached the gospel so that many had been gladdened by his voice, and miraculous powers had been vouchsafed to him, so that at his word, the sick had been healed, deaf ears had been opened, and the blind had been made to see. Nay, there is no doubt that he, who could not keep the devil out of himself, had cast devils out of others. Yet how are you fallen from Heaven, O Lucifer, son of the morning! He that was as a prophet in the midst of the people, and spake with the tongue of the learned, whose word and wonders proved that he had been with Jesus and had learned from him—he betrays his Master. Understand, my brethren, that no gifts can ensure grace, and that no position of honor or usefulness in the Church will necessarily prove our being true to our Lord and Master. Doubtless, there are bishops in hell, and crowds of those who once occupied the pulpit are now condemned forever to bewail their hypocrisy. You that are Church-officers do not conclude that because you enjoy the confidence of the Church, therefore there is an absolute certainty the grace of God in you. Perhaps it is the most dangerous of all positions for a man to become well known and much respected by the religious world, and yet to be rotten at the core. To be where others can observe our faults is a healthy thing, though painful; but to live with beloved friends who would not believe it possible for us to do wrong, and who, if they saw us err, would make excuses for us—this is to be where it is next to impossible for us ever to be aroused if our hearts be not right with God. To have a fair reputation and a false heart is to stand upon the brink of hell.

The Temporal Gifts of the World

Naked you did come into it, and it will take care you shalt take nothing out of it, for naked shall you go out of it again. Oh, man, you have accumulated knowledge until you have become a walking encyclopedia, but what shall you take with you? What difference shall there be between your hollow skull and that of the meanest peasant, when some wanton sexton, in some future year, shall take it up or split it with his spade? What shall you be the better for all those big thoughts that have stretched skull, and all those marvelous conceptions that have made it ache so much that you could scarcely carry it upon your shoulders? You will go back again to your fellow earth, and the worm shall eat you, and the philosopher shall taste no sweeter to his tooth than did the peasant; and, then, whether you be prince or king, or whether you be a poor, ignorant man, the worms shall make no distinction. You shall still rot—still be consumed; noisome gases and a handful of dust shall be your whole residuum.

What then can the world give? If it tried, it could not give you anything that would last; it cannot give you anything better than air. It can give you nothing that can pass into eternity with you. What though it follow you with the trumpet of fame? That trumpet cannot be heard halfway across the Jordan. If all the men in the world clapped their hands in your praise, not one angel, even on the very borders of the celestial world would observe the tumult of applause. The world can give you nothing that you can carry with you. You are at the best a packhorse that shall carry its burden till it ends its journey, and then it must lie down and die. You do but carry a burden on your back, and verily, death shall unload you ere you are suffered to enter another world.

How different is Christ in His gifts! What He gives, He gives forever. When He bestows mercies, they are lasting things; no shadows does He give, but real substance—no fancies, but eternal realities does He bestow. Oh, men of this world, when your gold is melted—when your diamonds have dissolved in gas—when your estates have gone—when your hopes are lost, and when your goods are destroyed, then shall the people of God begin to know their riches; then shall they shine forth as the sun in the kingdom of their Father.

The Nature of Sin

Sin! From your fruitful womb what myriads of ills proceed! What countless hosts of evils are the fruits of sin! How many are the sins themselves! Sins of *thought*—rebellious thoughts, proud thoughts, blasphemous thoughts, atheistic thoughts, covetous thoughts, lustful thoughts, impatient thoughts, cruel thoughts, false thoughts, thoughts of ill memory, and dreams of an unholy future; what swarms are there! However, the omission of thoughts, which should have been such as thoughts of repentance, gratitude, reverence, faith, and the like—these are equally numerous. With the double list, my roll is written within and without with a hideous catalogue. As the gnats that swarm the air at eventide, so numerous are the transgressions of the mind.

There are many within contemporary Christianity who believe that unregenerate man already understands the true nature of sin. They maintain that these people don't need to be confronted with the Law because they understand it in truth. While many readily acknowledge that lying, stealing, blasphemy, adultery (and even lust and hatred) are morally wrong, they cannot truly see sin without the Holy Spirit's helping hand under the floodlight of the Moral Law. The Apostle Paul (because of his conscience) no doubt knew that sin was morally wrong, but he made the statement that he had not known sin but by the Law (see Romans 7:7). The Law was the axe that cut off any hope of self-righteousness. It showed sin to be exceedingly sinful (see Romans 7:13) and left him without hope of salvation. It made him thirst for the righteousness that could only be found in Christ. It is with this instruction that the Law acts as a schoolmaster to bring us to Christ (see Galatians 3:24). The test of where someone's understanding is, is their answer to the question, "Do you think that you are a good person?" Most will say that they are morally good despite the fact that they acknowledge the sins of lying, stealing, etc. (see Proverbs 20:6).

Notice that Paul does "The Good Test" on the self-righteous Jews in Romans Chapter two. They already possessed the mirror of the perfect Law of liberty, but they had never looked into it themselves and seen sin in its true light (see Romans 2:18–20). So Paul turned the mirror towards them so that they could see themselves in truth. He used the Eighth Commandment and personalized it by asking, "You that preach a man should not steal, do you steal?" Then he used the Seventh: "You that say a man should not commit adultery, do you commit adultery?" Then the First and Second: "You that abhor idols, do you commit sacrilege?" He then told them that their hypocrisy caused others to break the Third Commandment by blaspheming.

How do we know that unrepentant man has no real knowledge of sin? The Scriptures tell us "There is none that understands, there is none that seeks after God" (Romans 3:11, italics added). It is the Law that helps us personalize our transgressions. It does what Nathan the prophet did for King David. It brings God and His standards into the picture and helps us throw ourselves before the throne of His mercy. It causes us to personalize our sin and say, "I have gone out of the way. I am together become unprofitable; I am not good. My throat is an open sepulcher; with my tongue I have used deceit. The poison of asps is under my lips. My mouth is full of cursing and bitterness. My feet are swift to shed blood. Destruction and misery are in my ways. And the way of peace have I not known. There is no fear of God before my eyes. My mouth is stopped by the Law, and I am therefore guilty before God. I have sinned and come short of the glory of God. But thanks be to God, I am freely justified by his grace through the redemption that is in Christ Jesus" (based on Romans chapter three).

While there are those that may be quick to say that some of these verses are not personably applicable, the true convert knows that the wickedness of his heart has never been put to the test. Think where your heart would take you if you knew that there was no God and therefore no Judgment Day. What gossip would come through your lips, what lost wallet wouldn't be returned, what person would be free from your lustful eyes? What jealousy and hatred wouldn't lead to murder … if you knew that you would never, could never be caught because there was no God and therefore no retribution?

That's what many believe, and that's why we see the sins of these verses played out in the everyday life of this wicked world—of which we were once a part. But after the Law has done its accusing work, with a broken and contrite King David, we can now say that God has had mercy on us, because of His loving kindness. According to the multitude of His tender mercies, He blotted out our transgressions. He washed us thoroughly from our iniquity and cleansed us from our sin. For we acknowledged our transgressions and our sin was ever before us. Against Him and Him only had we sinned and done evil in His sight. We were shapened in iniquity, when He desired truth in the inwards parts. But He made us clean. He washed us and made us whiter than snow. He hid his face from our sins, blotted out our iniquities and created a clean heart within us. ~ *Ray Comfort*

Encouragement to Preachers

The sermon preached by Peter at Pentecost was the arrow of the Lord's deliverance to three thousand, and there is no reason why the Lord should not cause one of ours to be the same. Three thousand cannot be converted if only a hundred are present to hear; but with this rest assembly, and thousands of smaller ones within gunshot, why should not the slain of the Lord be many? Assuredly, the divine Comforter can as readily bless three millions as three individuals.

The Necessity of Preaching

Suppose that we do not preach the gospel and warn the wicked man, so that he turns not from his iniquity. What then? Hear this voice: "He shall perish, but his blood will I require at thine hand." What will my Lord say to me if I am unfaithful to you? "Where is the blood of those people who gathered at Newington Butts? Where is the blood of that crowd that came together to hear you speak, and you did not preach the gospel to them?" Oh, it were better for me that I had never been born than that I should not preach the gospel! "Woe is unto me if I preach not the gospel" of Christ, for men perish where there is not the Word of God!

The Unpardonable Sin

One friend perhaps says, "I am afraid that I have committed the unpardonable sin." If you come to Christ, you have not, I know; for he who comes to Him, Jesus will in no wise cast out. He cannot, therefore, have committed the unpardonable sin. Come along with you, man, and if you are blacker than all the rest of the sinners in the world, so much the more glorious shall be the grace of God when it shall have proved its power by washing you whiter than snow in the precious blood of Jesus.

Genuine Conversion

If we labor for souls, we must not be content unless souls are really saved, for the apostle says, "For I bear them record that they have a zeal of God." Well, does not that satisfy you, Paul? They are zealous for God. They are red-hot. "No," says he, "not unless it is in the right way. They have a zeal of God, but not according to knowledge." We feel very thankful when we see tears stream down the cheek, but you know, people cry at the theater, and there is not much in it. Pray God it may not end in a shower of tears; but that the heart may bleed as well as the eyes weep. It may happen that we have induced our hearers to give up some outward sins. So far, so good. But it is written, "You must be born again;" and if this vital change is not experienced, all outward reformation will land them short of Heaven.

The Crucifixion

Cowardice! cowardice! cowardice, craven, base lies at your door, O humanity! The Christ who was like a sheep—harmless and defenseless—was treated as if He had been one of the wild beasts of the forest. Who could have had the heart to smite Him who gave His back to the smiters, and His cheeks to those who plucked off the hair? O humanity! If I stand at the bar to impeach you, I scarce know where to commence the indictment, and, having commenced it, I know not where to close it. How fallen, dishonored, infamous are you, O humanity! Low, depraved, heinous, indeed, have you become that you could put the Messiah Himself to death, and crucify the Lord of Glory.

How these words wonderfully express the thoughts that the Christian has as he reads the Gospels' accounts of the crucifixion. ~ *Ray Comfort*

A Clear Message

If we want men to be truly converted, we must set before them the plan of salvation very clearly and distinctly. I meet with hundreds of persons who have had some kind of work upon their hearts, but they tell me that they walk in a mist. They have not quite understood it. They felt that they were on the rock, but they were not quite sure what the rock really was. It is a good thing that our zeal for God should be according to knowledge, that we know what we believe, and why we believe it, and know that we are saved and how we are saved and why we are saved; for if there be a mistake here, it may be fatal.

False Converts

Who was it that added Judas, and Ananias and Sapphire, and Simon Magus, and Demas to the church? Who was it that stole forth by night and spread tares among the wheat? That evil spirit is not dead, he is still busy enough in this department, and continually adds to the church each as are not saved. His are the mixed multitude that infest the camp of Israel, and are the first to fall a lusting; his the Achane who bring a curse upon the tribes; his are those of whom Jude says, "Certain men crept in unawares who were before of old ordained to this condemnation." These adulterate the church, and by so doing, they weaken and defile it, and bring it much grief and dishonor.

Blinded Eyes

Though I heard the gospel from my childhood, and was brought up upon the very knee of piety, I did not understand what I must do to be saved till I heard that text preached from—"Look unto me, and be saved, all the ends of the earth." I do not believe that my ignorance was the fault of the preacher. It was certainly not the fault of my father or my mother, and not the fault of the Bible, which I had read through again and again; but it was the fault of these dim eyes, that I could not see. Go on! go on! you preachers of the Word. Spread abroad the knowledge of this great fact, that "He that believeth on the Son hath everlasting life."

The Purpose of the Law

The business of the Law is first to teach us our obligations to God. Let us ask ourselves if we have ever heard the Law teaching us in that way. Brethren, read the Law of Ten Commandments, and study each separate precept, and you will find that in those ten short precepts you have all the moral virtues, the full compass of your accountability to God, and of your relationship to your fellowmen. It is a wonderful condensation of morals. The essence of all just decrees and statutes lies there. Perfection is there photographed, and holiness mapped out. No one has ever been able to add to it without creating an excrescence, not a word could be taken from it without causing a serious omission. It is the perfect Law of God, and tells us exactly what we ought to be; if we are in any degree deficient, we are to that extent guilty before God. Now, when the Law comes to a man's conscience, it reveals to him the divine standard of right—holds it up before him—makes him look at it—and apprises him that the Commandments do not merely refer to acts and deeds, but with equal force to the words and thoughts from whence they proceed.

It is a perfect Law [see Psalm 19:7 KJV] of a perfect God that demands moral perfection. That is what we are commanded to warn every man, that we may present every man perfect in Christ Jesus. — *Ray Comfort*

Mortality

We do not realize our mortality unless we are startled into a recognition of it. We believe others to be mortal, and are not much surprised when they fall; but we have a secret notion that no axe will for the present be laid at our root. Yet reason would lead a man to say, "It happens to many suddenly to die; why should it not happen to me?"

This is one area that we often neglect as Christians—to confront men and women about their mortality. Spurgeon does this continually. None of us truly believes that we could die today or tomorrow. We put death way into the future. Most people have thoughts about their mortality, even if they don't air them.

A good way to open up spiritual things with the unsaved is to mention spiritual things (perhaps using a tract) and simply say, "Do you ever think about what happens after someone dies? What's on the other side?" Don't be afraid to reason with them about the fact that it is God and God alone that determines how long we live. If He says, "You fool, tonight your soul is required out you," we cannot resist His will. Tell them that God may lose patience with their continual rebellion and their procrastination, and let the fear of death spark the fear of God. ~ *Ray Comfort*

Science and the Bible

My friend, the philosopher, says it may be very well for me to urge people to read the Bible, but he thinks there are a great many sciences far more interesting and useful than theology. *Extremely obliged to you for your opinion, sir.* What science do you mean? The science of dissecting beetles and arranging butterflies? "No," you say, "certainly not." The science, then, of arranging stones and telling us of the strata of the earth? "No, not exactly that." Which science then? "Oh, all sciences," say you, "are better than the science of the Bible." Ah! sir, that is your opinion, and it is because you are far from God, that you say so.

But the science of Jesus Christ is the most excellent of sciences. Let no one turn away from the Bible because it is not a book of learning and wisdom. It is. Would you know astronomy? It is here; it tells you of the Sun of Righteousness and the Star of Bethlehem. Would you know botany? It is here; it tells you of the plant of renown—the Lily of the Valley and the Rose of Sharon. Would you know geology and mineralogy? You shall learn it here, for you may read of the Rock of Ages and the White Stone with a name graven thereon, which no man knows, saying he that receives it. Would you study history? Here is the most ancient of all the records of the history of the human race. Whatever your science is, come and bend o'er this book; your science is here. Come and drink out of this fair fount of knowledge and wisdom, and you shall find yourselves made wise unto salvation. Wise and foolish, babes and men, gray-headed sires, youths and maidens—I speak to you, I plead with you, I beg of you respect your Bibles and search them out, for in them you think you have eternal life, and these are they which testify of Christ.

Willful Ignorance

Ah, dear friends! I would to God they know the pearl of great price, the incomparable value of salvation by blood; for then would they reckon the highest glory of this present world as unworthy to be compared with the least delight of the kingdom of God. With many, this ignorance is *willful*. Nobody is so blind as the man that does not want to see, nobody so deaf as the man that does not wish to hear. Many are like the hogs in harvest —very deaf when they are told to go out of the cornfield. And so, when sinners run riot in their sins, they are very deaf indeed when they are told to quit them and fly to Christ for refuge. Some of you, perhaps, do not want to know too much. When you come to that part of the Bible that begins to touch your conscience, you say, "Shut that up." You will go on somewhere else. You do not want to know. Willful ignorance will bring terrible damnation. If there be salvation, and you do not want to know it, then you deserve to be cast away.

Hypocrisy

Those of you who say, "We do not want that sermon," are probably the persons who need it most. He who shall say, "Well, we have no Judas amongst us," is probably a Judas himself. Oh! search yourselves; turn out every cranny; look in every corner of your soul to see whether your religion be for Christ's sake and for truth's sake and for God's sake, or whether it be a profession that you take up because it is a respectable thing, a profession that you keep up because it keeps you up. The Lord search us and try us, and bring us to know our ways.

Reading the Scriptures

If this be the Word of God, what will become of some of you who have not read it for the last month? "Month, sir! I have not read it for this year." Ay, there are some of you who have not read it at all. Most people treat the Bible very politely. They have a small pocket volume, neatly bound; they put a white pocket-handkerchief around it, and carry it to their places of worship. When they get home, they lay it up in a drawer till next Sunday morning; then it comes out again for a little bit of a treat and goes to chapel; that is all the poor Bible gets in the way of an airing. That is your style of entertaining this Heavenly messenger. There is dust enough on some of your Bibles to write "damnation" with your fingers. There are some of you who have not turned over your Bibles for a long, long, long while, and what think you? I tell you blunt words, but true words. What will God say at last? When you shall come before Him, He shall say,

"Did you read my Bible?" *No.* "I wrote you a letter of mercy; did you read it?" *No.* "Rebel! I have sent you a letter inviting you to me; did you ever read it?" *Lord, I never broke the seal; I kept it shut up.* "Wretch!" says God, "Then you deserve hell. I sent you a loving epistle and you would not even break the seal; what shall I do to you?" Oh! let it not be so with you. Be Bible readers; be Bible searchers.

How wonderful it is to hear such powerful and sobering words. Never before in history has there been such a glut of Bibles. The average Christian bookstore has hundreds (if not access to thousands) of different versions for us to choose from—the big print version, small print, large Bibles, small Bibles, thin Bible, fat Bibles, Bibles for men, Bibles for women, versions for kids, for youth groups, for teens and for families. Yet, so few Christians read the Word every day without fail. They are not as Job, who esteemed the words of His mouth, "more than [his] necessary food." I would like to add two more versions that seem appropriate: The Neglected Version and The Damnation Version. ~ *Ray Comfort*

Divine Righteousness

Men, ignorant of God's righteousness, are said to be "going about to establish their own righteousness"—in other words, to set up the *poor idol* of their own righteousness. Man sees God's righteousness, and, instead of accepting it, he says, "I think I could match that. I will set up my own righteousness." There is a treasure of gold, and the man says, "No, I will not have that. I think that I could make a sovereign at home out of a bit of brass." Fool that he is! How shall he mimic God? If I were at Heaven's wide-open gate, and a voice should say, "Enter freely," and I replied, "No, I think I prefer the Surrey hills, or a place down by the seaside," what a fool I should be! but, even then, not so great a fool as when forsaking the righteousness of God, I want to set up my own. A human thing at best, how shall that match the divine righteousness? An imperfect thing at best, how shall I compare that with the perfect righteousness of Christ? A fading, floating thing, always apt to be damaged by the next moment's temptation, how can I be so foolish? A ridiculous thing, an ignominious thing, a filthy thing. Paul said that his righteousness, which was of the Law, was "blameless;" and yet he counted it dung that he might win Christ—dung, the most filthy thing. Here, scavenger, take it away! Have any of you any righteousness of your own? I do not believe that even the dustman would take it. He would say, "No, the carts are not for carting away man's righteousness; we have no place bad enough to shoot it into." Shoot it into the bottomless pit—nay, even there they have not any righteousness, for they know their true condition. Human righteousness is a great lie; it is filthy rags. Away with it from off the face of the earth!

The Law's Matchless Perfection

I warrant you it is a humbling day when a man gets to understand that fore very idle word that he has spoken, he will be brought to account; and when he hears again that his desires and imaginations will all come under divine scrutiny. How startled is the purest mind when it understands that whosoever looks upon a woman to lust after her hath committed adultery with her already in his heart, so that even glances of the eye and thoughts of the heart are offenses of the Law. The Law of God takes cognizance of the entire nature, and reveals the evil, which lurks in every faculty. The mere imagination of sin is sinful—the very conception of it, albeit that we should reject it, and never carry it into act, would still be a stain upon our minds, and render us impure before the thrice holy God. This is one of the first works of the Law—to show us what spotless purity it demands, and to reveal to us the matchless perfection, which alone can meet its requirements.

Open-Air Preaching

One of the earliest things a minister should do when he leaves college and settles in a country town or village is to begin open-air speaking ... No sort of defense is needed for preaching out of doors, but it would need very potent arguments to prove that a man had done his duty who has never preached beyond the walls of his meeting place.

The Awakened Conscience

The conscience of a man, when he is really quickened and awakened by the Holy Spirit, speaks the truth. It rings the great alarm bell. And if he turns over in his bed, that great alarm bell rings out again and again, "The wrath to come! The wrath to come! The wrath to come!"

Human Wisdom

I was in the Hall of Philosophers a little while ago, where were the busts of Socrates, and Plato, and Solon, and all the great men of former ages. But if they were all put together, of what small account were the maxims that they taught mankind for the promotion of real happiness and true goodness? Why, the sum total is nothing in comparison with that one sermon of the Christ of Nazareth, which He preached upon the Mount. That one sermon put into the scale outweighs the wisdom of Greece and Rome. And yet, when the Man had come who unselfishly, lovingly, tenderly, wisely would lead our fallen race into the paths of holiness, and onward to the goal of perfect felicity, what did humanity do but grind its teeth, and gather up its weapons and say, "Away with such a fellow from the earth; it is not fit that He should live!" Alas, human nature! How demented and imbecilic you are! The very beasts might lay claim to more sagacity and shrewdness than you have.

Salvation Verses

Every star in Heaven yields its ray of light to cheer the mariner upon the watery waste, but there are leaders among that sparkling host—stars of the first magnitude—whose golden lamps are so dexterously hung, and withal trimmed with such excessive care, that they offer waymarks to the wanderer by which he may be able to steer his vessel to the desired haven. So all the promises of Scripture are full of comfort, in their sphere, they glow and glisten with the warmth and light of love; but there are "bright particular stars," even among these; promises, conspicuous as Orion, brilliant as the Pleiades, fixed as Arcturus with his sons. Brethren, you know those soul-saving texts to which I refer, which are radiant with comfort, and have in them such a blessed combination of simple words and comforting sentences that they guide multitudes of sinners to the port of peace in Jesus Christ.

Heaven and Hell

Oh! that sweet scene beyond the clouds, sweet fields arrayed in living green, and rivers of delight. Are not these great things? But then, poor unregenerate son, the Bible says, if you are lost, you are lost forever; it tells you that if you died without Christ, without God, there is no hope for you, that there is a place without a gleam of hope, where you shall read in burning letters, "You knew your duty, but you did it not." It tells you that you shall be driven from His presence with a "Depart, you cursed." Are not these great things? Yes, sirs, as Heaven is desirable, as hell is terrible, as time is short, as eternity is infinite, as the soul is precious, as pains to be shunned, as Heaven is to be sought, as God is eternal, and as His words are sure, these are great things, things you ought to listen to.

The Mercy of God

Let me tell you that the mercy of God flows freely. It wants no money and no price from you, no fitness of frames and feelings, no preparation of good works or penitence. Free as the brook, which leaps from the mountainside, at which every weary traveler may drink, so free is the mercy of God.[45] Free, as the sun that shines, gilds the mountain's brow, and makes glad the valleys without fee or reward, so free is the mercy of God to every needy sinner. Free, as the air, which belts the earth and penetrates the peasant's cottage as well as the royal palace without purchase or premium, so free is the mercy of God in Christ.

> Someone once said that the branch that carries the most fruit, hangs the lowest. The closer we get to the light, the more we see our sin in truth. Blessed are they that mourn. They are blessed because they not only see their terrible sin, but they then see the glorious cross. Sin magnifies grace. How gracious God is to sinners. Those, who have a shallow understanding of sin, have a shallow understanding of mercy. — Ray Comfort

Just Damnation

I know that you have attended this Tabernacle ever since it was built, and listened to our ministry for years, but boast not of that; away with that as a ground of trust; pull off that garment. You have never failed in business; you have brought up your children well; you never swear; you were never a drunkard; midnight orgies never saw you mixed up in them. This is well, but I pray you, put not on this as your proper dress. The proper dress for a sinner to go to Christ in is sackcloth and the rope. "Well," says one, "I never will acknowledge that I deserve to be damned!" Then you never will be saved. "Well," says another, "I never will take the language of a great sinner upon my lips." Then you shall never be saved, for unless you are willing to confess that God may justly damn you, God will never save you. But if you feel in your heart tonight that if He sends your soul to hell, His righteous Law approves it well; if you wonder how it is that you are not in the pit, and marvel why such mercy should have been shown to you, come, brother, come. Come as you are, for you wear the true court-dress of a sinner. When a beggar goes out to beg at the door, should he put on a new black coat, a clean white cravat, and kid gloves? Nay, verily, let him clothe himself in tatters—the more rents he has, the better—for tatters are the livery of a beggar, and rags are the court-dress of a mendicant. So, come in your sins; come in your doubts; come in your hardness of heart; come in your impenitence; come in your deadness; come in your lethargy; come as you are—foul, vile, filthy, waiting for no amendment, but with a rope upon your neck, and a garment of sackcloth about your loins. Come now, come now; God help you to come.

It is the Law in the hand of the Spirit that convinces men and women that they are justly damned. Without the Law, they are left without the knowledge that sin is exceedingly sinful [see Romans 7:13]. This is why the contemporary Church must imitate Christ, Paul, and men like Spurgeon in their efforts to reach the lost. They must open up the spiritual nature of God's Law as Jesus did to show the world that it desperately needs God's mercy or it will be damned. — Ray Comfort

Good Works

Now, again, there are some other people who . . . do not care particularly about this covering for the head, but they think they will get a pair of slippers, and thus, cover their nakedness. "What do you mean by that?" says one. Well, good works. "Ah!" they say, "those doctrinal people, they look to the head. I do not care about the head. I shall look to the feet." And so, they look to the feet, and they make themselves very decent sort of people, too. They keep the Sabbath; they frequent the house of God; they read the Bible; they say a form of prayer; and they try to be honest, sober, and so forth. Very right.

I do not say a word against slippers, only that they are not a good covering for the whole man. I do not say a word against good slippers. Good works are very well, but they are not sufficient. Good works are like a pair of shoes, but do not let a man think a pair of shoes can become wide enough to cover his whole body. Such men are deluded. They think if their outward walks and conversation are good and right and proper that, therefore, their whole nakedness is covered. Oh! never delude yourselves into such an idea as that. Though you walk in the commandments of the Lord, blameless in the eyes of all men, yet so long as sin is in your heart, and the past sin of your life is unforgiven, you stand helpless, unclothed souls, in the estimation of God, and your garment is too narrow for you to wrap yourself in it.

Perfection Demanded

Do you want to be saved by your own righteousness? Do you know what kind of righteousness it must be? To be accepted, it must be perfect. That is to say, if you have committed but one sin, you have stained your character in the sight of God, and your hope of perfect righteousness is gone. God's Law requires obedience, from the first moment that the creature understands that Law, as long as ever that creature lives. Mark what it requires of you: "Thou shalt love the Lord your God with all your heart, and with all your soul, and with all your strength, and with all your mind." Have you done that? "And your neighbor as yourself." Have you done that? Why, there is not one of us who has done it. If we had kept the Law of God completely, from the first commandment to the last, from the first day until now, even that would not save us; for, if there were to be one sinful word or deed during the rest of life, it would spoil the whole, and God could not accept our righteousness.

When a man commits one sin, he is guilty of disobedience to all the commandments of God, for "he that offends in one point is guilty of all." Here is a chain containing twenty links. If I break one of them, I have broken the chain. True, there are nineteen perfect links, but if number twenty is snapped, down goes the cage over the mouth of the mine, and the miners are killed. Suppose that I should be required to produce a perfect vase of alabaster or clear crystal as a present to the Queen. But my servant-maid has chipped it just a little. What is to be done? I may possibly find somebody to use some patent cement, and fasten the little pieces in their places, but when all is done, it is chipped; it is not perfect; and if it must be perfect before royalty can accept it, I must got another vase, for this one will not do.

The Sweetness of Preaching Christ

And let me add to this that there is a very special sweetness about preaching Christ, in the public proclamation of His word. It may be that some brother here has the gift of speech, but has never used it for his Master. Let me put in my witness here. God's word has been unutterably sweet to my own heart, as I have believed it; it has been remarkably precious to me as I have confessed it as a Christian man; but still there is a something—I cannot tell you what—of singular delight about the preaching of this word. Oh, sometimes, when I have prepared my sermon, it has been bitter in my belly, but it has been as honey in my mouth when I have preached it to the great congregation gathered here! If I might choose my destiny, and if I had even to stop out of Heaven for the purpose, it would be Heaven to me, to be permitted always to be preaching Christ and the glories of His salvation; and I do not know that I should have any choice between that and Heaven. If I might be privileged to be, without ceasing, lauding and praising and extolling that dear Word of God, the Christ who was born at Bethlehem, if I might tell out to sinners everywhere that God is, in Him, making reconciliation, nay, that He has made reconciliation for all who believe in Him, this might be Heaven enough, at least for one poor heart, world without end.

"How sweet are your words unto my taste! yea, sweeter than honey to my mouth!" Try, brother, whether it will not sweeten your mouth if you begin to preach Christ. Perhaps you have been too quiet and too silent. Get up and speak for Jesus, and see whether the honey does not come into your mouth at once. In the olden time, they pictured the orator with bees buzzing round his lips, storing up the honey that dropped from his sweet utterances. This may be but a fable concerning the human talker; but certainly it is true of the man who preaches Christ, that his lips drop honey, and the more he speaks of his dear Lord and Master, and the less he tries with human eloquence to magnify himself, the more of sacred sweetness shall there be in every word that he utters.

The Daily Battle

Soldier of Christ, you have to struggle with yourself. My own experience is a daily struggle with myself. I wish I could find in me something friendly to grace, but hitherto I have searched my nature through, and have found everything in rebellion against God. At one time, there comes the torpor of sloth, when one ought to be active every moment, having so much to do for God and for the souls of men, and so little time to do it in. At another time, there comes the quickness of passion. When we would be calm and cool, and play the Christian, bearing with patience, there come the unadvised word and the rash expression. Anon, we are troubled with conceit, the devilish whisper—I can call it no less—"How well you have done! How well have you played your part!" This pride is the archenemy of our souls. Then will come distrust—foul and faithless—suggesting that God does not regard the affairs of men, and will not interpose on our behalf. Fresh forms of evil are generated in our own breasts, and this chameleon heart of ours, which never seems of one color but for a single moment, which is this and that by turns and nothing long, challenges us on all occasions, and against it we shall have perpetually to struggle. Unless we deny ourselves and lay violent hands upon the impulses of our nature, are shall never come to the place where the crowns are distributed to the conquerors.

Open-Air Preaching

You that preach Christ in the streets, go on preaching Him. I saw a man preaching the other day with no creature but one dog to listen to him, and I really thought that he might as well have gone home. But I met with a story yesterday, which I know to be true, and it showed me that I was making a mistake. There was a woman who for years had been in such dreadful despair that she would not even hear the gospel. She came to be very ill, and she said to one that called upon her, "You sent a man to preach under my window three months ago, and I got a blessing." "No," the friend said, "I never sent anybody to preach under your window." "Oh," she said, "I think you did, for he came and preached, and my maid said that there was nobody listening to him. I did not want to hear him; and as he made so much noise, my maid shut the window, and I lay down in bed; but the man shouted so that I was obliged to hear him; and I thank God I did, for I heard the gospel, and I found Christ. Did you not send him?" "No," said the good man, "I did not." "Well," she said, "then God did. There was nobody in the street listening to him; but I heard the gospel, and I got out of my despair, and I found the Savior, and I am prepared to die." Fire away, brethren! You do not know where your shot will strike, but "there's a billet for every bullet."

Zeal in Soul-Winning

Behold the altar, built of unhewn stones, and after God's own Law; behold the wood laid thereon; see the victim slain and the blood flowing; but you cannot make a sacrifice without fire—unless the fire from Heaven shall perfect the sacrificial preparations, all will be useless. Behold in the altar the figure of the man; he has faith, courage, love, and consecration; but if he lacks the fire of fervent zeal, his life will be a failure; he will remain an offering unconsumed, and consequently worthless and unaccepted. By this, indeed, may you know the genuine from the false when other things might raise a question. The false is like the altar of Baal, whereon there is much wood and a well-fed bullock, and around it are active genuflexions and vigorous ritualisms, but there is no true fire from Heaven; while the true is like the altar of Elias, upon which, in answer to fervent prayers, the hallowed flames descend. One of the first requisites of an earnest, successful, soul-winning man must be zeal. As well a chariot without its steeds, a sun without its beams, a Heaven without its joy, is a man of God without zeal.

Encouragement

As the fairest flower lies packed away within the little shriveled seed, and wants but time and sun to develop all its beauty, so perfection, glory, immortality and bliss unspeakable lie slumbering and hidden away within the grace, which God has given to all His people. "He that believeth in Him hath everlasting life." The life of Heaven is begun within the believer; it is germinating; it is daily developing; it shall in God's good time come to its absolute perfection.

Conscience and the Law

Conscience, when it is really awakened by the Law, confesses herself condemned, and ceases to uphold her plea of innocence. How can it be otherwise when the Law is so stern? Then, peradventure, the man will say, "I mean to do better in the future;" to which the Law replies, "What have I to do with that? It is already due that you should be perfect in the future; and if thou should be perfect, in what way would that wipe out your old offenses? You have only done what you ought to have done." But the man cries, "I do repent of having done wrong." "Ay," says the Law, "but I have nothing to do with repentance." There is no provision in the Ten Commandments for repentance. Cursed is the man who breaks the Law; and that is all that the Law has to say to him. Over the top of Sinai, there were flames exceeding bright, and a trumpet sounded exceeding loud, but there were no drops of the rain of pity there. Storm and tempest, thunderings and lightnings appalled the people, so that they trembled in the camp, and such must be the sights and sounds we witness as long as we are under the Law.

Think of the function of civil law. If a man commits a serious crime, stands guilty before the judge, and says, "I will not do it again," the law can't help him. That's not its purpose. It simply stands as his accuser and calls for his punishment. He shouldn't look to the law for mercy, but to the judge. — *Ray Comfort*

The Sinful Imagination

If you had never committed one single act of sin, yet the thought of sin, the imagination of it would be enough to sweep your soul to hell forever. If you had been born in a cell, and had never been able to come out into the world, either to commit acts of lasciviousness, murder, or robbery, yet the thought of evil in that lone cell might be enough to cast your soul forever from the face of God. Oh! there is no man here that can hope to escape. We must every one of us bow our heads before God, and cry, "Guilty, Lord, guilty—every one of us guilty—'Cursed is *every one* that continues not in *all things* which are written in the book of the Law to do them.'

"When I look into your face, O Law, my spirit shudders. When I hear your thunders, my heart is melted like wax in the midst of my bowels. How can I endure you? If I am to be tried at last for my life, surely I shall need no judge, for I shall be my own swift accuser, and my conscience shall be a witness to condemn."

The "work of the Law" is written on every heart. Conscience affirms the truth of the Commandments (Romans 2:15).
— Ray Comfort

Audible Prayer

It is not necessary to pray with the voice. It is sometimes highly undesirable that you should pray aloud; but yet, as a rule, you will find it greatly advantageous to yourself to use your voice as well as your mind in prayer. I speak what I have often proved. I am accustomed to praying without uttering a single sound, but I find a relief and a stimulus in occasionally "crying aloud." In a lone spot where I shall not be heard, I find it an intense delight to pour out my heart aloud, using words and exclamations whereby the spirit expresses itself with freedom and force. I think that the Savior, who was intensely human, felt much rest in the unrestrained pouring out of His heart and soul before His Father. He was supremely human as He was certainly divine; and I do not doubt that it was a comfort to Him to arouse the hills with His praises, startle the glens with His groans, and put a tongue into every bush and tuft by His strong cryings and tears. All nature was akin to Him, and the desert places were meet chambers for His great soul, wherein as in His own house, "the holy child Jesus" might speak with the Father face to face. I commend to you who would attain to high communion with the Eternal that, as often as you can, you get so far afield as to be able to pray aloud, and use the unrestrained voice in prayer. "My voice shalt thou hear in the morning, O God."

Gratitude

Gratitude is the only fountain of acceptable service; without it, the streams are far too defiled to flow in the paradise of God.

Make the Cross the chief object of your gratitude. In Galatians 6:14, Paul said that it was the only thing in which he gloried. This is because all other sources of joy may be taken from us (as it seems they were from the apostle). However, nothing can separate us from the love of God that was expressed in the Cross. It is our source for an eternal fountain of gratitude, and gratitude is the prime motivation for evangelism. — *Ray Comfort*

The Filthiness of Sin

Filth is *offensive* to all cleanly persons. We cannot bear close contact with a person who neglects the washing of his body or of his clothes, so as to become a living dunghill. However poor a man is, he might be clean; and when he is not, he becomes a common nuisance to those who speak with him or sit near him. If bodily filthiness is horrible to us, what must the filthiness of sin be to the pure and holy God! I cannot attempt to express the abomination of sin to God. He hates it with all His soul. If we are to be acceptable before God, there must be no keeping up of favorite sins, no sparing of darling lusts, no providing for secret iniquities; our service will be filthiness before God if our hearts go after our sins. He saith, "Be clean, that bear the vessels of the Lord." He would not have the vessels of His sanctuary touched with filthy fingers. Have we well considered this? Lay aside, then, all filthiness unless you wish to arouse the wrath of God.

Everlasting Kingdom

With Jesus as our monarch, we fear no revolution and no anarchy, for the Lord has established this kingdom upon a rock, and it cannot be moved or removed. When the sun and moon are blown out in darkness, and when the stars fall like the withered leaves of autumn, the kingdom in which we rejoice shall enjoy perpetual prosperity. As it is written, "Thy kingdom is an everlasting kingdom, and your dominion endureth throughout all generations."

The Preaching of Repentance

Let every man understand that he will never have remission of sin while he is in love with sin, and that if he abides in sin, he cannot obtain the pardon of sin. There must be a hatred of sin, a loathing of it, and a turning from it, or it is not blotted out. We are to preach repentance as a duty.[62] "The times of this ignorance God winked at, but now commands all men everywhere to repent." "Repent, and be baptized every one of you in the name of Jesus Christ for the remission of sins." He that has sinned is bound to repent of having sinned. It is the least that he can do. How can any man ask God for mercy while he abides in his sin?

We are to preach the acceptableness of repentance. In itself considered, there is nothing in repentance deserving of the favor of God, but the Lord Jesus Christ having come, we read, "He that confesseth and forsaketh his sin shall find mercy." God accepts repentance for the sake of His dear Son. He smiles upon the penitent sinner, and puts away his iniquities. This we are to make known on all sides.

We are also to preach the motives of repentance—that men may not repent from mere fear of hell, but they must repent of sin itself. Every thief is sorry when he has to go to prison; every murderer is sorry when the noose is about his neck. The sinner must repent, not because of the punishment of sin, but because his sin is sin against a pardoning God, sin against a bleeding Savior, sin against a holy Law, sin against a tender gospel. The true penitent repents of sin against God, and he would do so even if there were no punishment. When he is forgiven, he repents of sin more than ever, for he sees more clearly than ever the wickedness of offending so gracious a God.

We are to preach repentance in its perpetuity. Repentance is not a grace, which is only to be exercised by us for a week or so at the beginning of our Christian career. It is to attend us all the way to Heaven. Faith and repentance are to be inseparable companions throughout our pilgrimage to glory. Repenting of our sin and trusting in the great Sinbearer—this is to be the tenor of our lives; and we are to preach to men that it must be so.

We are to tell them of the source of repentance, namely, that the Lord Jesus Christ is exalted on high to give repentance and remission of sins. Repentance is a plant that never grows on nature's dunghill. The nature must be changed, and repentance must be implanted by the Holy Spirit, or it will never flourish in our hearts. We preach repentance as a fruit of the Spirit, or else we greatly err.

These words are refreshing. Nowadays, if repentance isn't neglected entirely by preachers, it is negated to a mere change of mind about God. There are some who discourage the preaching of "repentance" because they say, "The world doesn't understand the word." Then we should educate them until they do. We shouldn't dumb down our message, but instead lift up the understanding of those who, without repentance, will perish. — *Ray Comfort*

Faith Only in God

He will win the battle who knows how to begin on the low ground and to fight uphill by divine strength. Learn the wisdom, not of self-reliance, but of self-diffidence, for he that trusts in his own heart is a fool.

The Love of God

Perhaps, someone asks, "Do I rightly understand you, sir? I do not often go to a place of worship, but I was passing the Tabernacle, and just stepped in; now I am as bad as I well can be, you surely do not mean to say, sir, that God loves me, and such great sinners as I am?" Indeed, my dear friend, I do mean to say it, and to say it upon the authority of God Himself. "What! do you mean to tell me that God loves me as I am?" Yes, just as you are. "What! God loves an ungodly man?" Yes, here is a text to prove it, "God, who is rich in mercy, for His great love wherewith He loved us, even when we were dead in sins, hath quickened us together with Christ." Why, if He had not loved us when we were dead in sins, He would never have loved us at all, and still we should have remained dead in trespasses and sins. "Tis His great grace that lifts a beggar from the dunghill, and sets him among princes."

The Sacrifice

I do not think I can preach more, for a faintness has come over me, nor is there need for more if you will but chew the cud of this one precious truth: Jesus is the Lamb which God provided, and He is the Lamb, which God Himself presented at the altar. Yet, I must rouse myself to say a little more. Who was it that sacrificed the Lamb of God? Who was the priest on that dread day? Who was it that bruised Him? Who put Him to grief? Who caused Him the direst pang of all when He cried, "Why hast thou forsaken me?" Was it not the Father Himself? This was one point in the hardness of Abraham's test—"Take now your son, thine only son Isaac, whom thou lovest, and offer him for a sacrifice." He must himself officiate at the sacrifice. This the great Father did! He is the Lamb, the Lamb of God. And now today the bright side of this truth remains. He is the Lamb that God always accepts, must accept, glories to accept. Bring but Jesus with you, and you have brought God an acceptable sacrifice.

The Passover

It was to me the beginning of my life, that day in which I discovered that judgment was passed upon me in the person of my Lord, and that there is therefore now no condemnation to me. The Law demands death—"The soul that sinneth it shall die." Lo, there is the death it asks, and more. Christ, my Lord, has died, died in my stead: as it is written, "Who his own self bore our sins in his own body on the tree." Such a sacrifice is more than even the most rigorous Law could demand. "Christ our Passover is sacrificed for us." "Christ hath redeemed us from the curse of the Law, being made a curse for us." Therefore, do we sit securely within doors, desiring no guard without to drive away the destroyer; for, when God sees the blood of Jesus, He will pass over us.

Perishing Under a Pulpit

Many come here, Sabbath after Sabbath, to hear the gospel; the immense number and the constancy of it surprise me. I do not know why the multitudes come and crowd these aisles. When I preached yesterday in Worcestershire, and saw the thronging crowds in every road, I could not help wondering to see them, and the more so because they listened as though I had some novel discovery to make—they listened with all their ears and eyes and mouths. I could but marvel and thank God. Ah! but it is a dreadful thing to remember that so many people hear the gospel, and yet perish under the sound of it. Alas! the gospel becomes to them a savor of death unto death, and there is no lot so terrible as perishing under a pulpit from which the gospel is preached.

Humility

"That was a fine sermon," said one to Mr. Bunyan. The good man answered, "You are too late; the devil told me that before I left the pulpit." The archfiend soon suggests to God's servants sonic lofty notion, and they are tempted to appropriate to themselves the honor, which belongs to God only. Ah, what a fool I am that, even when I seek to be lowest at the feet of my Lord, I find myself satisfied with my humility! Do we not too often rather mimic humility than actually attain to it?

Messenger of Death

I cannot bear that one of you should die unforgiven. I look along these pews, and I remember some of you a good many years ago; you were then in a hopeful state, but you have not received Christ yet. Most faithful hearers you have been, but you have not been doers of the word. Do not think that I charge you too severely. Have you repented and believed? If not, woe is me that I should bear to you a message, which will be a savor of death unto death unto you because you refuse it, for how shall we escape if we neglect so great salvation? When it has been freely proclaimed to us year after year, what will become of us if we reject it? Do not still refuse to come to Jesus. Do not make me a messenger of death to you. I implore you, receive the message of mercy, and be saved.

Unchanging Holiness

Under the New Testament, God is not an atom less severe than under the old; and under the covenant of grace, the Lord is not a particle less righteous than under the Law. We are so saved by mercy that no sin goes unpunished. The Law is as much honored under the gospel as under the Law. The substitution of Jesus as much displays the wrath of God against sin as even the flames of hell would do. While the Lord is merciful, infinitely so, and His name is love, yet still our God is a consuming fire, and sin shall not live in His sight.

There are some who, in their ignorance, say that God is wrath-filled in the Old Testament and merciful in the New. They paint Him as having two natures. Yet, the New Testament Cross of Calvary stands as the ultimate and bloody display of God's fierce wrath against a rebellious world.
— Ray Comfort

Self-righteousness

We are naturally prone to account ourselves very good. Our own opinion of ourselves is seldom too low; most generally it is a rather high one. But just as a stern pedagogue would say to a boy who was getting a little proud, "Come along, sir; I must take you down a little"; so the Law takes us down. It says, "Look at that precept; you have not kept that; and consider this other precept, for you appear to have forgotten it." "Look," says the Law, "you talk about your holiness, but have you loved the Lord your God with all your heart, and all your soul, and all your might? And have you loved your neighbor as yourself?" And then, when conscience, which is a great friend of this pedagogue, replies, "Indeed, I have done nothing of the kind," the conviction of sin comes home to the soul, and sadness reigns. You will tell me, "This is very unpleasant,—to be made to feel that you are sinful." Ay, but it is very necessary. There is no getting to Christ in any other way. Christ died for sinners, and if you are not sinners, what interest can you have in His death? Why should you think that He died for you? You must be convinced of your sinfulness before you can possibly realize the value and need of salvation. It is the business of the Law to lay before you the straight line, that you may see your crooks, and put before you the pure gold, that you may discern the humbling fact that what you thought to be pure metal is only so much worthless dross. It is the part of this pedagogue to bring you down, to humble you, and make you feel how sinful you have been.

Such words are a very pleasant tonic to those who evangelize biblically. For an understanding of this biblical principle, see hell's Best Kept Secret, The Way of the Master, *and* What Did Jesus Do? — *Ray Comfort*

Concern for the Lost

They wander in on a Sunday morning, sit down, get their hymn books, listen to the prayer without joining in it, hear the sermon, but might almost as well not have heard it, go home, get through the Sunday, go into business. With them there is never any secret prayer for the conversion of men, no trying to talk to children or servants or friends about Christ, no zeal, no holy jealousy, no flaming love, no generosity, no consecrating of the substance to God's cause! This is too faithful a picture of a vast number of professing Christians. Would it were not so.

I have found from experience that often God has condescended to use the message called Hell's Best Kept Secret *to awaken those in this state. [To obtain copies, see details at the end of this publication.] It is wise, when giving it to those for whom you are concerned, to say something like, "I would love to know your opinion of this teaching," rather than "You need to listen to this." — Ray Comfort*

Burden for the Lost

If sinners will be damned, at least let them leap to hell over our bodies. And if they will perish, let them perish with our arms about their knees, imploring them to stay. If hell must be filled, at least let it be filled in the teeth of our exertions, and let not one go there unwarned and unprayed for.

Do we really believe that sinners will be damned forever? Do we think about their fate very often, if ever? Or do we busy ourselves in the work of the Lord, and never bother to implore them to come to the Savior? In general, the modern pulpit is deathly silent when it comes to the horrors of hell. When do we hear preaching about the reality of the Lake of Fire or of the terrible wrath of God? Such themes aren't popular with modern preachers. They never have been. They are not popular with me. Other topics are more attractive, but preachers must not ignore the fate of the lost, because if we do, we run the risk of it also being ignored in the pews.

How we fall short of having the passion we should. How would we react if we saw a huge line of blind men walking towards a thousand foot cliff, and one by one falling headlong onto jagged rocks below? Wouldn't we put ourselves between them and the cliff? Wouldn't we put our arms around them to hold them back? Wouldn't we implore them and scream at them to turn around? Yet we don't warn or plead with those whose fate is infinitely worse than that of those who would fall onto jagged rocks. Our passive preaching, and *careful not to offend* vocabulary betray our apathy and our unbelief. If we don't *implore* the world to turn from sin it's because we don't truly believe God's Word. We mustn't. We cannot be so deathly cold, so evil-hearted as to not care. We haven't let the reality of hell sink into our minds and soften our hard hearts. The fact of its existence should horrify us beyond words, and then it should be reflected in our prayers and in our preaching.

The Danger of Prosperity

Did not some of you, at one time, the moment you awoke in the morning, begin communing with God? Were there not red-letter days, when, from morning light to evening shade, you were in fellowship with the Most High? You had your burdens, but you always carried them to Jesus; and you had your joys, but you always shared them with Him. You lived for Him; your heart was warm towards Him; you walked with Him in constant communion, but, now, can you really live without even thinking of Him? Can you be happy without thinking of your God? Have you a better house than you used to have, and more money, more friends, and more of this world's good things; and do you now forget your God, and go the whole livelong day without any communication between your soul and Him? Ah, then, you have indeed gone down in the world, and up; you are getting poorer and poorer; God help you! If you had come to me, and told me that you had lost everything, but that you loved Jesus better, I should have sympathized with you because of your trouble, but I should have congratulated you upon your grace. But now that you have got on so well in the world that you do not love your Lord as you once did, I can only pity you because of your dreadful prosperity, and mourn over the fearful loss, which you have experienced.

Let Down Your Nets

There is no exclusion put upon any tribe or clan; no classes are laid under ban; no individuals are exempted. Therefore, Church of Christ, by the love you bear to your crucified Master, by His wounds and death for you, and by His living love to you, seek out the lost and gather together the outcasts. You fishers of men, launch out into the deep and let down your nets for a draught. You sowers of holy seed, go abroad and sow the untrodden wastes. You consecrated builders, break away from old foundations and lay fresh groundwork for a larger temple for your God and King. Surely, the Spirit of love in a church will suggest this.

Witnesses of Christ

Remember, if you are not witnesses for God, you will be prisoners at His bar. You must either occupy the witness stand for God, or else take the prisoner's place, to be tried and found guilty.

Judgment and love are the great themes of the Bible. The Fall came about because of Justice. If God wasn't just, He would have ignored sin. But He judged it. He proclaimed the death sentence upon the sinful human race. Judgment is justice expressed, and without the justice of God, there would be no Cross of Calvary. It happened because justice and love are part of God's eternal character. That's why it is biblical to express spiritual truth in legal terms, something Spurgeon does in this thought. We are witnesses for Christ. If we are not witnessing for Him, then we have never been acquitted from the courtroom of eternal justice. We are no doubt still guilty before the Judgment Bar of the Judge of the Universe. — Ray Comfort

The New Birth

Do not suppose that you are personally right in the sight of God because you have had a godly mother and father, or godly grandparents. Christ's message to all who have not been regenerated by the Holy Spirit is, "Ye must be born again." True religion is personal; it is a thing that concerns each man himself.

The Breath of Mortal Man

I recollect walking out to preach nigh unto forty years ago, just when I began my witnessing for the Lord Jesus. As I trudged along with a somewhat older brother, who was going to preach at another village station, our talk was about our work, and he said to me, "Does it not strike you as a very solemn thing that we two local preachers are going to do the Lord's work, and much may depend even upon the very hymns we give out, and the way in which we read them?" I thought of that, and I prayed—and often do pray—that I may have the right hymn and the right chapter, as well as the right sermon. Well do I remember a great sinner coming into Exeter Hall, and I read the hymn beginning, "Jesu, lover of my soul," and that first line pierced him in the heart. He said to himself, "Does Jesus love my soul?" He wept because he had not loved the Savior in return; and he was brought to the Savior's feet just by that one line of a hymn. It does make it the burden of the Lord when you see life, death, and hell, and worlds to come hanging, as it were, upon the breath of a mortal man by whom God speaks to the souls of his fellows.

Tell the Preacher

There was a man of God who had been a very distinguished preacher, and when he lay dying, he was much troubled in his mind. He had been greatly admired, and much followed. He was a fine preacher of the classical sort, and one said to him, "Well, my dear sir, you must look back upon your ministry with great comfort." "Oh, dear!" said he, "I cannot; I cannot. If I knew that even one soul had been led to Christ and eternal life by my preaching, I should feel far happier; but I have never heard of one." What a sad, sad thing for a dying preacher! He died and was buried; and there was a goodly company of people at the grave, for he was highly respected, and deservedly so. One who heard him make that statement was standing at the grave, and he noticed a gentleman in mourning, looking into the tomb, and sobbing with deep emotion. He said to him, "Did you know this gentleman who has been buried?" He replied, "I never spoke to him in my life." "Then what is it that so affects you?" He said, "Sir, I owe my eternal salvation to him." He had never told the minister this cheering news, and the good man's deathbed was rendered dark by the silence of a soul that he had blessed. This was not right. A great many more may have found the Lord by his means, but he did not know of them, and was therefore in sore trouble. Do tell us when God blesses our word to you. Give all the glory to God, but give us the comfort of it. The Holy Spirit does the work, but if we are the means in His hands, do let us know it, and we will promise not to be proud.

The Condemnation of the Law

The mount mentioned in our text was Mount Horeb or Sinai—the mount that burned with fire, the mount around which they set bounds so that, if so much as a beast touched the mount, it should be stoned or thrust, through with a dart. It was that mountain from which they heard the thunder pealing while the Law was being proclaimed in a voice so terrible that they entreated that they might not hear it any more. I believe there are some here—I had almost said that I hope there are—who have been long standing at the foot of Sinai. You have heard the thunder of that dreadful voice, and you have felt condemned; your soul is in bondage even now. If ever there was a slave in this world, you are one; you have the festers on you, and you have the cruel whip perpetually flagellating your conscience. Other slaves do have rest sometimes, but you get none; you are tortured and tormented; you are almost like the fiend himself when he walked through dry places, seeking rest, and finding none.

Well do I remember when I was in your present condition, and I was in it, oh, so long! And blessed was the day when my Lord said to me, "Thou hast dwelt long enough in this mount," and then I came to Calvary and the blood of sprinkling, and I had done with Sinai. Yet I have never felt regret that I lingered so long at the foot of Sinai. I shall regret it if any of you do so, but I do not regret it in my own case, because I think it was needful for one who was to be a public teacher, that he should have more depression of spirit and more trial than anybody else, that he might know the ins and outs of this matter in his own experience, and so be able to help others who may be tortured in a similar way. But there is no reason why you, my friend, should have this experience, for it may be that you are not to be a public teacher; and it would be well for you if, this very moment, the spirit of bondage were cast out of you and the Spirit of adoption took possession of your soul. You need not remain at the foot of Sinai, for, as I found out, *there is another hill called Calvary*. You need not listen to the threatenings of the Law, for there is another voice, the voice of the blood of Jesus, "which speaks better things than that of Abel." If you will, by simple faith, but listen to that voice, you will learn that it speaks peace, not punishment, and cries out for mercy, not for justice.

O tempted, distressed, despairing soul, thou hast dwelt long enough in Mount Sinai! At this glad hour, the silver trumpet proclaims a jubilee for you. Thine inheritance, which thou hast forfeited, has been redeemed; and you yourself, once sold into slavery, are now manumitted, for the price of your redemption has been paid to the utmost farthing.

Mixed Multitude

I have been frequently pained in reading sermons, and on the rare occasions when I have had the opportunity of hearing sermons, to note that they have been addressed to the whole congregation just as though all were Christians. It is too much the custom for ministers to address the whole assembly as "brethren," and to speak to a mixed multitude of men and women as if they all had a part and lot in spiritual things. It seems that if anywhere, certainly in the pulpit, there should be a wise and constant use of discrimination. The preacher should make his hearers clearly understand that there are some who fear God and some who fear Him not—some who are still dead in trespasses and sins, and others who are alive unto God through the quickening power of the

Holy Spirit. It would be a very wicked thing for me to delude you with the notion that you are all saved, for I cannot help fearing that some of you are not yet saved. The outward lives of some here are quite sufficient, evidence that they have never been sanctified by the Holy Spirit. Indeed, I feel sure that I am addressing some who would not venture to claim that they are Christians. They are too honest to do that, for they know that they are strangers to the saving power of the grace of God; and how dare these lips of mine call those the children of God who are, at present, the children of wrath, even as others? How can my tongue pronounce that to the gold, which I know is but dross? How can I speak to those of you who are living, and I fear will die, without a Savior, as though you had an equal interest in the precious blood of Jesus with those who believe in Him?

About Our Father's Business

Jesus is no idler or loiterer; He is about His Father's business, and you must march with quick step if you would keep pace with Him. As vinegar to the teeth and as smoke to the eyes are sluggards to active persons. Those, who have much to do have no fellowship with gossips, who drop in to while away the hours with chat. Jesus has no fellowship with you, who care not for souls that are perishing. He is incessantly active, and so must you be if you would know His love. There is a fierce furnace-heat beating upon everything today. Men are toiling hard to hold their own, and Jesus must not be served by slothful hearts. I am sure that I err not, from His mind, when I say to you, beloved, if you would know the Beloved fully, you must get up early and go afield with Him to work with Him. Your joy shall be in spending and being spent for Him.

Feeling Weakness

All men who are eminently useful are made to feel their weakness in a supreme degree.

Rarely do I approach a stranger to witness to him without a feeling of weakness. Fear sits on my shoulder like a sinister bird, and whispers words of inadequacy. But I have learned to thank God for fear, because without it, I wouldn't pray. I wouldn't bother. It is my own weakness that makes me pray. My weakness makes me whisper, "Help me, Lord," and thus becomes my strength. — *Ray Comfort*

Eating Our Honey

Why do you not go out to preach yourself? Some of you could, if you would. What are you doing? There are districts where there are tracts to be distributed. Do you know anything about house-to-house visitation? I speak to some who do nothing whatever, unless it be a little grumbling. I wonder whether we shall ever have a day such as the bees celebrate in its due season. You may, perhaps, have seen them dismissing the unproductives. It is a remarkable sight. They say to themselves, "Here are a lot of drones eating our honey, but never making any; let us turn them out." There is a dreadful buzz, is there not? But out they go. I do not propose either to turn you out or to make a buzz; but if ever those who do work for Christ should burn with a holy indignation against do-nothings, some of you will find the place too hot for you!

The Pain of the Cross

The placing of the cross in its socket had shaken Him with great violence, had strained all the ligaments, pained every nerve, and more or less dislocated all His bones. Burdened with His own weight, the august Sufferer felt the strain increasing every moment of those six long hours. His sense of faintness and general weakness were overpowering; while to His own consciousness, He became nothing but a mass of misery and swooning sickness. To us, sensations such as our Lord endured would have been insupportable, and kind unconsciousness would have come to our rescue. But in His case, He was wounded and *felt* the sword; He drained the cup and *tasted* every drop.

In late January of 2005, a Californian aerospace engineer and father of three found himself regaining consciousness after a railway accident that killed two other people in his compartment. He touched the back of his head and looked in horror at the blood on his hand. Thinking he was about to die, he wrote a short love letter in blood to his children and his beloved wife. His rescuers were brought to tears when they saw the bloody, scribbled note on the wall of the train. His wife said that Hallmark could never come up with a better card to express someone's love.

God wrote His love letter to humanity in the blood of His Son. There has never been such a display of love towards such unworthy creatures such as what we see at Calvary's Cross. Yet that love is hidden from the world. They see the cross, but they don't see the love. They don't see the love because they don't see their sin. They don't see their sin because the Church has failed to use God's Law to show them the true nature of sin. Listen to what Jonathan Edwards said about why the world is ignorant of sin: "But it is God's manner to show men the plague of their own hearts by some means or other before He reveals His redeeming love to their souls. While sinners are unconvinced, sin lies hid. They take no notice of it. But God makes the Law effectual to bring men's own sins of heart and life to be reflected on, and observed."
— Ray Comfort

The Pain of the Cross

Have any of you lately been racked with pain? Have you suffered acutely? Ah! then at such times, you know to some degree the price the Savior paid. His bodily pains were great, hands and feet nailed to the wood, and the iron breaking through the tenderest nerves. His soul-pains were greater still; His heart was melted like wax; He was very heavy; His heart was broken with reproach; He was deserted of God. Left beneath the black thunderclouds of divine wrath,

His soul was exceeding sorrowful, even unto death. It was pain that bought you. We speak of the drops of blood, but we must not confine our thoughts to the crimson life-floods, which distilled from the Savior's veins. We must think of the pangs, which He endured, which were the equivalent for what we ought to have suffered, what we must have suffered had we endured the punishment of our guilt forever in the flames of hell. But pain alone could not have redeemed us; it was by death that the Savior paid the ransom.

Excuses

The Law makes no diminution of its claims because of fallen human nature; and what is more, when the Law comes with power to a man's conscience, he does not himself dare to plead human nature, for of all pleas, that is one of the most fallacious. A man will say, "Well, I know I drank to intoxication, but that is merely gratifying an instinct of human nature." Now, just suppose that this drunkard, when he gets sober falls into the hands of a thief—will he not give the rogue in charge to a policeman? But what if the defense be set up that it was human nature robbed him? See what he will say about it. Says he, "I will get human nature locked up for twelve months if I can." He does not recognize soft speeches about human nature when anyone does wrong to him, and he knows, in his own soul, that there is no valid defense in such a plea when he does wrong to God.

Never Weep Over Sinners

And you, too, who are moral enough in your conversation, and regular in your attendance on the outward forms of religion, you who never weep over sinners, you who never pray for them, you who never speak to them, you who leave all that to your minister, and think you have nothing to do with it, the voice of your brother's blood crieth from the ground to Heaven.

Results of Preaching Judgment

For the last few months I have been led to blow the silver trumpet, sounding forth the love and mercy of our God in Christ. Many times in your hearing, I have preached a full Christ for empty sinners, and have set forth the freeness and graciousness of the divine proclamation, which in the gospel is made to the chief of sinners. I have not, concerning that point, shunned to declare unto you the whole counsel of God. But I feel that I must now blow a blast upon the rough ram's horn, for sometimes our congregations need to be reminded of the Law and terrors of God, and of the judgment to come. Our experience is that the preaching of judgment is greatly blessed of God. We have remarked that a very large number of conversions have occurred under those sermons in which the declaration of God's wrath against all iniquity has been the most plain and solemn. A thunderstorm clears the air; there are pestilences, which would gather beneath the wings of calm, which can only be purged away by the lightning flash.

The Birthday of the Soul

Trying to bring others to Christ does us good by renewing in us our old feelings, and reviving our first love. When I see an inquirer penitent for sin, I recollect the time when I felt as he is feeling; and when I hear the seeker for the first time say, "I do believe in Jesus," I recollect the birthday of my own soul, when the bells of my heart rang out their merriest peals, because Jesus Christ was come to dwell within me. Soul-winning keeps the heart lively, and preserves our warm youth to us; it is a mighty refresher to decaying love.

Sin's Attraction

Is sin so luscious that you will burn in hell forever for it?

How often do we hear sinners scoff and say that they would rather enjoy the pleasures of sin and the threat of hell doesn't deter their insanity? But think for a moment, when you slam your finger in a door or burn your flesh on a toaster: does the pain you feel, feel less painful because of a pleasurable memory? Not for a second. Every sinful memory may give lingering pleasure in this life, but it will not be entertained for a moment in the pain of hell. Not for a second.

— Ray Comfort

Restless for the Lost

Well do I remember when I first knew the Lord how restless I felt till I could do something for others. I did not know that I could speak to an assembly, and I was very timid as to conversing upon religious subjects, and therefore I wrote little notes to different persons setting forth the way of salvation, and I dropped these written letters with printed tracts into the post, or slipped them under the doors of houses, or dropped them into areas, praying that those who read them might be aroused as to their sins, and moved to flee from the wrath to come. My heart would have burst if it could not have found some vent. I wish that all professors kept up their first zeal, and were diligent in doing little things as well as greater things for Jesus, for often the lesser agencies turn out to be as effectual as those that operate upon a larger area. I hope that all of you young people who have been lately added to the church are trying some mode of doing good, suitable for your capacity and position, that by all means you may save some. A word may often bless those whom a sermon fails to reach, and a personal letter may do far more than a printed book.

Passion for the Lost

Passion for saving souls not only employs, but also draws forth the strength of the church; it awakens her latent energies, and arouses her noblest faculties. With so divine a prize before her, she girds up her loins for the race, and with her eye upon her Lord, presses forward to the goal. Many a commonplace man has been rendered great by being thoroughly absorbed by a noble pursuit, and what can be nobler than turning men from the road that leads to hell? Perhaps some of those ignoble souls who have lived and died like dumb, driven cattle might have reached the majesty of great fires if a supreme intent had fired them with heroic zeal and developed their concealed endowments. Happy is the man whose task is honorable, if he does but honorably fulfill it. Lo, God has given to His Church the work of conquering the world, the plucking of brands from the burning, the feeding of His sheep and lambs, and this it is which trains the church to deeds of daring and to nobility of soul.

Sin in Children

Any man who declares children to be born perfect was never a father. Your child without evil? You without eyes, you mean!

Understanding the true nature of personal sin is the key to raising children for Christ. — *Ray Comfort*

The Preaching of the Law

Those who preached the Law, as well as the gospel, in the Puritanic times were the most fruitful soul-winners. We find our blessed Lord and Master, whose heart was overflowing with compassion, and whose very nature was love, often dwelling upon the wrath to come; and indeed, His utterances are more telling and terrible than the most burning threatening from the lips of thundering seers of old.

Consecrated Christians

Oh, I could sigh to think of the capacities, which lie dormant in some Christians! It is sad to think how their children might grow up, and with God's blessing, become pillars in the House of the Lord, and perhaps ministers of the gospel under the influence of an earnest consecrated father and mother; but instead thereof, the dullness, the lukewarmness, the worldliness, and the inconsistencies of parents are hindering the children from coming to Christ, hampering them as to any great advances in the divine life, dwarfing their stature in grace, and doing them lifelong injury. Brethren, you do not know the possibilities, which are in you when God's Spirit rests upon you; but this much is certain: If you yourselves be called into a higher form of divine life, you shall then become mediums of blessing to your relatives. Your husband, your wife, your child, your friend, and the whole of your family shall be the better for your advance in spiritual things.

Great Preachers

God has raised up some apostolic spirits, whose presence in a nation is like the rising of the sun; darkness flies before them, and the light of salvation streams from them to tens of thousands. When they lift up their hands to preach, God gives them power to shake the gates of hell, and when they bend the knee to pray, they unlock the gates of Heaven. Men like Baxter with bursting hearts of love, or Joseph Alleine with glowing tongue or Whitfield with seraph's fire or Wesley with cherub's zeal: These are the men who bless their age and are most truly great.

The Preparation of the Law

I do not believe that any man can preach the gospel who does not preach the Law.

This concept is foreign to many in the contemporary church. They believe that their commission is simply to preach the gospel, based on Mark 16:15. However, biblical gospel proclamation is—Law to the proud and grace to the humble. No intelligent farmer sows seed onto hard soil. If he does so, he will reap a disappointing harvest. He first turns the hard soil, breaks it up, and then plants his good seed into the prepared soil. That is the simple principle of biblical evangelism. The seed of the gospel will yield a disappointing harvest if it is sown onto the hard, unprepared soil of the unregenerate heart. A wise preacher will take the time to do

what Jesus did, and prepare the soil of the heart with the Law of God. (This concept is dealt with in Hell's Best Kept Secret, The Way of the Master, *and* What Did Jesus Do?)
— Ray Comfort

By All Means Save Some

There is a door to each man's heart, and we have to find it, and enter it with the right key, which is to be found somewhere or other in the word of God. All men are not to be reached in the same way, or by the same arguments, and as we are by all means to save some, we must be wise to win souls, wise with wisdom from above. We desire to see them conquered for Christ, but no warrior uses always the same strategy. There is for one open assault, another a siege, for a third an ambush, for a fourth a long campaign. On the sea, there are great rams that run down the enemy, torpedoes under water, gunboats, and steam frigates. One ship is broken up by a single blow; another needs a broadside; a third must have a shot between wind and water; a fourth must be driven on shore. Even thus, must we adapt ourselves and use the sacred force entrusted to us with grave consideration and solemn judgment, looking ever to the Lord for guidance and for power. All the real power is in the Lord's hands, and we must put ourselves fully at the disposal of the divine Worker, that He may work in us both to will and to do of His good pleasure, so shall we by all means save some.

The Power of Sin

If you will not have death unto sin, you shall have sin unto death. There is no alternative. If you do not die to sin, you shall die for sin. If you do not slay sin, sin will slay you.

The word "sin" should never be divorced from the word "death." Sin is a devil dressed as an angel. It promises life, but brings death. — Ray Comfort

The Soul-Winner's Joy

Even if I were utterly selfish and had no care for anything but my own happiness, I would choose, if God allowed, to be a soul-winner, for never did I know perfect, overflowing, unutterable happiness of the purest and most ennobling order till I first heard of one who had sought and found a Savior through my means.

I was encouraged recently when I received a phone call from a woman who lives in Australia. She told me that 20 years earlier, she had been running along a beach in New Zealand when I ran alongside her and witnessed to her. She said that she abused me, but shortly afterwards was soundly saved. She had since led half her family to Christ, including her own father on his deathbed, and now she and her husband traveled together and preached the gospel. Never be discouraged. God is faithful to (in His time) bring

sinners to Himself. All we are called to do is plant the seed.
— *Ray Comfort*

Self-Righteousness

Nothing can damn a man but his own righteousness; nothing can save him but the righteousness of Christ.

Nothing can destroy self-righteousness like the Law. Learn how to use it to cut the root of the tree of self-righteousness. What a tragedy it is when Christians fail to use the Law to bring the knowledge of sin. Have you ever tried to do a job without using the right tools? Have you ever tried to screw in a screw with your thumbnail? Yet that's what the Church often tries to do when it fails to pick up the Law. The Law is a state of the art electric screwdriver. Its head is designed to fit the screw. It turns the head of the rebellious, self-righteous sinner in the way that he must go, if he is to be saved. — *Ray Comfort*

The Meaning of Repentance

Repentance is an old-fashioned word, not much used by modern revivalists. "Oh!" said a minister to me, one day, "it only means a change of mind." This was thought to be a profound observation. “Only a change of mind,” but what a change! A change of mind with regard to everything! Instead of saying, “It is only a change of mind,” it seems to me more truthful to say it is a great and deep change—even a change of the mind itself. But whatever the literal Greek word may mean, repentance is no trifle. You will not find a better definition of it than the one given in the children’s hymn:

“Repentance is to leave, The sins we loved before, And show that we in earnest grieve, By doing so no more.”

Red Hot Sermons

I have heard of a ship that was fired at by the cannon in a fort, but no impression was made upon it until the general in command gave the order for the balls to be made red-hot, and then the vessel was sent to the bottom of the sea in three minutes. That is what you must do with your sermons: make them red-hot. Nevermind if men do say you are too enthusiastic or even too fanatical. Give them red-hot shot. There is nothing else half so good for the purpose you have in view.

The Most Effective Sermons

The sermons that are most likely to convert people seem to me to be those that are full of truth, truth about the fall, truth about the Law, truth about human nature and its alienation from God, truth about Jesus Christ, truth about the Holy Spirit, truth about the Everlasting Father, truth about the new birth, truth about obedience to God and how we learn it, and all such great verities. Tell your hearers something, dear brethren, whenever you preach, tell them something, tell them something!

Unless you open-air preachers know the gospel from beginning to end, and know where you are in preaching it, you cannot preach with due emotion, but when you feel at home with your doctrine, stand up and be as bold and earnest and importunate as you please. Face the people feeling that you are going to tell them something worth hearing, about which you are quite sure, which to you is your very life. There are honest hearts in every outdoor assembly and every indoor assembly, too, that only want to hear honest beliefs, and they will accept them and be led to believe in the Lord Jesus Christ.

The Influence of Fear

I further believe, although certain persons deny it, that the influence of fear is to be exercised over the minds of men, and that it ought to operate upon the mind of the preacher himself. "Noah, moved with fear, prepared an ark to the saving of his house." There was salvation for this world from perishing in the flood in the fears of Noah. When a man gets to fear for others, so that his heart cries out, "They will perish; they will perish; they will sink to hell; they will be forever banished from the presence of the Lord," and when this fear oppresses his soul, weighs him down, and then drives him to go out and preach with tears, oh, then he will plead with men so as to prevail! Knowing the terror of the Lord, he will persuade men. To know the terror of the Lord is the means of teaching us to *persuade,* and not to speak harshly. Some have used the terrors of the Lord to terrify, but Paul used them to persuade.

A Plea to the Lost

A just God condemns the impenitent sinner, and just men assent to the Divine sentence. See then, O you ungodly ones that are present today, you often think our company a great nuisance, and perhaps while I am preaching, my alarming words annoy you. Ah, we shall not annoy you long. Does your mother tease you when she bids you seek the Lord? She will not tease you long. When I bring home the judgment to come, is the subject obnoxious to you? I shall not ask your patience long. We shall be separated; if you go your way and follow after sin and wrath, there will come a dividing time, and O let me say to you, you would give worlds if you had them; you would give them if they were solid diamonds, to hear again the voice that now fatigues you, and to listen once more to those plaintive invitations that vex you and spoil your mirth. Ah, how would you bless God if He would let you come back again and have once more those Sabbaths, which were so dull and dreary, and permit you to go up once more to the house of God, which now perhaps is like a prison-house to your vain and frivolous spirits. O sirs, I say you may well have patience with us for a little time and bear with our importunities, for we shall not plague you much longer. We beseech you to come to Jesus; we would pluck you by your garments and beseech you to flee from the wrath to come. Forgive us for being thus in earnest, for even if we should fail with you, you will soon escape the importunities of our love.

The Call of God

If God has called you to be a missionary, your Father would be grieved for you to shrivel down into a king.

Concern for the Lost

Herein is the folly of so many Christians—that, being wrapped up in the interest of their own salvation and taken up with their own doubts and fears, they feel little care and they take little trouble for others. They never seem to empty themselves out into the world that is around them, and never seem to get into a world bigger than the homestead in which they live. But when a man begins to think about others, to care for others, to value the souls of others, then his thoughts of God get larger. Then his consolations grow greater, and his spirit becomes more Godlike. A selfish

Christianity, what shall I call it but an unchristian Christianity, a solecism in terms, a contradiction in its very essence: You do not find the men who are anxious after others so often troubled as those who give no thought except to themselves. Mr. Whitefield, in his diary, tells of his times of depression, but they are comparatively few. When he is going from one "pulpit-throne" (as he calls it) to another—preaching all day long, hearing the sobs and vies of sinners, perhaps bearing the hootings and peltings of a mob, and sitting down as soon as he has done preaching in public to finish up his letters or to devote an hour to prayer—why, he has not time enough to get to desponding. He cannot afford space enough to be doubting his own interest in Christ. He is so engaged in his Master's service, and has so much of the blessing of God upon it, that he goes right on without needing to stop. Christian, may you get into the same delightful state, warm with love to Christ, fervent with zeal for the spread of His kingdom!

Save Some

Save some, O Christians! By all means, save some. From yonder flames and outer darkness, and the weeping, wailing, and gnashing of teeth, seek to save some! Let this, as in the case of the apostle, be your great, ruling object in life: that by all means, you might save some.

The Terror of Death

Oh! how solemn will be that hour when we must struggle with that enemy, Death! The death-rattle is in our throat—we can scarce articulate—we try to speak, the death-glaze is on the eye: Death hath put his fingers on those windows of the body and shut out the light forever; the hands well-nigh refuse to lift themselves, and there we are, close on the borders of the grave! Ah! that moment, when the Spirit sees its destiny; that moment, of all moments the most solemn, when the soul looks through the bars of its cage, upon the world to come! No, I cannot tell you how the spirit feels, if it be an ungodly spirit, when it sees a fiery throne of judgment, and hears the thunders of Almighty wrath, while there is but a moment between it and hell. I cannot picture to you what must be the fright, which men will feel, when they realize what they often heard of! Ah! it is a fine thing for you to laugh at me tonight. When you go away, it will be a very fine thing to crack a joke concerning what the preacher said, to talk to one another and make merry with all this. But when you are lying on your deathbed, you will not laugh. Now, the curtain is drawn, you cannot see the things of the future; it is a very fine thing to be merry. When God has removed that curtain, and you learn the solemn reality, you will not find it in your hearts to trifle.

Trials and Afflictions

If the clouds were not black, you might not expect rain. If your afflictions were not grievous, they would not be profitable. If your adversities did not really pain and trouble you, they would not be blessed to you. We have heard some people say, "If this trouble had come in such-and-such a shape, we would not have minded it." But, God meant you to mind it, for it was in your minding it that it was blessed to you. "The blueness of a wound," saith Solomon, "cleanseth away evil." When the stroke causes black and blue wounds, when really the spirit is thoroughly wounded, then the blessing comes. It is not merely said in the Scriptures that there is a needs-be for affliction. That is a great truth, but it is added that there is a needs-be that, the affliction should lower our spirits. Listen to the words: "Now for a season, if need be, you are in heaviness through manifold temptations." The needs-be is not merely for the temptation, but that you be in heaviness through the temptation—not for the iron only, but for the iron entering into your soul. If the child liked the rod, it would be no chastisement; and if the Christian loved his affliction while he was in it, and it seemed joyous to him, then it would be no affliction; but it is the very sharpness of it, the vinegar and gall that is the medicine that produces the good effect. The blackness of the cloud proves its fullness, and its fullness brings the shower.

Humility and Pride

The gate of Heaven, though it is so wide that the greatest sinner may enter, is nevertheless so low that pride can never pass through it.

Preaching—a Matter of Life and Death

Preaching the gospel is to us a matter of life and death; we throw our whole soul into it. We live and are happy if you believe in Jesus and are saved. But we are almost ready to die if you refuse the gospel of Christ.

Fishers of Men

To try to win a soul to Christ by keeping that soul in ignorance of any truth, is contrary to the mind of the Spirit; and to endeavor to save men by mere claptrap, or excitement, or oratorical display, is as foolish as to hope to hold an angel with bird-line, or lure a star with music. The best attraction is the gospel in its purity. The weapon with which the Lord conquers men is the truth as it is in Jesus.

The gospel will be found equal to every emergency; an arrow can pierce the hardest heart, a balm which will heal the deadliest wound. Preach it, and preach nothing else. Rely implicitly upon the old, old gospel. You need no other nets when you fish for men; those your Master has given you are strong enough for the great fishes, and have meshes fine enough to hold the little ones. Spread those nets and no others, and you need not fear the fulfillment of His Word, "I will make you fishers of men."

The Law of God

There is a war between you and God's Law. The Ten Commandments are against you. The first comes forward and says, "Let him be cursed. For he denies Me. He has another god beside Me. His god is his belly and he yields his homage to his lust." All the Ten Commandments, like ten great cannons, are pointed at you today. For you have broken all of God's statutes and lived in daily neglect of all His commandments. Soul, you will find it a hard thing to go at war with the Law. When the Law came in peace, Sinai was altogether on a smoke, and even Moses said, "I exceeding fear and quake!" What will you do when the Law of God comes in terror, when the trumpet of the archangel shall tear you from your grave, when the eyes of God shall burn their way into your guilty soul, when the great books shall be opened, and all your sin and shame shall be punished? Can you stand against an angry Law in that Day?

This is the most meaningful of Spurgeon's words for me [see Preface]. In 1982, I sat in my office and read these powerful truths for the first time. I had never heard of the Law being used in an evangelistic manner. As far as I was concerned, the Law had no real purpose. It was just something God instigated until He sent His Son to redeem humanity. The following weekend, I read Galatians 3:24 and it was as though a light on understanding burst into my mind and almost took my breath away. ["Wherefore the law was our schoolmaster to bring us to Christ, that we might be justified by faith"] ~ Ray Comfort

Preaching Christ

She is a traitor to the Master who sent her if she is so beguiled by the beauties of taste and forgets that to "preach Christ ... and Him crucified" is the only object for which she exists among the sons of men. The business of the Church is salvation of souls.

Driving at Men's Hearts

You and I must continue to drive at men's hearts till they are broken. Then we must keep on preaching Christ crucified until their hearts are bound up.

Broken by the Law

Now, if you have your hearts broken up by the Law, you will find the heart is more deceitful than the devil. I can say this myself: I am very much afraid of mine, it is so bad. The heart is like a dark cellar full of lizards, cockroaches, beetles, and all kinds of reptiles and insects, which in the dark we see not. But the Law takes down the shutters and lets in the light, and so we see the evil. Thus sin becoming apparent by the Law, it is written the Law makes the offense to abound.

Unconcern for the Lost

We need to be ashamed at the bare suspicion of unconcern.

Preaching the Law

I do not believe that any man can preach the gospel who does not preach the Law. The Law is the needle, and you cannot draw the silken thread of the gospel through a man's heart unless you first send the needle of the Law to make way for it.

Weep Over Sinners

Love your fellowmen, and cry about them if you cannot bring them to Christ. If you cannot save them, you can weep over them. If you cannot give them a drop of water in hell, you can give them your heart's tears while they are still in this body.

Unclean Thoughts

As I walked to this house of prayer tonight, and tried to concentrate my meditations upon the person and work of the Lord Jesus Christ, I could not help feeling how mysterious it is that the more we try to guide our thoughts into right channels, the more determined they seem to be to run towards evil. Have you not sometimes found that, even in your most hallowed moments, some unchaste and vile thought, which you abhor as you hate the very fiend himself, will suddenly come into your mind? Does not blasphemy at times intrude into your prayers? Does it not occasionally happen that the hymn you are singing suggests something the very reverse of praise to God, and that the text of the sermon, or some part of the discourse itself, becomes a peg upon which the devil hangs a temptation to sin? Alas! alas! our thoughts, if left to themselves, are as a cage of unclean birds or a den of wild beasts; and as Hercules needed to turn a stream of water to clean the Augean stable, our Lord Jesus Christ needed to pour rivers of water out of His own heart to cleanse the foul stable of our corrupt thoughts.

The Salvation of Souls

As the fisherman longs to take the fish in his net, as the hunter pants to bear home his spoil, as the mother pines to clasp her lost child to her bosom, so do we faint for the salvation of souls.

Do Something for Jesus

Show Him a proof of your love, and the best proof you can give is your own personal holiness and persevering effort to gather in His redeemed. Brother, sister, do something for Jesus. Do not talk about it; do it. Words are leaves; actions are fruits. Do something for Jesus; do something for Jesus today! Ere the sun goes down, think of some one action that may tend to the conversion of some one person, and do it with your might; let the object of the effort be your child, your servant, your brother, your friend—but do make the effort today. Having done it today, do it tomorrow, and every day, and doing it in one way, do it another way; and doing it in one state of heart, do it in another. Let your joy enchant; let your sorrow arouse; let your hope attract; let your changeful moods help you to attack sinners from different quarters, as your varying circumstances bring you into contact with differing persons. Be always awake. Turn yourself about as a gun on a swivel to reach persons who are found in any direction, so that some may fall wounded by the gospel's power. By all means, save some. God grant it may be so.

The Sin of Pride

How is it that you do not lay hold of Christ, since this is the only time when there is a probability that Christ can be laid hold of? I will tell you why it is. You do not love Christ; you love sin. Or else you are too proud to come to Christ; you think yourselves good enough, and you think that Christ is not for such as you are, but only for great sinners and the lowest of the low. O sirs, is your pride such a fine thing, that you will be damned in order to maintain its dignity? Throw your pride down, come as a sinner must come, and lay hold of Jesus Christ. Or if it be your sin, which hinders, may God, the Holy Ghost, help you to pluck out the right eye and cast off a right arm sooner than having two eyes and two arms to be cast into hellfire.

"But," saith one, "how may I lay hold on Christ?" May the blessed Spirit enable you to do it. Here it is: Trust Jesus Christ and you shall be saved. Conscious that you deserve His wrath, trembling because of His terrible Law, look to Jesus. There hangs a bleeding Savior. Methinks these eyes can see Him bleeding there; God eternal, He by whom the Heaven of Heavens was made, and the earth and the fullness thereof, takes upon himself the form of man and hangs upon the tree of the curse.

The Law—Guilty or Not Guilty?

Cursed is everyone who continues not in all things that are written in the book of the Law to do them." Unconverted man, are you guilty, or not guilty? Have you continued "in all things that are written in the book of the Law to do them?" Methinks you will not dare to plead, "Not guilty." But I will suppose for one moment that you are bold enough to do so. So then, sir, you mean to assert that you have continued in "all things, which are written in the book of the Law."

Surely, the very reading of the Law would be enough to convince you that you are in error. Do you know what the Law is? Why I will give you what I may call the outside of it, but remember that within it, there is a broader spirit than the mere words. Hear thou these words of the Law—"*Thou shalt have no other gods before me*." What! have you never loved anything better than God? Have you never made a god of your belly or of your business or of your family or of your own person? Oh! surely, you do not say you are guiltless here.

"Thou shalt not make unto you any graven image, or any likeness of anything that is in Heaven above, or that is in the earth beneath, or that is in the water under the earth." What! have you never in your life set up anything in the place of God? If you have not, I have, full many a time. And I wot, if conscience would speak truly, it would say, "Man, you have been a mammon-worshipper; you have been a belly worshipper; you have bowed down before gold and silver; you have cast yourself down before honor; you have bowed before pleasure; you have made a god of your drunkenness, a god of your lust, a god of your uncleanness, a god of your pleasures!"

Will you dare to say thou have never *taken the name of the Lord your God in vain*? If thou hast never sworn profanely, yet surely in common conversation, you have sometimes made use of God's name when you ought not to have done so. Say have you always hallowed that most holy name? Have you never called upon God without necessity? Have you never read His book with a trifling spirit? Have you never heard His gospel without paying reverence to it? Surely, you are guilty here.

And as for that fourth commandment, which relates to the keeping of the Sabbath—"Remember the Sabbath-day to keep it holy,"—have you never broken it? Oh, shut your mouth and plead guilty, for these four commandments were enough to condemn you!

"Honor your father and your mother." What! will you say you have kept that? Have you never been disobedient in your youth? Have you never kicked against a mother's love and striven against a father's rebuke? Turn over a page of your history till you come to your childhood. See if you cannot find it written there; ay, and your manhood, too, may confess that you have not always spoken to your parents as you should, or always treated them with that honor they deserved, and which God commanded you to give unto them.

"Thou shalt not kill"—you may never have killed any, but have you never been angry? He who is angry with his brother is a murderer; you are guilty here.

"Thou shalt not commit adultery." Mayhap you have committed unclean things and are here this very day stained with lust, but if you have been never so chaste, I am sure you have not been quite guiltless, when the Master says, "He that looks on a woman to lust after her, hath committed adultery already with her in his heart." Has no lascivious thought crossed your mind? Has no impurity ever stirred your imagination? Surely if you should dare to say so, you would be brazen-faced with impudence. And have you never stolen?

"Thou shalt not steal." You are here in the crowd tonight with the product of your theft mayhap; you have done the deed; you have committed robbery. But if you have been never so honest, yet surely there have been times in which you have felt an inclination to defraud your neighbor. And there may have been some petty or mayhap some gross frauds, which you have secretly and silently committed, on which the law of the land could not lay its hand, but which, nevertheless, were breaches of this Law.

And who dare say he has not borne false witness against his neighbor? Have we never repeated a story to our neighbor's disadvantage, which was untrue? Have we never misconstrued his motives? Have we never misinterpreted his designs?

And who among us can dare to say that he is guiltless of the last—"*Thou shalt not covet*"? for we have all desired to have more than God has given us; and at times our wandering heart has lusted after things that God has not bestowed upon us.

Why, to plead not guilty is to plead your own folly; for verily, my brethren, the very reading of the Law is enough, when blessed by the Spirit, to make us cry, "Guilty, O Lord, guilty."

Knowing the Word

If you wish to know God, you must know His Word. If you wish to perceive His power, you must see how He works by His Word. If you wish to know His purpose before it comes to pass, you can only discover it by His Word.

Concern for the Lost

I would freely give my eyes if you might but see Christ, and I would willingly give my hands if you might but lay hold on Him.

Eloquence Preachers

Let eloquence be flung to the dogs rather than souls be lost. What we want is to win souls. They are not won by flowery speeches.

Self-Righteousness

I would that this whip would fall upon your backs, that you might be flogged out of your self-righteousness and made to fly to Jesus Christ and find shelter there.

Preaching the Law

No man will ever put on the robe of Christ's righteousness till he is stripped of his fig leaves, nor will he wash in the fount of mercy till he perceives his filthiness. Therefore, my brethren, we must not cease to declare the Law, its demands, its threatenings, and the sinner's multiplied breaches of it.

Not the Word of Man

I recollect a story told of William Dawson, whom our Wesleyan friends used to call Billy Dawson, one of the best preachers that ever entered a pulpit. He once gave out as his text, "Through this man is preached unto you the forgiveness of sins." When he had given out his text, he dropped down to the bottom of the pulpit, so that nothing could be seen of him, only there was a voice heard saying, "Not the man in the pulpit; he is out of sight, but the Man in the Book. The Man described in the Book is the Man through whom is preached unto you the forgiveness of sins." I put myself and you and everybody else out of sight, and I preach to you the remission of sins through Jesus only. I would sing with the children, "Nothing but the blood of Jesus." Shut your eyes to all things but the cross. Jesus died and rose again and went to Heaven, and all your hope must go with Him! Come, my hearer, take Jesus by a distinct act of faith this morning! May God the Holy Ghost constrain you to do so, and then you may go on your way rejoicing! So be it in the name of Jesus.

Faithful Preaching

When anyone dies, I ask myself, "Was I faithful?" Did I speak all the truth? And did I speak it from my very soul every time I preached?

Admission of Sin

Have I got a lost man here? Lost man! Lost woman! Where are you? Do you feel yourself to be lost? I am so glad of it, for there is remission by the blood-shedding. O sinner, are there tears in your eyes! Look through them. Do you see that Man in the garden? That Man sweats drops of blood for you. Do you see that Man on the cross? That Man was nailed there for you. Oh! if I could be nailed on a cross this morning for you all, I know what you would do: You would fall down and kiss my feet, and weep that I should have to die for you. But sinner, lost sinner, Jesus died for you—for you; and if He died for you, you cannot be lost. Christ died in vain for no one. Are you, then, a sinner? Are you convinced of sin because you believe not in Christ? I have authority to preach to you. Believe in His name, and you cannot be lost. Do you say you are no sinner? Then I do not know that Christ died for you. Do you say that you have no sins to repent of? Then I have no Christ to preach to you. He did not come to save the righteous; He came to save the wicked. Are you wicked? Do you feel it? Are you lost? Do you know? Are you sinful? Will you confess it?

Reminding Men of Death

Men have been helped to live by remembering that they must die.

Godly Sorrow

Is there any holy salt in your tears? Is it sin that you weep for? Is it sin that you repent of? Every murderer repents at the gallows, they say—that is, he repents of being hanged, but he does not repent of having killed others. He might do the same thing again if he has the opportunity. We ought clearly to discern between the natural terrors that come of vivid descriptions of the wrath to come and that real spiritual touch of God, the Holy Ghost, that breaks and melts the heart and then casts it into another mould.

The Irksome Task

We must school and train ourselves to deal personally with the unconverted. We must not excuse ourselves, but force ourselves to the irksome task until it becomes easy.

Open-Air Preaching

The open-air speaker's calling is as honorable as it is arduous, as useful as it is laborious. God alone can sustain you in it, but with Him at your side, you will have nothing to fear.

Terrors of the Lord

Some have used the terrors of the Lord to terrify, but Paul used them to persuade.

Open-Air Preaching

The [street] preachers needed to have faces set like flints, and so indeed they had. John Furz says, "As soon as I began to preach, a man came forward and presented a gun at my face, swearing that he would blow my brains out if I spoke another word. However, I continued speaking and he continued swearing, sometimes putting the muzzle of the gun to my mouth, sometimes against my ear. While we were singing the last hymn, he got behind me, fired the gun, and burned off part of my hair." After this, my brethren, we ought never to speak of petty interruptions or annoyances. The proximity of a blunderbuss in the hands of a son of Belial is not very conducive to collected thought and clear utterance.

Light and Fire

If people are to be saved by a message, it must contain at least some measure of knowledge. There must be light as well as fire.

The Driving Power of the Gospel

God [has] appointed a day in which He will judge the world, and we sigh and cry until it shall end the reign of wickedness, and give rest to the oppressed. Brethren, we must preach the coming of the Lord, and preach it somewhat more than we have done, *because it is the driving power of the gospel*. Too many have kept back these truths, and thus the bone has been taken out of the arm of the gospel. Its point has been broken; its edge has been blunted. The doctrine of judgment to come is the power by which men are to be aroused. There is another life; the Lord will come a second time; judgment will arrive; the wrath of God will be revealed. *Where this is not preached, I am bold to say the gospel is not preached*. It is absolutely necessary to the preaching of the gospel of Christ that men be warned as to what will happen if they continue in their sins. Ho, ho, sir surgeon, you are too delicate to tell the man that he is ill! You hope to heal the sick without their knowing it. You therefore flatter them, and what happens? They laugh at you; they dance upon their own graves. At last they die! Your delicacy is cruelty; your flatteries are poisons; *you are a murderer*. Shall we keep men in a fool's paradise? Shall we lull them into soft slumbers from which they will awake in hell? Are we to become helpers of their damnation by our smooth speeches? In the name of God, we will not.

Sin Still Remembered by God

Come down from your high places and see the horrible pit in which you lie by nature. Think of your past lives, I pray you, of those days in which you found pleasure in walking after the flesh. I call on you to remember the sins of your youth, and your former transgressions of thought, word, and deed. If they are shut out who defile and are defiled, where are you? Where are you? For these sins of ours, though they were committed years ago, are nonetheless sinful today; they are as fresh to God as if we perpetrated them this very moment. You are still red-handed, O sinful man, though your crime was worked some twenty years ago. You are black, O sinner, still, though it be fifty years ago that your chief sin was committed; for time has no bleaching power upon a crimson sin. The guilt of an old offense is as fresh as though it were wrought but yester-morn.

The Battle with the Old Nature

We could weep our eyes out when we discover what a palate for pleasurable sin our old nature still retains; yea, a longing for the very sin of which we most bitterly repent and from which we most eagerly long to be delivered. How can we hope to enter Heaven if there be these appetites in us? They are there, and they defile! What can we do? There, too, is that vile thing called "pride." Why, some of us cannot be trusted with a pennyworth of success, but we are exalted above measure. Some of God's children cannot have ten minutes fellowship with Christ, but they must put on their fine feathers and crow right lustily because they feel themselves to be nearing absolute perfection.

Hope of Self-Salvation

How can such vain creatures be admitted among the glorified? Nor is this all, for sloth preys on many, and tempts them to shun God's service, and especially to shun the cross of Christ. Sloth is a rust, which has a sadly defiling power. We gather moth and mildew from inaction. Never is a man pure who is not zealous in the service of God. We rot to corruption if we lie still. How, then, shall we be admitted within the jeweled city? Ah, look within your heart, my brother—look steadily beneath the fair film of the surface and mark the inward evil, which it conceals. Judge not yourself alone when at your best, occupied with your prayers and praises and almsgivings, but look steadily into your soul at other times, and you shall see a loathsome mass of evil life, a seething corruption moving within your heart; for evil remains even in the regenerate; and this cannot enter Heaven. Thank God, it cannot. Even though the word of exclusion staggers me, sends me back as with a stunning blow, and makes me cry, "You shut me out, my God, by this your decree." Yet I feel that if it be so, the decree is right and just and good. "There shall in no wise enter into it anything that defiles." Amen and amen.

Now, I ask you whether this word of exclusion does not, in you who know its meaning, slay all hope of self-salvation? For, first, here are our past sins, and they defile and make us defiling. How are we to get rid of them? How can we wash out these polluting blots? Tears! So much salt water thrown away if looked upon as a bath for sin! Good works performed! They are already due to God.

How shall future discharge of debts repay the past? O, my God, if I have ever known what sin means, I have also known that it is impossible that its defiling nature should ever be changed, or that the pollution should ever be removed by any efforts of my own. I spoke with one the other day who said that she was seeking salvation by good works. I knew that she had performed self-denying acts of charity, and I asked her whether she felt nearer to the salvation at which she aimed. I knew that I spoke to a sincere, honest person, and her reply did not surprise me. She answered sadly, "The more I do, the more I feel I ought to do, and I am no nearer to the point I am aiming at." And so it is. The more a sincere heart does seek to serve God, the more it feels the shortcoming of its service of Him; and the more a person seeks after purity by his own efforts, the further he judges himself to be from it. Our standard rises as we rise towards it; our conscience becomes tender in proportion as we obey it; and so, in the nature of things, rest of heart comes not in that manner. Ah, there remains not beneath Heaven anything that can wash out the defilement of past sin save one only cleansing flood.

O sinful man, plunge your hands into the Atlantic and you shall crimson every drop of its tremendous waters and yet the stain shall be as scarlet as before. No, no, no. It is certain that no man can enter Heaven, by reason of his transgression and his sinfulness, except Omnipotence shall cleanse him.

This thought is often neglected in our witnessing. We tell sinners that good works don't wash away sin, but we neglect to tell them that any good works are but a result of the command to love our neighbor as ourselves. They are nothing of which to boast [see Ephesians 6:8–10]. The "Good" Samaritan wasn't "good" at all. He merely fulfilled the basic requirements of what the Law commands: he loved his neighbor as himself. — *Ray Comfort*

The Restlessness of the Ungodly

The sea cannot rest because it is the sea, and the sinner cannot be quiet because he is a sinner. How could you, O natural, unregenerate man, ever enter into the kingdom of Heaven as you are? You are not capable of it; it is not possible to you. Holiness has in it no attractions for you, since you love sin and the wages of it. You do not know God, and cannot see Him; for this is the privilege of the pure in heart and of them alone. You live in a world where everything has been made by the great Lord, and yet you do not perceive His hand, so great is your blindness. Shall blind men grope through the streets of the New Jerusalem? You are unacquainted with the simplest elements of spiritual things, for they can only be spiritually discerned, and you have no spiritual faculty. You are blind and deaf, yes, dead to God and Heavenly things—you know you are.

Sin's Power

That sin must die, or you will perish by it. Depend on it that sin, which you would save from the slaughter, will slaughter you.

Hardness of Heart

There are some of you of whom I almost despair. God can save you, but I cannot tell how He will do it. Certainly, the Word does not seem likely to be blessed. You have been called and entreated. Early and late, we have entreated you. Our bowels have yearned with tenderness for you, but hitherto in vain. God knows I have been hammering away at the granite, and it has not yielded yet. I have smitten the flint, and it is not broken. Some of you all but break the ploughshare; you are such rocks that it seems in vain to plough upon you.

Lack of Piety

Would that we had grace to cleave the clouds and mount into the pure blue sky of fellowship with Christ! We do not serve God as we should. We are as cold as ice when we should be like molten metal burning our way through all opposition. We are like the barren Sahara when we should be blooming like the garden of the Lord. We give to God pence when He deserves pounds, nay, deserves our heart's blood to be coined in the service of His Church and of His truth. Oh! we are but poor lovers of our sweet Lord Jesus, not fit to be His servants, much less to be His brides. If He had put us in the kitchen to be scullions, I fear we are scarce fit for the service, and yet He has exalted us to be bone of His bone and flesh of His flesh, married to Him by a glorious marriage covenant. O, brethren, God often calls us to higher degrees of piety, and yet we will not come.

Free From Their Blood

My anxious desire is that every time I preach, I may clear myself of blood of all men; that if I step from this platform to my coffin, I may have told out all I knew of the way of salvation.

Mistakes in the Bible

I do not hesitate to say that I believe that there is no mistake whatever in the original Holy Scriptures from beginning to end. There may be and there are mistakes of translation, for translators are not inspired, but even the historical facts are correct. Doubt has been cast upon them here and there, and at times with great show of reason—doubt, which it has been impossible to meet for a season, but only give space enough and search enough, and the stones buried in the earth cry out to confirm each letter of Scripture. Old manuscripts, coins, and inscriptions are on the side of the Book. Against it, there is nothing but theories, and the fact that many an event in history has no other record but that which the Book affords us.

The Book has been of late in the furnace of criticism, but much of that furnace has grown cold from the fact that the criticism is beneath contempt. "The words of the Lord are pure words." There is not an error of any sort in the whole compass of them. These words come from Him who can make no mistake, and who can have no wish to deceive His creatures. If I did not believe in the infallibility of the Book, I would rather be without it. If I am to judge the Book, it is no judge of me. If I am to sift it like the heap on the threshing-floor and lay this aside and only accept that, according to my own judgment, then I have no guidance whatever, unless I have conceit enough to trust to my own heart.

The Law and the Gospel

There is no point on which men make greater mistakes than on the relation that exists between the Law and the gospel.

Stubborn Sinners

There are men who cannot be convinced or persuaded; they doubt everything, and with closed teeth, they resolve not to believe, though a man declares it to them. They are encased in the armor of prejudice, and they cannot be wounded with the sharpest arrows of argument, though they profess great openness to conviction. What is to be done with the numerous clans who are related to Mr. Obstinate? You might as well argue with an express-train as with Mr. Obstinate. He runs on and will not stop, though a thousand should stand in his way. Will the words of God convince him?

There are some in this place today of whom I should have said—if I had known them before their conversions—that it was a vain task to preach the gospel to them; they so much loved sin and so utterly despised the things of God. Strangely enough, they were among the first to receive the Word of God when they came under the sound of it. It came to them in its native majesty, in the power of the Holy Ghost; it spoke with a commanding tone to their inmost heart; it threw open the doors that had long been shut up and rusted on their hinges, and Jesus entered to save and reign. These, who had defiantly brandished their weapons, threw them down and surrendered unconditionally to Almighty Love, willing believers in the Lord Jesus.

Brethren, we have only to have faith in God's Word, and speak it out straight, and we shall see proud rebels yielding. No mind is so desperately set on mischief, so resolutely opposed to Christ, that it cannot be made to bow before the power of the words of God. Oh, that we used more the naked sword of the Spirit! I am afraid we keep this two-edged sword in a scabbard, and somewhat pride ourselves that the sheath is so elaborately adorned. What is the use of the sheath? The sword must be made bare, and we must fight with it without attempting to garnish it. Tell forth the words of God. Omit neither the terrors of Sinai, nor the love-notes of Calvary. Proclaim the word with all fidelity, as you know it, and cry for the power of the Highest, and the most obstinate sinner out of håell can be laid low by its means. The Holy Spirit uses the word of God. This is His one battering ram with which He casts down the strongholds of sin and self in those human hearts with which He effectually deals. The Word of God will bear the tests furnished by the hardness of the natural heart, and it will by its operations prove its divine origin.

I Am Dumb

Now poor sinner, with all your sin about you, take this promise in your hands, go home tonight, or if you can, do it before you get home—go home, I say, upstairs, alone, down by the bedside, and pour out thine heart, "O Lord, all that man said is true. I am condemned, and Lord, I deserve it. O Lord, I have tried to be better, and I have done nothing with it all, but have only grown worse. O Lord, I have slighted Your grace. I have despised Your gospel. I wonder that You have not damned me years ago. Lord, I marvel at myself, that You suffer such a base wretch as I am to live at all. I have despised a mother's teaching; I have forgotten a father's prayers. Lord, I have forgotten You. I have broken Your Sabbath, taken Your name in vain. I have done everything that is wrong, and if You do condemn me, what can I say? Lord, I am dumb before Your presence."

Fired Himself

I have known what it is to use up all my ammunition, and then I have, as it were, rammed myself into the great gospel gun and fired myself at the hearers—all my experience of God's goodness, all my consciousness of sin, and all my sense of the power of the gospel.

Look to Him

Has God the Spirit taught you that you are accursed? Has He made you feel the bitterness of sin? Has He made you cry, "Lord, have mercy upon me, a sinner?" Then, my dear friend, Christ was cursed for you; and you are not cursed. You are not cursed now. Christ was cursed for you. Be of good cheer; if Christ was cursed for you, you cannot be cursed again. "Oh!" says one, "if I could but think He was cursed for me." Do you see Him bleeding on the tree? Do you see His hands and feet all dripping gore. Look to Him, poor sinner. Look no longer at yourself or at your sin. Look to Him and be saved. All He asks you to do is to look, and even that He will help you to do. Come to Him, trust Him; believe on Him. God the Holy Spirit has taught you that you are a condemned sinner. Now, I beseech you, hear this word and believe it. "This is a faithful saying and worthy of all acceptation—that Christ Jesus came into the world to save sinners."

Sinners to Christ

I would sooner bring one sinner to Jesus than unravel all the mysteries of the Word, for salvation is the thing we are to live for.

Hidden Sins Exposed by the Law

Even with the light of nature and the light of conscience and the light of tradition, there are some things we should never have believed to be sins had we not been taught so by the Law.

Challenge to the Unsaved

I need not, I think, prolong the service now, but I hope you will prolong it at your own houses by thinking of the matter. And may I put the question personally to all as you separate: Whose are you? On whose side are you? There are no neutrals; there are no betweenites. You serve either Christ or Belial. You are either with the Lord or with His enemies. Who is on the Lord's side this day? Who? Who is for Christ and for His cross, for His blood, and for His throne? Who, on the other hand, are His foes? Those who are not for Christ are numbered with His enemies. Be not so numbered any longer, for the gospel comes to you with an inviting voice—" Believe in the Lord Jesus Christ, and thou shalt be saved." God help you to believe and cast yourself upon Him now; and if you trust him, you are saved now, and you shall be saved forever. Amen.

Vanity, Vanity

I wish that I could put these questions before you, as they ought to be put. It needs the earnest seraphic voice of George Whitfield or the pleading tongue of Richard Baxter to plead with you, but yet I think I talk to rational men; and if it be a matter of arithmetic, it shall need no words of mine. I will not ask you to take your life at the longest that you expect it to be—at eighty, say—and crowd it full of all the pleasures you can imagine; suppose yourself in good health; dream yourself to be without business cares, with all that heart can wish. Go and sit upon the throne of Solomon if you will, and yet what will you have to say when it is all over? Looking back upon it, can you make more of it than Solomon did, when he said, "Vanity of vanities, all is vanity"—"All is vanity and vexation of spirit"? When you have cast up that sum, may I ask you to calculate how much you will have gained, if, in order to possess this vanity, you have renounced eternal happiness, and have incurred everlasting woe?

More Probing Needed

In many ministries, there is not enough of probing the heart and arousing the conscience by the revelation of man's alienation from God, and by the declaration of the selfishness and the wickedness of such a state.

Memory of a Godless Life

Will you turn over the leaves of your diary, now, dear friends, or fly upon the wings of memory to the hole of the pit whence you were dug. Did you not, O you who live close to Christ, did you not once despise Him? What company did you like best? Was it not that of the frivolous, it not that of the profane? When you sat with God's people, their talk was very tedious. If they spoke of divine realities and experimental subjects, you did not understand them; you felt them to be troublesome. I can look back upon some whom I know now to be most venerable believers, whom I thought to be a gross nuisance when I heard them talk of the things of God. What were our thoughts about? When we had time for thinking, what were our favorite themes? Not much did we meditate upon eternity; not much upon Him who came to deliver us from the misery of hell's torments,

Brethren, His great love wherewith He loved us was never laid to heart by us as it should have been. Nay, if we read the story of the crucifixion, it had no more effect upon our mind than a common tale. We knew not the beauties of Christ; we thought of any trifle sooner than of Him. And what were our pleasures? When we had what we called a day's enjoyment, where did we seek it? At the foot of the cross? In the service of the Savior? In communion with Him? Far from it; the further we could remove from godly associations, the better pleased we were. Some of us have to confess with shame that we were never more in our element than when we were without a conscience, when conscience ceased to accuse us and we could plunge into sin with riot.

Good Tracts

When preaching and private talk are not available, you need to have a tract ready ... Get good striking tracts, or none at all. But a touching gospel tract may be the seed of eternal life. Therefore, do not go out without your tracts.

There are many tracts available. However, make sure they contain the whole counsel of God. The most popular of tracts fails to open up the Moral Law as Jesus did, to mention the fact of Judgment day, or the reality of hell. Instead, they promise a wonderful new life in Christ. The promise is one of happiness rather than righteousness. — *Ray Comfort*

Hypocrisy

If any man's life at home is unworthy, he should go several miles away before he stands up to preach. When he stands up, he should say nothing.

The Profitableness of Affliction

I do not think that we ever pray with such fervor of supplication in our prosperity as we do in our adversity. And then how precious the promises become! As we only see the stars when the shadows gather at night, so the promises shine out like newly kindled stars when we get into the night of affliction. I am sure that there are passages of Scripture, which are full of consolation, the depths of which we do not even imagine yet, and we never shall know all that is in them till we get into the depths of soul trouble, which correspond with them. There are points of view from which scenery is to be beheld at its best; and, until we find out those points of view, we may be missing the sight of some of the most beautiful objects in nature. God leads us one way and another by our chastisements to understand and prize His promises. And, oh, dear friends, how should we ever know the faithfulness of God if it were not for affliction? We might talk about it and theoretically understand it; but to try to prove the greatness of Jehovah's love, and the absolute certainty of His eternal faithfulness—this comes not except by the way of affliction and trial.

I might talk on forever about the sweet uses of adversity, and not exhaust the subject. You experienced people of God know even more than I do about this matter, for some of you have done business on deeper waters than my barque has yet ploughed, and yet, methinks, my keel has passed over the deep places of the sea of trouble, and there may be deeper depths before me still. I have probably said sufficient to prove to you that chastening is a divine way of instructing us. You will find that, if you want the most Christ-like saints and the most deeply experimental believers, and the Christians who are best acquainted with the Word of God, you must look for them among those who are the most intimately acquainted with the fiery furnace and its burning heat.

The Fear of God

You must have, more or less, a distinct sense of the dreadful wrath of God and of the terrors of the judgment to come, or you will lack energy in your work and so lack one of the essentials of success.

True Zeal

If you never have sleepless hours, if you never have weeping eyes, if your hearts never swell as if they would burst, you need not anticipate that you will be called zealous. You do not know the beginning of true zeal, for the foundation of Christian zeal lies in the heart. The heart must be heavy with grief and yet must beat high with holy ardor. The heart must be vehement in desire, panting continually for God's glory, or else we shall never attain to anything like the zeal, which God would have us know.

The Lamb of God

Although I am too weak to preach to you as I desire, I feel great joy for myself in looking to the Sin-Bearer who has taken away my sin. How I wish that all of you felt the same! This is the pith and the marrow of my theology. But you must take the Lamb of God for yourselves. You must know Him for yourselves. You must believe in Him for yourselves, and He will surely take away that sin which now burdens you. He will take it right away, so that it shall never burden you again. He will blot it out. It shall cease to be. You shall be no more under condemnation, but shall be free from it forever. God help you to know Jesus, of whom I speak to you!

Shut Out of Heaven

Dear heart, this is a question I beg you to look to at once. You do not know how short a time you have left to you in which you may look into it. Some who were here but a Sabbath-day or so ago are now gone from us. Eleven deaths reported at one church meeting among our members! We are a dying people; we shall all be gone within a very short time. I charge you by the living God, and as you are dying men and women, see to it that you are not shut out, so as to hear the fatal cry, "Too late, too late, you cannot enter now." There shall be no purgation in eternity, and no possible way of entering in among the perfected, for it is written, "There shall in no wise enter into it anything that defileth." No crying, "Lord! Lord!" No striving to enter in, no tears, no, not even the pangs of hell itself, shall ever purge the soul so as to make it fit to join with the holy Church above, should it pass into the future state uncleansed. Shut out! shut out! O God, may that never be true of anyone among us, for Christ's dear name's sake, Amen.

Sugared Gospel

Avoid a sugared gospel, as you would shun sugar of lead. Seek that gospel which rips up and tears and cuts and wounds and hacks and even kills, for that is the gospel that makes alive again. And when you have found it, give good heed to it. Let it enter into your inmost being. As the rains soak into the ground, so pray the Lord to let His gospel soak into your soul.[141]

The Use of the Law

God be thanked when the Law so works as to take off the sinner from all confidence in himself! To make the leper confess that he is incurable is going a great way toward compelling him to go to that divine Savior, who alone is able to heal him. This is the whole end of the Law toward men whom God will save.

The Conscience

We love because He first loved us. Brethren, I was ready to perish under a sense of sin. I was all but damned. I felt the wrath of God surging in my soul like a sea of fire. I found no relief or comfort. Even the Word of God did not cheer me. They told me of believing in Jesus, but till I learned that this Jesus was God's great-appointed sacrifice for sin, I saw nothing in Him to cheer me. When I learned that He had borne the penalty and satisfied justice, then I found out the glorious secret, and my conscience was at rest. Conscience within us reflects, as in a mirror, the facts of the case as God sees them. God causes an awakened conscience to require that which His justice requires. The demand of the conscience is the echo of the demand of the divine government. Conscience requires atonement because the necessity of the case and the nature of God require it. When I learned that there was such an atonement provided, oh, then I rested most sweetly! I wish you all did so. You who have no atoning sacrifice to plead, how can you bear the weight of your sins? What will you do with them when the death-damp is on your brows? You for whom, according to your own creed, no debt was paid, no penalty endured, how will you answer Justice in her great and terrible day?

The Preacher's Work

The preacher's work is to throw sinners down in utter helplessness, so that they may be compelled to look up to Him who alone can help them.

The Law a Great Deluge

Beloved, the Law is a great deluge, which would have drowned the world with worse than the water of Noah's flood. It is a great fire, which would have burned the earth with a destruction worse than that which fell on Sodom. It is a stern angel with a sword, athirst for blood, and winged to slay. It is a great destroyer sweeping down the nations. It is the great messenger of God's vengeance sent into the world. Apart from the gospel of Jesus Christ, the Law is nothing but the condemning voice of God thundering against mankind. "Wherefore then serveth the Law?" seems a very natural question. Can the Law be of any benefit to man? Can the Judge who puts on a black cap and condemns us all, this Lord Chief Justice Law, can He help in salvation? Yes, He can; and you shall see how He does it, if God shall help us while we preach.

Now, if you are unrepentant, you have never obeyed your Maker. Every step you have taken has added to your crimes. When God has fanned your heaving lungs, you have breathed out your poisonous breath in rebellion against Him. How should God feel toward you? You have walked over the principles of righteousness with your unsanctified feet. You have lifted up your hands, filled with poisoned weapons, against the throne of the Almighty. You have spurned every principle of right, of love and of happiness. You are the enemy of God, the foe of man and a child of the devil in league with hell. Ought not God hate you with all His heart?

Yet, in the midst of your rebellion He has borne with you. All this you have done, and He has kept silent. Dare you think that He will never reprove?

Lo, I see, the Law given upon Mount Sinai. The very hill doth quake with fear. Lightnings and thunders are the attendants of those dreadful syllables, which make the hearts of Israel to melt. Sinai seems altogether on the smoke. The Lord came from Paran, and the Holy One from Mount Sinai; "He came with ten thousands of His saints." Out of His mouth went a fiery Law for them. It was a dread Law even when it was given, and since then from that Mount of Sinai, an awful lava of vengeance has run down, to deluge, to destroy, to burn, and to consume the whole human race, if it had not been that Jesus Christ had stemmed its awful torrent and bidden its waves of fire be still. If you could see the world without Christ in it, simply under the Law, you would see a world in ruins, a world with God's black seal put upon it, stamped and sealed for condemnation. You would see men, who, if they knew their condition, would have their hands on their loins and be groaning all their days. You would see men and women condemned, lost, and ruined. And in the uttermost regions, you would see the pit that is dug for the wicked, into which the whole earth must have been cast if the Law had its way, apart from the gospel of Jesus Christ our Redeemer.

My hearer, does not the Law of God convince you of sin? Under the hand of God's Spirit, does it not make you feel that you have been guilty, that you deserve to be lost, that you have incurred the fierce anger of God? Look here: have you not broken these Ten Commandments; even in the letter, have you not broken them? Who is there among you who has always honored his mother and father? Who is there among you who has always spoken the truth? Have we not sometimes borne false witness against our neighbors? Is there one person here who has not made to himself another god, and loved himself or his business or his friends more than he has Jehovah, the God of the whole earth? Which of you has not coveted his neighbor's house or his manservant or his ox or his donkey? We are all guilty with regard to every letter of the Law; we have all of us transgressed the Commandments. And if we really understood these Commandments, and felt that they condemned us, they would have this useful influence on us of showing us our danger, and so leading us to fly to Christ. But, my hearers, does not this Law condemn you, because even if you should say you have not broken the letter of it, yet you have violated the spirit of it? What, though you have never killed, yet we are told, he that is angry with his brother is a murderer.

This Law does not only mean what it says in words, but it has deep things hidden in its bowels. It says, "Thou shall not commit adultery," but it means as Jesus has it, "He that looketh on a woman to lust after her has committed adultery with her already in his heart." It says, "Thou shall not take the name of the Lord your God in vain." It means that we should reverence God in every place, and have His fear before our eyes, and should always pay respect to His ordinances and evermore walk in His fear and love. My brethren, surely there is not one here so foolhardy in self-righteousness as to say, "I am innocent." The spirit of the Law condemns us. And this is its useful property; it humbles us, makes us know we are guilty, and so we are led to receive the Savior.

The Use of the Law

Lower the Law and you dim the light by which man perceives his guilt. This is a very serious loss to the sinner rather than a gain, for it lessens the likelihood of his conviction and conversion. I say you have deprived the gospel of its ablest auxiliary [its most powerful weapon] when you have set aside the Law. You have taken away from it the schoolmaster that is to bring men to Christ ... They will never accept grace till they tremble before a just and holy Law. Therefore, the Law serves a most necessary purpose, and it must not be removed from its place.

The Broken Bottles of Science

We are invited, brethren, most earnestly to go away from the old-fashioned belief of our forefathers because of the supposed discoveries of science. What is science? The method by which man tries to hide his ignorance. It should not be so, but so it is. You are not to be dogmatical in theology, my brethren; it is wicked, but for scientific men, it is the correct thing. You are never to assert anything very strongly; but scientists may boldly assert what they cannot prove, and may demand a faith far more credulous than any we possess. Forsooth, you and I are to take our Bibles and shape and mould our belief according to the ever-shifting teachings of so-called scientific men. What folly is this! Why, the march of science, falsely so called, through the world may be traced by exploded fallacies and abandoned theories. Former explorers, once adored, are now ridiculed;

the continual wreckings of false hypotheses is a matter of universal notoriety. You may tell where the supposed learned have encamped by the debris left behind of suppositions and theories as plentiful as broken bottles.

Arguments Against the Bible

The only real argument against the Bible is an unholy life. When a man argues against the Word of God, follow him home, and see if you cannot discover the reason of his enmity to the Word of the Lord. It lies in some form of sin. He, whom God sends, cares nothing at all about human wisdom, so as to fawn upon it and flatter it; for he knows that "the world by wisdom knew not God," and that human wisdom is only another name for human folly.

Heavy Tidings

Everybody says, "Be quiet about the wrath to come, or you will have everybody down upon you." Be down upon me, then! I will not soften God's word to please anybody; and the Word of the Lord is very clear on this matter. If you receive not the Lord Jesus Christ, you will die in your sins. If you believe not in Him, you must perish from His presence. There is a day coming when you will die. After this, comes another day when you must appear before the judgment-seat of Christ, and all your actions shall be published, and you shall be judged for the things done in the body, whether they be good or whether they be evil. And then you shall receive the sentence of, "Come, you blessed," or, "Depart, you cursed."

Do you think we like to preach this? Do you think that it is any pleasure to the servant of God to deliver these heavy tidings? Oh, no! we speak in the bitterness of our spirit very often, but we speak because we dare not refrain. It is infinitely better that men should be told the truth than that they should be flattered by a lie into eternal ruin. He ought to have the commendation of all men, not who makes things pleasant, but who speaks things truly. Somebody is preaching of how to get people out of hell. I preach about how to keep them out of hell. Do not go there. Keep you clear of the fire, which never can be quenched. Escape for your lives; look not behind you; stay not in all the plain, but haste to Christ, the mountain of salvation, and put your trust in Him.

The Blindness of the Lost

Many will sit here tonight, who have, through a long life, committed a hundred sins of which they would be ashamed to be reminded, and yet they are not ashamed of them. They would only be ashamed to be found out; they are not ashamed of the sin itself. A man truly awakened by the Spirit of God feels the remembrance of his sin to sting him as with scorpions. He cannot bear it. But the great mass of people does a thousand wrong things, and yet they are not troubled, but feel quite at their ease. Some of you are probably within a very short time of death and judgment, and yet you can make sport of sin. How often does it happen that people come to the place of worship, and go their way, having rejected solemn appeals; and they will never hear any more! They have had their last warning. Oh, if they could but know that, during the week, they will fall down dead, or be laid aside by sickness, never to leave the bed again! Yet, they trifle on the brink of fate, on the very verge of everlasting woe. If you saw a man going straight onto the very brink of some dreadful precipice, and you saw him about to take another step, you would say, "That man is blind. I am sure that he is, or else he would not act like that." People do not go into terrible danger with their eyes open; yet, there are many of our fellowmen, perhaps many of ourselves, going right on carelessly and heedlessly to the very brink of the awful abyss without a thought of danger. They must be blind. This horrible peace of conscience, this quenching of the Spirit whenever conscience does stir itself, this playing and trifling with death and judgment prove that they are blind.

God's Dwelling Place

I know men think of their fretted roofs and of their lofty pillars in their cathedrals, and think these ensure the divine indwelling, but He is no more inside that building than outside. God is to be found on the loftiest mountain, as well as in the valley, and where the preacher stands upon a log of wood upon the village-green, the place is just as consecrated as though a thousand years it had heard nothing but the song of praise and the voice of prayer. There are no holy places now; these are done with. They are the beggarly elements of the Law, but in the living Church, built up of men and women who have been born unto God by His Spirit, there Jehovah peculiarly dwells—in Heaven and in the little Heaven below, in the midst of His elect people, whom He has ordained according to His purpose.

The Blackness of Sin

Soul! you have as yet no true idea of what sin is. God the Holy Spirit has never opened your eyes to see what an evil and bitter thing it is to sin against God, or else there would be no "buts." Picture a man who has lost his way, who has sunk into a slough; the waters and the mire are come up to his very throat. He is about to sink in it when some bright spirit comes, stepping over the treacherous bog, and puts forth to him his hand. That man, if he knows where he is, if he knows his uncomfortable and desperate state, will put out his hand at once. You will not find him hesitating with "buts," and "of," and "peradventures." He feels that he is plunged into the ditch, and would come out of it. And *you* apparently are still in the wilderness of your natural state. You have not yet discovered what a fool, although a wayfaring man, might see: that sin is a tremendous evil, that your sin is all destructive and will yet swallow you up quick and utterly destroy your soul.

The True Preacher

The burden, which the true preacher of God bears, is for God and on Christ's behalf, and for the good of men. He has a natural instinct, which makes him care for the souls of others, and his anxiety is that none should perish, but that all should find salvation through Jesus Christ. Like the Christ who longed to save, so does the true Malachi, or messenger of God, go forth with this as his happy, joyful, cheerfully-borne burden—that men may turn unto God and live.

Preach Christ

Preach Christ or nothing; do not dispute or discuss except with your eye on the cross.

Pulpit Work

I must not so preach the grace of God as to give latitude to sin. I must not so denounce sin as to drive men to despair. Our path is often narrow as a razor's edge, and we keep on crying in our spirit while we are speaking, "Lord, direct me! Lord, help me to deal wisely for You with all these souls!" The anxieties, which we feel in connection with our pulpit work, are enough to make us old before our time.

The Light of the Gospel

I would not give much for your religion unless it can be seen. Lamps do not talk, but they do shine.

The Burden of a Preacher

You cannot preach conviction of sin unless you have suffered it. You cannot preach repentance unless you have practiced it. You cannot preach faith unless you have exercised it. You may talk about these things, but there will be no power in the talk unless what is said has been experimentally proved in your own soul. It is easy to tell when a man speaks what he has made his own, or when he deals in secondhand experience. "Son of man, eat this roll." You must eat it before you can hand it out to others. True preaching is Artesian: it wells up from the great depths of the soul. If Christ has not made a well within us, there will be no outflow from us. We are not proper agents for conveying truth to others, if grace has not conveyed it to us. When we get God's word in our studies, we feel it to be a load, which bows us to the ground. We are, at times, obliged to get up and walk to and fro beneath the terror of the threatenings of God's word; and often are we forced to bow our knee before the glory of some wonderful word of the Lord, which beams with excessive grace. We say to ourselves, "These are wonderful truths. How they press upon our hearts!" They create great storms within us; they seem to tear us to pieces. The strong wind of the mighty Spirit blows through the messenger of God, and he himself is swayed to and fro in it as the trees of the forest in the tempest. Hence, even in the reception of the message of God, it is a burden.

Be Honest With Your Soul

Some of you, my hearers, have often been impressed and partially convinced of sin, but you have put off Christ with excuses. Will you bear with me while I solemnly assure you that at its core, your heart is at enmity to God? Your excuse may look very pretty, but it is as flimsy as it is fair. If you were honest with your own soul, you would say at once, "I do not love Christ; I do not want His salvation." Your put-offs, your false promises, your excuses are worthless; anyone with half an eye can see through them—they are so transparent. You are an enemy to God; you are unreconciled and content to be so. This truth may be unpalatable, but it is nevertheless most certain. May God help you to feel this, and may it humble you before His presence.

Discouragement

Believer, if the conversion of the world rested with the Church, if the outgathering of the elect depended upon us, it never would be done, but God makes us work for this end, and so He works first in us, and then He works with us. How this ought to encourage us to work! This little arm—what can it do? But that Eternal Arm—what can it not do? This tongue, how feebly can it speak; but the voice of Him who spake as never man spake, how persuasively can it speak? Our spirits, narrow and limited—what can they affect? But His unbounded Spirit, what cannot He perform? Oh! let everyone here, who has been serving his Master, bid farewell to everything like a discouraging or desponding thought. The great army of God is not defeated. It never can be. In the long run, it must conquer. And even those parts of the divine strategy of our great Commander, which looked like retreat, are only portions of His perpetual victory. He is fighting on and will win the battle, even to the end. It is a great consolation to the believer to know that Jesus lives, and lives in triumph. I do remember, and I cannot help repeating what I have told you before—I do remember, when in an hour of the most overwhelming sorrow through which a mind could pass, this one thing restored and comforted me. After that dreadful catastrophe in the Surrey Gardens, when my mind gave way, my sorrow was extreme, and I had almost lost my reason for some three weeks, and was desponding and brokenhearted. I was alone, walking in solitude, mourning and weeping as I did day and night. On a sudden, there came into my mind, as though it dropped from Heaven, this text: "Him hath God highly exalted and given him a name which is above every name that at the name of Jesus every knee should bow." You know the rest. The thought that crossed my mind was this: "I am one of His soldiers, and I am lying in a ditch to die. It does not matter; the King has won the victory—Christ has won the victory—Christ is to the fore. If I die like a dog, I care not. The crown is on His head. He is safely exalted." In a moment, I was happy; my trouble was gone; I found myself perfectly restored. I fell on my knees in a solitary place, praising God who, in infinite mercy, had made that text to be a balm to my spirit. Now there may be someone here who feels much as I did—disconsolate, cast down. If you really love Jesus, there is not a nobler balm for your care than this: He reigns; He is glorious; the government is not taken from His shoulders. Our King is no captive; our

Emperor has not yielded up His sword; our Prince Imperial is not banished; our Empire never fails; the city of Jerusalem is not besieged; there shall be no straitness of bread in her streets. "God is in the midst of her: she shall not be moved; God shall help her, and that right early." Let the heathen rage. Let the people and nations be moved. Let the whole earth rock and reel, and the mountains be carried into the midst of the sea. God is our refuge and strength, our very present help in time of trouble. God reigns, and the kingdom of Jesus is settled by an unchangeable decree. Therefore, lift up your heads, you saints, for your redemption draws nigh, and even now clap your joyful hands, and go back again to the conflict of life until your Master calls you home like true heroes, that henceforth shall know no fear, and shall never turn your backs in the day of battle. God grant it may be so for His name's sake. Amen.

The Day of Death

Dear friends, put all your days together; they shall not equal that last day which shall be to you the beginning of days of another sort. The day of our death is the beginning of our best days. Sometimes even that part of a dying day, which is spent on earth, is the best that the dying believer has ever lived. I have seen believers die, and if anything can convince a man of the reality of religion, of the truth of the Scriptures, and of the power of the Spirit, it is the death of saints.

Spurgeon's Conversion

I think that the best holy day I ever spent (yes, I think I must put it as high as that,) was the day of my conversion. There was a novelty and freshness about that first day, which made it like the day in which a man first sees the light after having been long blind. My conversion day, shall I ever forget it? —when my heart began to beat with spiritual life, and the lungs of my soul began to heave with prayer, the hands of my soul were stretched out to grasp my Lord, and the eyes of my soul beheld His beauty. Ay, that was a very blessed sight, but what will it be to see Him face to face?

These are the words of a man who had a genuine conversion. Is this your experience? Seriously consider the genuineness of your professed conversion. Did you truly repent of sin? Have you applied the spiritual nature of God's Law to your own conscience? Have you truly seen the love of Calvary's Cross? Did you come out of darkness into light? Were you made a new creature in Christ? Did He become the Source of your joy? Did faith explode in your heart? Did His Word become your very sustenance? Do you delight to do His will? Do you? If not, you may have had a false conversion, and it would be very wise to examine yourself and see if you are in the faith. If you are not sure about this, make your calling and election sure. Get on your knees and open your Bible at Psalm 51 and make King David's penitent prayer your penitent prayer. Don't get up off your knees until you know that you have passed from death to life. Do it with the thought that tomorrow you may be snatched into eternity. Nothing is as important as your eternal salvation. — *Ray Comfort*

Let Us Hate Sin

"Then did they spit in His face." O my Lord, to what terrible degradation are you brought! Into what depths you dragged through my sin, and the sin of all the multitudes whose iniquities were made to meet upon you! O my brothers, let us hate sin; O my sisters, let us loathe sin, not only because it pierced those blessed hands and feet of our dear Redeemer, but because it dared even to spit in His face! No one can ever know all the shame the Lord of glory suffered when they did spit in His face. These words glide over my tongue all too smoothly; perhaps even I do not feel them as they ought to be felt, though I would do so if I could. But could I feel as I ought to feel in sympathy with the terrible shame of Christ, and then could I interpret those feelings by any language known to mortal man, surely you would bow your heads and blush, and you would feel rising within your spirits a burning indignation against the sin that dared to put the Christ of God to such shame as this. I want to kiss His feet when I think that they did spit in His face.

The Sabbath

I am no preacher of the old legal Sabbath. I am a preacher of the gospel. The Sabbath of the Jew is to him a task. The Lord's Day of the Christian, the first day of the week, is to him a joy, and a day of rest, of peace, and of thanksgiving. And if you Christian men can earnestly drive away all distractions, so that you can really rest today, it will be good for your bodies, good for your souls, good mentally, good spiritually, good temporally, and good eternally.

Difficult Doctrines

I often get confused over doctrines that puzzle me. I see this to be true and that to be true, but how to reconcile the two, I know not; then the thought of the daybreak comes in so comfortably. "What you know not now, you shall know hereafter." Here it is not good for us to know all things. In some respects, it is the glory of God to conceal Himself, and He may well say to us—"I have many things to say unto you, but you cannot bear them now." But there it will be the glory of God to reveal Himself, and it will also be to our benefit, our minds being then fortified and strengthened to receive what we could not comprehend here below. Perhaps the glare of the divine light, if it comes to us here, even though tempered by the Mediator Himself, might be too much for these poor eyes of ours.

Hypocrisy

I am told that Christians do not love each other. I am very sorry if that be true, but I rather doubt it, for I suspect that those who do not love each other are not Christians.

Now is the Time of Salvation

Oh, sinner! it may be now or never with you. I know that God saves men at the eleventh hour, but I know also that there are many who are not saved at the eleventh hour, and that after such-and-such an hour has struck, many are given up to hardness of heart, permitted to be their own destroyers, without any checks of conscience or of the Holy Spirit—and such may be your case. The ticking of the clock always cries to men who know how to interpret its meaning. "Now, or never! Now, or never! Today on earth, tomorrow in eternity!" If you would have Christ, the only time to seek Him is today. "Today, if you will hear His voice, harden not your hearts." "For now is the accepted time, now is the day of salvation."

The Use of Fear

I further believe, although certain persons deny it, that the influence of fear is to be exercised over the minds of men, and that it ought to operate upon the mind of the preacher himself: "Noah ... moved with fear, prepared an ark to the saving of his house" (Hebrews 11:7).

Fruit of Conversion

Have you no wish for others to be saved? Then you are not saved yourself. Be sure of that.

I was delighted to find this theme in Spurgeon's preaching. It meant that I could quote him and say what I wanted to say without saying it. He had the courage to declare what I only thought for many years, but never preached for fear of sounding harsh in the pulpit. However, there is a strong biblical basis for believing that a person who maintains that he is saved, and yet has no concern for the lost cannot and should not rest in the hope that he is saved. How can he be converted? He who is saved supposedly loves his neighbor as himself. Love has concern when professed loved ones are in danger. If we don't warn them, we don't love them.
– Ray Comfort

The Law's Power

When once God the Holy Spirit applies the Law to the conscience, secret sins are dragged to light; little sins are magnified to their true size; and things apparently harmless become exceedingly sinful. Before that dread Searcher of the hearts and Trier of the reins makes His entrance into the soul, it appears righteous, just, lovely, and holy; but when He reveals the hidden evils, the scene is changed. Offenses, which were once styled peccadilloes, trifles, freaks of youth, follies, indulgences, little slips, etc., then appear in their true colors, as breaches of the Law of God, deserving condign punishment.

The World Under the Law

Those who are under the Law may well be horribly afraid because of the penalties, which are due through their many failures and transgressions. They have broken the Law, and are therefore in constant danger of judgment and condemnation. The careless try to shake off the thought as much as possible by putting off the evil day, by forgetting death, and by pretending to disbelieve in judgment and eternal wrath; but still more or less this thought disturbs them, a dreadful sound is in their ears. When men are once awakened, the dread of punishment for sin haunts them day and night, and fills them with terror; and well it may, for they are under the Law, and the Law will soon cast them into its prison, from which they will never escape. Every transgression and disobedience must receive a just recompense of reward.

The State of the Lost

All men are under the Law by nature, and consequently they are condemned by it because they have broken its commands; and apart from our Lord Jesus men are only reprieved criminals, respited from day to day, but still under sentence and waiting for the appointed hour when the warrant shall be solemnly executed upon them.

Personal Workers

We want in the Church of Christ a band of well-trained sharpshooters, who will pick the people out individually and be always on the watch for all who come into the place, not annoying them, but making sure that they do not go away without having had a personal warning, invitation, and exhortation to come to Christ.

The Birth of Jesus

Strange that the Lord of glory was not born in a palace! Princes, Christ owes you nothing! Princes, Christ is not your debtor; you did not swaddle Him. He was not wrapped in purple; you had not prepared a golden cradle for Him to be rocked in! Queens, you did not candle Him upon your knees; He hung not at your breasts! And you mighty cities, which then were great and famous, your marble halls were not blessed with His little footsteps! He came out of a village, poor and despised, even Bethlehem. When there, He was not born in the governor's house or in the mansion of the chief man, but in a manger. Tradition tells us that His manger was cut in the solid rock. There was He laid, and the oxen likely enough came to feed from the selfsame manger, the hay and the fodder of which were His only bed. Oh! wondrous stoop of condescension, that our blessed Jesus should be girded with humility and stoop so low! Ah! if He stooped, why should He bend to such a lowly birth? And if He bowed, why should He submit not simply to become the son of poor parents, but to be born in so miserable a place?

Let us take courage here. If Jesus Christ was born in a manger in a rock, why should He not come and live in our rocky hearts? If He was born in a stable, why should not the stable of our souls be made into a habitation for Him? If He was born in poverty, may not the poor in spirit expect that He will be their Friend? If He thus endured degradation at the first, will He count it any dishonor to come to the very poorest and humblest of His creatures, and tabernacle in the souls of His children?

The Bible

Defend the Bible? I would as soon defend a lion! Unchain it and it will defend itself!

The Law's Use

The Law is the surgeon's knife that cuts out the proud flesh that the wound may heal. The Law by itself only sweeps and raises the dust, but the gospel sprinkles clean water upon the dust, and all is well in the chamber of the soul. The Law kills; the gospel makes alive. The Law strips, and then Jesus Christ comes in and robes the soul in beauty and glory. All the commandments and all the types direct us to Christ, if we will but heed their evident intent.

Enmity with God

As long as I am at enmity with God, guilty of breaking His Law and liable to His righteous wrath, I dread His name and shrink from His presence. The soul, under the Law, stands as the Israelites did, far off from the mountain, with a bound set between themselves and the glory of God. Distance and separation are the natural conditions of all who are under the Law. Far hence, cries the heart of man, when it beholds God touching the hills so that they smoke; and when it hears the voice of God like a trumpet waxing exceeding loud and long, it beseeches that it may not hear such words anymore.

The Hour of Death

Lord, make me to know that I am so frail that I may die at any time—early morning, noon, night, midnight, cockcrow. I may die in any place. If I am in the house of sin, I may die there. If I am in the place of worship, I may die there. I may die in the street. I may die while undressing tonight. I may die in my sleep, die before I get to my work tomorrow morning. I may die in any occupation. But God grant I may never die a blasphemer. I may die with the cup of communion at my lips. I may die preaching. I may die singing. In all, grant I may die as I wish to die: doing your service for the love of Christ by the power of Your Spirit. Perhaps, as I stand here and readily speak, the arrow is on its way; soon may the hand He stretched, and dumb the mouth that lisps this faltering strain. Oh! may it never intrude upon an ill-spent hour, but find me wrapped in meditation, and hymning my great Creator, or serving my fellowman with love to God, or in some way so laboring that it shall not come to me as a thief in the night, but shall find me watching, ready for His advent.

Law Stirs Opposition

A man under the Law does not escape from the dominion of sin because the Law rouses the opposition of the human heart. There are a great many things that people never wish to do or think of doing till they are forbidden. Lock up a closet in your house and say to your wife and children, "You must never enter that closet, or even look into the keyhole."

Perhaps they have never wanted to look into the dingy old corner before, but now they pine to inspect it. A number of bylaws have lately been posted up as to the use of Clapham-common, and I am half afraid to read them, for fear I should want to break them. I dare say that many things, which I never desired to do, are now strictly prohibited, and I shall feel vexed with the commissioners for lessening my liberty. I should not wonder but what numbers of persons, who never visited the common before, will now become sinners against the new laws. Law, by reason of our unruly nature, excites opposition and creates sin, for what a man may not do, he immediately wants to do. He who is under the Law will never escape from the dominion of sin, for sin comes by the Law by reason of the iniquity of our hearts.

The Conscience

O soul! You are at war with your conscience. You have tried to quiet it, but it will prick you. Oh, there be some of you to whom conscience is a ghost, haunting you by day and night. You know the good, though you choose the evil; you prick your fingers with the thorn of conscience when you try to pluck the rose of sin.

True biblical evangelistic preaching probes the human conscience because it is here that we echo the great truth of the Moral Law. — *Ray Comfort*

Proportionate Thankfulness

We should be ten times more full of bliss if we were proportionately more full of thankfulness. We bury God's mercies, and then sigh for His comforts. If we recollect how near to death's dark door we once laid, and how the gates of hell were opened for us and fain would have closed upon us forever, then we should bless that Mighty Arm that plucked us like brands from the burning, and adore that matchless atonement that has delivered us from going down into the pit, because a ransom has been found.

Praying for the Profane

Give away a tract whenever you can. Better still, give a little book that will not be torn up, one that has a cover on it, for you will probably see it upon the table when you call again. Speak a word for the Master whenever it is possible, and offer a short prayer at every convenient opportunity. I think we should make it a rule, whenever we hear a foul or blasphemous word in the street—(and, alas! we constantly do so)—always to pray for the person who utters it. Perhaps then the devil might find it expedient not to stir up people to swear, if he knew that it excited Christians to pray. Try it at all events, and see whether it may not have a subtle power to stop the profanity, which is so terribly on the increase.

Contrition of the Lost

No sinner looks to the Savior with a dry eye or a hard heart. Aim, therefore, at heart breaking, at bringing home condemnation to the conscience and weaning the mind from sin. Be not content till the whole mind is deeply and vitally changed in reference to sin.

Demands of the Law

The men who think they have kept the Law of God are evidently very far from understanding its meaning. They have a very poor idea of the mind of God or they would not have thought that they had fulfilled the will of God with such a poor, miserable, hypocritical righteousness as theirs. The Pharisee thought he had kept the Law, for he fasted twice a week and paid tithes of all he possessed, and yet the same man could go and swallow a widow's house behind the door and do all sorts of abominable actions. It is clear that he had formed a shockingly low notion of true holiness; in fact, he had degraded the Law into a mere external ordinance, which took note of the outside of the cup and platter and left the inside full of filthiness.

The Sincerity of Prayer

The other night, I told you of a dear brother who said, when I exhorted my hearers to select somebody to pray for, that he had prayed for one person for twenty years, and that he is not converted yet. So I said to him, "Have you spoken to your friend personally about his soul? Have you made it your business to go down to his house, and tell him that you are anxious about him?" "No," he replied, "I cannot say that I have done so." "Well, then," I asked, "do you expect God to hear prayers of that kind? Suppose I were to pray that it might be a good harvest over in that field, and yet, for twenty years, I did not sow any corn there; the probability is that, when I did sow some, I should get my prayers answered, and gather in the harvest." If we pray for anything, God expects us to use the proper means of obtaining it; and if we neglect the means, we have no right to expect Him to believe in the sincerity of our prayer. If a father and mother pray for their children, but never pray with them, or speak to them personally about the welfare of their souls, they must not wonder if they are not brought to Christ.

The Greatest Blessing for Our Neighbor

What can be wiser than in the highest sense to bless our fellow men—to snatch a soul from the gulf that yawns, to lift it up to the Heaven that glorifies, to deliver an immortal from the thralldom of Satan, and to bring him into the liberty of Christ?

The Bitterness of the Cross

In the light of Calvary, sin does like itself appear; and what is the likeness of sin there? Why, the murderer of the Son of God—the murderer of the Prince of Life—the murderer of man's best Friend, whose only crime was this—"found guilty of excess of love," and therefore He must die. O sin, is this what you are? Are you a God-killing thing? I have heard of men being guilty of regicide, but what shall I say concerning Deicide? Yet sin virtually, and as much as it can, stabs at the Godhead, crying with the wicked husbandmen, "This is the heir; come, let us kill Him, and the inheritance shall be ours." This is the terrible character of sin—it will imbrue its hands in the blood of Him who is perfectly innocent and perfectly benevolent. It will take man's best Friend by the throat, condemn Him as if He were a felon, nail Him to a gibbet, and then stand and gaze at Him, and mock His very death-throes. There is nothing upon earth so devilish as sin. Oh, to what extremes of atrocity has sin not gone! And such is your sin and mine, to a greater or less degree. A sight of the cross, therefore, brings bitterness into the soul, because it shows us what sin is, and what are its ultimate issues and true designs if it could carry them out. Never do we smite upon our breast so hard as when we see the cross of Jesus. We are condemned at the mercy-seat even more fully than we are at the judgment-seat.

The Purpose of the Law

The Law also shows us our great need—our need of cleansing, cleansing with the water and the blood. It discovers to us our filthiness, and this naturally leads us to feel that we must be washed from it if we are ever to draw near to God. So, the Law drives us to accept Christ as the only Person who can cleanse us, and make us fit to stand within the veil in the presence of the Most High.

Theatrical Preaching

I believe that the most damnable thing a man can do is to preach the gospel merely as an actor and turn the worship of God into a kind of theatrical performance.

> *Dare I say that much of what we see on Christian television falls into this category? It is an embarrassment. If we refuse to preach the fear of the Lord, we will fall back into entertainment as a means of holding our hearers.* ~ *Ray Comfort*

The Blood

O my soul! never look for peace elsewhere and never be afraid of finding peace here. If today, O Christian, you have lost your confidence, if today you are conscious of having been false to your Lord, and of having done despite to His Spirit, if today you feel ashamed of the very name of a Christian because you have dishonored it, if today despair is ready to strangle your hope, and you are tempted to give it all up, yet come now, even now, to this precious blood. Do not think that my Savior can save merely the little sinners; He is a great Savior—mighty to save. I know your sins speak very loudly—ah! well they may. I hope you will hear their voices and hate them in the future, but they cannot speak so loudly as the blood of Jesus does. It says, "Father, Father, shall I die in vain? Father, I paid my blood for sinners, shall not sinners be saved? I was smitten for the guilty, shall the guilty be smitten, too?" The blood says, "O God, I have vindicated Your Law, what more do You demand? I have honored Your justice. Why should You cast the sinner into hell? O Divine Benignity! can You take two exactions for one offense, and punish those for whom Jesus suffered? O Justice! will You here avenge? O Mercy! when the way is cleared, will You not run to guilty sinners? O Love Divine, when the pathway is opened for You, will You not show Yourself to the rebellious and the vile?" The blood shall not plead in vain; sinners shall be saved, and you and I, I hope, among them to the praise and glory of His grace.

Wake Up, Sinner

You have sat in judgment on your own soul, put on the black cap, and read out your own sentence; you have put yourself upon the death-cart; you have adjusted the rope about your own neck; and you are about to draw the bolt and be your own executioner. Oh! weigh your words and measure your acts and wake up to a consciousness of what you are about. Do not take the leap in the dark. Look down the chasm first, and gaze a moment at the jagged rocks beneath which soon you must lie a mangled corpse. Now, ere you drink the cup, know the poison that is in the bottom of it. Make sure of what you are doing, and if you are determined that you will clasp your sins with the spasmodic and terrific grasp of a dying, drowning man. Then grasp your sins and lose your soul; then keep your sins and be damned! Hold fast to your iniquities and be dashed forever from the presence of the Eternal One. If it be horrible to hear, how much more horrible to do? If it be dreadful to speak, how much more solemn to perform in cold blood that which our lips have spoken.

The Young Prince

You remember the story of the young prince, who came into the room where he thought his dying father was sleeping, and put the king's crown on his head to see how it would fit him. The king, who was watching him, said, "Wait a little while, my son. Wait till I am dead." So, when you feel any inclination to put the crown of glory on your head, just fancy that you hear God saying to you, "Wait till I am dead, before you try on My crown." As that will never be, you had better leave the crown alone, and let Him wear it to whom it rightfully belongs.

Speaking in Earnest

You may depend upon it that you may make men understand the truth if you really want to do so; but if you are not in earnest, it is not likely that they will be. If a man were to knock at my door in the middle of the night, and when I put my head out of the window to see what was the matter, he should say, in a very quiet, unconcerned way, "There is a fire at the back part of your house," I should have very little thought of any fire, and should feel inclined to empty a jug of water over him.

Separated Life

Remember again, that our Lord Jesus Christ had a broad wall between Him and the ungodly. Look at Him; and see how different He is from the men of His time. All His life long, you observe Him to be a stranger and a foreigner in the land. Truly, He drew near to sinners, as near as He could draw, and He received them when they were willing to draw near to Him; but He did not draw near to their sins. He was "holy, harmless, undefiled, and separate from sinners." When He went to His own city of Nazareth, He only preached a single sermon, and they would have cast Him headlong down the hill if they could. When He passed through the street, He became the song of the drunkard, the butt of the foolish, the mark at which the proud shot out the arrows of their scorn.

At last, having come to His own, and His own having received Him not, they determined to thrust Him altogether out of the camp. So, they took Him to Golgotha, and nailed Him to the tree as a malefactor, a promoter of sedition. He was the great Dissenter, the great Nonconformist of His age. The National Church first excommunicated and then executed Him. He did not seek difference in things trivial, but the purity of His life and the truthfulness of His testimony roused the spleen of the ruler and the chief men of their synagogues. He was ready in all things to serve them and to bless them, but He never would blend with them. They would have made Him a king. Ah! if He would but have joined the world, the world would have given Him the chief place, as the world's prince said on the mountain, "All these things will I give you, if thou wilt fall down and worship me." But He drives away the fiend, and stands immaculate and separate even to the close of His life.

If you are a Christian, be a Christian. If you follow Christ, go without the camp. But if there be no difference between you and your fellowman, what will you say to the King in the Day when He comes and finds that you have on no wedding garment by which you can be distinguished from the rest of mankind?

The Atonement

God's acceptance of Christ is the sure guarantee of the salvation of those who accept His sacrifice. Beloved, when thine eye of faith is dim, when your eyeballs swim in a flood of tears and the darkness of sorrow hides much from your vision, then Jehovah sees the blood of His Son, and spares you. In the thick darkness, when you cannot see at all, the Lord God never fails to see in Jesus that with which He is well pleased, and with which His Law is honored. He will not suffer the destroyer to come near you to harm you, because He sees in Christ that which vindicates His justice and establishes the needful rule of Law. The blood is the saving mark. At this moment, this is the pressing question for each one in the company gathered in this house: Do you trust the divine propitiation or do you not? Bring to me what you will to prove your own personal excellence. I believe in no virtue, which insults the Savior's blood, which alone cleanses us from all sin. Rather confess your multiplied transgressions and shortcomings, and then take heart and hope; for there is forgiveness large and free for the very chief of sinners, through Him who has made peace by the blood of His cross.

O my hearer, guilty and self-condemned, if you will now come and trust in Jesus Christ, your sins, which are many, shall be all forgiven you, and you shall love so much in return, that the whole bent and bias of your mind shall be turned from sin to gracious obedience. The atonement applied to the conscience saves from despair, and then acting upon the heart, it saves from the love of evil. But the atonement is the saving sign. The blood on the lintel and on the two side posts scoured the house of the poorest Israelite; but the proudest Egyptian—yes, even Pharaoh on the throne—could not escape the destroyer's sword. Believe and live. Reject the atonement and perish!

How to Preach

Preach with this object, that men may quit their sins and fly to Christ for pardon, that by His blessed Spirit they may be renovated and become as much in love with everything that is holy as they are now in love with everything that is sinful.

God's Hatred of Sin

God Himself put Christ into the sinner's place through wondrous love to us, and as Christ stood in the sinner's place, though a sinner He could never be, God treated Him as if He were actually the sinner. See how the Father's wrath burns against human sin; He could not be angry with His well-beloved Son, but inasmuch as Christ stood in the sinner's place, God poured out the vials of His wrath upon Him just as if He had been guilty. Behold how the Father smites Him: These are His words, "Awake, O sword." Will not the rod suffice, great God? No. "Awake, O sword, against my shepherd, and against the man that is my fellow, saith the Lord of hosts. Smite the shepherd." But will not some common smiting be sufficient? No, to the very heart, He must be smitten, and Jesus must die the death of the cross that we may live forever. "How God must hate sin, then, and what wrath must fall upon me!" That is the convicted sinner's thought. "My sin is personal and actual, and not, like Christ's, imputed; and since it is my own, how can God continue to bear with me?"

The Chief Business

Soul-winning is the chief business of the Christian minister; indeed, it should be the main pursuit of every true believer. We should each say with Simon Peter, "I go a fishing," and with Paul our aim should be, "That I might by all means save some."

Unconverted in the Church

By all means, let us bring true converts into the church, for it is a part of our work to teach them to observe all things whatsoever Christ has commanded them, but still, this is to be done to disciples and not to mere professors; and if care be not used, we may do more harm than good at this point. To introduce unconverted persons to the church is to weaken and degrade it; and therefore an apparent gain may be a real loss.

Unhatched Chickens

What mean these dispatches from the battlefield? "Last night, fourteen souls were under conviction, fifteen were justified, and eight received full sanctification." I am weary of this public bragging, this counting of unhatched chickens, this exhibition of doubtful spoils. Lay aside such numberings of the people, such idle pretence of certifying in half a minute that which will need the testing of a lifetime.

The Terrors of the Lord

I hate to hear the terrors of the Lord proclaimed by men whose hard visages, harsh tones, and unfeeling spirits betray a sort of doctrinal desiccation—all the milk of human kindness is dried out of them.

The Love of God

Whatever I believe or do not believe, the command to love my neighbor as myself still retains its claim upon me, and God forbid that any views or opinions should so contract my soul and harden my heart as to make me forget this law of love! The love of God is first, but this by no means lessens the obligation of love to man; in fact, the first command includes the second. We are to seek our neighbor's conversion because we love him.

Slain by the Law

God never clothes men until He has first stripped them, nor does He quicken them by the gospel till first they are slain by the Law. When you meet with persons in whom there is no trace of conviction of sin, you may be quite sure that they have not been wrought upon by the Holy Spirit; for "when He is come, He will reprove the world of sin, and of righteousness, and of judgment."

Judgment Day

He that pleads for Christ should himself be moved with the prospect of the Judgment Day. When I come in at yonder door at the back of the pulpit, and the sight of that vast crowd bursts upon me, I frequently feel appalled. Think of these thousands of immortal souls gazing through the windows of those wistful eyes, and I am to preach to them all, and be responsible for their blood if I be not faithful to them. I tell you, it makes me feel ready to start back. But then fear is not alone. I am borne up by the hope and belief that God intends to bless these people through the Word, which He will enable me to deliver. I believe that everybody in that throng is sent there by God for some purpose, and that I am sent to effect that purpose.

The Open-Air Preacher

An open-air preacher, who has to go out quite alone, must be in a very unfortunate position. It is extremely helpful to be connected with an earnest living church, which will pray for you; and if you cannot find such a church where you labor, the next best thing is to get half-a-dozen brothers or sisters who will back you up, go out with you, and especially, pray with you.

Personal Witnessing

Every open-air preacher should not only address the hundreds, but he should be ready to pounce upon the ones, and he should have others with him who have the same happy art. How much more good would come of preaching in the streets if every open-air preacher were accompanied by a batch of persons who would drive his nails home for him by personal conversation!

Indifference

Let us save men by all the means under Heaven; let us prevent men going down to hell. We are not half as earnest as we ought to be. Do you not remember the young man, who, when he was dying, said to his brother, "My brother, how could you have been so indifferent to my soul as you have been?" He answered, "I have not been indifferent to your soul, for I have frequently spoken to you about it." "Oh, yes!" he said, "You spoke, but somehow, I think, if you had remembered that I was going down to hell, you would have been more earnest with me. You would have wept over me, and, as my brother, you would not have allowed me to be lost." Let no one say this of you.

Ignorant of Wrath

It seems to me, too, that you are ignorant altogether of what the wrath of God must be in the world to come. Oh! could I take you to that place where hope has ever been a stranger. If you could put your ear a moment to the gratings of those gloomy dungeons of which despair is the horrid warden—if I could make you listen to the sighs, the useless regrets, and the vain prayers of those who are cast away, you would come back affrighted and alarmed, and sure I am your "buts" would have been driven out of you. You would say, "Great God, if You will but save me from Your wrath, do what you will with me, I will make no conditions. I will offer You no objections. If I must cut off my right arm or pluck out my right eye, be it so, if from this place of woe, You will but save me. Oh! from this fire that never can be quenched, from this worm of endless folds, which can never die, great God deliver me.

No Hiding from God

But oh! sinner, there is no hiding from God. The mountains cannot cover you from Him, even if they would; neither can the rocks conceal you. See, then, at the very outset how this throne should awe our minds with terror. Founded in right, sustained by might, and universal in its dominion, look and see the throne that John of old beheld.

Rejection of the Gospel

Sirs, if you would be saved, you must have the blood of Jesus sprinkled upon you. He that believes not in Christ Jesus, in Jesus, the atoning sacrifice—must perish. The eternal God must repulse with infinite disgust the man who refuses the loving sacrifice of Jesus. Inasmuch as he counted himself unworthy of this wondrous sacrifice—this marvelous expiation, there remains no other sacrifice for sin and nothing for him but that eternal blackness and darkness and thunder, which were foreshadowed at Sinai. Those, who refuse the atonement that wisdom devised, love has provided, and justice has accepted, have signed their own death-warrant, and none can wonder that they perish.

Distribution of Tracts

I well remember distributing them in a town in England where tracts had never been distributed before, and going from house to house, and telling in humble language the things of the kingdom of God. I might have done nothing if I had not been encouraged by finding myself able to do something ... [Tracts are] adapted to those persons who have but little power and little ability, but nevertheless, wish to do something for Christ. They have not the tongue of the eloquent, but they may have the hand of the diligent. They cannot stand and preach, but they can stand and distribute here and there: these silent preachers ... They may buy their thousand tracts, and these they can distribute broadcast.

I look upon the giving away of a religious tract as only the first step for action, not to be compared with any another deed done for Christ, but were it not for the first step, we might never reach to the second. That first attained, we are encouraged to take another, and so at the last. There is a real service of Christ in the distribution of the gospel in its printed form—a service, the result of which Heaven alone shall disclose, and the Judgment Day alone shall discover. How many thousands have been carried to Heaven instrumentally upon the wings of these tracts, none can tell.

I might say, if it were right to quote such a Scripture, "The leaves were for the healing of the nations." Verily, they are so. Scattered where the whole tree could scarcely be carried, the very leaves have had a medicinal and a healing virtue in them; and the real word of truth—the simple statement of a Savior crucified and of a sinner who shall be saved by simply trusting in the Savior—has been greatly blessed. Many thousand souls have been led into the kingdom of Heaven by this simple means. Let each one of us, if we have done nothing for Christ, begin to do something now. The distribution of tracts is the first thing.

Seeking Out the Lost

There are thousands in London who never will be converted by the preaching of the gospel, for they never attend places of worship. Some of them do not know what sort of thing a religious service is. We may shudder when we say it: it is believed there are thousands in London who do not even know the name of Christ—living in what we call a Christian land, and yet they have not heard the name of Jesus. Thank God things are better than they were, but things are bad enough still. Brethren, you must go and see these things and mend them. To the lodging-houses, young men, you must carry the gospel, and to those thickly-peopled habitations, where every room contains a family, and not one room a Christian. I believe there is very much good to be done by house-to-house visitation—not by City Missionaries and Bible-women only, may God speed that noble body of laborers—but by all of you, by you that have position in society among your neighbors. Make yourselves free, and go and talk to them of Christ in the little houses that are near to you. As far as your time allows be a visitor, and if there be one dark part of the town known to you as the haunt of sinners, make it a point to use this agency of visitation from house-to-house. Let the lost sheep of Israel's house be sought out. Some will need special means before ever they can be found and brought in.

Praying for the Lost

Let me beg you, where all other means fail, to seek men by your prayers. As long as a man has one other man to pray for him, there is a hope of his salvation. If you in your daily supplications make mention of men—if you select special cases—if you bear their names before the Lord, you shall have the joy of seeing them turned from darkness to light, and they with you shall be a people "sought out." If a word of mine shall stir up but one of you to seek the Lord's hidden ones, my soul shall rejoice; and if every one of you shall register a vow in this house of prayer—"I will seek out some family today, and continue my work tomorrow, and the next day I will be seeking out others; I will not wait till they come to me to be taught, but go and seek them and compel them to come in, that the house may be filled, that the Church of God may have its full complement of Christ's chosen"—if you will do this, my soul shall be well content. If you have never been sought, then you will not seek others; if you have never tasted that the Lord is gracious, I shall not marvel that you neglect this work, but oh! by the hell from which you are delivered, by the Heaven to which you are going, by the blood that redeemed you from death and hell, by that gracious Spirit that quickened you and still keeps you alive, by every glorious promise that stimulates you in your onward career, I pray you spend yourselves and be spent in seeking souls.

Personal Salvation

Dear brethren, you ought to know, you can know, you can know now whether you are saved or not. At any rate, if I did not know myself to be saved, I would give no sleep to my eyes or slumber to my eyelids till I had found the Savior. If a shadow of a doubt about my being washed in the blood of Christ were on my soul, I would get to my knees and not rise from them until I did really know that Christ had saved me. If you are in doubt, and yet are content about your condition, I fear that you know nothing at all about the matter; for the true child of God, if he is in any doubt about his salvation, is uneasy till that doubt is gone. He cannot rest till he knows that he is saved; and, after all, that is not a very difficult thing to know, for we are told over and over again in this blessed Book that he who believes in Christ is not condemned, but has everlasting life. If you have believed in Him, you are not condemned. You have His own word for it. He who trusts to Jesus only, builds on a sure foundation. So, if you are trusting in Him, you may have the full assurance that you have passed from death unto life, and shall never come into condemnation. Do not, brother, go limping along all your life when you might run in the way of God's commandments. A good old minister, of my acquaintance, when people used to say to him that they hoped and hoped, and never got any further than that, was in the habit of replying, "You are always hoping, and hoping; I hope you will learn to run one of these days—to run without weariness in the ways of God."

The Terrors of Death

I have been told that, some years ago, there went into the chamber of horrors at Madame Tussaud's exhibition a young gentleman, who was foolish enough to put himself under the guillotine—in the place that had been occupied by criminals. As he lay there, with his bare neck exposed to the terrible knife, he was so struck with horror that he was unable to move, and people who went by thought he was one of the waxwork figures. He could not stir until someone took him away. And, oh! if you did but know where you readily are, with that dreadful axe of divine justice just above your head, you might well be paralyzed with horror! Only let your breath fail or your pulse stop, and down it descends to your utter destruction. But alas! you are insensible to these things. May the Spirit of God arouse you! May He make you feel your true position, and then I am sure you will not be content to remain a moment longer of a doubtful and undecided mind. Hearken, my friend. That sin of yours can be forgiven, for Jesus died for sinners. That heart of yours can be renewed by grace, for Jesus lives again. You can be delivered from the wrath to come, for Jesus has gone up on high to plead for just such sinners as you are.

Come to Christ

While I see the foot-tracks of my Master before me; while I see still more His gracious sanctions following my labors; while I behold His name magnified, His glory increased, and perishing souls saved (as thanks be to God we have witness every day); while this gospel warrants me; while the Spirit of God moves me; and while signs following do multiply the seals of my commission—who am I that I should stay myself for man, or resist the Holy Ghost for any flesh that breathes? Oh then, you chief of sinners, you vilest of the vile, you who are the scum of the city, the refuse of the earth, the dregs of creation, whom no man seeks after, you whose characters are destroyed and whose inmost souls are polluted, so black that no fuller on earth can whiten you, so debased that you have sunk beyond the hope of any moralist to reclaim you! come—come to Christ. Come at His own invitation. Come, and you shall be surely received with a hearty welcome.

The Cross

The man who has lived a life of service, at last dies a felon's death! Look upon His head girt with the crown of thorns! Mark well His cheeks where they have plucked off the hair! See the spittle from those scornful mouths, staining His marred countenance! Mark the crimson rivers, which are flowing from His back where they have scourged Him! See His hands and His feet, which are pierced with the nails, and from which ensanguined rills are flowing! Look to that face so full of anguish; listen to His cry, "I thirst, I thirst," and as you see Him there expiring, can you think that He will spurn the seeker? As you see Him turn His head and say to the dying thief by His side, "Today shalt thou be with me in paradise," you dare not belie Him so much as to deem that you may not come to Him. You will outrage your reason if you start back from Jesus crucified. The cross of Christ should be the hope, the anchorage of faith. You may come, sinner—black, vile, hellish sinner. You may come and have life even as the dying thief had it when he said, "Lord, remember me."

Thoughts of Death

Some of you never think of dying, and yet you should. You say you may live long. You may and you may not. If there were a great number of loaves upon this table, and you were to eat one every day; if you were told that one of those loaves had poison in it, I think you would begin every one with great caution; and knowing that one of them would be your death, you would take each up with silent dread. Now you have so many days, and in one of these days, there is the poison of death. I do not know which one. It may be tomorrow; it may not be until many a day has gone. But I think you ought to handle all your days with holy jealousy.

Confidence in God

O you, who are His people, fall back in confidence upon the God who has treasures of snow and hail and the dread artillery of storm and tempest! Most of you, my hearers, have never seen a great storm yet, or heard in its majesty the thunder of God's power. You must be in the tropics to know what these can be, and even then, you would have to say, "These are but parts of His ways." Oh, how the Lord can shake the earth, and make it tremble even to its deep foundations when He pleases! He can make what we call, "the solid earth" to be as weak as water when He does but lift up His finger. But all the power that God has—and it is boundless—is all in that right hand, which has been lifted high to Heaven in the solemn oath that He will save His people. Wherefore, lean upon God without the shadow of a doubt. He may well put all your fears to rest even by the thunder of His power.

God's Promises

A promise is nothing unless I have good security that it shall be fulfilled. It is in vain for men to promise largely unless their fulfillment shall be as large as their promise, for the largeness of their promise is just the largeness of deception. But here every word of God is true. God has issued no more notes for the bank of Heaven than He can cash in an hour if He wills. There is enough bullion in the vaults of Omnipotence to pay off every bill that ever shall be drawn by the faith of man or the promises of God. Now look at this one—"As your days, so shall your strength be." Beloved, God has a strong reserve with which to pay off this promise; for is He not Himself omnipotent, able to do all things? Believer, till you can drain dry the ocean of omnipotence, till you can break into pieces the towering mountains of almighty strength, you never need to fear. Until your enemy can stop the course of a whirlwind with a reed, till he can twist the hurricane from its path by a word of his puny lip, you need not think that the strength of man shall ever be able to overcome the strength, which is in you, namely, the strength of God. While the earth's huge pillars stand, you have enough to make your faith firm. The same God, who guides the stars in their courses, who directs the earth in its orbit, who feeds the burning furnace of the sun, and keeps the stars perpetually burning with their fires—the same God has promised to supply your strength. While He is able to do all these things, think not that He shall be unable to fulfill His own promise.

To Draw Near to God

To draw near to God, what does this mean? To draw near to God, brethren and sisters, implies first that we are reconciled to Him by the death of His Son. For a man to attempt to draw near to God while God is angry with him would be a species of insanity. As well might the moth draw near to the candle or the stubble approach the flame. God is "a consuming fire," and while our hearts are evil, there can nothing come of an approach to God but destruction. Before any one of us can draw near to God in acceptable prayer and praise, we must wash in the fountain that Christ has filled from His dying veins. Does thou believe in the atonement, my hearer? Believing in it, hast thou also received it? Do you rest your soul's salvation upon the accomplished mediatorial work of Jesus Christ? If not, you are such an enemy to God that you may by no means even think yourself capable of drawing near to Him. Your back is towards Him; and the faster you walk, the further from God will you journey; and your end will assuredly be to hear from Him the word, "Depart." You have been departing all your life. You shall go on departing throughout eternity, departing from the God whom you have despised and forgotten. Before, then, we can draw near to God, we must have come with repentance and faith to the cross, and have looked up to Him who bled thereon, and we must have accepted Him as our salvation. I ask you whether you can accompany me in the first step. Have you laid hold on eternal life in Christ Jesus?

Complacency of the Lost

Is it not a horrible thing that Satan leads men to say, "Do not trouble us with your gospel! Do not bother us with religion! Do not come here with your tracts! Let us alone!" They claim the wretched right to perish in their sins, the liberty to destroy their own souls. We know who rules when men speak thus: it is the prince of darkness, who makes them hate the light. Oh, my hearers, do not some of you say, "We do not want to be worried with thoughts of death and judgment and eternity; we do not desire to hear about repentance and faith in a Savior. All we want of religious people is that they will let us alone." This cruel kindness we cannot grant them. How can we stand by and see them perish?

Preach Boldly

Oh, you that preach Christ, preach Him boldly! No cowardly lips must proclaim His invincible gospel! Oh, you that preach Christ, never choose your place of labor;

never turn your back on the worst of mankind! If the Lord should send you to the borders of perdition, go there and preach Him with full assurance that it shall not be in vain.

Oh, you that would win souls, have no preference as to which they shall be. If you have a choice, select the very worst! Remember, my Master's gospel is not merely for the moralist in His respectable dwelling, but for the abandoned and fallen in the filthy dens of the outcast. The all-conquering light of the Sun of Righteousness is not for the dim dawn alone, to brighten it into the full blaze of day, but it is meant for the blackest midnight that ever made a soul to shiver as in the shadow of death. The name of Jesus is high over all, in Heaven and earth and sky. Therefore, let us preach it with authority and confidence, not as though it were an invention of men. He has said He will be with us, and therefore nothing, is impossible. The Word of the Lord Jesus cannot fall to the ground. The gates of hell cannot prevail against it. The pleasure of the Lord shall prosper in His hand. The Lord shall bruise Satan under our feet shortly.

The Two-Handed Sword

The foolishness of preaching will turn out to be the great proof of the wisdom of God. Brethren, you that teach in the school, or you that preach from the pulpit or distribute tracts or speak personally to individuals, you need not be afraid but what wisdom will exonerate herself from all charges and vindicate her own methods. You may be called a fool today for preaching the gospel, but that accusation, like rust on a sword, will wear off as you use the weapon in the wars of the Lord. The preaching of the Word soon puts down all clamors against itself. Those clamors mainly arise because it is not preached. No one calls the gospel effete where it is smiting right and left like a great two-handed sword. Our reply to the outcry about the failure of the pulpit is to get into it and preach with the Holy Ghost sent down from Heaven.

The Sinfulness of Pride

How great has been your pride! When Christ bids you believe on Him, take up His cross and follow Him, He tells you to do the best thing you can do, and then you set up your judgment in contradiction to Him. You say, "But." What! is Christ to mend His gospel by your whims? What! is the plan of salvation to be cut and shaped to suit you? Does not Christ know what is best for you, better than you do yourself? "Will you snatch from His hand the balance and the rod, rejudge His judgment, dictate to God, the Judge of all the earth? And yet, this is what you attempt to do ... Oh! you know not what is the quintessence of iniquity that lies within those words so easily spoken, but which will be so hard to get rid of on a dying bed—"I will follow you, but—"

Universal Revival

The fact is the Church has scarcely ever been in a state of universal revival since the day of Pentecost. There has been a partial moving among Christians every now and then, but the whole mass throughout has never burned and flamed with the earnestness, which the grand cause demands. Oh, that the Lord would set the whole Church on fire! We have no cause whatever for disappointment. In proportion to the little effort put out, great things have come to us; therefore let us get to our nets again, and say no more about the night in which we have toiled.

The Old Method

I remember well how some of our brethren used to talk to us. They said, "You preach the gospel to dead sinners; you bid them repent and believe. You might just as well shake a pocket-handkerchief over a grave and bid the corpse come out of it." Exactly so. They spoke the truth, but then I would delight to go and shake a pocket-handkerchief over graves and bid the dead live if Jesus bade me do so. I should expect to see the cemetery crack and heave from end to end if I were sent on such an errand by the Lord. I would accept the duty joyfully. The more absurd the wise men of our age make the gospel out to be, and the more they show that it is powerless to produce the end designed, the more will we persevere in our old method of preaching Jesus crucified.

Self-Righteousness

The natural self-righteousness of man prompts him to frame apologies. We are all the best men in the world according to our own gauge and measure. [See Proverbs 20:6 (KJV)]. If we could sit as judges upon ourselves, the verdict would always be, "Not guilty." Sin, which would be very shocking in another, is very venial in us; nay, what would be abominable in other men, becomes almost commendable in ourselves, so partially do we judge our own cases.

Free Salvation

To offer free salvation to men who are neither drunkards nor swearers—why, the thing is ridiculous. "The sermon was very good for Magdalens, for thieves, and such like, but not for us." No, you are too good to be saved. You need not a physician, because you are whole. Your own table has enough upon it; you do not need to come to this feast. But bethink you, I pray you, whether this be not all a mistake. In what are you better than other men, after all? Even if you do not indulge in open sins, does not your heart often go a-lusting towards evil? Does your tongue always speak that which is right and true? If you cannot remember sins of commission, what about the sins of omission? Have you fed the hungry? Have you clothed the naked? Have you taught the ignorant? Have you loved God with all your heart and soul and strength? Have you given Him all that He demands of you? Why you cannot say this: Now the perfection, the holiness, which

God demands in order to salvation, must be like a perfect alabaster vase. If there be a single crack or spot on it, all is spoiled. You may say, "Well, it is not much broken; we have not seriously damaged it." Nay, but God requires it to be perfect, and no matter how slight the damage it may have sustained, you cannot enter Heaven upon the footing of your good works—you are cast out forever. Hear these words, "By the deeds of the Law there shall no flesh be justified in His sight." "Cursed is every one that continues not in all things which are written in the book of the Law to do them," and "As many as are of the works of the Law, are under the curse." God save you from that false excuse.

Halting Between Two Opinions

Remember again, what it is you are trifling with. It is your own soul, the soul that can never die. You are trifling with a Heaven, which you will never see if you keep on with these excuses. You are trifling, sinner, with that hell, which must be your never-ending portion if you continue as you are. Can you play with hellfire? O, can you make sport of Heaven? Can you laugh at the blood of Jesus? You are really doing so while you are thus halting between two opinions. Now if you must play the fool, find something cheaper to play with than this.

Call to Trust in Christ

Now, I say, for the Scripture says, "Today is the accepted time; today is the day of salvation." The only way to end your excuses is not by praying or resolving, but by looking to Christ. There hangs the bleeding Savior on the cross, He dies as the just for the unjust to bring us to God. He suffers there, that sin may be forgiven. Look to Him, trust Him, and you shall be saved. My hearer, I give you now in God's name this invitation, this command: Trust your soul to Jesus, the Son of God, who suffered for sin, and you shall be saved. But mind this. I may never meet you all this side the grave, but I will meet you all at God's great day, and if you receive not Christ and trust in Him, I am clear of your blood. Upon my skirts your doom cannot fall. You have heard the gospel; you have been told to trust Jesus as you are; you have been assured that He is able to save to the uttermost those who come to Him. You have been bidden to come, and now on your own heads be your soul's rain if you come not. But may the Spirit of God take these things and apply them to your souls. May He be as a fire and as a hammer in your souls—as a fire to melt or as a hammer to break; and may you today with brokenness of heart, take Christ to be your Savior both now and forever. Amen.

Self-Deception

As I look around you, though there be full many who can read their title clear to mansions in the skies, yet along these pews what a considerable proportion there is of my hearers who are only deceiving their own selves! Well, sinners, I will make the road to hell as hard for you as I can. If you will be lost, I will put up many a chain and many a bar, and shut many a gate across your way. If you will listen to my voice, God helping me, you shall find it a hard way—that way of transgressors; you shall find it a hard thing to run counter to the proclamation of the gospel of Christ.

Procrastination

What! are you become like the silly sheep that goes willingly to his slaughter? Are the swallows and cranes more wise than you? For they know the senses and they judge the times, but you know not that your summer is almost over, that your leaves are falling in the autumn of your life, and that your dreary winter of despair and of hopelessness is drawing near. Souls, are these things fancies? If so, sleep while I preach of them. Are they dreams? Do I bring out these doctrines but as bugbears to alarm you as if you were some children in a nursery? No, but as God is true, are not these the most solemn realities that ever rested on the lip of man or moved the heart of hearer? Then why is it, why is it, why is it that you make light of these things still? Why is it that you will go your way today as you did before? Why will you say, "Well, the preacher has warned me faithfully, and I will think of it, but—I was invited and I will consider, but—I did hear the warning, but—?" Ah, souls, while you shall be saying, "But ...," there shall be another, "But ..." go forth, and that shall be, "But cut him down, why cumber he the ground?" Wake, vengeance, wake! The sinner sleeps. Pluck out your sword,

O Justice! let it not rest in its scabbard; come forth! Nay, nay, oh! come not forth devouring sword! oh, come not forth! O Justice, be still! O Vengeance, put away your sword, and Mercy, reign still! "Today, if you will hear His voice, harden not your hearts as in the provocation," but if you harden your hearts, remember He will swear in His wrath that you shall not enter into His rest. Oh! Spirit of God, do the sinner turn, for without you, he will not turn. Our voice shall miss its end, and he will not come to Christ.

Compassion for Souls

Let me beseech you to believe that it is needful as well as justifiable that you should feel compassion for the sons of men. You all desire to glorify Christ by becoming soul-winners—I hope you do—and be it remembered that, other things being equal, he is the fittest in God's hand to win souls who pities souls most. I believe he preaches best who loves best, and in the Sunday-school and in private life each soul-seeker shall have the blessing very much in proportion to his yearning for it. Paul becomes a savior of many because his heart's desire and prayer to God is that they may be saved. If you *can* live without souls being converted, you shall live without their being converted; but if your soul breaks for the longing that it has towards Christ's glory and the conversion of the ungodly, if like her of old, you say, "Give me children or I die," your insatiable hunger shall be satisfied; the craving of your spirit shall be gratified. Oh! I would to God there should come upon us a divine hunger, which cannot stay itself except men yield themselves to Jesus; an intense, earnest, longing, panting desire that men should submit themselves to the gospel of Jesus. This will teach you better than the best college training how to deal with human hearts. This will give the stammering tongue the ready word; the hot heart shall burn the cords, which held fast the tongue. You shall become wise to win souls, even though you never exhibit the brilliance of eloquence[231] or the force of logic.

This is an appropriate thought for us. After enriching our souls with Spurgeon's eloquence, we may aspire to such speech, but the reality is that Charles Spurgeon was unique. Our confidence rather should be in the power of the gospel, and in the help of God. ⁓ *Ray Comfort*

~Biography of~

Charles Haddon Spurgeon

1834–1892

From Boy Preacher to Prince of Preachers, Charles Haddon Spurgeon moved tens of thousands to trust Christ for their eternal salvation and left a treasure trove of sermons and writings that continue to move and touch his readers. And Spurgeon did all through great infirmities and trials, living humbly even as he became a world-renowned celebrity.

The 15-year-old boy entered the Primitive Methodist Church amid a howling snowstorm that had kept him from reaching his intended church. The unusual English storm also kept the preacher from reaching the church. Only a handful of hearty believers made it, and the young lad, Charles, joined them in the service with singing.

Charles describes the events this way:

> "At last, a very thin looking man, a shoemaker, went up into the pulpit to preach ... He was forced to stick to his Scripture text, for the simple reason that he had little else to say. The text was, 'Look unto me, and be ye saved, all the ends of the earth' (Isaiah 45:22).

"When he had managed to spin out 10 minutes or so, he was at the end of his tether. Then he looked at me under the gallery, and I daresay, with so few present, he knew me to be a stranger. Just fixing his eyes on me, as if he knew all my heart, he said, 'Young man, you look very miserable.' Well, I did, but I had not been accustomed to have remarks made from the pulpit on my personal appearance before. However, it was a good blow, struck right home. He continued, 'And you always will be miserable—miserable in life, and miserable in death—if you don't obey my text; but if you obey now, this moment, you will be saved.' Then, lifting up his hands, he shouted as only a Primitive Methodist could do, 'Young man, look to Jesus Christ. Look! Look! Look! You have nothing to do but to look and live.'

"I saw at once the way of salvation ... I had been waiting to do fifty things, but when I heard the word, 'Look!' what a charming word it seemed to me! Oh! I looked until I could almost have looked my eyes away. There and then the cloud was gone, the darkness had rolled away, and that moment I saw the sun; and I could have risen that instant, and sung with the most enthusiastic of them, of the precious blood of Christ, and the simple faith which looks alone to HIM ...

E'er since by faith I saw the stream
  Thy flowing wounds supply
    Redeeming love has been my theme
      And shall be till I die."

God's hand was in a snowstorm, an absent preacher, a faithful little shoemaker, and an aptly spoken word. And He brought forth the salvation of a man who would see tens of thousands of souls converted under his ministry, and tens of millions influenced by his writings that are reprinted and absorbed by Christians to this day. Once in the Kingdom, God lit a fire in Charles that would light the way for millions of people.

The bedraggled 15-year-old boy who heard the word of the Lord that day and looked up to see Jesus was Charles Haddon Spurgeon, often called the Prince of Preachers, a teacher and man who lived the Word and was used by God.

Young Beginnings

Spurgeon's Christian roots can be traced back to persecuted Dutchmen who fled to England centuries earlier only to find different persecution. Job Spurgeon was imprisoned in 1677 for six years and had all of his belongings confiscated for attending a worship service not sanctioned by the Church of England. A few years after being released from prison, he was sent back for the same offense.

Spurgeon's father and grandfather were both strong Christians and Congregationalist ministers.

Into this godly heritage, Charles Haddon Spurgeon was born June 19, 1834 in Kelvedon, Essex, England—the first of 17 children. Interestingly, as an infant, he was sent to live with his grandparents and stayed with them until he was six years old. There, he was given a complete youngster's understanding of Scriptures, and by age six he had learned to love John Bunyan's classic *Pilgrim's Progress*.

Back with his parents, he grew up in a home with strong Puritan teachings and faithful, restrained lives to match. There was no known hypocrisy in his parents' lives. And the Spurgeons did not allow it in their offspring. By outward standards, he and his siblings were exemplary children.

Little Charles once lost his pencil and decided to buy one at the store on credit. When his father found out, he gave him a lecture on the sins of debt that he never forgot.

> "I was marched off to the shop like a deserter marched into barracks, crying bitterly all down the street and feeling dreadfully ashamed, because I thought everybody knew I was in debt. The farthing was paid amid solemn warnings, and the poor debtor was set free like a bird out of a cage."

Spurgeon spent some time at a boarding school, and here we see a flash of his occasional fieriness. When he first started there, he knelt to pray before going to bed and was pelted by other boys with slippers and other items. He arose and struck at the mocking boys to his right and then to his left. After several were knocked down, the others stopped and stayed still. Then he knelt back down and returned to his prayers. He reported not being interrupted again.

From his earliest days, Spurgeon struggled with the sin in his life. Although his sinfulness might appear small from the outside, it weighed heavily on the boy's heart. No doubt at least part of this reason was all the talk and teaching in the home of fallen nature. In addition to Scripture, Spurgeon was reared on the writings of John Bunyan and Richard Baxter, making him keenly aware of the soul's struggle with sin. He had a sharp sense of the justice of God.

> "Sin, whatever it might be to other people, became to me an intolerable burden. It was not so much that I feared hell as that I feared sin, and all the while I had upon my mind a deep concern for the honour of God's

> name. I felt that it would not satisfy my conscience if I could be forgiven unjustly, but then there came the question, how could God be just and yet justify me, who had been so guilty?"

During that cold Sunday morning in January 1850, Spurgeon was making his way toward his own church, but the fateful snowstorm forced him to the Primitive Methodist Church where the faithful cobbler showed him the way to salvation through the words of the prophet Isaiah.

Spurgeon, of course, knew the Gospel well from his upbringing, but God chose to use a vehicle outside his family to draw him to His Son. It was the longing of his heart, and Christ filled it.

> "I do from my soul confess that I was never satisfied till I came to Christ ... Since that dear hour when my soul cast itself on Jesus, I have found solid joy and peace, but before that all those supposed gaieties of early youth, all the imagined joy and ease of boyhood, were but vanity and vexation of spirit to me. That happy day when I found the Saviour and learnt to cling to His dear feet was a day never to be forgotten by me, an obscure child, unknown, unheard of. I listened to the word of God, and that precious text led me to the Cross of Christ."

Spurgeon attended Oxford for a while. However, because he was not a member of the Church of England, he was not allowed to earn a degree. But he studied diligently, and his keen mind was obvious. And he was free to preach as he desired, taking part in street preaching.

Spurgeon was never able to keep his joy and the basic message of the Gospel to himself. It spilled out of him naturally. Almost immediately, he set out as a servant of God, putting his hand to the plow and not looking back. There was nothing too small or trivial; he only wanted to do God's will. The Lord began him small, found him faithful, and in a stunningly short time, brought him to great things.

> "The very first service which my youthful heart rendered to Christ was the placing of tracts in envelopes, and then sealing them up, that I might send them. I might have done nothing for Christ if I had not been encouraged by finding myself able to do a little. Then I sought to do something more, and from that something more, and I do not doubt that many servants of God have been led on to higher and nobler labours for their Lord, because they began to serve Him in the right spirit and manner."

His spirit was to share Christ in any way he could—writing verses on a scrap of paper and leaving it for someone to find.

> "I could scarcely content myself even for five minutes without trying to do something for Christ."
>
> Nothing could stop him.
>
> "It may be that in the young dawn of my Christian life, I did imprudent things in order to serve the cause of Christ, but I still say, give me back that time again, with all its imprudence and with all its hastiness, if I may but have the same love to my Master, the same overwhelming influence in my spirit, making me obey my Lord's commands because it was a pleasure to me to do anything to serve my God."

Deceived Onto the Path of Greatness

Spurgeon was actually tricked into his first sermon. James Vinter, who headed the Local Preachers' Association in Cambridge, heard of Spurgeon's success giving the closing address after Sunday school. Vinter invited Spurgeon to accompany a man to the village of Teversham where he was to preach. Enroute, Spurgeon said he would be praying for him, and the man stopped in surprise. He had never preached, he said, and never intended to. He assumed Spurgeon was preaching and suggested that if he were not, they should turn back.

Spurgeon realized he had been tricked, but he decided to give a message anyway, even though he was completely unprepared and had never preached. He chose the Scripture "Unto you therefore which believe He is precious" on which to preach, and God greatly blessed the 16-year-old. When he finished, a woman's voice piped up and asked, "Bless your dear heart. How old are you?" Spurgeon very solemnly replied, "You must wait till the service is over before making such inquiries. Let us now sing."

And so the boy preacher was launched at 16. Within 18 months of his conversion, Spurgeon was made pastor of the small Waterbeach Baptist Chapel.

He said he became a Baptist because of studying the New Testament in Greek. "According to my reading of Holy Scripture, the believer in Christ should be buried with Him in baptism, and so enter upon his open Christian life."

Spurgeon's mother once proclaimed, "Ah, Charles! I often prayed the Lord to make you a Christian, but I never asked that you become a Baptist."

Spurgeon with a smile responded quickly, "Ah, mother! The Lord has answered your prayer with His usual bounty, and given you exceeding abundantly above what you asked or thought."

England was in a state of considerable spiritual darkness, with corruption and apathy in the Church of England. While there were firm remnants of Christianity, the overall picture was dismal. The Rev. Desmond Morse-Boycott of the Church of England wrote:

> "England was a land of closed churches and unstoled clergy ... The parson was often an absentee, not infrequently a drunkard ... The rich went to church to doze in upholstered curtained pews fitted with fireplaces, while the poor were herded together on uncomfortable benches."

The small town of Waterbeach was in a similarly, spiritually dilapidated state. But God was with the 17-year-old pastor, and the work of Charles Spurgeon began to bear fruit almost immediately. The thatched-roof church was soon crammed with people, and some men who were the lowest and most noxious in the village became great blessings in the church.

Many of the villagers helped out their young pastor with his needs, knowing that the tiny amount of income he was provided could not support even such a modest lifestyle. Spurgeon was determined to stick it out as long as God desired it. He seemed to want little for himself and truly delighted in the changed lives of those in the village.

> "I can testify that great numbers of humble country folk accepted the Saviour's invitation, and it was delightful

> to see what a firm grip they afterwards had on the verities of the faith. Many of them became perfect masters of divinity. I used to think sometimes that if they had degrees who deserved them, diplomas would often be transferred and given to those who hold the plough handle or work at the carpenter's bench."

This attitude toward the simple man remained with Spurgeon, a country boy himself, who remained comfortable and approachable by any class even when he became a worldwide name.

He spent three years in Waterbeach and although a mere teenager most of the time, the church and the village flourished under his care and ministering. He wrote:

> "It was a pleasant thing to walk through that place when drunkenness had almost ceased, when debauchery in the case of many was dead, when men and women went forth to labour with joyful hearts, singing the praises of the ever-living God."

New Park Street: Great Church, Little Preacher

In November 1853, the young man received an invitation to preach a Sunday service at New Park Street Chapel in London. New Park Street was famous among Baptists and Londoners and most Christians as a place of great godly influence and preaching in the 1700s. Spurgeon thought at first it was a mistake. Why would such a great church be interested in this little, country lay preacher?

But after he determined that the invitation was indeed not an error, he replied in sincere humility, informing them that he was only 19 and had never preached in a large church. He went on to say he had a prior commitment for the date they requested and offered December 11. The New Park Street deacons accepted.

New Park Street Chapel was symbolic of the decline in Baptist churches in England in the middle 1800s. The once vibrant church was a shell of its former glory. Few congregations in the whole of London topped 300 people, and all the talk was of the decline in church attendance. In fact, the Baptist denomination was divided on several issues.

Spurgeon arrived in London on a cold and dreary day, staying in a tiny little apartment where the other young men boarding there ridiculed him for claiming that he would be preaching at New Park Street. He felt completely alone, without a friend in the city. When he tried to sleep, it was torture in the cramped room with the cacophony of horses and cabs all night. He already hated London.

And yet he considered that perhaps God was in all of it. When he arrived at New Park Street the next morning, he was in awe of the magnificent building, and wondered how such a sophisticated and perhaps critical congregation would receive him. But more surprises were in store. As the time of the service approached, the great chapel did not fill up. In fact, it was dotted with just a few souls. It felt practically empty.

Spurgeon rose and spoke on "Every good gift and every perfect gift is from above and cometh down from the Father of Lights, with Whom is no variableness neither shadow of turning." Every thread of Spurgeon's preaching led up to the Cross. He did not preach on moral issues or anything in modern debate. He simply preached Christ crucified and let everything else fall as it may.

The people seemed unsure of the young preacher who knew Scripture so well and seemed to already have a vast wealth of knowledge and experience. But when the evening service came about, everyone returned and brought a good number more with them. He preached from Revelation, "They are without fault before the throne of God."

In one day, his future and the church's future were cemented together. He was invited to pastor the church. And while he could not accept immediately, and did not treasure leaving his flock in Waterbeach, he received peace from God to take the position.

Spurgeon Breaks the Mold

Spurgeon was not one to simply go with the flow. But he also understood the need for discipline and submission.

An example from his first months at New Park Street Chapel demonstrates this vividly. He was not truly ordained when he accepted the New Park Street pulpit. It was suggested there be a formal ordination service over which one of London's ordained ministers would preside. Spurgeon thoughtfully replied in a long letter to the deacons.

He opposed the ordination ceremony. His calling was from God, and he had already recognized his ministry. He objected to the concept of ministers passing on power from one to another and believed it was completely up to the local church. But, he was willing to submit to the church leadership if they felt his ceremonial ordination to be critically important: "It will be submission. I shall endure it as a self-mortification in order that you may all be pleased. I would rather please you than myself."

The ordination ceremony never took place. Spurgeon also broke the mold of tradition by discouraging references to himself as "Reverend" or even "Pastor," and by discarding the long, black frock of ministers and wearing plain clothes. These changes were severely criticized by other ministers, who believed they ought to be set apart from the flock. Moreover, Spurgeon broke through the heavy academic style of preaching so in vogue. He chose instead to speak directly to his listeners in words that could not possibly be misunderstood.

But it was not the insistence on outward changes that brought people to hear Spurgeon; it was the message of Jesus Christ crucified and arisen, and the need for Him alone for salvation. And the people came and came. Soon, not only was the once nearly empty chapel filled, but the street outside was blocked on Sundays for the overflow crowd to listen to this very young man of God.

Soon it became evident that larger space was necessary. They turned to the Music Hall in the Royal Surrey Gardens. This was a huge step, because the building housed up to 12,000 people. Spurgeon and William Olney—the man who was instrumental in bringing Spurgeon to London—feared it might have been far too large and they would have looked silly. But where they were simply could not work any longer, so they pressed forward.

Terror, Flight, Disorder and Death

It was a disaster that first night in October 1856. The Music Hall was jammed to capacity, such as it never was with secular performances. But after a Scripture reading and prayer, the wicked had their planned moment. Someone shouted, "Fire!" and another shouted, "The balcony is giving way!" Several others shouted similar fears. A panic erupted among the people and as they pressed toward the doors, seven people were killed, trampled by others desperately trying to flee a perfectly safe building.

The *British Banner wrote:* "At the most solemn moment of the occasion, the wicked rose in their strength, like a whirlwind, sin entered, followed by terror, flight, disorder and death!"

It seemed clear to everyone that it was a staged effort by evil-doers to wreck the work of God—everyone except Spurgeon, who to the end of his life wanted to "hope there was no concerted wickedness."

Spurgeon, only 22 years old, was devastated. The burden of it overwhelmed him. He became sick and was unable to preach for a couple of Sundays. But gradually his strength returned, and along with it his speaking became as powerful as ever. And the church was able to make good use of Music Hall afterward.

Eventually, however, a new building of their own was needed. In 1861, they built the Metropolitan Tabernacle, which still stands in London today. It was a huge structure that comfortably seated 3,700, with room for another 2,000 to squeeze in, which they normally did.

Charles in Love

Susannah Thompson was a "greatly privileged favourite" of William Olney, who was the lead Deacon and responsible for bringing Spurgeon to London. And so she saw Spurgeon preach his first three sermons at New Park Street Chapel.

Despite her Christian upbringing, she had never professed her faith in Christ, although she was very well aware of her need for the Saviour.

During a Sunday evening sermon about a year before Spurgeon arrived, the preacher spoke on "The word is nigh thee, even in thy mouth, and in thy heart," and the light dawned in Susannah's soul. She wrote:

> "The Lord said to me, through His servant, 'Give me thine heart,' and, constrained by His love, that night witnessed my solemn resolution of entire surrender to Himself."

But she records that she grew cold and indifferent to the things of God, and was in such a state when Spurgeon took the pulpit.

Some of their early connections are shrouded in personal privacy that eludes history. But she writes that quite unexpectedly, Spurgeon gave her an illustrated copy of *The Pilgrim's Progress*, the John Bunyan book that had meant so much to him since childhood. He inscribed it, "Miss Thompson, with desires for progress in the blessed pilgrimage, from C.H. Spurgeon, April 20, 1854."

In June 1854, the two were providentially seated next to each other at a party. Spurgeon handed a book written by Martin Tupper to Susannah and asked about a quotation in it: "Seek a good wife of Thy God, for she is the best gift of His Providence."

She blushed slightly, then heard him whisper the question, "Do you pray for him who is to be your husband?" There was a pause, and then Spurgeon asked her if she would take a walk with him. In August, they were engaged and they married on January 8, 1856.

The home they made was modest, and they took care to avoid any excessive displays. Their homes in town and later in Westwood were seemingly open to everyone: to missionaries, preachers and visitors from around the world. And they gave generously to those in need. The estimates from a review of their accounting books found that they gave away about five times as much as they kept for themselves. That's more than an 80 percent "tithe."

The Spurgeon's twin boys—Thomas and Charles—were born September 20, 1856. They were tremendous blessings to their parents and became preachers and leading men of God themselves. But the birth left Susannah an invalid in her home for 15 years. Yet her joy and that of her husband did not diminish.

"She was a fine example of the triumph of sanctified will over physical suffering," J.C. Carlile wrote in *Charles Spurgeon, The Great Orator*. "Even in pain, she dictated many letters to other sufferers and helped bear the burdens of ministries of all denominations who had fallen on evil times."

Out of the money she saved in frugal housekeeping, she began the Book Fund, which financed thousands of books of Bible study for pastors around the world. She also found money for soup kitchens, clothing for the children of poorly paid village ministers, and the individual needs of untold numbers of people.

Despite her fragile health, Susannah proved to be the ideal partner for Spurgeon, loving and serving the Lord first and sharing a spiritual intensity that helped buoy him when he needed it. Despite her extended illness, she did not seem to be a major burden on her husband. On the contrary, she was his helpmate.

Prince of Preachers

Spurgeon brought a whole new method to preaching. He did not strive for the flowery speech of the humanists or the rhetoric of the High Calvinists. Nor did he muddle through, as did many of the rural preachers. He spoke simply and from the depth of his heart and his intellect, but it was not to impress man. It was to impress upon man the glory of God, the fallen sinning state of each of us and the salvation of Christ.

"His ideal was that of the fisherman," wrote Carlile, who was a student under Spurgeon. "He lowered his net to catch fish; he baited his hook, not for decorative purposes but to secure souls."

Spurgeon never took his eye off the Word. God's great truths defined everything for him, and they informed his preaching. He wanted to make people clearly understand him. There would be no fogs in his preaching.

"Sermons should have real teaching in them, and their doctrine should be solid, substantial and abundant," Spurgeon wrote. "The world still needs to be told of its Saviour and of the way to reach Him."

Spurgeon did not do much on the spur of the moment. Occasionally he gave sermons without preparation—such as his first one. But most of the time he was intent on always finding just the right words and meanings to make his point clear. He wanted to use illustrations to make the points from ancient Scripture real to his listeners. He was very willing to quote other great men of God, from Bunyan to John Knox to Richard Baxter. And so he labored over every sermon, always starting at the beginning—with prayer. In speaking to students at his Pastors' College, he put it very clearly to them:

> "I frequently sit hour after hour praying and waiting for a subject, and this is the main part of my study; much hard labour have I spent in manipulating topics, ruminating upon points of doctrine, making skeletons out of verses and then burying every bone of them in the catacombs of oblivion, sailing on and on over leagues of broken water till I see the red lights and make sail direct to the desired haven.
>
> "Unstudied thoughts coming from the mind without previous research, without the subjects in hand having been investigated at all, must be of a very inferior quality, even from the most superior men, and as none of us would have the effrontery to glorify ourselves as men of genius or wonders of erudition, I fear that our unpremeditated thoughts upon most subjects would not be remarkably worthy of attention at all.
>
> "Our sermons should be our mental lifeblood—the outflow of our intellectual and spiritual vigor; or, to change the figure, they should be diamonds well cut and well set, precious intrinsically and bearing the marks of labour. God forbid that we should offer to the Lord that which costs us nothing."

And there you have the heart of C.H. Spurgeon on preaching. Notice that it does not include anything other than what is driving the preacher to preach. There is nothing on methods or deliveries or services. Where is the heart of the man expounding on the Word of God? That was the question for Spurgeon. When asked once about how he attracted so many people while other churches were dormant or dwindling, he answered:

> I did not seek them. They have always sought me. My concern has been to preach Christ and leave the rest to His keeping.

That was his heart.

Although it would not be his style, Spurgeon could certainly point to the results of preaching Christ first and Him crucified, preaching from deep study and prayer, and preaching for the glory of the Lord and not the preacher.

The Tabernacle For a Growing Congregation

The church needed a new home, and although the Music Hall worked for a while, the leadership knew that they needed to build. Spurgeon's vision was for a Greek structure. He felt there were no sacred languages other than ancient Greek and Hebrew. He believed that a Christian church should not be a Gothic structure, but should be Grecian.

The Metropolitan Tabernacle was completed in 1861—the largest church in the world at the time, holding nearly 6,000 people. Predictably, Spurgeon was criticized for building such a monumental edifice. He was charged with puffing himself up and being ostentatious. It was also said that the money could have been better spent on the poor. But the charges of egotism and ostentation evaporated when the church opened and filled up twice every Sunday. And as for helping the poor, Spurgeon's personal giving and books open for review shamed any critic. The couple's 80 percent tithe put to rest the lie that he was making himself rich through the Tabernacle.

At one point, an American lecture bureau invited him to come to America to tour all major cities and give 50 lectures. They offered to pay all expenses, plus $50,000—which would be a quarter million dollars today. Spurgeon wasn't interested. Ever keeping his eye on the Master's will, he quickly replied, "I can do better. I will stay in London and try to save 50 souls."

He was comfortable, but given his position of worldwide prominence and influence, and particularly the sales of millions of his books, his lifestyle was very modest. He could have lived as a king, but lived *for* the King and allowed his riches to be stored up in heaven rather than on earth.

Winning Souls From His Knees

Spurgeon did not desire to take church members from other congregations; he wanted to get the lost into the Tabernacle and into the Kingdom. By always preaching Christ and salvation, he knew he never missed the opportunity for a lost soul to hear the Gospel.

The soul-winning ways of Spurgeon began where everything began with him: in prayer. The Tabernacle was known as a church that prayed. Spurgeon may have set the example for many in later years, but the leadership had made the commitment before he arrived. The remnant that sought him out were on their knees, paving the way. That critical resolution was never lost.

No doubt many people came to hear Spurgeon out of curiosity, but saved or lost, they all heard a Christ preached that captured them.

Bob Ross wrote that Spurgeon "plainly preached the Word,

pressing the Law and the Gospel upon his hearers—the Law to convict and break the hardened, and the Gospel to heal the broken."

He loved God and he loved his fellow men. Here is how he concluded one of his sermons:

> He that believeth not shall be damned. Weary sinner, hellish sinner, thou who are at the devil's castaway, reprobate, profligate, harlot, robber, thief, adulterer, fornicator, drunkard, swearer ... listen! I speak to thee as to the rest. I exempt no man. God hath said there is no exemption here. Whosoever believeth in the name of Jesus Christ shall be saved. Sin is no barrier. The guilt is no obstacle. Whosoever, though he were black as Satan, though he were guilty as a fiend—whosoever this night believes shall every sin forgiven, shall every crime effaced, shall every iniquity blotted out; shall be saved in the Lord Jesus Christ, and shall stand in heaven safe and secure. That is the glorious gospel. God apply it home to your hearts and give you faith in Jesus.s

New Park Street went from 232 members when Spurgeon arrived to more than 5,000 about 10 years later. It was the largest independent congregation in the world—independent of denominations, but dependent on the King of kings. Prime Minister Gladstone, many members of the royal family, members of Parliament, and dignitaries from around the world visited the Tabernacle. But no matter who was in attendance, like Baxter and others before him, the message had to remain the same. All were sinners; all needed Christ or were condemned eternally. No one from the rag-tag orphan to the king escaped the equation.

People swarmed to him to hear the Truth. No numbers were kept, because Spurgeon did not use the modern altar call. He did not request a public decision. He simply quoted Scripture to believe in Christ and be saved. But even without the numbers, the fruits were quite clear. The growth of the church was primarily new believers. He planted several other churches in the London area, offshoots of the Tabernacle.

> From the very early days of my ministry in London, the Lord gave such an abundant blessing upon the proclamation of His truth that whenever I was able to appoint a time for seeking converts and inquirers, it was seldom, if ever, that I waited in vain; and usually, so many came, that I was quite overwhelmed with gratitude and thanksgiving to God.

Spurgeon's Legacy of the Pen

Spurgeon always loved to write. As a child, he planned his own magazine and wrote articles for it. This gift carried on until his death, leaving a godly legacy to future generations through both his preaching and writings.

From early on, there was such demand for the words he gave that his sermons were printed and distributed in England and the United States. The first ones were bound up and 500 printed. They disappeared so fast, more were printed until about 6,000 were distributed. Later more than 200,000 booklets with his sermons were printed.

Probably the most popular books he wrote were a little series entitled *John Ploughman's Talk*. More than 300,000 volumes were printed and sold very quickly. Subsequent printings added greatly to that number.

His writings encouraged lay believers and instructed ministers. But mostly, they were meant for the average man.

There was more that Spurgeon accomplished. In 1856 he started the Pastor's College with only one student. It grew steadily until about 100 young men were enrolled to become ministers of the gospel. The College also housed the Stockwell Orphanage with boys' and girls' schools overseen by Spurgeon and supported by funds he helped raise.

He published a monthly magazine called the *Sword and the Trowel,* beginning in 1865, in which he essentially continued preaching Christ, but also touched on issues of doctrine within the church.

His autobiography lists 78 books he wrote and published, in addition to the sermons and the magazine.

Calvinist Without Apology

Spurgeon was an unapologetic Calvinist, in that he believed what Calvin believed. But he disliked the term, because it took the focus off the Saviour. He simply agreed with Calvin's theology, and believed that the Puritan fathers had come closest to Scriptural truth.

> We know nothing of the new ologies; we stand by the old ways ... Believing that the Puritanic school embodied more gospel truth in it than any other since the days of the apostles.
>
> He defined Calvinism in its simplest terms this way:
>
> If anyone should ask me what I mean by a Calvinist, I should reply, "He is one who says, Salvation is of

> the Lord." I cannot find in Scripture any other doctrine than this. It is the essence of the Bible. "He only is my rock and my salvation." Tell me anything contrary to this truth, and it will be heresy; tell me a heresy, and I shall find its essence here, that it has departed from this great, this fundamental rock-truth, "God is my rock and my salvation."

The Protestant pastors were generally evangelical, but they were weak in their doctrine. And the result was clear in the lives of church members. Spurgeon wanted to set the church back on the rock-hard path of strong doctrine.

Spurgeon said:

> My daily labor is to revive the old doctrines of Gill, Owen, Calvin, Augustine and Christ ... The old truth that Calvin preached, that Augustine preached, is the truth that I preach today, or else I would be false to my conscience and my God. I cannot shape truth; I know of no such thing as paring off the rough edges of a doctrine. John Knox's gospel is my gospel. And that gospel which thundered through Scotland must thunder through England again.

In his day, however, not unlike today, there were elements from Hyper-Calvinists to Arminians who found fault with Spurgeon's doctrine. Knowing Scripture so well—he had much of it committed to memory—and knowing the writings of the church fathers intimately, he was able to aptly defend his doctrines.

But while willing to do it, he did not like the arena of battling other believers over issues of doctrine. He preferred the bottom line.

> If I am asked to say what my creed is, I think I must reply, 'It is Jesus Christ' ... Jesus Christ, Who is the sum and the substance of the Gospel, Who is in Himself all theology, the Incarnation of every precious truth, the all-glorious embodiment of the way, the truth and the life.

He urged listeners, "Do not make minor doctrines main points," but stick with the theme of grace from God through Jesus. Yet he could discuss the most minute doctrines in great detail and earnestness, and they were apparently important to him.

Battling the Erosion and Corrosion of the Down-Grade

By the late 1880s, there was an insipid falling away from God's Truth that infected many churches, including the Baptists. Some ministers openly preached against the infallibility of the Bible, the deity of Christ and eternal salvation. Those few were censured by the Baptist Union. But many others did so more surreptitiously. In the light of great scientific discoveries, these learned men began to question portions of Scripture or elements of the Trinity. They cast themselves as progressive and modern. Some found a new understanding in the theories of Charles Darwin, and pointed to what they felt were contradictions between Scripture and science—choosing science as their guide. Their congregations followed.

Carlile wrote:

> The pulpit was charged with silent surrender to the radical betrayal of the evangelical foundations of the Christian faith.

A blind eye was turned toward this apostasy within the Baptist Union and other denominations. It became known as the "Down-Grade" controversy.

Spurgeon at first thought it was an exception here and there. But he soon began to see a rapid spread of these ideas and was alarmed at the sudden infusion within his own denomination. Spurgeon was a very sick man by this point, and in fact, was only a few years from death. He likely knew it. And so there was no personal gain for him to enter into such a burgeoning fray at the end of his life. In fact, it probably taxed his failing strength.

Nonetheless, he felt compelled to defend the Gospel. After a number of private conversations and correspondences with men he thought were reducing Scripture, and with S.H. Booth, the secretary of the Baptist Union, he brought the issue into the open in an 1887 *Sword and the Trowel* article. In the magazine, he issued a general warning to readers of the defection from the Truth that was riddling the Nonconformist churches.

Spurgeon laid out three charges: 1) The infallibility of Scripture from God was denied, 2) the way of salvation through Christ was not preached, and 3) hell was denied, as was any eternal punishment for sin. It went right to the heart of the Gospel.

Just how deeply the unbelief had ensnared the church became obvious with the response. Many in the camp of science vigorously attacked Spurgeon over religion. He was also attacked through Christian publications and even the pulpit. And shockingly, at the next annual meeting of the Baptist Union, the issue was ignored. There was complete silence.

After repeated attempts to get the Baptist Union to confront the issue, Spurgeon felt he had no choice. He withdrew from the union. By unanimous vote, the congregation of the Tabernacle followed him. This was a blow to the union, as Spurgeon was by far the best-known Baptist preacher, and his congregation many times larger than any other. After several private attempts to get Spurgeon to return, the union passed a motion of censure against him—almost unanimously.

Booth claimed that Spurgeon had never brought the matter up with him. Spurgeon was stunned and was ready to produce the written documentation between Booth and him as evidence that the matter had indeed been thoroughly explored. But Booth insisted that those were private correspondences. As easily as Spurgeon could have proved his position and Booth's hypocrisy, he honored his old friend, and in spite of the betrayal, never revealed the letters. Without the proof, he undermined his own credibility. He also lost a friend. This was a painful split, because Spurgeon and Booth had been close for many years. To Booth's credit, Spurgeon knew he was trying to keep the controversy from blowing up and dividing the union. But it was unacceptable compromise for Spurgeon.

The censure passed by the Baptist Union was a deep wound for Spurgeon. But he had set out his path of defense of Scripture and would not turn back. He was absolutely militant about God's Word. But however strong his heart was in the matter, his body was not up to the battle. The controversy wore down his feeble frame even further, hastening the inevitable.

Suffering with Christ

Like so many great men and women of God, Spurgeon tasted of immense physical suffering. And much of his suffering was brought on by his zeal to push himself to the brink and beyond to do God's good will.

Arnold Dallimore wrote of the schedule that took its toll on Spurgeon's body:

> Although he began full of youthful vigor he labored to such an extent that his health soon was drained. He preached 10 times a week on the average, often in places that were far removed from London. He oversaw his Pastors' College, his orphanage and almshouses, and bore the responsibility of raising the funds to keep them all vibrant and healthy. Every Monday he edited a sermon preached the previous day to prepare it for the press and each month he produced his magazine. He was also constantly producing books.

By the age of 30, he was already showing the signs of the stress. The painful disease of gout developed. Over the years, he would be in such agony that he was bed-ridden and unable to move. Many of his sermons were preached through obvious pain. He would use his cane and, with the help of church members, mount the podium to preach. Frequently, once he embarked upon the word of God, the pain seemed to dissipate, and he became animated and energetic until he was finished.

Spurgeon's views on his physical suffering are not those of many Christians today. He saw suffering as a gift from God. Without his suffering, he never could have been the comforting and sympathetic man that he was to the sick and downtrodden.

His son, Charles Jr., wrote:

> I know of no one who could, more sweetly than my dear father, impart comfort to bleeding hearts and sad spirits. As the crushing of the flower causes it to yield its aroma, so he, having endured in the long continued

> illness of my beloved mother, and also constant pains himself, was able to sympathize most tenderly with all sufferers.
>
> Spurgeon knew this truth intimately.

"In the matter of faith healing, health is set before us as if it were the great thing to be desired above all things. Is it so? I venture to say that the greatest earthly blessing that God can give to any of us is health, with the exception of sickness. Sickness has frequently been of more use to the saints of God than health has."

Spurgeon at Rest, at Last

In his last years, Spurgeon spent some wintertime in Menton, in South France, to help his ailing body. That is where he was in January 1892. He was very sick, yet he could not help but hold little services with just the handful of friends and family. He had spoken to the great throngs of thousands, but he would expound the word of God to any group, no matter how small.

Wilson Carlile was with Spurgeon in his last days, and it was clear that the Down-Grade issue was still on his heart.

> When he was dying at the East Bay, Menton, my wife and I went to his family prayers, which he took though in bed. He prayed for all the wandering sheep, concluding, "Thou, Lord, seest the various labels upon them and rightly regardest them by the mark of the Cross in their hearts. They are all Thy one fold.'"

Spurgeon crossed the River Jordan January 31, 1892, and entered into the loving arms of the Master whom he served so diligently on this earth. Typical of his humility and understanding of man's heart, he had left the request: "Remember, a plain stone. 'C.H.S.' and no more; no fuss."

He knew that a monument would be to him, and not to his Saviour. On his casket was this inscription:

> In ever loving memory of Charles Haddon Spurgeon, born at Kelvedon, June 19, 1834, fell asleep in Jesus at Menton, January 31, 1892. I have fought a good fight, I have finished my course, I have kept the faith.

Indeed he did. —By Rod Thomson

Illustration Portfolio

The Birthplace of Charles H. Spurgeon
June 19, 1834 in Kelvedon, Essex, England

Rev. John Spurgeon
father of C.H. Spurgeon

Eliza Spurgeon
mother of C.H. Spurgeon

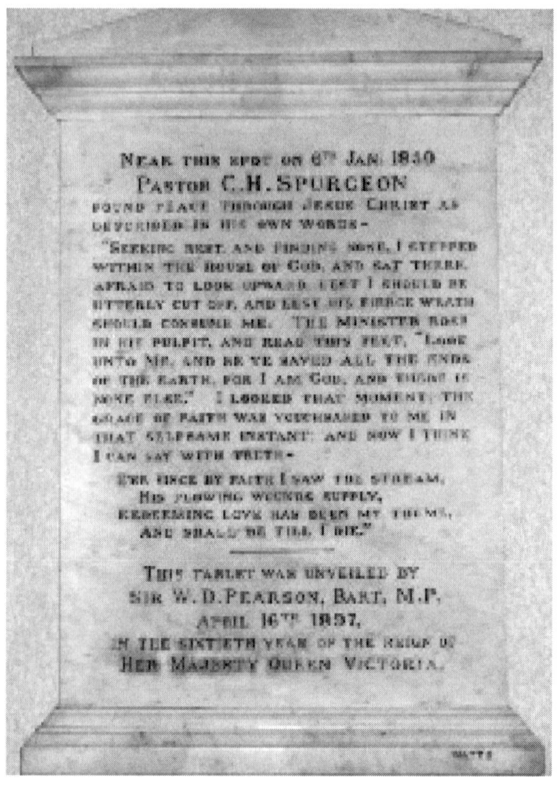

Near this spot on 6th Jan. 1950
Pastor C.H. Spurgeon
found peace through Jesus Christ as described in his own words –
"Seeking rest, and finding none, I stepped within the House of God, and sat there, afraid to look upward, lest I should be utterly cut off, and lest His fierce wrath should consume me. The minister rose in his pulpit, and read this text, "Look unto Me, and be ye saved all the ends of the Earth, for I am God, and there is none else."
I looked that moment: the grace of faith was vouchsafed to me in that selfsame instatnt; and now I think I can say with truth –

E'er since by faith I saw the stream,
His flowing wounds supply,
Redeeming love has been my theme,
And shall be till I die."

This tablet was unveiled by
Sir W.D. Pearson, Bart, M.P.
April 16th 1897.
in the sixtieth year of the reign of
Her Majesty Queen Victoria

Above: The cottage where Mr. Spurgeon preached his first sermon at age 16.

Left: Susannah Tompson became Mrs. Charles Spurgeon on January 8, 1856. Despite fragile health, she was a strong partner to her husband and his ministry.

Below: The Spurgeons lived a comfortable but modest life at Westwood, and used the majority of their income to help ministers, the poor, and people in need.

WESTWOOD

The New Park Street Chapel
Spurgeon accepted his first pastorate in December 1853, at the age of 19.

Music Hall in the Royal Surrey Gardens
In spite of a disasterous beginning, the congregation used this building as a meeting place for five years.

THE METROPOLITAN TABERNACLE
Above: Completed in 1861, the new home of the Park Street congregation was built in the Greek style. It was the largest church in the world at the time and held nearly 6,000 people.
Left: Spurgeon sometimes needed to be helped into the pulpit because of the pain he suffered from gout.

Stockwell Orphanage

Spurgeon oversaw and raised funds to support the Boy's School and Girl's School at Stockwell Orphanage (*above*), as well as the Pastor's College he founded (*bottom*).

The Pastor's College

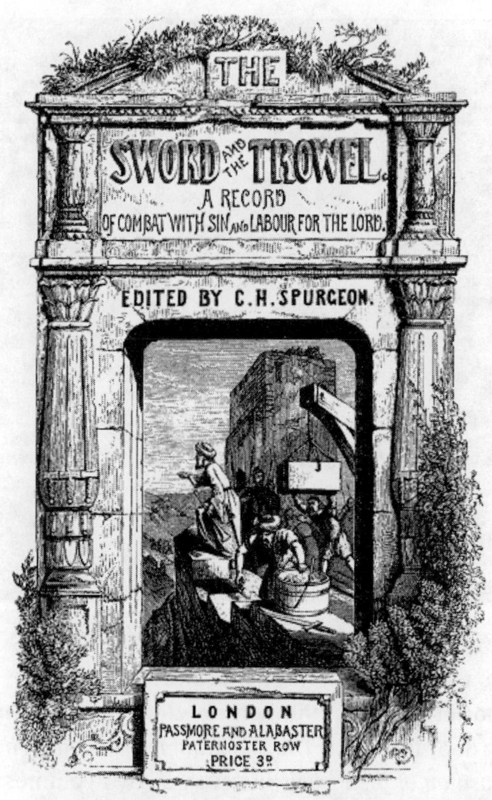

THE SWORD AND THE TROWEL
Spurgeon published this monthly magazine beginning in 1865, in which he essentially continued preaching Christ, but also touched on issues of doctrine within the church.

Spurgeon in his study at Westwood, his family home.

Spurgeon's study at Westwood (*above*) contained more than 12,000 volumes. Mr. Spurgeon's work was enormous. Besides editing and furnishing most of the matter for his monthly magazine, *The Sword and Trowel*, since January 1, 1865, he wrote *The Saint and His Saviour*, *The Treasury of David, an Exposition of the Psalms* in seven octavo volumes; *The New Park Street Pulpit* and the *Metropolitan Tabernacle Pulpit*, which contains about two thousand of his weekly sermons from 1855 to 1889, making thirty large volumes. Also *Lectures to My Students*, *Commenting and Commentaries*, *John Ploughman*, the *Cheque Book of the Bank of Faith*, and various other publications.

Mark XVI. 14.

This shows us the way in wh we must deal with unbelief in ourselves, & in others. It is a sin & should be treated as such. Jesus wd not have upbraided had not this been the case.

In the case before us they had repeated testimonies, from their own brethren, & backed by his own word — but we have even more guilt for we know him to be risen & yet doubt.

I. Let us consider its evil in itself

Suppose some one doubted us.
Think of who he is & what he has done.
Consider his near & dear relation to us.
The many times in wh we have doubted
And upon the same matter.
Where his promises forbade unbelief
Despite our own declarations.
What have we believed in preference?

II. Let us observe the evils wh it causes

It grieves the Spirit of God.
It causes distress in our own hearts
It weakens us for action or suffering
It depresses others.
It leaves an ill impression on sinners
It cannot but gender to bondage.

III. Let us reflect upon its sinfulness where it reigns

It gives God the lie.
It argues hatred in the heart
It is the sign of utter moral death.
It is the essence of hell.

SERMON NOTES

This one page of handwritten notes is all Spurgeon took with him into the pulpit when he preached the sermon titled "Unbelievers Upbraided."